100
Most Popular
Children's Authors

Popular Authors Series

The 100 Most Popular Young Adult Authors: Biographical Sketches and Bibliographies. Revised First Edition. By Bernard A. Drew.

Popular Nonfiction Authors for Children: A Biographical and Thematic Guide. By Flora R. Wyatt, Margaret Coggins, and Jane Hunter Imber.

100 Most Popular Children's Authors: Biographical Sketches and Bibliographies. By Sharron L. McElmeel.

100 Most Popular Picture Book Authors and Illustrators. By Sharron L. McElmeel.

100 Most Popular Picture Book Authors for the Year 2000. By Sharron L. McElmeel.

100
Most Popular
Children's Authors

Biographical Sketches and Bibliographies

Sharron L. McElmeel

1999
Libraries Unlimited, Inc.
Englewood, Colorado

Libraries Unlimited, Inc.
P.O. Box 6633
Englewood, CO 80155-6633
1-800-237-6124
www.lu.com

Library of Congress Cataloging-in-Publication Data

McElmeel, Sharron L.
    100 most popular children's authors : biographical sketches
and bibliographies / Sharron L. McElmeel.
        xxxi, 495 p. 19x26 cm. -- (Popular authors series)
    Includes bibliographical references and index.
    ISBN 1-56308-646-8 (cloth)
    1. Children's literature, American--Bio-bibliography--
Dictionaries. 2. Children's literature, English--Bio-bibliography--
Dictionaries. 3. Authors, American--Biography--Dictionaries.
4. Authors, English--Biography--Dictionaries. I. Title. II. Title:
One hundred most popular children's authors.   III. Series.
PS490.M39   1998
810.9'9282--dc21   98-41942
    [b]   CIP

For Jack, who makes this possible

Contents

Introduction

Sharing Author Information and Motivating Readers

One effective way of motivating young readers to increase reading is to connect them with a favorite author and provide background information about the author and the author's writing. Educators, in their efforts to promote and evaluate reading, often ask students to respond to a book through activities that demonstrate having read and understood the material. One of the most valuable responses is wanting to read another book by the same author. Connections between the author and what students are reading promote more reading and students' own writing. Creating increasingly self-motivated readers and writers is the ultimate goal.

This book provides information about authors most read by young readers in elementary or middle school. Information is biographical, accompanied by a selected book list and suggestions for more reading about the author. Other reference sources include these popular authors as well, most often through a multivolume set of references that are written over a period of years. Thus, to obtain information on the current most popular authors students needed access to several volumes of a reference work. Even with that access, the information for authors profiled in early volumes is seriously out of date. Every effort has been made to have the information about each of the authors included in this book be as up-to-date and accurate as possible.

For more than a dozen years I have profiled authors and illustrators in books and periodicals. I have interviewed hundreds of authors and have listened to many of them speak at national or state conferences. For authors included in this book, I have relied heavily on my previous writings, interview notes, and notes from their presentations at conferences. Quotes are from these sources. Further research updated recent publication information and future plans of the authors.

Although I have included selected book lists as part of each author's chapter, I did so only to provide readers with a sample of titles to associate with the author. As each author continues to write (even books by Laura Ingalls Wilder are been adapted, repackaged, and republished), new books are added each publishing season. Readers wishing to have a complete and up-to-date list of a particular author's publications can now access that information in minutes by going to the Library of Congress's Catalog on the World Wide Web. The catalog can be accessed at http://www.loc.gov. Suggestions for further reading include articles and, where appropriate, websites that provide more information about the author and the author's writing. Do keep in mind that although websites can often provide up-to-date information, the sites can also disappear quickly. All the websites listed here were accessible during the three months before the manuscript was completed. When you access the website, you may wish to print a personal copy of an "author file" for future reference.

Some choices for author inclusion seem obvious. As an educator, I have worked with over 12,000 young readers choosing and selecting books to read and enjoy. Authors such as Laura Ingalls Wilder have enjoyed a high level of popularity for decades. Some names are new, but most likely will not be as long lasting as Wilder. Beverly Cleary has been another constantly popular author for at least two decades. She was also at the top of the survey used to confirm our choices.

The list of authors selected for inclusion was based, in general, on the results of a national 1997 survey designed to identify the 100 most important authors and illustrators in children's literature. Survey responses came from both teachers and students. The results were reported originally in *Library Talk* (January/February 1998).

The 1997 survey was based on one survey conducted by Don Gallo in 1988. In the spring of 1989, Gallo published the survey results of 41 educators who had served as officers of the Assembly on Literature for Adolescents (ALAN) of the National Council of Teachers of English. Lin Buswell and I decided to expand the population invited to participate, and to include younger groups of readers.

The first major step was to construct a preliminary list of authors and illustrators. The criteria for choosing authors and illustrators to share with young readers seem to be as numerous as the authors themselves. No person or group can create an uncontroversial list of authors and illustrators that all children must read before passing through a specific age or grade. Any list leaves out some local favorites—every choice is relative. Any selection is bound to show biases of the group making the preliminary selections. We attempted to diversify selections and reflect current trends in children's literature. We narrowed the list by using the advice of hundreds of educators and students.

Upon publication of the survey for "authors of novels/information books for young readers" in a national journal, completed forms began to arrive. The survey attracted participants from 41 states, two Canadian provinces, and Saudi Arabia. More than 3,000 completed surveys were submitted and clear patterns began to emerge.

Recognized by over 98 percent of respondents, Beverly Cleary topped the list. No other author received recognition by more than 90 percent of respondents. The next group included: Judy Blume, R. L. Stine, and E. B. White and was recognized by 80 percent or more of respondents. Three more were recognized by 70 percent or more of the respondents. This group included Roald Dahl, A. A. Milne, and Laura Ingalls Wilder. Sixteen authors were recognized by 50 percent or more of the respondents while an additional eleven were recognized by 40 percent or more. Among the top 27 (those recognized by 40 percent or more) were contemporary writers such as Shel Silverstein and Lois Lowry, as well as classic writers such as Lewis Carroll and C. S. Lewis. The remainder were recognized by a lesser percentage of respondents but none by less than 16 percent. We included other authors based on years of observation and informal interviews with young readers.

Because of the types of books written or the nature of biographical information, author-information demanded a slightly different treatment in their respective chapters. I felt that some of the book lists needed to be annotated—a brief indication of the book's topic/theme—while others seemed self-explanatory based on the title or genre written by the author. So, while each author chapter has standard information—biographical sketch and a section titled "Books and Notes" —the "Books and Notes" section will vary somewhat in format. In the same way, the "For More Information" sections also vary depending on available information.

In each case I have attempted to provide information that will entice readers into the books mentioned. I hope you will find here those special motivational connections between young readers and a particular author and author's books. Connecting books and authors and readers is the ultimate goal.

Sharron L. McElmeel
Cedar Rapids, Iowa

David A. Adler

**New York, New York
April 10, 1947**

📖 Cam Jansen Mysteries

📖 Picture Book
Biographies Series

About the Author
and the Author's Writing

It was a two-and-a-half-year-old nephew, visiting one Sunday, who nudged David Abraham Adler into the world of children's books. "[He] asked me one question after another. I tried to keep up with him, to answer all his questions, but he didn't stop. Often he didn't even wait to hear my answer to one question before he asked me another. When he left, I wrote some of his questions in my journal along with my answers. That led to my first book, *A Little at a Time* [Random, 1976]. It's the story of a small boy going for a walk to a museum with his grandfather and continually asking questions. It was while I was teaching that I wrote my first book for children."

The book had no punctuation at all, no periods or commas, and was all dialogue. He sent the book to Random House "because Random House had the most children's books on the shelves in the stores."

Since that year, Adler has written many kinds of books with several publishers. He says, "I've written a few riddle and puzzle books. I've also written science, math and economics books and biographies." A biography of Golda Meir, *Our Golda, the Story of Golda Meir* (Viking, 1984) was his first biography. He used a very old set of encyclopedias in his research for that book. That set of encyclopedias and other rare books have been used in his research. In addition to his popular mystery/adventure series, Adler is well known for his Picture Book Biography series and has written several focusing on traditions and holidays in Jewish culture. Puzzles, rebuses, and riddles are also popular subjects for Adler's writings.

David A. Adler was born April 10, 1947 in New York City. He was the second of six children—four boys and two girls. His parents "always encouraged us to be individuals." Individuals they were. One brother attempted to make rock candy by keeping a string dangling in a jar of sugar water. A second brother sterilized dirt, desalinized ocean water, and boiled bayberries. His family viewed David as "the creative one." His family hung several of his paintings and drawings in the home. Together, the Adler children collected baseball cards, bottle caps, campaign buttons, stamps, coins, and historic newspapers. And, Adler's family all loved books. The family went to the library every Friday afternoon.

Robert McCloskey's *Homer Price* was one of David's favorite books. David's father was continually adding bookcases to hold the family books. Later, Adler's brother, Eddie, began building bookcases. Of his childhood Adler says, "I grew up in a large house filled with brothers, sisters, and books. My first stories were ones I made up to tell my younger brothers and sisters. I'm married now and like to tell stories to my children, but I also try to be a good listener and a good observer."

As a child Adler read many kinds of books but did not plan on writing; he envisioned himself becoming a major league baseball player. Although he was good in the field, he wasn't a powerful hitter. When faced with a fastball, he couldn't hit at all. So, he thought it might be nice to be a U.S. senator. Instead of becoming a major league baseball player or senator, Adler entered the advertising field in his early twenties. He also earned an undergraduate degree in economics and education, and obtained a graduate degree in marketing from New York University. For a time he was a financial writer, and he says, "I was a cartoonist before I was a writer. I was a math teacher, arts and crafts teacher, and a waiter, too."

Since that first book, Adler has settled in to writing for children. Among his most popular titles are those in the Cam Jansen series and the Picture Book Biography series. The Cam Jansen series has been translated into Dutch, German, and Japanese. Several of Adler's Picture Book Biographies are available in Spanish.

Much of Adler's fiction comes from real life, although he uses "creative license." During school visits, Adler explains that authors "continually adapt real people and true events into their fiction so that not everything written occurs as it actually takes place." He gets ideas from many people and events in his own life, his family, students he meets at presentations, and librarians who suggest book needs. He never uses the real name of a person who inspired an idea, but on occasion, someone recognizes him- or herself in a book. When his then eight-year-old son Michael read the first three chapters of Adler's manuscript for *Benny, Benny, Baseball Nut* (Scholastic, 1987), he recognized himself and told his father, "Dad, this is me!" Adler confirms that "the main character in the book, *Benny, Benny, Baseball Nut* is based on my eldest son, a real baseball enthusiast."

Other books evolve from life events. When Adler was six years old, a neighbor's boy convinced Adler that a jar of brown liquid was a magic potion. That incident became the inspiration for *I Know I'm a Witch* (Holt, 1988). The mischievous boy from Adler's childhood became the book's female main character. Adler became lost while traveling in Yugoslavia and had a strange experience that, many years later, became the basis for a title in the Cam Jansen series, *Cam Jansen and the Mystery of Flight 54* (Viking, 1989).

His writing goes through drastic rewrites. When he visits schools he often takes huge reproductions of some of the beginning pages of a book, pages at various stages of his revisions, so that he can share the revision process.

The first title in the Cam Jansen series is *Cam Jansen and the Stolen Diamonds* (Viking, 1980). Adler originally wrote the manuscript featuring a male character, but after several revisions the main protagonist evolved as red-haired Jennifer "Cam" Jansen, a girl with a photographic memory. Her friend Eric is the oldest of four children and thus is cast as a nurturing child who helped care for the younger children in his family. Cam, on the other hand, was an only child and exhibited many traits often attributed to male characters—adventurous and headstrong. Adler says, "[Cam] is based on an elementary school classmate. Cam Jansen's sidekick, the timid Eric Sheldon, is based on myself."

Cam Jansen and Eric Sheldon solve crimes in the Cam Jansen series. Adler's plots take Cam and Eric into some suspenseful moments as they attempt to unravel clues and solve crimes. Adler says, "It's not easy to come up with crimes that don't involve violence." Most often the crime is robbery. The plot must not be so simple that readers can figure out the crime in the first two chapters, but must not be so complex that the story doesn't make sense by the time the reader gets to the end.

Eric's twin sisters, Donna and Diane, become two of four stars in a second mystery series, Fourth Floor Twins. The other two characters are Gary and Kevin Young, a second set of twins. Together the four find a stolen sculpture, track down a missing suitcase (and the youngest Sheldon sibling) on the Silver Ghost Express, solve the mystery of the man in the blue hat, and participate in a sand castle contest—while hot on the trail of a dog napper.

A third mystery series began with *Jeffrey's Ghost and the Left-Over Baseball Team* (Holt, 1984). Next came mysteries featuring Herman "Houdini" Foster and his cousin Janet, who solve crimes in the Houdini Club Magic Mysteries, published by Random House, among others.

Adler has written a number of riddle books that are attractive to primary-age readers. He tackles animal riddles, spooky riddles, riddles for Thanksgiving, school American History riddles. Of the time he wrote these books he says, "I was difficult to live with. . . . I kept asking my family the most awful riddles and some that I still think are terrific."

While most readers expect a writer to research nonfiction titles (and of course, Adler does), many do not realize that fiction books also require research. For example, to make Cam Jansen realistic—she has a photographic visual memory—Adler read much about people who have photographic memories. The plot for each Cam Jansen book requires research for the specific events that take place. For example, during the writing of *Cam Jansen and the Mystery of the Carnival Prize* (Viking, 1984), Adler centered some action around a rigged carnival game. He researched carnival games and determined that a game *could* be rigged in the manner he described. Eventually, he created a model of the game and took it to his editor at Viking to prove that the rigging method was possible.

Adler has been known to write some chapters in the quiet of the Hewlett-Woodmere Public Library, but also writes at home on his computer. He is prolific, having over 140 entries in the Library of Congress catalog. During 1997, five publishers released a total of ten Adler books. His writing versatility is evident in the titles released. *Hiding from the*

Nazis (Holiday, 1997), for example, is the true story of Lore Baer, who as a four-year-old Jewish child was placed with a Christian family in Dutch farm country. Another title, *Easy Math Puzzles* (Holiday, 1997), took Adler back to his puzzle/riddle era. A Cam Jansen mystery was released, as well as a book in an offshoot series, Young Cam Jansen, and three titles in the Picture Book Biography series. Additional titles released in 1997 included: a title in the Houdini Club Magic Mystery series, a story about Chanukah, and a biography about Lou Gehrig for older readers. The previous year eight titles were released: four mysteries, two Picture Book Biographies, a book about fractions, and *The Kids' Catalog of Jewish Holidays* (Jewish Publication Society, 1996).

A new series of books featuring Andy Russell as the main character is based on his middle son, Edward. "He is an interesting boy with interesting questions such as, 'Daddy, what if the Wright brothers had been Siamese twins? What would the cockpit of an airplane look like now?' The family in the books are based on our family."

Within a twenty-year time span, Adler has authored more than 150 children's books, including mysteries, biographies, riddles, science and math books, and books about the Holocaust. These have won numerous awards and have been translated into Braille, British English, Chinese, Danish, Dutch, German, Hebrew, Japanese, Spanish, and Swedish.

For many years David A. Adler has lived in Woodmere, New York, with his spouse, Renee. They have three sons—Michael Seth, Edward Ranan, and Eitan Joshua. Among David Adler's favorite things are: the colors green, yellow, blue, and gray; kiwis; dolphins; July 4th; Thanksgiving; and Passover. He says if he were not a writer that he would want to be "a comedian—a *real funny* one." "I feel very fortunate; I love the work I do. Most times, it doesn't seem like work at all."

Books and Notes

Adler has written more than 150 books. The books in these selected lists are representative of titles he has written in that category. Annotations/notes are included where content is not adequately indicated by title.

Biographies—
Picture Book Series

Since the early 1980s Adler has authored almost thirty titles about U.S. presidents and other historical figures such as: Eleanor Roosevelt, Helen Keller, Harriet Tubman, Rosa Parks, and Jesse Owens.

A Picture Book of Amelia Earhart. Illustrated by Jeff Fisher. (Holiday, 1998).

A Picture Book of Davy Crockett. Illustrated by John and Alexandra Wallner. (Holiday, 1996).

A Picture Book of Robert E. Lee. Illustrated by John and Alexandra Wallner. (Holiday, 1994).

A Picture Book of Sitting Bull. Illustrated by Samuel Byrd. (Holiday, 1993).

A Picture Book of Thurgood Marshall. Illustrated by Robert Casilla. (Holiday, 1997).

Biographies for Intermediate Readers

Although very well known for his series of Picture Book Biographies, Adler also writes biographies for an older, intermediate audience.

Benjamin Franklin—Printer, Inventor, Statesman. Illustrated by Lyle Miller. (Holiday, 1992).

Lou Gehrig: The Luckiest Man. Illustrated by Terry Widener. (Harcourt, 1997).
Includes information about Gehrig's struggle with the terminal disease amyotrophic lateral sclerosis (AML, or Lou Gehrig's disease).

Math, Science, and Puzzles

David Adler earned an undergraduate degree in economics and was, at one time, a mathematics teacher. Those interests most likely stimulated his books that explain mathematical and science concepts, as well as titles that focus on economics. His several books of rebuses, riddles, and puzzles seem to combine his interest in mathematics and mysteries.

Easy Math Puzzles. Illustrated by Cynthia Fisher. (Holiday, 1997).

Fraction Fun. Illustrated by Nancy Tobin. (Holiday, 1996).

Shape Up: Making Shapes, Eating Polygons. Illustrated by Nancy Tobin. (Holiday, 1998).

Mystery Series

Cam Jansen Adventure Series

Adler's first mystery series featured a fifth-grade girl, Jennifer Jansen (nicknamed Camera, Cam for short) because of her photographic memory that helps her and her friend Eric solve mysteries. The first two titles in this series, *Cam Jansen and the Mystery of the Stolen Diamonds* and *Cam Jansen and the Mystery of the U.F.O.*, launched the series in 1980. Since then, more than a dozen titles in the series have been published.

Cam Jansen and the Chocolate Fudge Mystery. Illustrated by Susanna Natti. No. 14. (Viking, 1993).

Cam Jansen and the Triceratops Pops Mystery. Illustrated by Susanna Natti. No. 15. (Viking, 1995).

Cam Jansen and the Ghostly Mystery. Illustrated by Susanna Natti. No. 16. (Viking, 1996).

Cam Jansen and the Scary Snake Mystery. Illustrated by Susanna Natti. No. 17. (Viking, 1997).

Fourth Floor Twins Series

Twins Donna and Diane Sheldon, who first appeared in the Cam Jansen Adventure series as Eric's younger sisters, and another set of twins, Gary and Kevin Young, team up in this mystery series.

The Fourth Floor Twins and the Sand Castle Contest. Illustrated by Irene Trivas. (Viking, 1988).

Young Cam Jansen Series

The Young Cam Jansen books feature Cam Jansen as an eight-year-old girl who solves mysteries. The first two titles published in the series were:

Young Cam Jansen and the Lost Tooth. Illustrated by Susanna Natti. Viking Easy-to-Read, Level 2. (Viking, 1997).

Young Cam Jansen and the Missing Cookie. Illustrated by Susanna Natti. Viking Easy-to-Read, Level 2. (Viking, 1997).

Houdini Club Magic Mystery

Adler created an easy-to-read mystery series for Random House. The series features Herman "Houdini" Foster and his cousin Janet, who solve crimes together in their urban setting. The series is part of Random House's First Stepping Stone Books.

Lucky Stars. Illustrated by Heather Harms Maione. (Random House, 1996).

Magic Money. Illustrated by Heather Harms Maione. (Random House, 1997).

Jewish Culture and Themes

David Adler has created informational books about Jewish culture and traditions as well as retellings of tales that focus on Jewish themes or true-life accounts of the Holocaust.

Chanukah in Chelm. Illustrated by Kevin O'Malley. (Lothrop, 1997).
Mendel is told by the rabbi to get a table for the Chanukah menorah, but Mendel makes the task more difficult than it should be.

Child of the Warsaw Ghetto. Illustrated by Karen Ritz. (Holiday, 1995).
Profiles the life of Froim Baum, a child who lived in the ghetto during the Jewish Holocaust (1939–1945).

Hiding from the Nazis. Illustrated by Karen Ritz. (Holiday, 1997).
The true story of a four-year-old Jewish child, Lore Baer, who lives with a Christian family in a Dutch farm country to avoid persecution by the Nazis.

For More Information About/By the Author

Articles

Adler, David. "Meet the Author: A Letter to Students from Mystery-Author Extraordinaire." *Instructor* 105, no. 3 (October 10, 1995): 74.

Earl, Robin. "Writing Is Child's Play for 5 Towner." *Nassau Herald* (NY) (January 16, 1986): Part II, p. 1.

Lloyd Alexander

◆ Science Fantasy

Philadelphia, Pennsylvania
January 30, 1924

📖 The Prydain Chronicles
📖 The Westmark Trilogy

About the Author
and the Author's Writing

At the age of fifteen, Lloyd Alexander declared that he was going to be a poet and writer. "My parents were horrified when I told them I wanted to be an author," he says. They wanted him to do something sensible, to find some sort of useful work. But Alexander was a reader and wanted to be a writer. He loved the work of Shakespeare, Dickens, Twain, and the world's mythologies. King Arthur was his hero. Alexander had no idea of how to find useful work and no idea of how to become a poet.

His parents could not afford to send him to college, so after graduating from high school in 1940, Alexander went to work. He worked as a bank messenger as one of his first jobs and managed to attend Lafayette College for a time. After one term he joined the U.S. Army to fight in World War II. He was stationed in Texas, Maryland, and across the Atlantic in Wales. During these tours he worked in the artillery, the

Army band (he played cymbals), and in first-aid. He found Wales "an enchanted world." From Wales he was sent to France, where he joined the Seventh Army in Alsace-Lorraine, the Rhineland, and southern Germany. Here, he was a staff sergeant in combat intelligence, and finally, after the war, was attached to a counter-intelligence unit in Paris. He was discharged while in France and stayed on to attend the Sorbonne. He met his wife, Janine Denni, in Paris, and together, with her young daughter Madeleine, they returned to the United States, settling in Drexel Hill, near Philadelphia. Alexander began to write, despite the fact that he had no formal training. His first efforts were aimed at an adult audience. Few were published, so he earned his living as a cartoonist, advertising writer, layout artist, and editor and writer for a small magazine. At night he pursued writing. After seven years of rejections, he succeeded in getting a novel published. During the next ten years he wrote for adults. Eventually, he turned his attention and talent to books for young readers.

In the late 1950s he began to research material for a time-travel book. The book, *Time Cat: The Remarkable Journeys of Jason and Gareth* (Holt, 1963), featured Jason and his magic cat, Gareth. With the wink of an eye Gareth takes Jason to nine faraway places in history. Alexander extensively researched each geographical location and each time period. During the research he "stumbled across a collection of Welsh tales, *The Mabinogion.*" Two volumes of medieval stories soon took him back to all of the heroes, games, and dreams. He could again envision the castles, mountains, and valleys of an enchanted land. That was the beginning of the Prydain Chronicles—the Wales that he had discovered years before. The Welsh research never did make it into *Time Cat,* but it did lead Alexander into a much longer fantasy. The fantasies were set in a land, Prydain, much like the land of Wales.

The Prydain Chronicles began with *The Book of Three* (Holt, 1964) and filled four more titles. The final book in the chronicles, *The High King* (Holt, 1968), earned the coveted Newbery Award for Alexander in 1969. The series became the basis for an 82-minute Disney movie, *The Black Cauldron,* in 1985, and spawned Disney books based on the movie. The film, according to the All-movie Guide, was "a morbid affair and as a result was the first Disney feature cartoon to earn a PG rating." Due to the popularity of the Alexander books, the film grossed more than $21 million. But because the film was animated in precomputer days, it took Disney animators more than ten years to produce. The gross fell short of the estimated $25 million it is said to have taken to put the movie on the screen.

Throughout the chronicles, protagonist, Taran, the Assistant Pig-Keeper, struggles against evil forces that are attempting to destroy Prydain. The Prydain Chronicles are sword-and-sorcery-type stories, but even in the fantasy the stories contain elements of Alexander's own life. His wife, Janine, has suggested that Alexander grumbles like the character Doli, and Alexander admits that he is, like Fflewddur Fflam, an outrageous stretcher of the truth. The chief protagonist is an Assistant Pig-Keeper and would-be warrior, Taran. Of him Alexander says, "I admit that the dreams of the Assistant Pig-Keeper were much like mine as a child." For a number of years the Alexanders' living room has housed an ancient harp, still with a broken string, on the mantelpiece. It is difficult to tell if that harp is owned by Fflewddur Fflam, the would-be bard, or by Alexander himself.

Younger readers will find a taste of the Prydain Chronicles through two picture-book tales created from incidents in the novels. *Coll and His White Pig* (Holt, 1965) is based on an event that occurs in *The Book of Three*. Another picture book, *The Truthful Harp* (Holt, 1967), tells the tale of King Fflewddur Fflam. The late Evaline Ness illustrated each of the picture books.

Completing the Chronicles left Alexander with a sense that the creative experience had somehow changed his life. Looking for a way to convey that idea, Alexander created the story of Sebastian. Sebastian is a young man who seeks to become the fourth fiddler in a noble household, and after being rejected, sets out to see the world. Sebastian, himself, becomes a metaphor for the creative process and the demands that process makes on individuals. *The Marvelous Misadventures of Sebastian* (Dutton, 1970) earned Alexander his second major award, the 1971 National Book Award.

The Chronicles ended with *The High King*, but in 1973 Alexander collected six short stories, *The Foundling and Other Tales of Prydain* (Holt, 1973; Puffin, 1996), dealing with events that preceded the birth of Taran, a key figure in the author's five works on the Kingdom of Prydain.

In the 1980s Alexander created another mythical kingdom for the Westmark Trilogy. Theo, a printer's apprentice, examines the principles of honor, justice, and freedom of the press, all while trying to avoid the tyranny of the kingdom's chief minister. In *Westmark* (Dutton, 1981) Theo flees from criminal charges and falls in with a charlatan, his dwarf attendant, and Mickle, an urchin girl, who travels with them in the kingdom of Westmark. They ultimately arrive at the palace, where the king is grieving over the loss of his daughter. During the course of *The Kestrel* (Dutton, 1982), Theo helps Mickle to assume her rightful place as princess. To do that, all Theo's talents are needed, as well as those of his former companions. *The Beggar Queen* (Dutton, 1984) details the efforts of the king's uncle who plots to overthrow the new government of Westmark and bring an end to the reforms instituted by Mickle, now Queen Augusta, Theo, and their companions.

In 1986 Alexander published a story about sixteen-year-old Vesper in *The Illyrian Adventure* (Dutton). As an orphan she has a guardian, and together they research an ancient legend and become entangled in a dangerous rebellion. Further adventures take the pair to Central America, a grand duchy in Europe, a remote country of Jedera, and finally to the Pennsylvania countryside.

Alexander says, concerning the connection between his writing and life, "While I use parts of my own personality in creating most of my characters, and some of my wartime experiences, most particularly in the Westmark Trilogy, some actual objects have found their way into many books." Those objects include "my ancient Welsh harp in the Prydain chronicles [and] a 300-year-old cabin in Drexel Hill in *The Philadelphia Adventure* [Dutton, 1990]. The flute, paint box, bronze bowl, and other objects carried by Jen in *The Remarkable Journey of Prince Jen* [Dutton, 1991] were those I owned as a child." The objects "came from my father's oriental importing business." While working on *The Iron Ring* (Dutton, 1997) he always kept a brass Hindu statuette on his work table.

In recent years, Alexander has contributed to *The Big Book for Peace* (Dutton, 1990) and to a collection of a dozen scary stories by Newbery Award–winning authors, *A Newbery Halloween* (Delacorte, 1993).

One of Alexander's stories waited fifteen years to be published. He tells the story of *The Fortune-Tellers* (Dutton, 1992). "While cleaning old papers and assorted junk from under the eaves of the attic, Janine found a manuscript I had written 15 years earlier. It was a short fable I had put temporarily aside, to begin another project. By then, my attention was elsewhere; I forgot about it. It somehow got put in with a stack of papers which, finally, ended up in the attic. But, having patiently waited all those years, the story was published as a picture book with gorgeous illustrations by Trina Schart Hyman." The story is about a carpenter in the West African country of Cameroon who goes to a fortune-teller and finds the predictions about his future coming true in an un-usual way. That the story is set in Cameroon seemed to be a fortunate match with illustrator Trina Schart Hyman. Hyman's daughter, Katrine, married an African prince and went to live in Cameroon—providing Trina with ample opportunity to research the flora and fauna of the country.

Lloyd Alexander and his wife, Janine, continue to reside in the Drexel Hill area. Alexander says, however, "there is no hill, unless you count the bump in the road across from the barber shop." He begins his writing early in the morning (sometimes as early as 4 A.M.) and, when he feels he has done all he can, he stops. Sometimes he sneaks back to bed. Alexander says that he is "thinking horizontally." His wife calls it "snoozing." He has mentored area writers and has introduced some, in-cluding Donna Jo Napoli, to editors at Dutton. The Alexanders continue to enjoy their cats (some have appeared in his books). The couple's 1996 Christmas card combined Alexander's interest in drawing and music in his sketch showing himself holding a violin. Few will think of Alexander as a musician, but many will remember him as a master storyteller. About his interests and pastimes Alexander says, "Mozart's music is a great passion; so is playing the violin, which I do amazingly badly. I love reading, British style crossword puzzles, and drawing silly cartoons for my own amusement."

Always a reader, Alexander's message for those who read his books is, "Read! Read every book you can get. Each book we read adds another dimension to our lives."

Books and Notes

Lloyd Alexander has contributed to more than 40 books. The books in the selected list are representative of his fantasy titles. Annotations/notes are in-cluded where the content is not ade-quately indicated by title or when the title has not been annotated within the biographical information.

The Prydain Chronicles

The Book of Three (Holt, 1964).

The Black Cauldron (Holt, 1965).

The Castle of Llyr (Holt, 1966).

Taran Wanderer (Holt, 1967).

The High King (Holt, 1968).

The Westmark Trilogy

Westmark (Dutton, 1981).

The Kestrel (Dutton, 1982).

The Beggar Queen (Dutton, 1984).

Adventures of Vesper

The Illyrian Adventure (Dutton, 1986).
The first tale featuring Vesper, a fearless sixteen-year-old orphan, and her guardian who find themselves in the middle of a dangerous rebellion during their research of an ancient legend. Set in 1872.

The El Dorado Adventure (Dutton, 1987).
During a visit to South America to inspect her real-estate holdings, seventeen-year-old Vesper attempts to stop the building of a canal that would destroy the homeland of a native tribe.

The Drackenberg Adventure (Dutton, 1988).
The year is 1873, and seventeen-year-old Vesper Holly and her guardians must face their archenemy, Dr. Helvitius, in the pursuit of a lost art treasure. The obscure European grand duchy is threatened with annexation by a neighboring kingdom.

The Jedera Adventure (Dutton, 1989).
Vesper and her guardians face danger, in the remote country of Jedera, when they attempt to return a valuable book borrowed years ago by Vesper's father.

The Philadelphia Adventure (Dutton, 1990).
The year is now 1876, the eve of the Centennial Exposition in Philadelphia, and twenty-year-old Vesper finds herself clashing once again with Dr. Helvitius. His evil schemes plunge all of them into danger in the wild Pennsylvania countryside.

Other Titles

The Fortune-Tellers. Illustrated by Trina Schart Hyman. (Dutton, 1992).
After going to a fortune-teller, a carpenter in the West African country of Cameroon finds that the predictions are coming true in unusual ways.

The House of Gabbaleen. Illustrated by Diane Goode. (Dutton, 1995).
Tooley is eager to reverse his "bad luck," so he ignores his cat's warnings and invites a greedy little man into his home. His hopes of bettering his fortunes are dashed.

The Arkadians (Dutton, 1995).
An honest young man joins together with a poet-turned-jackass and a young girl with mystical powers in an attempt to escape the wrath of a king and the wicked soothsayers.

Time Cat: the Remarkable Journeys of Jason and Gareth (Holt, 1963; Puffin, 1996).
With a wink of his eye, Gareth, a magic cat, can take Jason on a time trip to a faraway land in a historical time period. Together they have nine adventures.

The Iron Ring (Dutton, 1997).
Young King Tamar, driven by his sense of *dharma* or honor, begins a quest during which he encounters talking animals, wicked and honorable kings, demons, and "the love of his life."

For More Information About/By the Author

Articles

Alexander, Lloyd. "Fools, Heroes & Jackasses: The 1995 Anne Carroll Moore Lecture." *School Library Journal* 42, no. 3 (March 1, 1996): 114–16.

Alexander, Lloyd. "The Fortune-Tellers: Acceptance Speech for the Boston Globe-Horn Book Award." *Bulletin for the Center of Children's Books* 70, no. 1 (January 1, 1994): 46–47.

Alexander, Lloyd. "A Letter to the Class From: Lloyd Alexander." *Trumpet Club Notes* (November/December 1985): 2.

Reasoner, Charles. *A Teacher's Guide to the Paperback Editions of The Prydain Chronicles by Lloyd Alexander* (Dell, 1982).

Avi

Mystery and Suspense ◆ Adventure ◆ Fantasy ◆ Ghost stories

**New York, New York
December 23, 1937**

📖 *The True Confessions of Charlotte Doyle*
📖 *Nothing But the Truth*

About the Author
and the Author's Writing

His teachers covered his writing papers with red ink marks. He was told that he would not (or could not) become a writer. So why did he? Because he was told he couldn't! Avi struggles with dysgraphia—a learning disability in writing. He left words out of sentences and added others where they didn't make sense. He spells words incorrectly (even though he knows how to spell them correctly). Until the eighth grade Avi was in the same class as his twin sister. Emily was considered smart. His older brother went to college at the age of fifteen. Avi's school performance did not compare well with his siblings. He was viewed as "being sloppy and erratic, and not paying attention." He endured unending criticism, but despite that, he kept trying. He liked what he wrote and actually did fairly well in science. But when he was sent to a science high school, he failed. His parents enrolled him in a small private school, and it was there that an English teacher insisted that he get help with writing. By the time he was seventeen, he knew that he wanted to be a writer. Since then, he has earned acclaim as a Newbery Honor Award–winning author and has garnered many other awards for his books for young readers.

Edward Wortis was born December 23, 1937, five minutes before his sister, Emily. His sister began to call him Avi—no one seems to know why, but the name stuck. Their father, Joseph, was a psychiatrist, their mother, Helen Zunser, a social worker. The family spent a lot of time reading, and every night they read to Avi. On Fridays the family would go to the library. Every birthday brought at least one gift book. Avi says, "I loved to read. Still do." Avi was reading by the time he was five years old and has never stopped. For a time he also thought he wanted to play baseball, but he wasn't very good. Besides, something inside him pulled him toward writing.

His grandfather, a Russian immigrant, often told him stories about American history—how wonderful the country was—and he recounted the wonderful traditions associated with being in America. Avi came to regard history with a sense of *story*. His entire family seemed to be a family of storytellers. Avi's paternal grandmother was French and raised in Alsace-Lorraine. When she was six or seven years old, the Germans marched into Alsace during the Franco-Prussian war of 1870. She often told vivid stories of those days.

Avi also loved to draw, and his parents, who enjoyed photography, encouraged him to become a sculptor. But *he* wanted to write. Avi struggled through school, but with the help of an understanding tutor he began to understand his abilities and cope with his dysgraphia. He attended the University of Wisconsin, where he earned an undergraduate degree in 1959 and a masters degree in 1962. Two years later he received a second masters degree in library science from Columbia University. For twenty-five years he worked as a librarian at the New York Public Library, the Lambeth Public Library in London, and Trenton State College in New Jersey, where he was also an assistant professor. During this time he married Joan Gabiner and they had two sons, Shaun and Kevin.

His writing career began early. At first he wrote plays, but when his oldest son was born, he began to tell stories for younger readers. His first book, *Things That Sometimes Happen* (Doubleday, 1970), was based on a storytelling game he played with Shaun. Shaun would tell his dad what he wanted a story to be about, and Avi would create a tale using those characters or objects. That storybook became the catalyst for Avi's writing career. Since *Things That Sometimes Happen*, Avi has only written for young readers. After Avi and his wife divorced, he married again, this time to Coppelia Kahn. A stepson, Gabriel Kahn, also entered his life.

During his own childhood in the 1940s, Avi read picture books, novels, many comic books, and listened often to kids' radio. Like many youngsters, Avi listened to adventure stories. He loved all the radio heroes—the Lone Ranger, Captain Midnight, the Green Hornet, and the Sky King. In fact, he often *lived* their stories. Avi later wrote a book, *Who Was That Masked Man Anyway?* (Orchard, 1992), which incorporated those radio heroes into the plot. Frankie, the chief protagonist, is the boy Avi would have liked to have been. The story is told with dialogue and is very funny. Avi says, "I think [it is] my funniest book."

Other books come from bits and pieces of Avi's life. During high school, Avi was captain of the soccer team. Unfortunately, they never won a game. *S.O.R. Losers* (Bradbury, 1984) is based on those experiences.

Avi brought together a relative's request for a funny book and the fact that some friends had just bought an old railway station in North Brookfield, Massachusetts, and mixed those ideas with inspiration he got by reading a lot of "old" children's books. The result was *Emily Upham's Revenge* (Pantheon, 1978; Morrow, 1992).

An abridged version of a Shakespeare play performed in his sons' elementary school nudged Avi to write *Romeo and Juliet: Together (and Alive) at Last* (Orchard, 1987), and his interest in Poe inspired *The Man Who Was Poe* (Orchard, 1989).

Avi's favorite reading material was comic books. When his sons were young they loved them too—so much that one son, Shaun, had a superhero costume party for his fourth birthday. One guest came as the Green Lantern, complete with a jade ring borrowed from his mother. During that party, the boy lost the ring in the grass. Those ideas all came together in *No More Magic* (Pantheon, 1975). Later the same interest in comic books helped Avi create the format for *City of Light, City of Dark* (Orchard, 1993). Avi read all the comic books he could get hold of, but his mother refused to let him read scary ones in the house. While he was working on this story, he remembered all the comic books that he had read. Soon, he decided that a comic book format would be the best way to tell the tale. He worked closely with the illustrator, Brian Floca, to create a visual tale.

For a time Avi and his family lived in Lambertville, New Jersey, and in New Hope while he worked at Trenton State College. Two of his historical novels are set in that region. *Night Journeys* (Pantheon, 1979; Beech Tree, 1994), set in Solebury, tells the story of runaway indentured servants. The book's sequel, *Encounter at Easton* (Pantheon, 1980; Beech Tree, 1994), continues the story by telling about the servants and children who help the indentured servants escape.

New Jersey and New England provide the general setting for several other novels as well. *Captain Grey* (Pantheon, 1977; Morrow, 1993) takes place on the New Jersey coast during the 1780s. A sign proclaiming the site of a skirmish along the side of a New Jersey highway inspired another book, *The Fighting Ground* (Lippincott, 1984; Harper, 1987).

Avi encountered the subject of *The Barn* (Orchard, 1984) while photographing old barns in northern California. The story of Ben, who attempts to save his father by building the barn, ended up in 1855 Oregon, not California.

During school visits Avi is often asked where he gets his ideas. His answer is that, "Everyone has ideas. The bigger question is what do you do with your ideas?" He explains that two of his sons are rock musicians and fashion their ideas into music. His sister, Emily, takes her ideas and writes poems. His brother uses his ideas to help him understand science. "And I take my ideas and turn them into stories."

Avi has written books as diverse as his reading interests. He has written comedy, mystery, adventure, fantasy, animal tales, ghost stories, and young adult coming-of-age tales. He also writes novels in comic book form, dialogue, documentary style, and historical novels.

In 1997 Avi wrote a story, *Keep Your Eye on Amanda!*, about twin raccoons. But this story is unlike any others. Avi is selling the story chapter by chapter to newspapers. The first newspaper to publish the story was the *Colorado Springs Gazette Telegraph*. As a child Avi remembers reading a story in installments in the newspaper, and that sense of joy and anticipation inspired Avi to re-create the newspaper serials common in the nineteenth and early twentieth centuries. The story is set in the Boulder area, where Avi moved in 1995. Soon some of the area raccoons found his home, entered an open window, and went on a rampage that found its way into Avi's story.

Avi brings many experiences to his writing. In addition to his work as a librarian and writer, he has interests in photography, reading, hiking, running, camping, making bread, and playing cricket. During his full-time librarian days, he found time to research and write by going in to work early, using a lunch hour, staying an extra hour, and working at night and weekends. Writing was almost compulsive. Because his writing time was episodic, so was much of his writing. Now, Avi has an office with a computer, where he writes about six hours a day. He says he needs absolute quiet to work. Writing one book often takes a year or more and he rewrites as often as ten or fifteen times. He sets more short-term than long-term goals—five pages a day, rather than 300 pages a summer.

Today, Avi lives in Boulder, Colorado, where he has learned how to ski and ride horses. He also enjoys photography and cooking. Avi's son Shaun is a rock musician in the Boston area, and his other son, Kevin, lives and manages rock bands in San Francisco. Kevin has a young daughter named Ruby.

Avi's message to people who want to write is consistent: "[T]he key to writing is reading. The more you read, the better your writing can be."

Books and Notes

Avi's novels start fast and grab the reader immediately. He prefers to begin with strong dialogue and includes real-life conflicts. Avi has written over 49 novels in many genres. His books' narrative style relies heavily on emotional suspense, imagery, irony, and contradiction. His most popular books are adventure, mystery and suspense novels and humor books. Historical facts and settings are included in many of his books. While he says that he hated "being a student and hated to study," he has a degree in history and read novels as a way to immerse himself in the subject.

The following are selected titles classified by genre.

Adventure

The Barn (Orchard, 1994).
A family, three children and their father, are homesteading in 1855 Oregon. Then disaster strikes. Their father's building of the barn becomes the symbol for recovery.

Beyond the Western Sea, Book 1: The Escape from Home (Orchard, 1996).

Beyond the Western Sea, Book 2: Lord Kirkle's Money (Orchard, 1996).
A gallery of unforgettable characters flee Ireland in the 1850s, encounter stolen money in London, and search for their immigrant father in America.

Captain Grey (Morrow, 1993).
The only thing standing in the way of Captain Grey's reign of havoc and revenge along the New Jersey coast is Kevin. A tale from the 1780s.

Animal Tales

Poppy (Orchard, 1995).
This tale began as a story about a great horned owl, Mr. Ocax, who wanted to rule Dinwood Forest. It became a book about Poppy, a deer mouse, who challenges the bully, Mr. Ocax.

Poppy and Rye (Avon, 1998).
This sequel follows the adventures of Poppy the deer mouse. In this tale, the home of a family of golden mice is threatened by beavers.

Fantasy

Bright Shadow (Bradbury, 1985; Aladdin, 1994).

Morwena has the last five wishes in the land, but when they are used, she must die. How will she use the wishes?

Perloo the Bold (Scholastic, 1998).

A peaceful scholar is chosen to succeed Jolaine as the leader of the furry underground Montmer people. Perloo finds himself in danger when Jolaine dies and her evil son attempts to seize control.

Tom, Babbette & Simon (Macmillan, 1995).

Three fantasy tales filled with magic and transformation.

Ghost Stories

Devil's Race (Lippincott, 1984).

Tom's namesake was the personification of evil, and now he wishes to invade the current century, come back to life, and take over the body of today's Tom, an unusually nice teenager.

Mystery

The Man Who Was Poe (Orchard, 1989).

Poe's help is sought to find Edmund's mother and sister, but Poe is looking for a solution to the mystery he is writing.

No More Magic (Pantheon, 1975).

A search for what is real, and what is fantasy.

Who Stole the Wizard of Oz (Knopf, 1981).

Becky has been accused of stealing a rare children's book from the town library. Intent on clearing herself, she and her twin brother, Toby, discover clues from children's books help solve the mystery.

Humorous Stories

Emily Upham's Revenge (Pantheon, 1978; Morrow, 1992).

A melodrama set in 1870s New England has pious Emily teaming up with an irreverent Seth to outwit thieves.

History of Helpless Harry (Morrow, 1995; Beech Tree, 1995).

Harry takes on the villain in a comedy-filled mystery that pits good against evil.

S.O.R. Losers (Bradbury, 1984).

The South Orange River Middle School soccer team is filled with boys who are required to be a member. While they may be "losers," they do have a lot of laughs.

Other

What Do Fish Have to Do with Anything? Short Stories (Candlewick Press, 1997).

A collection of tales: *What Do Fish Have to Do with Anything?*; *The Goodness of Matt Kaizer*; *Talk to Me, Teacher Tamer*; *Pets, What's Inside*; and *Fortune Cookie*.

Finding Providence: The Story of Roger Williams (Harper, 1997).

A short "I can read chapter book" biography of Roger Williams. Williams lived in the 1600s and, when forced to leave the Massachusetts Bay Colony, he traveled south, founding Providence, Rhode Island, with the help of the Narragansett Indians.

For More Information About/By the Author

Articles

Avi. "The Child in Children's Literature." *Horn Book* 69, no. 1 (January/February 1993): 40–50.

Avi's Home Page. URL: http://www.avi-writer.com/ (Accessed August 1998).

Broderick, Kathy. "Avi." *Booklinks* 6, no. 4 (March 1997): 56+.

Brooks, Kathleen. "The Truth Will Not Set You Free If You Have a Chance to Speak, or a Contradiction in Terms." *ALAN Review* 23, no. 2 (Winter 1996): 32+.

Elleman, Barbara. "Book Strategies: Nothing But the Truth, a Documentary Novel by Avi." *BookLinks* 1, no. 3 (January 1992): 60+.

Marinak, Barbara. "Author Profile: Avi." *The Book Report* (March/April 1992): 26–28.

Winarski, Diana L. "Avi on Fiction." *Teaching PreK–8* 28, no. 1 (September 1997): 62–64.

Books

Markham, Lois. *Avi* (Learning Works, 1996).

James Matthew Barrie

◆ Fantasy

Kirriemuir, Scotland
May 9, 1860–June 19, 1937

📖 *Peter Pan*

About the Author
and the Author's Writing

Scottish-born J. M. Barrie was known as a playwright and novelist. He was best known for his play *Peter Pan* (1904). He was the third son and ninth child of weavers David and Margaret Barrie. After attending Glasgow Academy and Dumfries Academy, Barrie entered Edinburgh University in 1878, where he earned a masters degree. Barrie worked as a journalist in Nottingham and later in London. By the 1880s he was writing novels.

The Little Minister (1891) became his first major success. The romantic plot involved a shy preacher and an outgoing woman who marries him. The first of Barrie's plays was produced in 1891. Barrie continued as both a novelist and playwright. In 1896 his novel *Sentimental Tommy* was published. It featured an overactive imagination. The following year, 1897, a dramatized version of *The Little Minister* brought Barrie fame and wealth. Due to his success as a literary writer Barrie left journalism and devoted himself to plays and novels.

In 1902 Barrie's fantasy novel *The Little White Bird* was published by Scribner's. The boy hero Peter Pan first appeared in that novel. The novel (and the character) was so popular that Barrie fashioned several chapters into a play titled *Peter Pan* (1904). The play is the best-known version of the story.

Peter Pan does not want to grow up and he escapes to Never-Never Land. Peter Pan meets the three Darling children, Wendy, John, and Michael, in a visit back to the human world. Peter Pan convinces the three children to return with him and Tinker Bell to Never-Never Land. Their adventures include encounters with a crocodile, the Indian princess Tiger Lily, and pirate Captain Hook. Two years later several more chapters were adapted into a second play, *Peter Pan in Kensington Gardens*, and in 1911 Barrie penned a narrative form of the play as *Peter Pan and Wendy*.

The Library of Congress contains more than 150 entries relating to J. M. Barrie's *Peter Pan*, including musical scores, plays, movies, and books about the boy who would not grow up. Scott Gustafson illustrated the latest complete and unabridged version of the story, published by Viking in 1991.

In 1953 Walt Disney released a twenty-two minute animated edition of the story chronicling the adventures of Peter and Wendy, Michael, and John Darling as they encounter Captain Hook on the enchanted island of Neverland. Peter Pan was played by Betty Bronson. Seven years later Disney released a 104-minute animated edition of the swashbuckler fantasy with Mary Martin in the lead role. This version brought the story into most households. Mary Martin originally starred in Broadway's musical version of Sir J. M. Barrie's *Peter Pan* in 1953. The play was so popular that it was restaged for television and aired on NBC's *Producer's Showcase* (March 7, 1955). It returned to television the following year, and eventually the producers sought to videotape the production. Mary Martin performed the lead once again, and on December 8, 1960, the video version was first telecast. Musical highlights of the play included "First Star to the Left, Then Straight On Till Morning," "I've Gotta Crow," "I'm Flying," "I Won't Grow Up," and "Ugg-a-Wugg." "Neverland" and "Hook's Waltz" were included in the video production.

The film was quickly dubbed a classic and shown several times in the 1970s. In 1989 the film was retelecast (complete with the then re-tired NBC Peacock logo) to a new audience. The 1989 release was re-edited to accommodate extra commercials. Currently, the original (and complete) version of the 1960 *Peter Pan* is available on videocassette.

Various other versions, or portions, of the play have been offered to the public. In 1992 Fox Television Network authorized a 23-minute release based on its afternoon adventure-show version. *Peter Pan & the Pirates: Demise of Hook* was billed as "an exciting animated episode." In 1992 Steven Spielberg directed a 142-minute tale of a grown-up Peter Pan titled *Hook* (TriStar). Robin Williams played Peter Pan and Dustin Hoffman played Hook. Peter Pan must "find his true self" to rescue his children from the hands of the evil Captain Hook. Julia Roberts was cast as Tinker Bell. The film grossed more than $119 million domestically.

Copies of the movie posters advertising *Peter Pan* are available for purchase from movie memorabilia companies. Carousel Publishing offered personalized books focusing on a search for Wendy's brothers. Because the original tale is now considered public domain, hundreds of spin-offs exist. A version (now copyrighted by Duncan Research because of their inclusion of notes and explanations) is posted on the Internet.

In 1934 Barrie's book *The Little Minister* became the basis for a film, *The Little Minister*, which starred Katharine Hepburn as Babbie and John Beal as the pastor. Although the play version (1897) had brought Barrie fame and wealth, the film version was only mildly acclaimed.

Barrie married Mary Ansell in 1894 and divorced in 1909. They had no children. However, Barrie wanted his story of Peter Pan to benefit children as much as possible and thus donated his rights to *Peter Pan* to a London children's hospital. Barrie did not write much later in life but continued to receive honors based on his earlier works. He wrote his best-known works early in his career. In 1913 King George V made Barrie a baronet, and he received the Order of Merit in 1922. James Matthew Barrie died in London on June 19, 1937.

Books and Notes

Fantasy

The Little White Bird or, Adventures in Kensington Gardens (Longwood Press, 1977).
　　Reprint of the 1902 edition published by Scribner's (NY).

Peter Pan. Illustrations by Jan Ormerod. (Viking, 1988).

Peter Pan. Illustrations by Trina Schart Hyman. (Bantam, 1981).

Peter Pan: The Complete Book. Introduction by Michael Patrick Hearn. Illustrations by Susan Hudson. (Tundra Books, 1988).

Peter Pan. Illustrated by Michael Hague. (Henry Holt, 1987).

Peter Pan. Josette Frank, ed. Illustrated by Diane Goode. (Random House, 1983).

Peter Pan in Kensington Gardens and Peter and Wendy. Peter Hollindale, ed. (Oxford, 1991).

For More Information About/By the Author

There seem to be few, if any, contemporary articles about James Matthew Barrie and his writings. However, various quotes extracted from his writings provide a rich perspective.

Quotes

"Nothing is really work unless you would rather be doing something else."

"The printing press is either the greatest blessing or the greatest curse of modern times, sometimes one forgets which."

"Shall we make a new rule of life from tonight: always try to be a little kinder than is necessary."

"When the first baby laughed for the first time, the laugh broke into a thousand pieces and they all went skipping about, and that was the beginning of fairies."

"To die will be an awfully big adventure."

"It's a sort of bloom on a woman. If you have it, you don't need to have anything else; and if you don't have it, it doesn't matter much matter what else you have."

"Life is a long lesson in humility."

Patricia Beatty

◆ Historical Fiction

Portland, Oregon
August 26, 1922–July 9, 1991

📖 *Charley Skedaddle*

📖 *Eben Tyne, Powdermonkey*

📖 *Who Comes with Cannons?*

About the Author
and the Author's Writing

Patricia Beatty's writing career emerged from boredom while living in London, England. Her writing began as a hobby, but soon became a career.

Beatty was born Patricia Robbins in Portland, Oregon, on August 26, 1922—seven months and four days after John Beatty, who was born January 22, 1922, in the same hospital. Though their mothers were casual acquaintances during Patricia and John's childhood, the two did not really become acquainted until attending Read College. Both earned undergraduate degrees from Read College in 1944, and then attended graduate school at the University of Idaho and the University of Washington in Seattle. Before marrying John Beatty on September 14, 1950, Patricia Beatty taught high school English and history in Coeur d'Alene, Idaho. Beatty first wrote about pioneers and Indians. She wrote without much success for years, although by 1960 a small publisher in Caldwell, Idaho, had published *Indian Canoe-Maker* (Caxton Printers, 1960). The book focused on the Quileute Indians.

Their daughter, Ann Alexandria, was born in 1957. In 1959, the Beatty's moved to London. Motivated by the setting and boredom, Beatty began to write about eighteenth-century England. Her novel, *At the Seven Stars* (Macmillan, 1963), was set in 1752 London and marked the first collaboration with her husband. John Beatty, specialized in English history, so Patricia chided him into helping her. Together they wrote six more novels set in England.

Between those books she wrote on her own as well. She penned historical novels set in the American West in the late 1800s and early 1900s. *Bonanza Girl* (Morrow, 1962; reissued 1993) was the first book published in this setting. In the 1960s she produced *The Nickel-Plated Beauty* (Morrow, 1964), *Me, California Perkins* (Morrow, 1968), and six other titles set during the turn of the century. She used her writing skills as a means to teach history.

After leaving England, the Beattys moved to California, where Patricia taught a children's writing class for the University of California at Los Angeles Extension Department.

During their writing, the Beattys checked facts and words diligently. For example, the main character in *Champion Towers*, Penitence Hervey, tells her own story. The dialogue and narrative had to reflect a seventeenth-century culture. The Beattys were careful to create Penitence's dialogue using language that would have been used at the time. Just before sending the manuscript to the publisher, they realized that because they had written the story in first person, the narrative also had to reflect the times. They checked and rechecked each word, a project that consumed them both for three hours a day for six weeks. They used their two-volume *Shorter Oxford English Dictionary on Historical Principles* and a concordance to the King James version of the Bible. During the process they established some guidelines for their decisions. If Shakespeare used a word similarly, the word stayed. If a word appeared in the Bible with the same meaning, the word stayed. And if the *Oxford English Dictionary* listed the word as late as 1665, the word stayed.

The rationale for the 1665 publication date was that a word certainly would have been used in common language prior to its inclusion in the 1665 dictionary. Sometimes they had used a word as a verb and during their checking process found that the word was only a noun in the 1600s. Then they had to search for a synonym.

Military terms were particularly troublesome and were central to the descriptions of the Battle of Worcester, for example. Military *patrols* were *scouting parties*, and *passwords* were *watchwords*.

Other terms were corrected to reflect appropriate usage—*fireplace* became *hearthfire;* horses did not *whinny*, but they did *neigh;* characters would not have suffered from *rheumatism*, but might have suffered from *arthritis*. At one point in the story they mentioned a secret passage that was accessed through a *Spanish knob*, but discovered that during the period of the story setting, the knob did not exist. Three hundred years ago people entered rooms and houses by using latches and strings.

The same detailed research characterized the novels written by Patricia. Her writing featured California settings and the Civil War period. Riverside, California, was the setting for at least two titles, *The Bad Bell of San Salvador* (Morrow, 1973) and *The Queen's Own Grove* (Morrow, 1966).

John Beatty died in 1975, and two years later Patricia Beatty married Carl J. Uhr. Her most popular titles were published in the 1980s. *Eben Tyne, Powdermonkey* (Morrow, 1990), a book of Civil War history, coauthored with Phillip Robbins, and *Jayhawker* (Morrow, 1991), a story dealing with the early years of the Civil War, are included on many lists of Civil War novels.

Patricia Beatty's writing career spanned three decades and resulted in more than fifty entries in the Library of Congress catalog. Patricia Beatty died July 9, 1991, in Riverside, California.

Books and Notes

Once a history teacher, Patricia Beatty continued that role as a writer. She wrote first about life in England, and then colonial America. Her best-known books are generally considered to be about life during the Civil War.

Civil War

Charley Skedaddle (Morrow, 1987).
    After deserting the Union Army during a battle, Charley, a twelve-year-old Bowery boy from New York, encounters a hostile, old Virginia mountain woman.

Eben Tyne, Powdermonkey (Morrow, 1990).
    Written with Phillip Robbins. Eben Tyne, a thirteen-year-old, becomes part of the Confederate Navy to help the crew of the *Merrimack* break the Union blockade of the Norfolk, Virginia, harbor.

Jayhawker (Morrow, 1991).

Early during the Civil War, Lije Tulley becomes a Jayhawker. The teenage Kansas farm boy becomes an abolitionist raider who slips into the neighboring state of Missouri to spy in an effort to help the antislavery movement.

Who Comes with Cannons? (Morrow, 1992).

A Quaker twelve-year-old girl from Indiana is living with relatives in North Carolina and discovers that they are running an Underground Railroad station during the beginning of the Civil War (1861).

English Setting

Holdfast (Morrow, 1972).

Written with John Beatty. During the reign of Elizabeth I, an Irish orphan is taken both from her beloved wolfhound and her homeland. She yearns for both.

Master Rosalind (Morrow, 1974).

A young woman disguises herself as a boy in order to play feminine roles in the theater during the time of Shakespeare.

Pirate Royal (Macmillan, 1969).

A bondservant, jailed for theft, joins a band of pirates and then earns a pardon and praise from the King of England for service to Henry Morgan, famous buccaneer.

Western United States of America

Bonanza Girl (Morrow, 1962, 1993; Beach Tree, 1993).

A widow and her two children head for the gold-mining region in Idaho to find jobs and begin a new life.

Me, California Perkins (Morrow, 1968).

Mrs. Perkins sends her husband to the bachelor quarters to show her displeasure with him and the appalling conditions in the uncivilized silver-mining town. Only Mrs. Perkin's determined daughter can intervene.

Red Rock over the River (Morrow, 1973).

Set in Ft. Yuma, Arizona, during the 1880s, Dorcas becomes involved in the escape of an outlaw from the prison across the river.

For More Information About/By the Author

Articles

Beatty, Patricia. "Writing the Historical Novel for Young Readers." *The Writer* 102, no. 3 (March 1, 1989): 17+.

John Bellairs

Marshall, Michigan
January 17, 1938–March 8, 1991

📕 *The Curse of the Blue Figurine*

📕 *The House with a Clock in Its Wall*

About the Author
and the Author's Writing

Asked about his favorite things, John Bellairs said, "I love ghost stories, coffins, bones, spells, Latin, cathedrals, darkness, castles, England, cobalt blue, Christmas, Italian food, the moon, secret passages, and wizards like Gandalf. I'm also a Red Sox fan." Most of his favorite things seemed to have ended up in his books.

John Bellairs was born in Marshall, Michigan, and most of his childhood was spent just twelve miles from the cereal capital of the world, Battle Creek. In Marshall, Bellairs was surrounded by many unusual enormous old houses. Bellairs included these old houses into his many books. But Bellairs's imagination filled the houses with strange happenings that, "If they didn't occur, I wish they had."

After graduating from high school, Bellairs earned an undergraduate degree from Notre Dame in 1959 and a masters degree in English from the University of Chicago in 1960. He began his career as an English teacher. He taught at the College of St. Teresa in Winona, Minnesota, and Shimer College in Mount Carrol, Illinois. Seven years later, motivated by the success of his first book, Bellairs turned to writing full-time. He traveled to England for six months. His writing did not sustain him, however, and he returned to teaching. He sailed back to the United States on the *Queen Elizabeth* and settled in New England. It was during this time that he meet Priscilla Braids at an Easter party.

They married on June 24, 1968, and took up residence in an old New Hampshire farmhouse. Bellairs became completely acquainted with the White Mountains. He taught English at Emmanuel College in Boston, and later joined the English faculty at Merrimack College in North Andover, Massachusetts.

He began writing children's books with *The House with a Clock in Its Wall* (Dial, 1973). This book, and those that followed, allowed Bellairs to return to full-time writing. The family, now including their son, Frank, moved to Haverhill, Massachusetts. By the early 1980s, Bellairs and Priscilla had divorced. Bellairs and his son continued to live in Haverhill in their frame house with a cozy porch. Bellairs died there of a heart attack on March 8, 1991.

Bellairs's writing included settings from his childhood. His boyhood hometown, Marshall, became New Zebedee in a series that included *The House with a Clock in Its Wall* (Dial, 1973), *The Figure in the Shadows* (Dial, 1975), and *The Letter, the Witch, and the Ring* (Dial, 1976). Readers who visit Marshall often feel as if they have landed right in the middle of Bellairs's New Zebedee. *The House with a Clock in Its Wall* is known as the Cronin Mansion. The books are a mix of teenage concerns and the supernatural, a mix that results in chilling tales for young readers.

The first few pages of the series concern Lewis Barnavelt, a shy, geeky young man who is on his way to meet his uncle for the first time. He is unable to keep friends and his attempts to find new friends bring some eerie (and magical) moments. Lewis grows to love and respect the unique Uncle Jonathan. The poker game in the front parlor with Mrs. Zimmerman is more than it appears. The book is full of chills and episodes from the commonplace to the supernatural. This series was followed by one beginning with *The Treasure of Alpheus Winterborn* (Dial, 1978).

The Treasure of Alpheus Winterborn is set in Hoosac, a town modeled after the real town of Winona. Myra Eells, the "bird-like" public librarian, meets Anthony Monday over magazines in a drugstore and listens. He grows to trust and respect her, and together they search for treasure. In the sequel, *The Dark Secret of Weatherend* (Dial, 1984), the two friends find themselves opposing a demon, Anders Borkman, who wishes to destroy humanity to develop a pure race. In spite of Borkman casting a spell on Anthony and Miss Eells, they find a way to outwit and conquer him.

The Curse of the Blue Figurine (Dial, 1983) began yet another series, this one set in the White Mountains of New Hampshire, not far from Bellairs's Massachusetts home. In addition to the settings, many ordinary experiences come from Bellairs's life—the experiences with bullies, the scaredy-cat kid Lewis, and the grownups (a father who owned a saloon and a mother who was constantly worried about money).

Most, if not all, of Bellairs's books have a recognizable pattern. The protagonist, usually a young teenager, makes a mystical goof, and with the help of friends or someone older, the protagonist comes to terms with the situation. His books are filled with everyday incidents, elements of science fiction, philosophical crises, cozy scenes, and mysterious happenings.

From 1980 until his death in 1991, John Bellairs lived in Haverhill, Massachusetts, where he wrote full-time. Bellairs left behind two unfinished manuscripts and plot outlines for two more novels. Bellairs's son, Frank, asked longtime Bellairs's fan Brad Strickland to complete the two partial manuscripts and to write the two novels based on the plot outlines. The titles, *The Ghost in the Mirror* (Dial, 1993), *The Vengeance of the Witch-Finder* (Dial, 1993), *The Drum, the Doll, and the Zombie* (Dial, 1994), and *The Doom of the Haunted Opera* (Dial, 1995) are listed as being "by John Bellairs, completed by Brad Strickland." Jonathan Abucejo, a devoted fan of Bellairs's work, has said, "I wasn't too sure what 'all' he had completed. . . . I couldn't really tell from the style where John Bellairs stopped and where Brad Strickland began." Since then, Brad Strickland has written additional books based on the characters created by Bellairs.

Johnny Dixon is the chief protagonist in the Strickland novels *The Hand of the Necromancer* (Dial, 1996) and *The Bell, the Book, and the Spellbinder* (Dial, 1997).

The characters that live in Bellairs's novels seem destined to live in Brad Strickland's books; Strickland "has set out to write the kind of stories he likes to read."

Books and Notes

John Bellairs wrote books set in three locations—New Zebedee, Michigan; Hoosac, Minnesota; and Duston Heights, Massachusetts (White Mountains).

Books Set in New Zebedee (Marshall), Michigan

Rose Rita and Lewis Barnavelt are the main characters. Lewis Barnavelt's parents were killed in an automobile accident, and he was sent to live with his Uncle Jonathan in New Zebedee. Lewis is a shy, chubby, blond-haired boy who has difficulty making friends. His efforts at friendship with Tarby, a popular athlete, are unsuccessful. He does, however, meet Rose Rita Pottinger, and they become best friends. *The Ghost in the Mirror* is a time-travel book that takes place in 1828 Stonebridge, Pennsylvania. *The Vengeance of the Witch-Finder* includes several episodes set in the Barnavelt Manor (near Dinsdale, England). The complete series includes:

The House with a Clock in Its Wall (Dial, 1973).

The Figure in the Shadows (Dial, 1975).

The Letter, the Witch, and the Ring (Dial, 1976).

The Ghost in the Mirror. Completed by Brad Strickland. (Dial, 1993).

The Vengeance of the Witch-Finder. Completed by Brad Strickland. (Dial, 1993).

The Doom of the Haunted Opera. Completed by Brad Strickland. (Dial, 1995).

Books Set in Hoosac (Winona), Minnesota

Anthony Monday is a gangly young man who most often wears cutoff jeans, sneakers, an old soiled white T-shirt, and a red leather cap with a crumpled bill. One day at the local drugstore he meets Miss Eells, the town's head librarian. They become friends rather quickly, and soon Anthony has an after-school job in the town's library. She listens as he tells his fears (dogs) and likes (mysteries). His favorite authors are John Dickson Carr, Agatha Christie, and Sir Arthur Conan Doyle. His hobby is coin collecting, and he is always searching for a boxfull of Brasher doubloons or 1822 five-dollar gold pieces. *The Mansion in the Mist* takes place in Hoosac, Minnesota, and on a Northern Canadian island on Shadow Lake. The books featuring Anthony Monday and Miss Eells include:

The Treasure of Alpheus Winterborn (Dial, 1978).

The Dark Secret of Weatherend (Dial, 1984).

The Lamp from the Warlock's Tomb (Dial, 1988).

The Mansion in the Mist (Dial, 1992).

Books Set in Duston Heights, Massachusetts (White Mountains)

John Michael Dixon and Professor Childermass are best friends. "Johnny" is living with his grandparents in Duston Heights because his mother died of cancer and his father serves in the Air Force. Johnny is rather shy and normally avoids kids his own age. He often reads adult nonfiction books about archaeology and is very good in science, Latin, and literature—interests he shares with Professor Childermass. There are references to Shakespeare and the works of the Dutch master painters, Rembrandt and Ruysdael. Their adventures include episodes in the White Mountains, the Boy Scout camp, the hotel run by Glomus's sister, St. Michael's church, and Johnny's hometown, Gildersleeve, Massachusetts. *The Hand of the Necromancer* and *The Bell, the Book, and the Spellbinder* were written by Brad Strickland but feature Bellairs's characters and settings.

The Curse of the Blue Figurine (Dial, 1983).

The Mummy, the Will, and the Crypt (Dial, 1983).

The Spell of the Sorcerer's Skull (Dial, 1984).

The Revenge of the Wizards Ghost (Dial, 1985).

The Eyes of the Killer Robot (Dial, 1986).

The Trolley to Yesterday (Dial, 1989).

The Chessmen of Doom (Dial, 1989).

The Secret of the Underground Room (Dial, 1990).

The Drum, the Doll, and the Zombie. Completed by Brad Strickland. (Dial, 1994).

The Hand of the Necromancer. By Brad Strickland. (Dial, 1996).

The Bell, the Book, and the Spellbinder. By Brad Strickland. (Dial, 1997).

For More Information About/By the Author

Articles

Abucejo, Jonathan. ©1996. *The Compleat Bellairs.* URL: http://www.pitt.edu/~jamst125.bellairs.htm (Accessed September 1997).

Site includes an introduction, lycaeum, codex, other spooky links, et cetera, and accolades. Biographical information about both John Bellairs and Brad Strickland is included.

Judy Blume

◆ Contemporary Realistic Fiction

**Elizabeth, New Jersey
February 12, 1938**

📖 *Superfudge*

📖 *Are You There God? It's Me Margaret*

About the Author and the Author's Writing

When she was growing up, she dreamed of being a cowgirl, a detective, a spy, a great actress, or a ballerina. Her mother was a homemaker, and her father a dentist. Neither of those careers interested her, nor did writing. It never occurred to her that there were people who could make a living writing. She did love to make up stories, while playing with paper dolls, bouncing balls, and practicing her piano lessons.

Judy Blume grew up to become a celebrated writer. Her book *Are You There God? It's Me Margaret* (Bradbury 1990; 1970) is still read twenty years later. *Tales of a Fourth-Grade Nothing* (Dutton, 1972) was published to wide acclaim and was followed by *Superfudge* (Dutton, 1980), which earned Blume a $500,000 advance against royalties.

Blume was born Judy Sussman on February 12, 1938, in Elizabeth, New Jersey. She grew up in a house on Shelly Avenue, a house her family moved to when Blume was two years old. On rainy days Judy would sit on the closed-in porch and play with her dolls or in the house's garret, where she imagined strange creatures creeping out of the attic's corners. She loved to perform and directed a production of *Stop the Music*. She wore an Old Gold Girl costume made by her father, Dr. Sussman. Her mother often took Judy to the pubic library in Elizabeth. She loved her favorite book, *Madeline* by Ludwig Bemelmans, so much that she hid it in her kitchen toy drawer so her mother would not be able to return it to the library. She memorized the words in the book and pretended to read it. Later, she was proud to be able to read *Madeline* and the backs of cereal boxes. In school she was in the "bluejay" reading group, and by second grade she was in the "robin" reading group. Stories she chose for herself at the library were much more interesting than the Dick, Jane, and Spot stories. When she was young, she was afraid of the canary flapping in the cage, the dark, being alone, thunderstorms, the attic, and a stained-glass window. She was shy, but loved to entertain people. She studied ballet and modern dance.

When Judy was in third grade she moved to Miami, Florida, with her mother and brother for the winter. The warm climate was supposed to help her brother's kidney condition. Judy missed her father, but did make some wonderful friends. In her teen years Judy spent summers at a Connecticut camp, Camp Kenwood. She made more friends and learned how to swim. She read all the Oz books, the Nancy Drew mysteries, and Maud Hart Lovelace's Betsy-Tacy books.

She attended an all-girl school, Battin High School. She was a co-feature editor of the high school paper. She remembers during her junior year that her English teacher encouraged her to use creativity in her writing. Her best friend was Mary Sullivan during those days of pony tails and pink buck shoes. The two skipped senior prom to go to June Week at the Naval Academy in Annapolis. Judy's date did not realize she was Jewish, and when he found out, his attitude changed. The weekend was a disaster, but Judy and Mary have remained lifelong friends.

After high school Judy entered Boston University, but returned home after contracting a serious case of mononucleosis. She entered New York University after her recovery. Those years began her beatnik or "bohemian" phase. During this time her parents moved from Elizabeth to Westfield, New Jersey. Judy Sussman met John Blume, a law school graduate. They were engaged, but before they married her father died. He was only fifty-four years old. The couple married a few months later, and their daughter, Randy (Randy Lee), was born in 1961. The first book Judy bought for her daughter was *Madeline*. Two years later, their son, Larry (Lawrence Andrew), joined the family.

To bring some interest into her life in suburban Scotch Plains, New Jersey, Judy tried writing pop songs and designed felt appliqué banners for children's rooms. Bloomingdale's purchased several hundred dollars worth of the banners, but she then became allergic to the glue that she was using.

Her next endeavor was children's writing, when her children were still preschoolers. After many rejections, she was on the verge of quitting when she decided to take a one-semester graduate class titled "Writing for Children and Teenagers." When the class ended, she took it again. By the end of the second session, her rejections had turned into checks. Blume wrote the first draft of *Iggie's House* (Bradbury, 1970) while taking the course. *Trailblazer* magazine published *Iggie's House* in serial installments. Reilly & Lee Publishers accepted her first book, *The One in the Middle Is the Green Kangaroo* (1969), and Bradbury Press published *Iggie's House* as a novel.

Within six years Blume's writing career flourished, but her marriage was failing. In 1975, during a flight to accept a book award, Judy Blume met Tom Kitchens. Judy and John separated shortly after that trip, and Judy, her son, and her daughter moved to Princeton, New Jersey.

At the time, Tom Kitchens worked for the National Science Foundation in Washington, D.C., giving out grants. As the two became acquainted, Judy and her children moved to London, and Judy and Tom Kitchens married there in May of 1976. After Kitchens was reassigned to the United States, the family moved to Los Alamos, New Mexico. She had trouble starting a new book, so she rented an office downtown above a bakery in an attempt to convince herself that she had a real job—writing. By noon she would give in to the delicious aromas from the bakery, and she would rush downstairs to purchase two glazed doughnuts. After a few months and gaining a few pounds she moved her writing back home. Later, the family moved to the more cosmopolitan Santa Fe. It took her over two years to complete a book for older readers, *Wifey* (Putnam, 1978), while she and Kitchens attempted to sandwich their successful careers into one home life. The marriage lasted three years.

Eventually Blume moved back to New York City, nearer her editors and publishers. She has written twenty-one books, including two titles listed for young adults, and two as adult titles. Her books have been translated into twenty languages and have sold over 65 million copies. She receives thousands of letters yearly and has received more than ninety awards, including more than thirty "children's choice" awards throughout the United States, Australia, England, and Germany. In 1996 she was the recipient of the American Library Association's Margaret A. Edwards award for lifetime contribution to the field of literature for young adults.

In 1994 and 1996 a television series began based on the stories about Fudge, Sheila, and their families from *Tales of a Fourth-Grade Nothing*, *Superfudge*, *Fudge-a-mania* (Dutton, 1990), and *Otherwise Known as Sheila the Great* (Dutton, 1972). CBS broadcast the series during 1997. During the 1997–98 season, the Kennedy Center sponsored a national touring company play based on *Tales of a Fourth-Grade Nothing*. The play appeared in Maryland, Pennsylvania, New York, Wisconsin, Texas, Florida, California, and several states between. While her books often grow from events in her life, events in her life also bring her characters to life.

Her books often have neurotic mothers, and her dentist father's influence is shown in many of her characters that "brush their teeth." The character Fudge is based her own lovable son, Larry. Larry never swallowed a turtle—that idea came from a newspaper article. *Tiger Eyes* (Bradbury, 1981) explored her emotions when her father died at a relatively young age. *Freckle Juice* (Macmillan, 1985; 1971) reflects events surrounding her daughter's invention of a concoction she used to wash her face every day—hoping it would bleach away the freckles. Most of her stories are set in New Jersey, the state where she grew up. *Tiger Eyes* was set in New Mexico, and her two years in Connecticut provided the setting for *Just as Long as We're Together* (Orchard Books, 1987) and *Here's to You, Rachel Robinson* (Orchard Books, 1993). *Fudge-a-mania* appeared after a summer in Maine.

Reality and fiction mix in other ways. Blume once gave her character Margaret a formal dinner birthday party. She invited everyone involved with the book, as well as some of her old sixth-grade friends. She and her husband owned a country house named Sally's Camp, a reference to her husband's nickname for her, a nickname based on her character Sally J. Freedman. The Martha's Vineyard camp is an island getaway with two lots, five cabins, and acres of leeway for dreaming. The camp comes complete with rowing boats named for other characters in her novels.

Judy Blume currently lives in a spacious Upper West Side apartment near Riverside Park with her husband, George Cooper, and a seventeen-year-old Calico cat. Cooper is an author of nonfiction writing about historical crimes. In 1997 he programmed, designed, and created graphics for Judy Blume's official website on the World Wide Web. According to her "official bio" at her website, "He thinks Judy is lucky because she gets to make things up. Judy thinks it would be fun to research and discover stories, like George." Together they have three grown children, Amanda, Randy, and Larry, and "one incredible grandchild."

Books and Notes

Judy Blume has written books for every age group—from preschool to adult. The following are notes and selected titles representing each category. For a complete listing see the Library of Congress website at http://www.loc.gov/.

Picture Books

Judy Blume broke into the field of children's books with *The One in the Middle Is the Green Kangaroo*. Her books are characterized (as are several of her novels) with sibling rivalry. The text for *The Pain and the Great One* originally appeared in *Free to Be . . . You and Me,* a collection of stories conceived by Marlo Thomas and developed and edited by Carole Hart and others (McGraw-Hill, 1974).

Freckle Juice. Illustrated by Sonia Lisker. (Macmillan, 1985; 1971).

The One in the Middle Is the Green Kangaroo. Illustrated by Irene Trivas. (Bradbury, 1991; 1969).

The Pain and the Great One. Illustrations by Irene Trivas. (Bradbury, 1984; 1974).

Primary/Intermediate Novels

Fudge is a irresistible little brother based on Blume's son, Larry. She has said, "Larry was what you would call an *interesting* child." He dumped peas on his head in restaurants, and, if the family had had a turtle, "I'm sure he would have eaten it." Sheila is the chief protagonist in *Otherwise Known as Sheila the Great.* Fudge and Sheila's families are both involved in *Fudge-a-mania* with interesting results.

Fudge-a-mania (Dutton, 1990).

Otherwise Known as Sheila the Great (Dutton, 1972).

Superfudge (Dutton, 1980).

Tales of a Fourth-Grade Nothing (Dutton, 1972).

Middle-Grade Novels (Selected)

Are You There God? It's Me Margaret has probably been the most discussed and most banned coming-of-age novel this century. Even though more than 20 years old, it is still widely read by preteens searching for clues to their own sexuality. Her other titles for this age group also deal with aspects of growing up.

Are You There God? It's Me Margaret (Bradbury, 1990; 1970).

Here's to You, Rachel Robinson (Orchard Books, 1993).

Iggie's House (Bradbury, 1970).

Starring Sally J. Freedman as Herself (Bradbury, 1982; 1977).

Young Adult Novels

When Marilee Foglesong, chair of the Margaret A. Edwards Award Committee (1996), called Blume to tell her that she was the recipient for *Forever*, Blume reports that she replied, "Really? That's not my best book." She feels that *Tiger Eyes* is the better book, but she was appreciative of the award in any case. The working title for *Tiger Eyes* was "When the Lizards Run," a fact that might provide some discussion. Which is the better title? Why was the title changed to *Tiger Eyes*? Judy Blume is the founder and trustee of the Kids Fund, a charitable and educational foundation that is supported by royalties from many of her books, including *Letters to Judy*.

Forever (Bradbury, 1975).

Letters to Judy: What Kids Wish They Could Tell You (Pocket, 1987).

Tiger Eyes (Bradbury, 1981).

For More Information About/By the Author

Articles

Blume, Judy. "Blume in Love." *Metropolitan Home* 26, no. 5 (September 1, 1994): 84.

Blume, Judy. "1996 Margaret A. Edwards Acceptance Speech Forever— A Personal Story." *Journal of Youth Services in Libraries* 10, no. 2 (Winter 1997): 148.

Blume, Judy, and Richard M. Lerner. "Tweens and Teens." *Family Circle* 107, no. 14 (October 11, 1994): 82.

Dillin, Gay Andrews. "Judy Blume: Children's Author in a Grown-Up Controversy." *Christian Science Monitor* (December 10, 1981): B6+.

Garber, Stephen. "Judy Blume: New Classism for Kids." *English Journal* 73, no. 5 (April 1984): 56–59.

Goodman, Kenneth S. "Look What They've Done to Judy Blume!: The 'Basalization' of Children's Literature." *The New Advocate* 1, no. 1: 29–41.

"Judy Blume Forever." *Teen Voices*. URL: http://www.bostonwomen. com/blume.html (Accessed July 1997). [Teen Voices, 316 Huntington Avenue, Boston, MA 02115; 617-262-2434.]

Judy Blume's Home Base. ©1997, 1998. URL: http://www.judyblume. com (Accessed August 1998).

MacCann, Donnarae. "The Blume/TON Interview—A Reply." *Top of the News* 35 (Fall 1978): 33–38.

Neary, John. "The 'Jacqueline Susann of Kids' Books,' Judy Blume, Grows Up with an Adult Novel." *People* 10, no. 16 (October 16, 1978): 47–54.

"Old Values Surface in Blume Country." *Interracial Books for Children Bulletin* 7, no. 5 (1976): 8–10.

Oxford Student Publications Limited. ©1997. *Cherwell Online.* "Hilary 1997 Issue 1: Comment: Superfudge and Apple Pie." URL: http://cherwell. ospl.co.uk/archive/Hilary1997/ Issue1/comment/header2.html (Accessed August 1998).

Raymond, Allen. "Judy Blume Tells It Like It Is. . . ." *Early Years* (May 1984): 22–25.

"Some 'Isms' Revisited, Answers from Blume Country: An Interview with Judy Blume." *Top of the News* 34 (Spring 1978): 233–43.

Steinberg, Sybil. "PW Interviews: Judy Blume." *Publishers Weekly* (April 17, 1978): 6–7.

Sutton, Roger. "An Interview with Judy Blume Forever . . . Yours." *School Library Journal* 42, no. 6 (June 1996): 24–27.

Michael Bond

◆ Animal Fantasy

**Newbury, England
January 13, 1926**

📖 *A Bear Called Paddington*
📖 *Here Comes Thursday*

About the Author
and the Author's Writing

During the Christmas season in 1957, Michael Bond found a small, lonely stuffed bear on a London department store shelf. He purchased the bear as a stocking stuffer for his wife and, because they lived near Paddington Station, the bear was named Paddington. Ten days later, the story of *A Bear Called Paddington* was finished. The book was published the same year as the Bonds' daughter, Karen, was born—1958. Michael Bond did not intend to become a children's writer.

He was a member of the Royal Air Force in 1943, working as a navigator. Two years later he was transferred to the Army. Later, he was stationed in Egypt and wrote in his spare time. He sent a short story to a London paper. They actually bought it, but he could not find anywhere to cash the check. Nevertheless, the check encouraged him that he *was* a writer. He was not able to support himself or his wife, Brenda Mary

Johnson, on the money from writing, so he joined the British Broadcast Corporation (BBC) as a television cameraman. During his cameraman years, he spotted Paddington Bear. The first book was such a success that Bond retired from the BBC in 1965 and became a full-time writer. In less than ten years he published eight books about Paddington and three books about Thursday, a mouse. He continued to write for a bevy of British periodicals and has written for television aired in Europe, North America, and in several Asian countries.

Michael Bond was born in Newbury, England, on January 13, 1926, but lived there for only the first six months of his life. The rest of his childhood was spent in Reading—years filled with newts, guinea pigs, and a dog. He cycled, read, and went to school rather unwillingly. Once grown, he drew a cartoon and sent it off to *Punch*—his first effort to get published. That was also his first rejection. Later, he joined the Air Force and turned to writing in an effort to "create something."

Books and Notes

Michael Bond created three major series of books. The first about Paddington Bear, the lovable, engaging bear found at Paddington Station in London with a "Please Look After This Bear" tag around his neck. When the Browns discover him on the railway platform, they take him into their home. Bond wrote eleven titles about Paddington, and, with Alfred Bradley, collected seven short plays based on Michael Bond's play, *The Adventures of Paddington*.

Paddington Bear Series

A Bear Called Paddington. Illustrated by Peggy Fortnum. (Houghton, 1958).

Paddington Helps Out. Illustrated by Peggy Fortnum. (Houghton, 1961).

Paddington at Large. Illustrated by Peggy Fortnum. (Houghton, 1963).

Paddington at Work. Illustrated by Peggy Fortnum. (Houghton, 1967).

Paddington Goes to Town. Illustrated by Peggy Fortnum. (Houghton, 1968).

Paddington Takes the Air. Illustrated by Peggy Fortnum. (Houghton, 1971).

More About Paddington. Illustrated by Peggy Fortnum. (Houghton, 1972).

Paddington Abroad. Illustrated by Peggy Fortnum. (Houghton, 1972).

Paddington Takes to TV. Illustrated by Peggy Fortnum. (Houghton, 1974).

Paddington on Top. Illustrated by Peggy Fortnum. (Houghton, 1975).

Paddington on Stage. Adapted by Alfred Bradley and Michael Bond. Illustrated by Peggy Fortnum. (Houghton, 1977).

Paddington Takes the Test. Illustrated by Peggy Fortnum. (Houghton, 1979).

Paddington Bear Books for Early Readers

The original Paddington stories were written in a chapter-book/novel format appropriate for the late primary or middle-grade reader. However, because the Paddington character holds great appeal for the younger reader, several of the episodes in the Paddington novels have been adapted into picture books, board books, and other formats that appeal to the preschool and early primary reader.

Audio Cassette

"The Paddington Audio Collection." Performed by Michael Bond (four books on cassette). (Harper, 1991).

Board Book Titles

Paddington at the Seashore (Harper, 1992).

Paddington Bear (Harper, 1992).

Paddington Goes Shopping (Harper, 1992).

Paddington in the Kitchen (Harper, 1992).

Paddington Takes a Bath (Harper, 1992).

Paddington Bear (Harper, 1992).

Paddington's Garden (Harper, 1993).

Paddington's Magical Christmas (Harper, 1993).

Paddington's Things I Do (Harper, 1994).

Paddington's Things I Feel. Illustrated by John Lobban. (Harper, 1994).

Picture Book Format

Paddington Bear and the Christmas Surprise. Illustrated by R. W. Alley. (Harper, 1997).

Toy Books/Rebus/ Changing Picture Book

Paddington Bear: A Lift-the-Flap Rebus Book (Harper, 1996).

Paddington Goes on a Picnic (Harper, 1995).

Paddington Makes a Mess (Harper, 1995).

Paddington's First Bath (Harper, 1995).

Paddington's New Room. Illustrated by Nick Ward. (Harper, 1995).

Olga da Polga Series

In 1971 Bond developed another character, this time a guinea pig that entered the Bond household as a birthday present for Bond's daughter, Karen. The guinea pig came from Basingstoke. Many of the things that take place in the book did happen to the real Olga. Michael Bond has said that he especially likes these stories because Olga was such an important part of the family—and because the stories were some of his best work. All four stories are collected in one volume: *The Complete Adventures of Olga da Polga* (Delacorte, 1983).

The Tales of Olga da Polga. Illustrated by Hans Helweg. (Macmillan, 1973).

Olga Meets Her Match. Illustrated by Hans Helweg. (Hastings House, 1975).

Olga Carries On. Illustrated by Hans Helweg. (Hastings House, 1977).

Olga Takes Charge. Illustrated by Hans Helweg. (Kestrel, 1982).

Adventures of Thursday

A mouse called Thursday is the main character in several other titles.

Here Comes Thursday (Lothrop, 1967).

Thursday in Paris (Lothrop, 1969).

Thursday Rides Again. Illustrated by Beryl Sanders. (Lothrop, 1969).

Thursday Ahoy! Illustrated by Leslie Wood. (Lothrop, 1970).

For More Information About/By the Author

Articles

Gooding, V. Kathleen. *A Bear Called Paddington.* URL: http://www.umcs. maine.edu/~orono/collaborative/bear. html (Accessed September 1997).
    Site includes a book summary, activities appropriate for grades 2–6, and suggestions for technology integration.

Hopper, June. "The Artist Who Drew Paddington Bear." *The Junior Bookshelf* 60, no. 6 (December 1, 1996): 219.

Bill Brittain

◆ Fantasy

**Rochester, New York
December 16, 1930**

📖 *The Wish Giver*
📖 *The Wizards and the Monster*

About the Author
and the Author's Writing

William E. Brittain, better known by the name that appears on all of his books, Bill Brittain, is a master at capturing readers and drawing them into his fantastical settings. "I love 'em," says Brittain. *The Wish Giver* (Harper, 1983) is the second in a series about the imaginary village of Coven Tree, where the natural and the supernatural exist. The first, *Devil's Donkey* (Harper, 1981) is his favorite. "It began the Coven Tree yarns, and Coven Tree is my village. I created it; I populated it; and I love it. I wish I could live there."

In real life, Bill Brittain lives in Asheville, North Carolina. For 32 years, most of them at Lawrence Junior High School on Long Island, Brittain was an English/remedial reading teacher. He and his wife, also a teacher, moved to Asheville in 1986 after he retired.

During his teaching career he wrote in his spare time and, now, even after having authored 13 published children's books, he doesn't consider himself to be a professional writer. He says, "The whole writing thing is more of a hobby that kind of took off." He began writing mystery short stories for the *Ellery Queen* and *Alfred Hitchcock* magazines in 1964. Fredric Dannay of *Ellery Queen* became his mentor. "Back in the 60s I began writing short mystery stories for magazines and sold about 75 of them. I tried an adult mystery book, but about 30 publishers turned it down. A couple of them, however, said I seemed to be writing for a younger audience. So I tried a book for young people."

Wishing fascinated Brittain, and he began to speculate about the power of wishes as well as the danger of wishes being granted. He began imagining the "ultimate" wish after hearing his students dream aloud for "a motorcycle, a good mark in science, that the class would end, and that the teacher would drop dead." The idea of a farm boy amassing all the world's money delighted him and he began to speculate about the consequences. That idea brought about *All the Money in the World*. Harper & Row, now HarperCollins, accepted that first novel for publication in 1979. Later the idea of three youngsters getting their wishes in unexpected ways was something that seemed to come naturally for Brittain. Those ideas resulted in *The Wish Giver: Three Tales of Coven Tree*. *The Wish Giver* became a Newbery Honor Book in 1984. Coven Tree and the villages in other books have all been based, with modifications, on Brittain's home community of Spencerport. And as for the characters, he says, "While I've never met a witch or demon, the farming backgrounds are ultra-authentic. Many characters are based on people I've known. Tommy Donahue in *Who Knew There'd Be Ghosts?* is me, pure and simple."

Bill Brittain was born December 16, 1930, in Rochester, New York, and raised in the small farming community near Spencerport in upstate New York. One of his favorite books while growing up was the tale of a young boy who lived on a farm in a cranberry bog in the Kingdom of Didd. When this young boy attempted to show respect for the king by removing his hat, the hat refused to be removed. No matter how many times Bartholomew removed the hat from his head, another hat appeared. This caused much trouble and anxious moments for the young boy. The story was Dr. Seuss's *The Five Hundred Hats of Bartholomew Cubbins*. Brittain still admires the book and the writer. "If I could handle language and ideas half as well as is done in this book, I'd have such a swelled head I'd never get my hat on."

Brittain says that his first book, *All the Money in the World*, is still going strong. "With twelve more published books completed (and some rejections) I still write because I want to, and not because I have to." But he says, "One awful thing I've learned in this business is that writing is work! Oh, the first draft is fun. I get to make up all those characters and give 'em the most unlikely problems to solve. But making editorial changes is pure drudgery. If it weren't for the fact that these changes improve the work tremendously, I wouldn't stand for it. On the other hand, I can't think of any other occupation that is so tremendously satisfying." When a member of the Newbery Committee called him in 1984 to inform him of his Newbery Honor Award for *The Wish Giver*, he says, "I made something of a fool of myself, demanding to know who was *really* calling and scoffing at the announcement the poor woman was trying to get across. When I finally realized the caller was serious, I was most embarrassed. Fortunately [she] had a marvelous sense of humor about the whole thing."

Two of Brittain's most recent books, *The Wizards and the Monster* and *The Mystery of the Several Sevens*, "are about Merlin, King Arthur's magician, who comes back as a substitute teacher in modern times. Merlin is based on John Van Alstyne, a friend of mine."

Brittain and his wife, Ginny, whom he describes as "a diplomatic, discerning critic of my material as I write it," live in Asheville. Their grown children, Jim and Susan, reside in New Jersey and Buffalo, New York, respectively. In addition to writing, which he says he often finds excuses not to do, he likes "working around the house, playing golf, carving little wooden figures, and trying to stay out of trouble." He says he also "plays a mean game of ping-pong."

Books and Notes

Bill Brittain created books set in Coven Tree and wrote about Merlin's magician coming back to modern times as a substitute teacher. Each of his books are peopled by characters who, on the surface, appear very normal, but often turn out to have special characteristics that lure the reader into their situation.

Tales from Coven Tree

These tales are set in the imaginary village of Coven Tree, where both the natural and the supernatural exist.

Devil's Donkey (Harper, 1981).
Book one—Old Magda the witch manages to convince Dan'l Pitt that magic in Coven Tree does exist.

The Wish Giver: Three Tales of Coven Tree (Harper, 1983).

Book two—Three young believers in magic make a wish, a wish that is guaranteed to give them exactly what they ask for. The wishes do come true, in an unusual and unexpected manner.

Dr. Dredd's Wagon of Wonders (Harper, 1987).

Book three—Their deal with Dr. Dredd for the services of a rainmaker draws the drought-stricken town of Coven Tree into a devastating struggle with the forces of evil.

Professor Popkin's Prodigious Polish: A Tale of Coven Tree (Harper, 1990).

Book four—Professor Popkin's magical furniture polish seems to make strange and mysterious things happen in the community of Coven Tree.

Merlin, King Arthur's Magician

King Arthur's magician, Merlin, comes to modern times as a substitute teacher; Merlin and two spunky fifth-graders involve themselves in mystery and adventure.

The Wizards and the Monster (Harper, 1994).

Becky and Simon dream of having adventures with magic and monsters. When they discover that Mr. Merlin is their substitute teacher, they are sure their adventures are about to begin.

The Mystery of Several Sevens (Harper, 1994).

Who stole the seven dwarfs' bag of gold is a mystery that has plagued fairy tale readers for decades. When Mr. Merlin magically transports Becky and Simon to fairyland, they set out to solve the riddle (and the mystery).

The Parnell Mansion

The old, run-down mansion is a favorite hangout for three buddies, Tommy Donahue, Harry the Blimp, and their friend Books. In each tale, the three friends overhear ghosts in the mansion and save the mansion from those claiming it for development.

Who Knew There'd Be Ghosts? (Harper, 1985).

Tommy, Harry the Blimp, and Books join forces with two lively ghosts to save a historic but run-down mansion from being destroyed by a crooked antiques dealer.

The Ghost from Beneath the Sea (Harper, 1992).

When the Parnell mansion is threatened by developers who want to turn it into an amusement park, Tommy, Harry, and Books join forces with a trio of ghosts to outwit the plan.

Miscellaneous Fantasy Titles

Each of these tales are fantastical in nature. *All the Money in the World* was Brittain's first children's novel. *Shape-Changer* was awarded Connecticut's "Nutmeg Book Award," a children's choice award, and the Nevada Young Readers' Award (Young Reader Category), both in 1997.

All the Money in the World (Harper, 1979).

Quentin wishes for all the money in the world and gets a pack of troubles too.

The Fantastic Freshman (Harper, 1988).

A magic charm grants fourteen-year-old Stanley his deepest desire, to be a VIP in his high school, but not without complications.

My Buddy, the King: A Novel (Harper, 1990).

Tom Quilt saves the life of King Tokab of Mokobway when he chokes on a frankfurter. The incident binds a friendship that becomes stronger as they outwit a plot to do in the king.

Shape-Changer (Harper, 1994).

A shape-changing policeman tries to recapture an alien master criminal who can also change form.

Wings: A Novel (Harper, 1991).

Ian's newly sprouted wings are an embarrassment to his politically ambitious father. The only ones who might be able to help seem to be the class outcast Anita and her eccentric mother.

For More Information About/By the Author

No articles located. See general biographical sources.

Anne Evelyn "Eve" Bunting

Contemporary Realistic Fiction ◆ Picture Book Fiction

Maghera, County Derry, Ireland
December 19, 1928

- 📖 *The Wall*
- 📖 *Smoky Night*
- 📖 *Sixth-Grade Sleepover*

About the Author
and the Author's Writing

Ireland, Scotland, and the United States (California) have all been home to author Eve Bunting. She was born in Ireland in 1928, the daughter of Sloan Edward and Mary Bolton. Her father was a product merchant. At the age of nine she was sent to a boarding school in Belfast. By 1945 she had graduated from Belfast's Methodist College and entered Queen's University, also in Belfast. It was at Queen's University that she met Edward Davison Bunting. They married April 26, 1951, and soon moved to Scotland, where they lived for nine years. Three children were born in Scotland, Christine, Sloan, and Glenn.

After Scotland, in 1958, the family moved to the United States, settling first in San Francisco where Ed's brother was living. After about a year, Ed was offered a job as a hospital administrator in Los Angeles, so the family moved to Pasadena. They bought a house on a tree-lined street, a home where the family has lived for more than thirty years. The dining room looks into the backyard gardens and the swimming pool. Eve Bunting became a naturalized citizen of the United States in 1967.

Bunting's writing career began as her children left home, and she began wondering about her own time. She says, "In 1971 I was facing the 'empty nest syndrome' with no prospects of much that would be worthwhile or entertaining for me for the rest of my life. At that time I didn't know of the wonder of grandchildren." Her husband was busy with his career, and Eve was looking for something to do. She spotted a Pasadena City College brochure and a course, "Writing for Publication." "I'd always liked to write, though I had never in my wildest dreams considered 'being a writer.' It worked out well." To date she has had more than 140 titles published. Her usual pen name is Eve Bunting, but she has also used "Evelyn Bolton" and "A. E. Bunting."

Bunting's writing has ranged from picture books to books for intermediate and young adult readers. She has also published a number of articles and short stories as well. For a time, she also taught writing classes at the University of California.

Eve Bunting has said that she writes "when I feel like it, but fortunately I feel like it everyday." She devotes four to five hours each day to writing. Information is carefully thought out before she begins the actual writing. She works in the library in her house. She does not use a computer, but after writing her notes, she types the story on a typewriter. Using a pencil and paper, she jots down her many ideas for characters and plots. She describes the pencil point of her pencil as the "character insertion subunit" and the eraser end as the "character deletion subunit." She writes on only the left side of the paper, saving the right side for second thoughts and insertions. After her first draft, she reads the story with a tape recorder to identify places where the sentence flow needs to be corrected. After revisions, the manuscript is sent off to an appropriate editor.

Eve Bunting was forty-three, and her children teenagers, before her first book, *The Two Giants* (Ginn, 1972), was published. The book, with illustrations by Eric von Schmidt, told the story of a scheduled fight between the Irish giant, Finn McCool, and the Scottish giant, Culcullan. Their fight leads to the construction of the Giant's Causeway in the Irish sea. It was a story that Bunting thought everyone knew, but quickly realized that the tale, often told by the Shanachies (storytellers) in Ireland, was not as well known in the United States.

That Irish folktale was the first of Bunting's many Irish connections. The reader may not be aware of the connections, but the themes in Bunting's books are often ones that have grown from her homesickness or the rich storytelling heritage that surrounded her as a child. "Much of my background in Ireland finds its way into my books, as does a certain amount Irish phrasing and Irish philosophy." For example, "In *Market Day* [Harper, 1996], that is my little town in Ireland that I write about."

A book she calls her "Irish book" was published in 1995. That book, *Spying on Miss Müller* (Clarion), was the book that she "always wanted to write." "[I] knew my experiences at the boarding school would make a pretty good book, and my editor at Clarion encouraged me, for years, to write it. The school is real, although I did change its name. And a lot of people in it are real or a mixture of real people." At Alveara boarding school in Belfast, at the start of World War II, thirteen-year-old Jessie must deal with her suspicions about a teacher whose father was German. Eve herself had been at boarding school during World War II when one of the teachers was treated horribly because she was suspected of being German. Eve Bunting says, "In the book *Spying on Miss Müller*, I am Jessie."

Eve Bunting is acutely aware of the actions and events going on around her. Since the beginning of her writing career, she has averaged six or seven books a year, and many of them reflect some current societal issues. Media accounts and discussions of those issues and events are like seeds that grow into full-fledged stories, stories reflecting the societal concerns of the times. *Sharing Susan* (Harper, 1991) deals with a twelve-year-old girl who finds out that she was switched at birth. Susan has to deal with both sets of parents and their desire to have her in their family. Susan's biological parents live in Laguna Niguel, which is where the Buntings' son Sloan teaches school.

Surrogate Sister (Lippincott, 1984) is the story of sixteen-year-old Cassie, who struggles with her mother's decision to give birth to a child for another couple. Cassie struggles with her resentment of the couple who will eventually raise and love her sibling.

The topics of suicide, abuse, and running away are blended into a tender love story in *If I Asked You, Would You Stay?* (Harper, 1984). A young man, Crow, brings Valentine back to a secret room in an about-to-be-torn-down, condemned building where he lives and hides. Together the two persevere and cope with life's situations.

Latchkey children are the topic in *Is Anybody There?* (Lippincott, 1988), a book that focuses on Marcus Mullen. His mother, a widow, must work full-time. One afternoon just before Christmas break, Marcus discovers that his hidden key is missing. At first Marcus suspects the garage apartment tenet is responsible, but he discovers that the secret is completely different.

Bunting does not restrict sensitive social issues and topics to her novels, as appropriate issues appear in her picture books, as well. Shortly after the Los Angeles riots, Bunting penned a title, *Smoky Night* (Harcourt, 1994), that dealt with a young boy, Daniel, and his mother, who find themselves in the middle of a riot. When their apartment is set on fire, Daniel loses his beloved cat, Jasmine. Daniel is left to wonder "Why?" and his mother is left with no good answer. The book's illustrations, created by David Diaz, earned him a Caldecott Award. Bunting got the idea for this book on the first night of the Los Angeles riots. She had been speaking at an author program in a Pasadena library, and when she came out she sensed something different, even in Pasadena. By the time she got home, the television was filled with riot scenes. She began to think about the effect the riots would have on a child caught in the middle of such horrible pandemonium. The day after the riots, she started making notes and writing the book. After several false starts, she finished it in just one month. "That book and it's subject matter are dear to my heart since I live close to Los Angeles."

The undercurrent of prejudice in that book is also the reason Bunting and her family left Ireland. She saw, firsthand, the prejudicial relationships between the Catholics and Protestants in her homeland and did not want to raise her children in "that kind of atmosphere." So, they emigrated to America. One of her first books was *Terrible Things* (Harper, 1980), an animal allegory of the Holocaust.

Homelessness is the topic of *Fly Away Home* (Clarion, 1991), a story that deals with a family unable to afford housing on the father's part-time janitor's pay. Andrew's mother has died, and Andrew and his father reside in the local airport. They wash in the airport bathroom, and eat in the airport cafeteria. Andrew dreams of flying free to a new home, just as the bird trapped inside the airport escapes.

The Wall (Clarion, 1990) deals with the aftermath of the Vietnam War; *The Wednesday Surprise* (Clarion, 1989) focuses on adult illiteracy; and *A Day's Work* (Clarion, 1994) deals with migrant workers. *The Wednesday Surprise* began as a story that a librarian in Pasadena told about her grandmother, Katina. Illiteracy also infused another novel, *Sixth-Grade Sleepover* (Harcourt, 1986).

Favorite things also creep into Bunting's writings. Her favorite holiday is Halloween, so it is no surprise that she has written books such as *Scary, Scary Halloween* (Clarion, 1986) and *In the Haunted House* (Clarion, 1990). Her grandchildren also give her ideas for books. *No Nap* (Clarion, 1989) and *Perfect Father's Day* (Clarion, 1991) feature a little girl, Susie, whose reluctance to nap and idea of a perfect Father's Day share favorite things straight from Bunting's grandchildren.

Bunting's favorite book is impossible to identify. "Many of my books [26] have won state awards voted on by children." She says, "I love each of them for different reasons." If she did not like what she had written, she wouldn't have written the book at all.

Books and Notes

Eve Bunting writes for the picture book audience and books for older readers. Her fiction is laced with bits and pieces from events in her own life and the lives of her children. The range of her books includes ghost stories (yes, Eve Bunting does believe in ghosts), adventure stories, and books about sharks and whales. She has addressed homelessness, the Holocaust, the plight of migrant workers, the Vietnam War, the death of a friend, and urban violence, while providing books that engage young readers and motivate them to reach out to more books and reading.

Eve Bunting and her husband, Ed, live in Pasadena, where they enjoy visits from their sons and daughter and four granddaughters (including a set of twins). When Eve is not writing, she is likely to be found swimming, reading, or walking. But, wherever she goes, there is most likely a pencil and paper close by. A list of Eve Bunting's books would include more than one hundred sixty books. The following are selected titles.

Picture Books

The Blue and the Gray. Illustrated by Ned Bittinger. (Scholastic, 1996).

Clancy's Coat. Illustrated by Lorinda Bryan Cauley. (Warne, 1984).

The Day the Whale Came. Illustrated by Scott Menchin. (Harcourt, 1998).

A Day's Work. Illustrated by Ronald Himler. (Clarion, 1994).

December. Illustrated by David Diaz. (Harcourt, 1997).

Ducky. Illustrated by David Wisniewski. (Clarion, 1997).

Flower Garden. Illustrated by Kathryn Hewitt. (Harcourt, 1994).

Fly Away Home. Illustrated by Ronald Himler. (Clarion, 1991).

Ghosts Hour, Spooks Hour. Illustrated by Donald Carrick. (Clarion, 1987).

Happy Birthday, Dear Duck. Illustrated by Jan Brett. (Clarion, 1988).

I Am the Mummy Heb-Nefert. Illustrated by David Christiana. (Harcourt, 1997).

Market Day. Illustrated by Holly Berry. (Harper, 1996).

Night Tree. Illustrated by Ted Rand. (Harcourt, 1991).

On Call Back Mountain. Illustrated by Barry Moser. (Blue Sky Press, 1997).

The Pumpkin Fair. Illustrated by Eileen Christelow. (Clarion, 1996).

Smoky Night. Illustrated by David Diaz. (Harcourt, 1994).

So Far from the Sea. Illustrated by Chris Soentpiet. (Clarion, 1998).

Some Frog! Illustrated by Scott Medlock. (Harcourt, 1997).

Sunflower House. Illustrated by Kathryn Hewitt. (Harcourt, 1996).

Train to Somewhere. Illustrated by Ronald Himler. (Clarion, 1996).

Valentine Bears. Illustrated by Jan Brett. (Clarion, 1983).

The Wall. Illustrated by Ronald Himler. (Clarion, 1990).

Books for the Intermediate/ Middle-Grade Reader

Coffin on a Case (Harper, 1992).

The Ghost Children (Clarion, 1989).

If I Asked You, Would You Stay? (Harper, 1984).

Is Anybody There? (Lippincott, 1988).

Janet Hamm Needs a Date for the Dance (Clarion, 1986).

Karen Kepplewhite Is the World's Best Kisser (Clarion, 1983).

Our Sixth-Grade Sugar Babies (Harper, 1990).

Sharing Susan (Harper, 1991).

Sixth-Grade Sleepover (Harcourt, 1986).

Someone Is Hiding on Alcatraz Island (Clarion, 1984).

For More Information About/By the Author

Articles

"Meet the Author: Eve Bunting." Supplement to *Instructor* (September 1992).

Raymond, Allen. "Eve Bunting: From Ireland with Love." *Early Years* (October 1986): 38–40.

Weiss, Stephanie. "Eve Bunting: Suitable for Children?" *NEA Today* (April 1995): 7.

Videos

"A Visit with Eve Bunting." [Video: 1/2-inch VHS, 1/2-inch BETA, or 3/4-inch tape]. (Houghton Mifflin/Clarion, 1991).

Betsy Byars

◆ Contemporary Realistic Fiction

Charlotte, North Carolina
August 7, 1928

- 📖 *The Summer of the Swans*
- 📖 *Bingo Brown's Guide to Romance*
- 📖 *Coast-to-Coast*
- 📖 Herculeah Jones Mystery series
- 📖 Blossom Family Series

About the Author and the Author's Writing

Mickey Mouse, Maurice Sendak, bubble gum, and Betsy Byars all share one thing in common—the year of their birth, 1928. Betsy Cromer Byars was born in Charlotte, North Carolina, on August 7, 1928. Her father was a cotton-mill worker in Hoskins, North Carolina. They lived for a while in the city and later in the country. Her country days were filled with animals—a goat, a rabbit, a rooster, and a dog. As a child she wanted to work in a zoo and take care of rejected baby animals. But, she also loved reading. At Christmas her family often gave her books. When she spied the packages under the tree, she would sneak the books one-by-one, read them, and put them back. She couldn't wait to find out about the story.

Byars spent most of her early life in the southeastern United States. For two years she attended Furman University in Greenville, North Carolina, and then returned home to attend Queens College, where she earned an undergraduate English degree in 1950. She and Edward Byars married shortly after, and he resigned his teaching job at Clemson College to enter graduate school in Urbana, Illinois.

While the Byars were living in Illinois, Betsy began writing. Popular magazines accepted her articles and eventually she began to write books for children. Although she began writing in 1956, it wasn't until 1968 that she considered herself self-supporting. When her children were young, she wrote daily. She would sit down at her typewriter after her children left for school, and continue until they returned at three o'clock.

Byars sold her first pieces, Erma Bombeck–type essays, to magazines. In 1962 one of her books, *Clementine* (Houghton), was published. Her second book was published three years later.

After Ed Byars completed his doctorate in theoretical and applied mechanics, the Byars moved to Morgantown, West Virginia, where he taught at West Virginia University. The family lived there for many years, and the surroundings provided Betsy with ideas for her novels. In 1971 she received the Newbery Award for *The Summer of the Swans* (Viking, 1970). She had the idea for the book from tutoring learning-disabled children. The swans idea came from an article about the swans swimming on the university lake.

Many of her ideas came from newspaper stories. *After the Goat Man* (Viking, 1974) evolved from a Morgantown newspaper article about a man who did not want to move to make way for highway construction. In the story some children help the old man fight for his land. An article about a lost sandhill crane provided the beginning for *The House of Wings* (Viking, 1972). When Byars was a child, a stranger wandered by the house and showed her how to brush her teeth with a cherry twig. That incident appeared in *The House of Wings*. Camping with her family produced a chance encounter with a fox, which became *The Midnight Fox* (Viking, 1968)—a story of the transformation of a boy by his encounter with a black fox trapped on his aunt and uncle's farm.

Many of her children's experiences as well as her own childhood experiences entered other stories. During her third-grade year, she contended with two bullies, the Fletcher brothers. The two became one character, Marv Hammerman, in *The 18th Emergency* (Viking, 1973).

She wanted to call the character Fletcher, but the real bully brothers are still alive. She was scared of what they might do, not what they did.

A friend's chance comment about children sneaking into their back-yard swimming pool inspired *The Night Swimmers* (Delacorte, 1984). And, when Byars spotted ninety-year-old twins, dressed alike, in a local grocery store, she knew she had characters for her book *The Pinballs* (Harper, 1977). The twins became the Benson sisters. The plot evolved from conversations with a friend who placed children in foster care. Similar conversations about a home for battered women resulted in the development of *Cracker Jackson* (Viking, 1985). In Byars's story, Cracker attempts to stop a man's wife abuse.

In the early 1980s Byars got her first personal computer. She was intrigued and asked her son to do some illustrations. The illustrations inspired *The Computer Nut* (Viking, 1984). Her Scottie dog became a character in the book.

Now that her children are grown, her writing schedule is less structured. She only writes when she has an idea, and then just two or three hours daily. She jots down ideas anywhere, and then completes the writing at her computer. One thing remains the same: She still does a lot of rewriting. Her writing comes in four stages—staring at her thumbnail, head writing, the writing, and finally reading what has been written and making something out of it.

In 1988 her thirtieth book, *The Burning Questions of Bingo Brown* (Viking), was published. Several books were made into TV specials. In Richard F. Abrahamson's article in *Journal of Reading*, Byars states that *The Night Swimmers* was well done, but the producers changed the name to *Daddy, I'm Your Mama Now*. Byars felt the Walt Disney film of *The Pinballs* was done quite well, but that the film version of *The Summer of the Swans* literally butchered the story.

During their years in Illinois, the Byars became interested in soaring—high class gliding. Much of their summers were spent flying, and for thirty-five years Betsy flew with her husband as the pilot. In 1984 she obtained her own pilot's license. Her first plane was a Cessna 152 in her favorite color, yellow. In March 1987 she and her husband flew coast-to-coast in a 1940 J-3 Cub. That experience resulted in a book, *Coast-to-Coast* (Delacorte, 1992), a story of a young girl and her grandfather as they cross the country coast-to-coast.

In 1986 her first book, *The Not-Just-Anybody Family*, about the Blossom family, was published by Delacorte. She wrote the sequel almost immediately. Previously, she had thought that authors waited until there was great demand for a sequel, then it was written. There was a great demand for a sequel to *The Pinballs*, but by then Byars had written two other books, and had lost the style of *The Pinballs*. Eventually, she created the Herculeah Jones Mystery series.

After his tenure at West Virginia University, Ed Byars went to Clemson University in Clemson, South Carolina, and the family moved there. Says Betsy, "I now live on an airstrip in South Carolina. My four children, Laurie, Betsy Ann, Nan, and Guy are married and I have seven grandchildren. My husband and I are pilots, and we fly a lot." One of Byars's children, Betsy Ann (Betsy Duffey), is an accomplished children's book writer. Betsy Duffey has published eighteen books, including several titles about a boy and his dog, Lucky, and the Pet Patrol series.

Books and Notes

Blossom Family Series

The title of the first book came from a humorous incident. The family breaks into the jail to get grandfather out. When someone asks them why they broke *into* jail, why they hadn't walked through the front entrance like anybody else, Maggie replied, "We Blossoms have never been just anybody." The saga of the Blossoms continued through several titles.

The Not-Just-Anybody Family (Delacorte, 1986).

The Blossoms Meet the Vulture Lady (Delacorte, 1986).

The Blossoms and the Green Phantom (Delacorte, 1987).

A Blossom Promise (Delacorte, 1987).

Wanted—Mud Blossom (Delacorte, 1991).

Herculeah Jones Mystery Series

The chief protagonist in each of these books is Herculeah Jones, a supersleuth who cracks mysteries with her best friend, Meat.

Tarot Says Beware (Viking, 1995).
The two friends investigate the murder of a palm reader.

Dead Letter (Viking, 1996).
Herculeah finds a mysterious note in the lining of a secondhand coat.

Death's Door (Viking, 1997).
An attempted murder brings the two friends to *Death's Door*, a mystery bookstore.

Disappearing Acts (Viking, 1998).
A search for Meat's long-lost father comes about while the two friends investigate a dead body in a comedy club.

Easy-to-Read Chapter Books

Although the majority of books by Byars are moderate-reading chapter books, she has authored some easy-to-read titles.

Two books are about "Ant," whose real name is Anthony, the younger brother of the narrator. The Golly Sisters are May-May and Rose, who have humorous adventures as they travel West.

Ant Plays Bear. Illustrated by Marc Simont. (Viking, 1997).

The Golly Sisters Go West. Illustrated by Sue Truesdell. (Harper, 1985).

The Golly Sisters Ride Again. Illustrated by Sue Truesdell. (Harper, 1994).

Hooray for the Golly Sisters! Illustrated by Sue Truesdell. (Harper, 1990).

My Brother, Ant. Illustrated by Marc Simont. (Viking, 1996).

Miscellaneous Titles

These earlier books are generally appropriate for middle-grade readers.

The Animal, the Vegetable, and John D. Jones (Delacorte, 1982).

The Burning Questions of Bingo Brown (Viking, 1988).

The Cartoonist (Viking, 1978).

Cracker Jackson (Viking, 1985).

The Cybil War (Viking, 1981).

The Pinballs (Harper, 1977).

The Summer of the Swans (Viking, 1970).

For More Information About/By the Author

Articles

Abrahamson, Richard F. "Books for Adolescents: Reviews." *Journal of Reading* 1, 30, no. 1 (November 1986): 179.

"The Booklist Interview: Betsy Byars." *The Booklist* 89, no. 10 (January 15, 1993): 906.

Byars, Betsy. "Ladders and Authority: Creating the Gift." *Journal of Youth Services in Libraries* 7, no. 2 (Winter 1994): 141.

Scales, Pat. "Betsy Byars' *The Summer of the Swans*." *Booklinks* 6, no. 2 (November 1996): 16+.

Books

Byars, Betsy. *The Moon and I* (J. Messner, 1991; Beech Tree, 1996).
Recounts humorous anecdotes from her childhood, including adventures with a blacksnake. She explains how she writes a book.

Usrey, Malcolm. *Betsy Byars* (Twayne, 1995).

Lewis Carroll
(Charles Lutwidge Dodgson)

◆ Fantasy

Daresbury-in-Cheshire, England
January 27, 1832–January 14, 1898

📖 *Alice's Adventures in Wonderland*
📖 *Through the Looking Glass*

About the Author
and the Author's Writing

Charles Lutwidge Dodgson was born in England in 1832 at the parsonage at Daresbury in Cheshire. His father was an Anglican clergyman, Charles Dodgson. His mother was Frances Lutwidge Dodgson, who gave Charles her birth name as his second name.

When Charles was eleven the family moved to Croft in North Yorkshire and a year later Charles was sent to a boarding school, Richmond School. It was there that Charles's potential as a mathematician became apparent. From 1846 to 1849 Charles was enrolled at Rugby. During this time he devised ways to entertain his siblings. He created magazines with stories, poems, and drawings. Later, he entered Christ Church in Oxford and worked to obtain a college Mastership. During those five years he continued to write and draw. One of his writings, in a work titled,

"Mischmasch," included a four-line verse that was to become the first verse of his later nonsense poem "Jabberwocky."

In 1855 two significant events occurred in Dodgson's life. Henry Liddell came to be the dean of Christ Church, and Dodgson was introduced to photography by his friend Reginald Southey and his uncle during summer vacation. Dodgson met Liddell's children, Harry, Lorina Charlotte, Alice, and Edith, in February 1856.

Before long, Dodgson was visiting the deanery to take pictures of the girls. Mrs. Liddell asked Dodgson not to take any more photographs, and he took it as a hint that he was around too much. But in the winter of 1856–57, the Liddells took a trip abroad and the children stayed in the deanery in the care of their governess, who allowed Dodgson to visit as often as he liked. After the Liddells returned, Dodgson continued to visit and take them on boating trips on the Thames.

Dodgson had originally intended to become a priest, but did not pursue the theological road beyond ordination as a deacon. He did, however, continue his academic and writing career. In 1860 he published two mathematical books. The following year, he completed another and started four more. He was also writing for a magazine, *The Train*, using the signature "BB." The editor asked Dodgson for a full pseudonym. Dodgson sent him four choices—Edgar Cuthwellis, Edgar U. C. Westhall, Louis Carroll, and Lewis Carroll. The editor choose Lewis Carroll, which had been derived by Dodgson by Latinizing and reversing his given names: Lutwidge = Ludovicus = Lewis; Charles = Carolus = Carroll. He used this pseudonym for the first time for a poem, "Solitude."

Dodgson was always more comfortable in the company of children. He gave parties for them, and took them to the theater and on boating trips.

Dodgson and his friend Robinson Duckworth took the daughters of Dr. Henry Liddel on a boating trip in the summer of 1862. Several years later, Dodgson would recall that it was on the 4th of July in 1862 that the Alice stories were "born." In August the Liddell daughters and Dodgson made two more river trips, and more adventures were added to the Alice stories.

By February 1863 Dodgson had written 18,000 words and began to negotiate with publishers. He added another 17,000 words and changed the title of the manuscript from "Alice's Adventures Under Ground" to "Alice's Adventures in Wonderland." Dodgson added his own drawings, but later asked John Tenniel, a cartoonist for *Punch*, to create the illustrations. Tenniel agreed in May 1864. Dodgson contracted with Tenniel for the illustrations, and not only paid him personally, but gave Tenniel detailed instructions regarding them.

Dodgson wanted the book published by Christmas of 1864, but Tenniel did not complete the illustrations until June 1865. Dodgson paid for the first printing of 2,000 copies himself. Dodgson presented Alice Liddell with her own white vellum-bound copy. Tenniel, however, did not like the printing job on the illustrations, and Dodgson ordered a new edition. Five thousand copies of the new edition were sold in 1866.

Dodgson recalled all copies from the first printing after a few had been sold or distributed by presentation. He regained all but ten copies, kept two himself, and distributed the remaining thirty-six recalled copies to hospitals. A second edition of *Alice*, more to the author's and illustrator's standards, was published by Macmillan in 1866.

The 1,952 copies remaining from the first edition were sold to Appleton in New York. The sale was authorized by Dodgson on April 10, 1865. Appleton had new title pages printed by Oxford press for 1,000 copies and those title pages were "tipped-in." Those were bound in England and shipped to the United States. The remaining 952 copies, the third issue, were shipped to New York in sheets and bound with a new title page printed in America. The American issue of the first edition was bound in the same red cloth as the first issue—the front cover showed Alice holding a pig, with the Cheshire Cat appearing on the back cover.

Mrs. Liddell had become concerned about her daughters' relationship with Charles Dodgson and discouraged Dodgson's presence. From July 1863 to December he saw little of them and rarely ever after that date.

Dodgson busied himself with other things. In 1867 he took his only trip abroad, with his friend Henry Liddon to Russia. The following June his father died, and he moved to a house in Guildford. This was also the period when he began to plan a follow-up to the "Alice's Adventures in Wonderland" story. Eventually he wrote a manuscript titled "Through the Looking Glass and What Alice Found There."

In 1869 he published *Phantasmagoria and Other Poems*, an entertaining collection comprising thirteen humorous poems and thirteen serious ones. In 1876 a long nonsense poem, "The Hunting of the *Snark*," appeared. His book royalties enabled him to teach fewer classes, and he spent summers at Eastbourne on the seacoast with his child-friends.

By 1880 Dodgson began to feel that others disapproved of his photography, especially his enthusiasm for photographing young girls. He gave up the hobby and turned almost completely to writing. In 1881 he gave up his lectureship at Christ Church and devoted his days to his mathematical and logic writings, his religious thoughts, and his children's stories. In 1885 *A Tangled Tale*, designed to interest children in mathematics, was published. By this time he had written seven books on logic or mathematics, and nine others dealing with games, puzzles, or children's stories. The fairy story, *Sylvie and Bruno*, was published in 1889 and its sequel, *Sylvie and Bruno Concluded*, was published four years later.

Between 1860 and 1897 Dodgson produced over 180 articles, booklets, leaflets, and pamphlets, as well as his Alice writings and his photography books. His books demonstrated his diverse abilities to write on a range of topics. His topics showed creativity and eclecticism. However, it seems that none of his writings ever came close to gaining the popularity and income generated from his Alice stories and his poetry. His poetry is often included as part of anthologies. Some of the more popular poems include "Jabberwocky," "The Lobster Quadrille," and "The Walrus and the Carpenter."

Dodgson loved anagrams (words whose letters can be rearranged to spell another word or words) and often included anagrams in his writing. A contemporary of Dodgson signed his writings and artwork with the moniker, "E. M. Anon." Some scholars have speculated that Dodgson is likely E. M. Anon because of his love of anagrams, and the fact that E. M. Anon spelled backwards is "no name."

Many who analyze Carroll's writings have found hidden anagrams and sometimes even sinister messages. These findings seem to be overzealous. However, Chinese officials did not cite any sinister hidden meaning when they banned *Alice in Wonderland* in 1931. The book was banned because the Governor of Hunan Province decided that there were grounds enough: "Animals should not use human language," and it was "disastrous to put animals and human beings on the same level."

In 1898, on January 14, Charles Lutwidge Dodgson died of bronchitis at his family home in Guildford.

Books and Notes

By far the most popular of Carroll's writings were *Alice's Adventures in Wonderland* and *Through the Looking Glass*. The tales are often referred to as *Alice in Wonderland*. Prior to 1968 it seems that most of the editions of Carroll's writings for children were published with Sir John Tenniel's (1820–1914) illustrations. A few editions were created with new illustrations by Eve Le Gallienne, Arthur Rackham, and Leonard Weisgard. In recent decades, however, many have illustrated Carroll's stories and poems. Graeme Base, a well-known Australian illustrator, has illustrated Carroll's "Jabberwocky." And Tony Ross, Diane Goode, Anthony Browne, Michael Hague, and Barry Moser have all created their own illustrated versions of *Alice in Wonderland* (1865).

Alice in Wonderland has become so well known that words and phrases from the book are part of everyday speech. For example, people are said to "grin like a Cheshire Cat" or to be "as mad as a March hare."

Through the Looking Glass (1871) introduced some new characters into Alice's adventures—Jabberwock dragon, Tweedledee and Tweedledum, and the Walrus and Carpenter. Tenniel's illustrations helped to popularize the characters.

Quotes

"Take some more tea," the March Hare said to Alice very earnestly. "I've had nothin yet," Alice replied in an offended tone, "so I can't take more." *Alice in Wonderland*, Chapter 6

"Twinkle, twinkle little bat, How I wonder what you're at! Up above the world you fly, Like a tea-tray in the sky." *Alice in Wonderland*, Chapter 7

For More Information About/By the Author

Articles

Birenbaum, Joel M. *Lewis Carroll Home Page*. URL: http://www.lewiscarroll. org/carroll.html (Accessed September 1997).

Books

Stoffel, Stephanie Lovett. *Lewis Carroll in Wonderland* (Abrams, 1997).

Matthew F. "Matt" Christopher

Sports Biography ◆ Sports Fiction

**Bath, Pennsylvania
August 16, 1917–
September 20, 1997**

- *Double Play at Short*
- *All-Star Fever*
- *On the Ice with—Wayne Gretzky*
- Peach Street Mudders Series

About the Author and the Author's Writing

At the age of 21, Matt Christopher was one of the athletes selected to play in a fund-raising exhibition game against the major league team the New York Giants. He batted twice and got one hit against Johnny Wittig. That spring he played Class C minor league baseball with Smiths-Falls, Ontario, Canada, a New York Yankee farm team. Later, he returned to play with a team he had played for earlier, the Freeville-Dryden baseball team, and was named the team's most valuable player (MVP).

Several years earlier, during high school, Christopher had played baseball, football, and soccer, and had already begun to think about writing. He had become a reader, and liked detective, horror, aviation, and sports books. He thought it would be wonderful to be able to earn a living writing those books. Christopher first concentrated on writing detective stories. He wrote one story a week for ten months. And before his first story sold, he had found time to marry, play more sports, and work. He sold his first story, "The Missing Finger Points," to *Detective Story* magazine for $50 in 1941.

He was successfully selling both adult and children's articles and short stories to magazines while holding a full-time job at General Electric in Syracuse, New York. During a conversation with a librarian there, Christopher was encouraged to develop a baseball story idea into a children's book. The librarian had told him that sports stories were very popular. Although he successfully published his first adult mystery novel, *Look for the Body* (Phoenix, 1952), he continued writing for children. Two years later *The Lucky Baseball Bat* (Little, Brown, 1954) was published. It remained in print for 25 years, and then was reissued in a shorter version as a "Springboard Book." Christopher has over 110 book entries in the Library of Congress catalog. In addition to books, Christopher has published over 275 short stories and articles in over 60 adult and children's periodicals. He wrote stories for a school reading program and audio-recorded many of the short stories. In his articles he has written about many subjects, including the Bermuda Triangle and Neil Armstrong, the first man on the moon.

Christopher's own sports background provided the beginnings for many of his books, but people and events in his life provided ideas as well. For example, his book *Ice Magic* (Little, Brown, 1973) involves a toy hockey game that duplicates the real game before the games occur. Matt Christopher said, "I got the idea for *Ice Magic* after my brother, Rudy, designed an ice hockey game." When he was well past his own playing days, Christopher gleaned ideas for writing by attending kids' and adult sports events. He would watch how players reacted; he watched teammates and fans, and listened to coaches and players. Many observations made their way into his books and stories.

Matthew F. Christopher was born in Pennsylvania in 1917 and grew up as the eldest child in a family of seven boys and two girls. His parents, Fred and Mary (Vass) Christopher, were immigrants, his mother from Hungary and his father from Italy. Neither attended school beyond the fourth or fifth grade. The family lived first in Pennsylvania, and when Christopher was just eight years old, the family moved to Ithaca, New York. There were few books in his childhood home, and his brothers and sisters seemed to care little about reading (Christopher read very little during his childhood), but they did enjoy sports. In their younger days the children played baseball with broom handles and tennis balls. Matt recalled those games in an author interview brochure distributed by Little, Brown and Company, *The Matt Christopher Sports Pages: The Official Publication of the Matt Christopher Fan Club.* "We had four to seven players on a team, never more than that because there weren't more kids than that in the whole town. Girls played too. And some had throwing arms and hitting eyes that were just as good as the boys. For bases we used flat rocks, and when we swung at a pitched ball, we swung with the intention of driving it as far up the hill as we could." As the players grew older, they moved from the garden plot area to the field nearby. In the field they had to contend with cow manure. "It was not a problem as long as we kept our eyes open!" His high school coach and principal attempted to obtain a baseball scholarship to Cornell for Christopher. He lacked one necessary mathematics course, but his family was too poor to enroll him in night school to obtain that credit. His parents felt college was for "rich kids, not for the poor like him." However, Christopher continued to play ball and at the age of nineteen signed a professional baseball contract. He was released just two months later. He continued to play semi-pro ball, stopping only when permanently sidelined by a knee injury. In the course of his writing career, Christopher wrote about many different sports—baseball, football, soccer, swimming, dirt bike racing, and others. He said, "Baseball is my favorite sport."

He married Catherine "Cay" M. Krupa on July 13, 1940, and settled down to work for various companies. He worked for the National Cash Register Company in Ithaca, and also for General Electric, among others. He and Cay raised four children, Martin "Marty," Pamela "Pam," Dale, and Duane. He wrote in the evenings after work and on weekends. After his twelfth book was published, Christopher felt secure enough with his writing career to quit his other jobs and become a full-time writer.

Eventually the family settled in Rock Hill, South Carolina. For most of his writing career, Christopher was able to write three to four books a year. In recent years that schedule has been reduced to one to three books a year. In 1985 Christopher's work was slowed by a brain tumor, but after radiation treatments he expressed pleasure that "[it] did not hinder my writing one single bit." When he was not writing, he enjoyed watching television shows, such as *Matlock* and *Murder, She Wrote*, or live sports events. He also enjoyed easy-listening music on the radio, reading, and visiting with his ten grandchildren and three great-grandchildren. During the last few years, Christopher did not make many school visits, but he and his wife Cay would often invite young readers and their parents to stop by their home in Rock Hill, South Carolina. In 1997 the benign tumor returned. The day before he returned to the hospital, he was jotting down ideas for even more books. Matt Christopher died in South Carolina, on September 20, 1997, at the age of eighty. According to Cay Christopher, Matt Christopher "has enough manuscripts at Little Brown to ensure that his books will continue to be published for several years." He left a wonderful legacy to children.

Books and Notes

Matt Christopher's earliest books focused mainly on the game, and little attention was given to the characters' lives outside of the ball park or off the basketball court. As Christopher's writing developed, fantasy, science fiction, and mystery became elements in many of his books. His characters are still involved in sports, but also express conflicts caused by societal pressures.

Animal Tales

Matt Christopher included adventure and a sense of suspense in each of his animal tales. For example, a blind boy is the chief protagonist in *Stranded*, a story about his surviving a shipwreck with his dog on an uninhabited Caribbean Island. *Desperate Search* is the story of two pets lost in a blizzard, and the two boys who search for them.

Desperate Search. Illustrated by Leslie Morrill. (Little, Brown, 1973).

Stranded. Illustrated by Gail Owens. (Little, Brown, 1974).

Sports Biographies

Within the past few years, Christopher researched fact books about sporting events and professionals. His books about great sports events (and the professionals involved) combined his knowledge and research abilities to share biographical information about athletes. For example, Christopher detailed events surrounding Bill Wambsganss's 1920 world series unassisted triple play, Babe Ruth's last three home runs, the major league debut by fifteen-year-old Joe Nuxhall, Willie Mays's 1954 world series catch, Ted Williams's final at-bat, Reggie Jackson's 1977 world series home runs, Dave Dravecky's comeback game, Kirk Gibson's 1988 world series pinch-hit home run, and Jim Abbott's no-hitter.

At the Plate with—Ken Griffey, Jr. (Little, Brown, 1997).

Great Moments in Football History (Little, Brown, 1997).

On the Court with—Andre Agassi (Little, Brown, 1997).

On the Field with—Emmitt Smith (Little, Brown, 1997).

On the Ice with—Wayne Gretzky (Little, Brown, 1997).

Jokes and Riddles

Baseball Jokes and Riddles. Illustrated by Daniel Vasconcellos. (Little, Brown, 1996).

Football Jokes and Riddles. Illustrated by Larry Johnson. (Little, Brown, 1997).

Mystery

While Christopher's several mystery and detective stories also include his perspective on sports, the books focus on a mystery. *Top Wing* focuses on a player's father who is blamed for a fire, and *Pressure Play* involves the origin of threatening letters to a player who seems to be spending too much time with his video hobby.

Pressure Play. Illustrated by Karin Lidbeck. (Little, Brown, 1993).

Top Wing. Illustrated by Marcy Ramsey. (Little, Brown, 1994).

Peach Street Mudders Series

This series of short chapter sport stories are just right for readers in the late primary or early intermediate reading stage. Each protagonist must deal with a conflict on the ball field and in his off-the-field life. Each book features a different member of the Peach Street Mudders.

All-Star Fever: A Peach Tree Mudders Story. Illustrated by Anna Dewdney. (Little, Brown, 1995).

The Catcher's Mask: A Peach Tree Mudders Story. Illustrated by Bert Dodson. (Little, Brown, 1998).

Shadow over Second: A Peach Tree Mudders Story. Illustrated by Anna Dewdney. (Little, Brown, 1996).

Stranger in Right Field: A Peach Tree Mudders Story. Illustrated by Bert Dodson. (Little, Brown, 1997).

Sports Fiction

The majority of Christopher's sports books were written from the male point of view. He did however, write two titles from a female viewpoint. *Supercharged Infield* (Little, Brown, 1985) is a mixture of sports and mystery. Penny Farrell, an outstanding softball player, finds herself attempting to uncover the reason for the strange behavior of two teammates who have unexplainably turned into super athletes. *Red-Hot Hightops* (Little, Brown, 1987) is the story of Kelly, who finds herself a confident and aggressive basketball player whenever she puts on a mysterious pair of red sneakers. When readers asked Christopher to write more books from a female point of view, he said, "My publisher says my girls' books do not sell as well."

The Comeback Challenge. Illustrated by Karen Meyer. (Little, Brown, 1996).

The Dog That Pitched a No-Hitter. Illustrated by Daniel Vasconcellos. (Little, Brown, 1988).

The Dog That Stole Home. Illustrated by Daniel Vasconcellos. (Little, Brown, 1993).

Fighting Tackle. Illustrated by Karin Lidbeck. (Little, Brown, 1995).

Little Lefty (Little, Brown, 1959; 1993).

Long Stretch at First Base. Illustrated by Foster Caddell. (Little, Brown, 1960).

The Lucky Baseball Bat. Illustrated by Dee DeRosa. Springboard Book. (Little, Brown, 1991). Originally published as a longer novel in 1954.

Man Out at First. Illustrated by Ellen Brier. Springboard Book. (Little, Brown, 1993).

Shoot for the Hoop. Illustrated by Karen Meyer. (Little, Brown, 1995). Originally published as *Sink It, Rusty* in 1963.

The Winning Stroke. Illustrated by Karin Lidbeck. (Little, Brown, 1994).

Zero's Slider. Illustrated by Molly Delaney. Springboard Book. (Little, Brown, 1994).

For More Information About/By the Author

Articles

LeMar, David M. "Grappling with the Shortage of Young-Adult Wrestling Fiction." *English Journal* (November 1991): 87–89.

Little Brown Books for Children Website. URL: http://www.littlebrown.com/ (Accessed November 1997).
    Go to the "Little Brown Books for Children" link and then search that section of the site for "Christopher, Matt."

Fan Club

Join the Matt Christopher Fan Club. Members receive a copy of "Matt Christopher Sports Pages" and an official fan club card. Send a self-addressed, business (no. 10) envelope with $1 to: Matt Christopher Fan Club, c/o Little, Brown and Company, 34 Beacon St., Boston, MA 02108.

John Ciardi

◆ Poetry

Boston, Massachusetts
June 24, 1916–March 30, 1986

📖 *The Hopeful Trout and Other Limericks*

📖 *The Monster Den: or Look What Happened at My House—and to It*

About the Author
and the Author's Writing

John Anthony Ciardi (CHAR dee) first wrote poetry for adults. He began to write for children when he and his wife lived with his mother, sister, and his sister's three children. Later, he wrote poetry for his own children, Myra Judith, John Lyle Pritchett, and Benn Anthony.

Ciardi was born on June 24, 1916, in Boston, Massachusetts, where his immigrant parents lived near relatives in the crowded north side tenements. The family had a view of the Old North Church steeple. John's father was an insurance agent and was killed in a car accident when John was just three years old. Shortly after, John's mother moved the family to Medford, Massachusetts, where he spent the rest of his childhood. At home Ciardi spoke Italian, but at school he learned and used English. After completing high school in Medford, Ciardi attended Bates College in Lewiston, Maine, where he became friends with Edmund Muskie. Muskie later became a U.S. senator. Ciardi did not do particularly well at Bates and transferred to Tufts University in Medford where he received an undergraduate degree in 1938. He graduated *magna cum laude*. The poet John Holmes influenced Ciardi at Tufts. Ciardi received a Hopwood Scholarship for study at the University of Michigan. He earned a masters degree in 1939. That year also marked some of the earliest recognition of his poetry.

During World War II, Ciardi served as a sergeant in the U.S. Air Force. He was a gunner aboard a B-29. In 1946, after the war, he married Myra Judith Hosttetter and entered teaching. He spent twenty years teaching English at Kansas City University, Harvard, and Rutgers, then resigned to become the poetry editor of the *Saturday Review*. He continued as editor until 1972. While at Harvard, as the Briggs Copeland Professor, his colleague Theodore Morrison asked him to teach poetry at Bread Loaf. He accepted, and the relationship continued for twenty-six years. He was a poetry editor, critic, and author of many books of poetry for adults. He published over forty books. He left the academic world in 1961, to write full-time and take advantage of his popularity as a national lecturer and speaker.

When Ciardi's daughter was in kindergarten, he wanted to write a book that she could read. He wrote thirty-one poems and gathered them into one volume, titled *I Met a Man* (Houghton, 1961). That was the first book his daughter read completely. She made crayon drawings for each poem. The poems on the first pages are easy to read while the poems that come later increase in reading difficulty. Because Ciardi's daughter loved the book so much, it became his favorite as well.

Children inspired ideas for other poetry books. Their young antics provided him with spoofs included in *The Monster Den* (Lippincott, 1966; Wordsong, 1991). Because the situations are so universal and are executed with a sophisticated sense of humor, both adults and children enjoy the poems. *The Monster Den* is dedicated to Benn, Jonnel, and Myra. Sometimes Ciardi referred to his older son, John Lyle, as Jonnel—a name derived from "John L.," which many used to distinguish son from father.

More poetry collections followed. A much anthologized poem, "Mummy Slept Late and Daddy Fixed Breakfast," was included in a collection, *You Read to Me, I'll Read to You* (Lippincott, 1962). Just one year before his death, *Doodle Soup* (Houghton, 1985) was published. The book contained thirty-eight humorous verses, including "The Best Part of Going Away Is Going Away from You," "The Dangers of Taking Baths," and "Why Pigs Cannot Write Poems."

In 1990 Houghton posthumously published a collection of his poems in a volume titled *Mummy Took Cooking Lessons and Other Poems*. The book introduces many silly characters—Betty Bopper, a popcorn popper; Captain Cuff, a man who is very, very rough; and a fireproof man, Dirty Dan Ploof. Merle Nacht created black-and-white illustrations that complement the freshness of Ciardi's poems. Another volume of poems, *The Hopeful Trout and Other Limericks* was published by Houghton in 1989. Susan Meddaugh illustrated the forty-one limericks in that collection.

John Ciardi continued to write poetry for adults and children throughout his life. He died of a heart attack in Metuchen, New Jersey, on Easter Sunday, March 30, 1986.

Books and Notes

John Ciardi's poetry earned a number of awards, but the award most significant to his children's writings is the National Council of Teachers (NCTE) of English Award for Children's Poetry. The NCTE award is currently given every three years and is based on the poet's body of writing. Ciardi received that award in 1982 and joined earlier recipients David McCord, Aileen Fisher, Karla Kuskin, Myra Cohn Livingston, and Eve Merriam. His poems are laced with humor and a sense of humility for human frailties.

Doodle Soup. Illustrated by Merle Nacht. (Houghton, 1985).

Fast and Slow: Poems for Advanced Children of Beginning Parents. Illustrated by Becky Gaver. (Houghton, 1975).

The Hopeful Trout and Other Limericks. Illustrated by Susan Meddaugh. (Houghton, 1989).

I Met a Man. Illustrated by Robert Osborne. (Houghton, 1961).

The Man Who Sang the Sillies. Illustrated by Edward Gorey. (Lippincott, 1961).

The Monster Den: or Look What Happened at My House—and to It. Illustrated by Edward Gorey. (Lippincott, 1966; Wordsong/Boyds Mills, 1991).

Mummy Took Cooking Lessons and Other Poems. Illustrated by Merle Nacht. (Houghton, 1990).

Someone Could Win a Polar Bear. Illustrated by Edward Gorey. (Lippincott, 1970; Wordsong/Boyds Mills, 1992).

You Know Who. Illustrated by Edward Gorey. (Lippincott, 1964; Wordsong/Boyds Mills, 1992).

You Read to Me, I'll Read to You. Illustrated by Edward Gorey. (Lippincott, 1962).

For More Information About/By the Author

Articles

"Echoes: Poems Left Behind." *Northwest Review* 28, no. 2 (1990): 128.

Books

Cifelli, Edward M., ed. *John Ciardi: A Biography* (University of Arkansas Press, 1997).

Cifelli, Edward M., ed. *The Selected Letters of John Ciardi* (University of Arkansas Press, 1991).

Beverly Cleary

◆ Contemporary Realistic Fiction

McMinnville, Oregon
April 12, 1916

📖 *Ramona the Pest*

📖 *Henry Huggins*

About the Author
and the Author's Writing

In Portland, Oregon, a library is named in honor of Beverly Cleary, and bronze statues of three of her book characters stand in a park near Grant School. In 1993 Cleary accepted an honorary doctorate from Cornell College in Mt. Vernon, Iowa. She has received numerous children's choice awards. Her books have been translated into fourteen languages and used as the basis for several television specials. Movies featuring Henry Huggins have traveled as far as Japan, Sweden, and Denmark. The Ramona series has traveled worldwide, as well. *Ralph S. Mouse* (Morrow, 1982), *The Mouse and the Motorcycle* (Morrow, 1965), and *Runaway Ralph* (Morrow, 1970) are well-loved books and popular videos. In 1984 Cleary was awarded the Newbery Award for *Dear Mr. Henshaw* (Morrow, 1983). She has also been awarded the Catholic Library Association Regina Medal (1980) and the University of Southern Mississippi's Silver Medallion (1982). Few people have passed through childhood without encountering Ramona, Beezus, Henry, and all the other boys and girls on Klickitat Street.

Beverly Cleary was born in McMinnville, Oregon, on April 12, 1916. Her father, Lloyd Bunn, was a fruit farmer, and her mother, Mabel Atler Bunn, was a teacher-turned-housewife. The family lived in a thirteen-room house built by the children of pioneers. In the early 1920s, her family's farming business failed, and, before she was seven, her family had moved from the eighty-acre farm in Yamhill to the big city of Portland. The big city frightened Beverly. "What a shock. The school room had forty children." She discovered chicken pox, small pox, and tonsillitis, and the humiliation of being in the "Blackbird" reading group. Her first-grade teacher punished children by putting them under her desk at her feet. She whipped their hands with a metal-tipped pointer if the child was thought not to be paying attention. "At the end of the first grade, I escaped to second grade." Her second-grade teacher was quite the opposite—kind, understanding, and patient. Her mother always told her reading was fun, and by the time Cleary finished second grade and moved on to the third, she had discovered books and the public library. Money was scarce, but she could always find books at the public library, her favorite place to be. She read everything she could get her hands on. She especially enjoyed funny stories. "I decided that someday when I grew up, I would write them."

Her teachers considered her a gifted storyteller, but when it was time to go to college, Beverly followed her mother's advice and studied for a "more dependable line of work." She studied library science at the University of California at Berkeley and later at the University of Washington. At school she met Clarence Cleary, an accountant. They eloped in 1940. She found work in Yakima, Washington, and her first book began to take shape. At the time, she was working with a "little band of parochial-school boys," who, for the most part, were nonreaders. They were searching for books they wanted to read, books about "kids like us." During World War II she was Post Librarian at the Oakland Army Hospital. Ten years later she started working at home. She complained to her husband that there were never any sharp pencils in the house, so he brought home a pencil sharpener. She wrote a humorous, believable story about a boy named Henry Huggins and his flea-ridden dog, Ribsy. One episode tells about two boys' attempt to take their dog home on the bus. The book, *Henry Huggins*, was published in 1950 by Morrow and garnered instant praise. For the next twenty-five years, Cleary wrote an average of one book a year. In 1955 she and Clarence became parents to twins—a son, Malcolm, and a daughter, Marianne. They provided inspiration for several books, including the stories featuring Janet and Jimmy, *The Real Hole* (Morrow, 1986) and *Two Dog Biscuits* (Morrow, 1986), as well as a book for older readers, *Mitch and Amy* (Morrow, 1967). Cleary describes herself as "your basic middle-class housewife" writing about "middle-class America, which, in my experience, is pretty much the same no matter what one's color may be." She likes to think that the color of the characters in her books are "the color of the reader."

The books about Henry Huggins took place on Klickitat Street in Portland, Oregon, and featured Henry and all his neighborhood friends, including Beezus and Ramona. Beezus and Ramona soon had their own books.

Cleary entered the world of miniature fantasy—popularized by E. B. White's *Stuart Little* and by Mary Norton's *The Borrowers*—when she wrote *The Mouse on the Motorcycle*. She was inspired when her son, Malcolm, received a miniature toy motorcycle during a stay in a London hotel. Upon returning to California, a neighbor found a mouse in a garden bucket. It seemed just the right size for riding the toy motorcycle. Before long, she had created the first draft for *The Mouse and the Motorcycle*. Most of the episodes came from the London experience, but Cleary set the story in California, a setting that was more familiar.

In the eighties Cleary slowed her pace. She no longer appears at conferences or schools. However, she does attend special occasions. For example, she was a surprise speaker at the ribbon-cutting ceremony for the reopening and rededication of the Central Library in Portland on April 8, 1997. The library was rededicated and renamed in her honor. Her remarks were brief. She spoke first of the grandeur of the library and her awe of all it contained. She recounted some of her early visits to the library as a child, and about the Yamhill library that her mother started. She pondered how she, as a six-year-old, might feel about entering the present library for the first time.

In 1993 she traveled to Iowa to receive an honorary Ph.D. from Cornell College in Mt. Vernon, Iowa. On that occasion she said that her goal in writing was "unpretentious." She first strived to write stories "that children will enjoy." Other guidelines she attempts to follow are: "never try to teach," and "never try to be funny." If humor is not natural, the book may not appeal to young readers. She also feels that one should "avoid being trendy," and "never get into a position of having to write for money."

Her new books often begin on January 2, because that was the date she began her first book, *Henry Huggins*. She writes in longhand first and later types the manuscript, editing from the typed copy. Writing generally takes two or more months and the editing lengthens the time to more than six months before the manuscript is ready to send to the editor. There are several revisions and edits before the manuscript is sent to a "good typist," and finally is sent to her editor at William Morrow Publishers.

For many years the Clearys lived in Carmel, California, in a modest house sitting cozily beneath trees on a peaceful street. Their carefully tended garden took over the backyard, filling it with trees, flowers, and vegetables. Now, Clarence and Beverly reside in a condominium. Her family consists of her husband and "one son, one daughter, one grandson, and one granddaughter." They have no pets, but Cleary often sees a skunk outside their window on summer evenings. She writes at a desk in the corner of the bedroom with a view of the mountains, trees, and a squirrel that entertains onlookers by popping out of the ground and pulling nasturtiums into his hole. Cleary generally writes from after breakfast to noon. She gets more letters than she can answer, sometimes 100 or more a day.

When she is not writing, she reads on the living room couch, in airports, and while waiting for appointments. She enjoys needlework, *Masterpiece Theater*, and listening to her favorite musician, her daughter, who is a cellist.

On October 13, 1995, over 1,000 people came to downtown Portland, Oregon, for the dedication of the Beverly Cleary Sculpture Garden for Children. For several years a nonprofit group of people, including author Eric Kimmel and his wife, Doris, led a fund-raising effort to commemorate Beverly Cleary's books. "The Friends of Henry & Ramona Committee" sold T-shirts and tote bags to raise the money for the garden. The sculpture garden concept was developed and Lee Hunt, a Portland artist, was commissioned to create bronze statues of Ramona, Henry, and Ribsy. Ramona is depicted in a raincoat with a fountain at her feet. A fountain beneath Ribsy's feet allows him to splash through the water. The bronze statues, nearly life-size, are situated on a concrete slab in Grant Park on NE 33rd Avenue between Knott Street and Broadway, adjacent to Grant High School. Around the slab are plaques engraved with the titles of Cleary's books that take place in Portland. The titles include all the Henry Huggins books, Ribsy, Otis Spofford, and all the books involving Ramona and Beezus.

Lee Hunt also created two terra-cotta busts of Ramona, one showing Ramona smiling smugly, and one depicting her as being very mad. They are now in the Gresham Regional Library.

Books and Notes

Books About Henry

Henry and Beezus (Morrow, 1952).

Henry and the Clubhouse (Morrow, 1962).

Henry and the Paper Route (Morrow, 1957).

Henry Huggins (Morrow, 1950).

Books About Ramona

Beezus and Ramona (Morrow, 1955).

Ramona and Her Father (Morrow, 1978).

Ramona the Pest (Morrow, 1968).

Ramona Quimby, Age 8 (Morrow, 1981).

Other Titles

Dear Mr. Henshaw. Illustrated by Paul O. Zelinsky. (Morrow, 1983).

The Hullabaloo A B C. Illustrated by Ted Rand. (Morrow, 1998).

The Mouse and the Motorcycle. (Morrow, 1965).

Ralph S. Mouse. Illustrated by Paul O. Zelinsky. (Morrow, 1982).

Runaway Ralph. (Morrow, 1970).

Strider. Illustrated by Paul O. Zelinsky. (Morrow, 1991).

For More Information About/By the Author

Articles

Bauer, Caroline Feller. "Laura Ingalls Wilder Award Presentation: July 1, 1975." *Horn Book* 51 (August 1975): 359–60.

Beverly Cleary Home Page. URL: http://www.teleport.com:80/~krp/cleary.html (Accessed September 1997).
Site has links to book information, biographical sketches of the author and her book characters, frequently asked questions, and more.

Beverly Cleary Sculpture Garden for Children! URL: http://www.multnomah.lib.or.us/lib/kids/cleary.html (Accessed September 1997).
Site shows statues at the garden and provides background information about Cleary and the garden's creation.

"Booklist Interview: Beverly Cleary." *Booklist* 87, no. 4 (October 15, 1990): 448.

Cleary, Beverly. "The Laughter of Children." *Horn Book* 58 (October 1982): 1–10.

Cleary, Beverly. "Laura Ingalls Wilder Award Acceptance." *Horn Book* 51 (August 1975): 361–64.

Fitzgibbons, Shirley. "Focus on Beverly Cleary." *Top of the News* 33 (Winter 1977): 167–70.

Paterson, Katherine. "Ramona Redux." *Washington Post Book World* (October 9, 1977): E-6.

Roggenbuck, Mary June. "Profile: Beverly Cleary—The Children's Force at Work." *Language Arts* (January 1979): 55–60.

Books

Cleary, Beverly. *A Girl from Yamhill* (Morrow, 1988).

Autobiography covers the author's life from childhood through high school years and her growing interest in writing.

Cleary, Beverly. *My Own Two Feet: A Memoir* (Morrow, 1995).

Autobiographical continuation of *A Girl from Yamhill*. Follows her life through college, early librarian jobs, her marriage, and the writing and publication of her first book, *Henry Huggins*.

Eth Clifford
(Ethel Rosenberg)

Animal Fantasy ◆ Contemporary Realistic Fiction

New York, New York
December 25, 1915

📖 Jo-Beth and Mary Rose
Series
📖 Flatfoot Fox Series
📖 Harvey Series
📖 *The Rocking Chair Rebellion*
📖 *The Remembering Box*

About the Author
and the Author's Writing

Born on Christmas day in 1915, Eth Rosenberg was born Ethel Clifford in Manhattan. The family soon followed her father's job to New Jersey, and then to Philadelphia. As a seven-year-old, she walked two miles to school and picked up seckel pears on the way. The one-room schoolhouse sat between a pear orchard and an apple orchard. At noon Clifford sat with her back against a tree and read. Her father died when Eth was just eight years old and her mother moved the family to Brooklyn to be near family. Clifford recalls the time of her father's death as a "defining moment of childhood." That is when she retreated into the world of fiction—a world that gave her power to create and control people and situations. *Alice in Wonderland*, the Louisa May Alcott series, and all the titles by Charles Dickens were among her favorite books. She also read the Bobbsey Twins books, the Tom Swift books, and the Frank Merriwell books, because her older brothers were reading them.

At the age of seventeen, Eth Clifford met David Rosenberg, who loved books as much as she did. They married October 15, 1941, and together founded the David-Stewart Publishing Company in Indiana. The company published a wide range of books and educational materials. Clifford also wrote. Her first successes were short stories and a couple of adult books. Then one night David overheard Eth telling their daughter, Ruthanne, one of her many stories. He encouraged her to write these stories down, and a career began that has lasted more than four decades. During most of her writing career she worked full-time and wrote in the evenings or during weekends. Her work included everything from typist to switchboard operator. Finally, she became a full-time writer and editor. She retired from publishing, but continues to write projects for children.

Her early children's books were picture and early reader books. She later wrote longer novels for intermediate-age readers. One of her early novels, *The Year of the Three-Legged Deer* (Houghton, 1972), tells of a trader who marries a Lenni Lenape Indian. They and their two children suffer an intolerance and bigotry that eventually rip the family apart. After several historical novels, Clifford turned to contemporary fiction in *The Rocking Chair Rebellion* (Houghton, 1978). Opie, a fourteen-year-old, reluctantly volunteers at a home for the aged. There she meets a former neighbor, Mr. Pepper, who is an unwilling guest in the home. Mr. Pepper and some other residents decide to buy a house and set up a home for themselves in Pepper's old neighborhood. The current neighbors resist the establishment of a "home" in their neighborhood until Opie's lawyer father takes the case and works out a resolution.

Clifford's story ideas come from everywhere. Watching a television interview of a twelve-year-old boy who entered college gave her the idea that developed into *I Hate Your Guts, Ben Brooster* (Houghton, 1989). "Often, however," Clifford says, "the best ideas just seem to spring into my mind from out of nowhere!"

A trip to a Toronto island park inspired the third book in the Mary Rose and Jo-Beth series. In that story, *Just Tell Me When We're Dead* (Houghton, 1983), Mary Rose and Jo-Beth's runaway cousin is on an amusement park island with suspects in a robbery. Mary Rose and Jo-Beth are able to help solve the mystery.

Harvey's Horrible Snake Disaster (Houghton, 1984) was written after Clifford "read two different articles, spaced weeks apart, both of which intrigued me. One was about a herpetologist whose python had escaped from its cage and wrapped itself around the driver, who then tried to explain the incident to a judge. The other was about a woman who was frightened by a snake in a tub, was being taken downstairs by paramedics, one of whom accidentally tripped and dropped the woman." Clifford used those articles as a foundation for Harvey and his troublesome cousin, Nora. She says, "[I] had great fun creating the book!"

Stories told her by her mother from Eth's childhood found their way into *The Remembering Box* (Houghton, 1985), a book about a warm and loving relationship between a young Jewish boy and his grandmother. Memories of a blind man she remembered from childhood inspired *The Man Who Sang in the Dark* (Houghton, 1988). Clifford says, "*The Man Who Sang in the Dark* was autobiographical. However, the end was fiction! It seemed to me, however, that it needed a happy ending. Young readers especially want to know that problems can be solved somehow. In letters they write to me, they often comment on their relief that this was so!" Each of Clifford's books is fast-moving, full of characterization, humorous.

During the years in Indiana, Eth Clifford and her husband wrote several historical works about the state. One title, *Living Indiana History: Heartland of America* (David-Stewart, 1965), was used for many years in Indiana classrooms. Eth Clifford is generally considered an "Indiana author." She has contributed several of her manuscripts and papers to the Kerlan Collection, housed in the Walter Library of the University of Minnesota; to the Division of Rare Books and Special Collections of the University of Wyoming; and to the Bicentennial Library of California State College in California, Pennsylvania. In the early 1980s the Rosenbergs moved to North Lauderdale, Florida, and later to North Miami Beach. For a number of years they have been instrumental in organizing an annual conference in children's literature held in south Florida. In 1987 Clifford received a State of Florida artist's fellowship award for her work in children's literature.

The Rosenbergs have one daughter, Ruthanne, and six grandchildren. Clifford says, "When I'm not writing, I *read*. And buy books! I am an inveterate book buyer, so that books seem to be spilling over in every corner. I enjoy being with my grandchildren, who often have sleepover visits with me. I'm happy to say each and every one of them is a devoted reader."

Books and Notes

Eth Clifford's books are a zany mix of humor and serious themes, mysteries, and relationships. Her characters are often quick-witted, likable, and are sure to spend time in situations with which every child can identify.

Jo-Beth and Mary Rose Series

Eth Clifford's series about Jo-Beth and Mary Rose began with *Help! I'm a Prisoner in the Library*. When their father's car runs out of gas, two girls find themselves accidentally locked overnight in the public library. They find and help an injured librarian who lives upstairs, and their father rescues all of them the next morning. In the next book in the series, the girls find themselves in a deserted ghost town with a very lifelike ghost. In yet another title, a runaway cousin and bank robbers manage to enter the fracas.

The Dastardly Murder of Dirty Pete (Houghton, 1981).

Help! I'm a Prisoner in the Library (Houghton, 1979).

Scared Silly (Houghton, 1988).

Harvey Series

A humorous series filled with mysterious events features Harvey Willson and sometimes his pest of a cousin, Nora. Each adventure involves an animal— snake, monkey, parrot, and raccoon.

Harvey's Horrible Snake Disaster (Houghton, 1984).

Harvey's Marvelous Monkey Mystery (Houghton, 1987).

Harvey's Mystifying Raccoon Mix-Up (Houghton, 1994).

Harvey's Wacky Parrot Adventure (Houghton, 1990).

Flatfoot Fox Series

This series for somewhat younger readers serves up mysterious fare in an easy-to-read chapter format. The books involve cases ranging from finding the owl's missing "whoooo" to finding Otter's missing child. Flatfoot's sidekick is Secretary Bird. Reviewers have said that *Flatfoot Fox and the Case of the Missing Schoolhouse* is "perhaps the funniest and best yet" and that Flatfoot Fox uncovers "the truth in the best Sherlock Holmes tradition."

Flatfoot Fox and the Case of the Bashful Beaver. Illustrated by Brian Lies. (Houghton, 1995).

Flatfoot Fox and the Case of the Missing Schoolhouse. Illustrated by Brian Lies. (Houghton, 1997).

Flatfoot Fox and the Case of the Missing Whoooo. Illustrated by Brian Lies. (Houghton, 1993).

Flatfoot Fox and the Case of the Nosy Otter. Illustrated by Brian Lies. (Houghton, 1992).

Other Titles

Family for Sale (Houghton, 1996).

Never Hit a Ghost with a Baseball Bat. Illustrated by George Hughes. (Houghton, 1993).

The Remembering Box. Illustrated by Diane Diamond. (Houghton, 1985).

The Rocking Chair Rebellion (Houghton, 1978).

For More Information About/By the Author

No articles located. Check general biographical references.

Christopher Collier

◆ Historical Fiction

**New York, New York
January 29, 1930**

📖 *My Brother Sam Is Dead*
📖 *Jump Ship to Freedom*
📖 Drama of American History
Series

About the Author
and the Author's Writing

Christopher Collier has taught grade seven through doctoral candidates since 1955, and has been writing books for young readers since the early 1970s. Christopher Collier, known as "Kit" to his friends, says, "I love teaching and see my books as extensions of my *teaching* life." His books, often written in collaboration with his brother, James Lincoln Collier, usually begin with an idea that he has for teaching a concept to readers. "I was teaching eighth grade and thought that kids would learn better and remember more if they learned history through really exciting, but true, novels."

Once Collier identifies the historical period and general setting, he begins to research. No detail is too insignificant to check—the weather, the terrain of the locations, food eaten, clothing worn, and utensils used. As he begins to think about the story, he identifies characters and creates a complete profile of those that might be included in the story. Even the characters' names are researched to ensure that the name would have been used at the time. Collier takes copious notes concerning descriptions of the characters, exact details of the settings, and each event or action included in the story. "It is amazing that some of the episodes in our books that are true are the most unbelievable. In one book, two men are swept off an 18th-century brigantine—and with the next wave, one of them is swept back on again. Amazing, but it really happened. Some of the things we make up are easy to believe, but they never happened at all. Truth is often more interesting than fiction. A combination of both is what makes our books historical fiction." "Almost everything we put in our books really did happen to someone, though not always to the people who live in our stories."

To interpret events and authenticate details, Christopher (and his brother James) visit the sites used in the manuscript. For example, when the Colliers were writing about the decapitation of the slave Ned in *My Brother Sam Is Dead* (Scholastic, 1974), they visited the site of the decapitation and measured relative distances so that every move and action would be portrayed as accurately as possible. They even verified the words of the British officers and quoted those in the book.

The Colliers' books are sometimes criticized for the portrayal of women, children, and slaves as subordinate, and for the lifestyles that include heavy drinking and broken families caused by death portrayed in their books. During that period, African Americans were also referred to as "niggers." Christopher Collier explains that not using that term would have made their writing less credible. Similarly, to avoid representing the subservient role women, children, and slaves had in society would have created an inaccurate portrait of the times.

In one scene originally included in *My Brother Sam Is Dead*, two male characters were depicted as conversing while washing dishes. During the Revolutionary period, males would not have been washing dishes, so the scene was changed to have them go to the barn to take care of the animals. The process of finding history, dating it, and making the details accurate is described by Collier as "historiography." In the collaborative process, Christopher's role is to make the books reflect the time period, while James's is to create an interesting and exciting text.

Christopher Collier has said that one of the most difficult aspects of writing about a historical period is determining how the people then living spoke. While writing *My Brother Sam Is Dead*, the Colliers decided to have the characters use modern speech, partly to make the book easier to read and partly because they did not know how people during that time period actually spoke.

Christopher Collier was born on January 29, 1930, to Edmund Collier, a writer, and Katharine Brown Collier. He earned an undergraduate degree from Clark University in Worcester, Massachusetts, served two years in the military, married, earned a masters degree, and then earned a doctorate from Columbia University. Collier and his wife had two children. The couple later divorced. Collier and his second wife, Bonnie, whom he married in 1969, added another son to the family.

For a time Collier taught junior high in the Greenwich and New Canaan, Connecticut, public schools. In 1958 he began teaching history at Columbia University in New York City, and later taught at the University of Bridgeport in Connecticut. In 1981 he was named a professor of history at the University of Connecticut, Storrs. He is also the Connecticut State Historian. In addition to his writing for children, Christopher Collier has written or contributed to several historical articles and books for university presses and historical organizations, such as the Bridgeport Museum of Art, Science, and Industry, and the Connecticut Humanities Council. Some recent projects have included research on Connecticut Indians for the Connecticut Attorney General, and on gun control for the Office of the Public Defender. He often presents keynote speeches at meetings such as the Connecticut Association of Boards of Education, the Connecticut Association of School Superintendents, and the "Judges" Institute (members of the Connecticut Bench).

Christopher Collier has lived in Connecticut most of his life. Presently Collier says, "I live with my wife Bonnie, a librarian. I have three grown-up children, Edmund Quincy 'Ned,' Sally McQueen, and Christopher Zwissler. I am Professor of History at the University of Connecticut. One son is a lawyer; the other is a graduate student in architecture; and my daughter is a librarian." When not studying history or writing, "I play trumpet in a swing band, ice dance, play ice hockey, tennis, water ski, and swim. I also read a great deal."

Books and Notes

While Christopher Collier has written or contributed to several historical pieces, his children's writing is in collaboration with his brother, James Lincoln Collier. Each of the books listed in the following selected lists are coauthored by James Lincoln Collier.

Set During the Revolutionary War

Conflicts inherent in the times are included in each book set during the American Revolution. *My Brother Sam Is Dead* focuses on the division between established authority and loyalty to ideological principals, *The Bloody Country* deals with the incompatibility between human values and property values, and *The Winter Hero* deals with the conflict between economic need and ideological commitment.

The Bloody Country (Scholastic, 1976).

My Brother Sam Is Dead (Scholastic, 1974).

The Winter Hero (Scholastic, 1978).

The Arabuses (Set in Post-Revolutionary Days)

Each title attempts to describe the way free blacks and slaves lived in the North during the post-revolutionary era, from 1781 to 1790. The books deal with slaves being used as bargaining chips during the drafting of the Constitution, relative intelligence and ability, and the powerlessness of the most powerless of all the people in the postwar era, female slave children.

Jump Ship to Freedom (Delacorte, 1981).

The War Comes to Willie Freeman (Delacorte, 1982).

Who Is Carrie? (Delacorte, 1984).

Civil War Era

The Colliers first became known for their accurate portrayal of African Americans and their role during and immediately after the Revolutionary War. Recent titles have stretched their research and writing beyond the Revolutionary War. *The Clock* takes place in 1810 Connecticut. *With Every Drop of Blood* is the story of fourteen-year-old Johnny, who, while trying to transport food to Richmond, Virginia, is caught by a black Union soldier.

The Clock. Illustrated by Kelly Maddox. (Delacorte, 1992).

With Every Drop of Blood: A Novel of the Civil War (Delacorte, 1994).

Drama of American History Series

Christopher and James Collier collaborated on a ten-volume series of history books focusing on the circumstances of the English colonization of Virginia, the evolution of slavery, an examination of the events and personalities involved in creating the Constitution of the United States, the westward expansion, and the War of 1812. *The Cotton South and the Mexican War, 1835–1850* examines how the southwestern portion of the United States was created out of land settled first by Native Americans, taken by the Spanish, and then used as a pawn between the North and the South prior to the Civil War. The titles include: *The Paradox of Jamestown, 1585–1700*; *Pilgrims and Puritans, 1620–1676*; *Clash of Cultures: Prehistory–1638*; *The French and Indian War, 1660–1763*; *The American Revolution, 1763–1783*; *Creating the Constitution, 1787*; *Building a New Nation, 1789–1803*; *The Jeffersonian Republicans, 1800–1820*; *The Age of Jackson, 1821–1850*; *The Cotton South and the Mexican War, 1835–1850*. All published by Benchmark Books, 1998.

For More Information About/By the Author

Articles

McElmeel, Sharron. "Author! Author! Christopher Collier and James Lincoln Collier." In *Educator's Companion to Children's Literature, Volume 1: Mysteries, Animal Tales, Books of Humor, Adventure Stories, and Historical Fiction* (Libraries Unlimited, 1995): 128–31.

Raymond, Allen. "Jamie and Kit Collier: The Writer and the Historian." *Teaching K–8* (January 1988): 35–38.

James Lincoln Collier

Historical Fiction ◆ Nonfiction ◆ Books about music

**New York, New York
June 27, 1928**

- 📖 *My Brother Sam Is Dead*
- 📖 *Jump Ship to Freedom*
- 📖 Drama of American History Series
- 📖 *Jazz: An American Saga*

About the Author
and the Author's Writing

James "Jamie" Lincoln Collier was born June 27, 1928, in New York, New York. His parents were Edmund Collier and Katharine Brown Collier. At the age of twenty-two, he earned an undergraduate degree from Hamilton College. His younger brother, Christopher, turned to teaching as his vocation, while James turned his creativity toward the worlds of music and writing.

As a freelance writer, James has authored articles for major publications on diverse topics, including children's fears, anxiety, and jazz and jazz musicians. His articles have been published in *Reader's Digest*, *Publishers Weekly*, and *TV Guide*. His books for young readers range from science fantasy to books about music and related topics.

While Jamie is an accomplished writer in his own right, he is perhaps best known for the historical fiction written in collaboration with his brother, Christopher. Christopher Collier feels that as a teacher there must be a better way to teach history than using "dull, dull textbooks." For fifteen years, Christopher Collier attempted to persuade Jamie to collaborate with him to write a book of historical fiction. Jamie finally agreed, and their first collaboration, *My Brother Sam Is Dead* (Scholastic, 1974), was published. After collaborating on six novels set during the American Revolution, Jamie and Christopher wrote a novel set in 1810, *The Clock* (Delacorte, 1992), and a Civil War novel, *With Every Drop of Blood: A Novel of the Civil War* (Delacorte, 1994). More than twenty years after their first novel was published, the two collaborated on a series of ten titles, Drama of American History, for Benchmark Books.

Generally, Christopher Collier generates the original idea that rises from a topic he wants to teach. He sketches an outline and then researches the book. He searches incidents, details of weather, characters' names—anything that might enter into a story dealing with the topic he has generated. Christopher then sends the package of information to Jamie, who writes the first draft. If information is needed for the first draft, Jamie indicates that by putting in the code "TC," meaning "to come." When that draft is sent back, Christopher researches the gaps then returns it to Jamie again. Sometimes details—the patterns on dishes that might have been used in that time period, for example—must be researched. Mention of the day's weather is even verified. The two writers then meet to produce the near-final draft. Jamie's job is to make the text exciting; Christopher's job is to make sure the text is accurate in every detail.

In addition to the historical novels, Jamie Collier has written a number of other titles for young readers, including biographies of Louis Armstrong and Duke Ellington, and a history of jazz. These music books blend Jamie Collier's career in music and jazz playing with his freelance writing career. Generally, these works contain detailed technical information and deal with musical motifs and patterns of compositions and work.

Jamie Collier married in 1952. He and his wife, Carol, became the parents of two sons, Geoffrey Lincoln and Andrew Kemp. They later divorced, and Jamie married Ida Potash. After living for a number of years in Greenwich Village in New York, Jamie Collier now lives in Pawling, a town in the southeast corner of Dutchess County bordering Connecticut on the east, and Putnam County to the south. Pawling is sixty-seven miles north of New York City. Pawling is a pre-Revolutionary town settled in 1728, and could be the setting for one of the Collier brothers' Revolutionary war novels. In the fall of 1778, George Washington stayed there waiting for the British to attack either Boston or West Point. The Quaker meeting house on Quaker Hill was built in 1749 and became a hospital for soldiers in the Revolutionary War.

Books and Notes

James Lincoln Collier has written dozens of articles, several adult books, and books about music, musicians, and popular young adult topics. Critics give him mixed reviews of his music titles, citing his "sociological observations," which in some critics' view tend to diminish rather than illuminate the personalities of the musicians he profiles. Others cite the overly technical passages and the author's sometimes questionable assertions as stumbling blocks for the general reader. All in all, Collier's popularity seems to be rooted in his collaborative work with his brother. (See the entry "Christopher Collier" for more bibliographical information.)

Books About Music and Music-Related Topics

Duke Ellington (Collier Books, 1993; Originally published by Macmillan, 1991).

Jazz: An American Saga (Henry Holt, 1997).

Louis Armstrong: An American Success Story (Collier Books, 1993; Originally published by Macmillan, 1985).

Set During the Revolutionary War

These books, set in the Revolutionary War and each dealing with a major conflict of the time, are coauthored with his brother, Christopher Collier.

The Bloody Country (Scholastic, 1976).

My Brother Sam Is Dead (Scholastic, 1974).

The Winter Hero (Scholastic, 1978).

The Arabuses (Set in Post-Revolutionary Days)

Coauthored with his brother, Christopher, each title attempts to describe the way free blacks and slaves lived in the North during the post-revolutionary era, from 1781 to 1790.

Jump Ship to Freedom (Delacorte, 1981).

The War Comes to Willie Freeman (Delacorte, 1982).

Who Is Carrie? (Delacorte, 1984).

Civil War Era

Each book is coauthored with Christopher Collier. The Clock is set in 1810, and With Every Drop of Blood is set during the Civil War.

The Clock. Illustrated by Kelly Maddox. (Delacorte, 1992).

With Every Drop of Blood: A Novel of the Civil War (Delacorte, 1994).

Drama of American History Series

Christopher Collier and James L. Collier have collaborated on a ten volume series of history books. Titles include: *The Paradox of Jamestown, 1585–1700*; *Pilgrims and Puritans, 1620–1676*; *Clash of Cultures: Prehistory– 1638*; *The French and Indian War, 1660–1763*; *The American Revolution, 1763–1783*; *Creating the Constitution, 1787*; *Building a New Nation, 1789–1803*; *The Jeffersonian Republicans, 1800–1820*; *The Age of Jackson, 1821–1850*; *The Cotton South and the Mexican War, 1835–1850*. All published by Benchmark Books, 1998.

For More Information About/By the Author

Articles

McElmeel, Sharron. "Author! Author! Christopher Collier and James Lincoln Collier." In *Educator's Companion to Children's Literature, Volume 1: Mysteries, Animal Tales, Books of Humor, Adventure Stories, and Historical Fiction* (Libraries Unlimited, 1995): 128–31.

Raymond, Allen. "Jamie and Kit Collier: The Writer and the Historian." *Teaching K–8* (January 1988): 35–38.

Ellen Conford

**New York, New York
March 20, 1942**

- 📖 *Strictly for Laughs*
- 📖 *The Alfred G. Graebner Memorial High School Handbook of Rules and Regulations*
- 📖 Jenny Archer Series

About the Author and the Author's Writing

Ellen Conford, teaching at a ten day summer institute for writers, was attempting to convince the participants, mostly teachers, that they needed to teach in the classroom and write to entertain. On the seventh day, she met a participant who told her that he and his eleven-year-old niece were avid readers of her books. He also said Conford always followed his niece's three rules for good writing:

- ✓ Don't bore me.
- ✓ Don't make it stupid.
- ✓ Don't treat me like a child.

In thirteen words a fan had summed up the essence of Conford's view on writing for young readers.

Ellen Conford began writing in third grade knowing she would be a writer. She never took a writing course, and she was not taught writing fiction in school. She says, "From the time I got my own library card in second grade, I read. Eight books a week, every week, as long as I was in school. I loved it. I would have read more than eight books, but that was the limit we were allowed. I learned how to write fiction from reading what other authors had written."

Conford's style is light-hearted, crisp, and humorous. She haunts shopping malls to listen to kids speak. Her dialogue is always lively and helps build the profile of each of her characters.

She says she "writes books I would like to read. Plot is just an excuse to write about the characters I'm interested in." She writes mostly about witty girls, aged 11 to 16, who often deliver humorous one-liners. Some protagonists could pass as stand-up comedians. In fact, the main character in *Strictly for Laughs* (Pacer/Putnam, 1985) is a stand-up comic who tries to use comedy routines to get the guy (in this case a boy named Peter). Conford relates that the book came about when "Beverly Horowitz, the then editor at Pacer, suggested that I write a book about a group of kids who have a cable television show and devise a contest to increase viewer interest. I thought it was an idea with great comic possibilities, so I wrote a book about three kids who do a local radio show and have trouble stirring listener interest, but as I am more interested in character than plot, I devised Joey."

Ellen Conford was born March 20, 1942, in New York City, the daughter of Harry and Lillian (Pfeffer) Schaffer. She grew up in New York and attended Hofstra College (now Hofstra University) on Long Island, from 1959–1962. For more than two decades she has been a full-time writer. She says, "My first book was published in 1971. Before that I had poetry and short stories published in magazines." *Impossible Possum* (Little, Brown, 1971) was her first book, inspired when she visited the public library with her then four-year-old son and decided that she could write something better than what was available. She wrote the book for the primary-age reader, and although it was successful, she soon turned to writing for intermediate and middle-grade readers. Conford's acquaintances have given her ideas for the people and events in her books. Her book *Crush* (HarperCollins, 1998) is a "collection of short stories about Valentine's Day and is based a good deal on people and events from my high school and college days. Some of the characters in the stories are very much like my friends—and enemies—from my teenage years." Her characters are, in general, adolescents who look at life with a little humor. Conford consciously avoids serious, painful situations, preferring to deal with problems that adolescents encounter every day. She says, "My most satisfying moments as an author are when I get letters from kids who say, 'I never liked reading before I read one of your books. Now I've learned that reading can be *fun*, not work, or something you just have to do in school.' When someone tells me that, I feel that I *really* made a difference in some one's life; that I've influenced a person who will have a lifelong habit of reading and thinking and acquiring knowledge needed for the making of critical and ethical reasons."

Three of her titles have become video/television movies. *Dear Lovey Heart* became a Walt Disney movie in 1989; *Girl with E.S.P.,* based on *And This Is Laura*, was made into a television movie/video for ABC Wide World of Learning in 1980; and *The Alfred G. Graebner Memorial High School Handbook of Rules and Regulations* was filmed for a Learning Corporation production released in 1984.

Ellen Conford is married to David Conford, an English professor at the State University of New York at Farmingdale. Their son, Michael, is married to Gloria Nightingale. Conford's extended family includes several other writers. "I have a large family of aunts, uncles, and cousins (my mother was one of nine children) and several of my cousins are writers. Almost all of my mother's family has writing talent. Some are professionals; some just write for fun."

When Conford is not writing she says, "I love to read, do needlework, watch old movies, play Scrabble, cook, and collect cookbooks." Among her favorite foods are lobster, artichokes, asparagus, and profiteroles with chocolate sauce for dessert. The Confords live in Great Neck, New York.

Books and Notes

Ellen Conford writes books aimed at readers in grades 2–4, for intermediate readers in grades 4–6, and for older readers in grades 6–8+. The American Library Association has named several of her books to the notable book list and to *School Library Journal's* Best Books of the Year.

Jenny Archer Series

In the 1990s Conford wrote several chapter books for the late primary or early intermediate reader, books starring an unforgettable character, Jenny Archer.

Can Do, Jenny Archer. Illustrated by Diane Palmisciano. (Springboard/ Little, Brown, 1991).

If she wins a can collecting contest, she will win the chance to direct a class movie and risk losing a friend.

Nibble, Nibble, Jenny Archer. Illustrated by Diane Palmisciano. (Springboard/ Little, Brown, 1993).

The status of the commercial Jenny hopes to make is in question once Jenny finds out the "snack" she likes so well was intended for gerbils.

Get the Picture, Jenny Archer. Illustrated by Diane Palmisciano. (Springboard/Little, Brown, 1994).

Her imagination runs wild as she takes candid photographs in her neighborhood.

A Job for Jenny Archer. Illustrated by Diane Palmisciano. (Springboard/ Little, Brown, 1988).

In an effort to earn money, and convinced her family is poor, Jenny puts her family's house up for sale.

A Case for Jenny Archer. Illustrated by Diane Palmisciano. (Springboard/ Little, Brown, 1988).

Jenny's interest in mysteries leads her to view her neighbors with suspicion and begin investigating them.

Jenny Archer, Author. Illustrated by Diane Palmisciano. (Springboard/ Little, Brown, 1989).

Enhanced episodes make for interesting reading in Jenny's autobiography.

What's Cooking, Jenny Archer? Illustrated by Diane Palmisciano. (Springboard/Little, Brown, 1989).

A new business and preparing lunch for her friends at school includes many comic mishaps.

Jenny Archer to the Rescue. Illustrated by Diane Palmisciano. (Springboard/Little, Brown, 1990).

In an effort to use her newly learned first-aid skills, Jenny creates some of her own emergencies.

Books for Late Primary/ Intermediate Readers

Dear Mom, Get Me Out of Here (Little, Brown, 1992).

The Luck of Pokey Bloom (Archway, 1983).

My Sister the Witch. Illustrated by Tim Jacobus. (Troll, 1995).

Norman Newman and the Werewolf of Walnut Street. Illustrated by Tim Jacobus. (Troll, 1995).

Books for Older Readers

Crush (HarperCollins, 1998).

The Frog Princess of Pelham (Little, Brown, 1997).

I Love You, I Hate You, Get Lost (Scholastic, 1994).

For More Information About/By the Author

Articles

Bugniazet, Judith. "Ellen Conford: Biography and Books." *The ALAN Review* 14, no. 1 (Fall 1986): 23–24.

Conford, Ellen. "I Want to Make Them Laugh." *The ALAN Review* 14, no. 1 (Fall 1986): 21–23.

Keller, John G. "Ellen and Me, or The Editor as Fisherman's Wife." *Elementary English* 51, no. 6 (September 1974): 791–96.

Pam Conrad

Historical Fiction ◆ Contemporary Realistic Fiction ◆ Picture Book Fiction

**Brooklyn, New York
June 18, 1947–
January 22, 1996**

📖 *Prairie Songs*
📖 *Stonewords*
📖 *The Tub People*
📖 *Zoe Rising*

About the Author and the Author's Writing

Pam Conrad's first young adult book, *Prairie Songs* (Harper, 1985), was named the winner of the 1986 International Reading Association Children's Book Award and one of the 1985 ALA Best Books for Young Adults. After that time, she wrote dozens of other award-winning books. *Stonewords* (Harper, 1990), won the 1991 Edgar Allen Poe Award for Best Juvenile Mystery and was a 1990 Boston Globe-Horn Book Honor Awardee. She also was the author of several well-received picture books, including *The Tub People* (Harper, 1989) and *The Rooster's Gift* (Harper, 1996).

Pam Conrad was born Pamela Stumpf in Brooklyn, New York. Her father, Robert F. Stumpf, was a teacher, and her mother, Doris Dowling Stumpf, was a businesswoman. Pam's childhood homes were in Maspeth, New York, and when she was seven, her family moved to Valley

Stream, Long Island, New York. That was a year of milestones. Pam contracted chicken pox, and, during her recovery, her mother gave her a pencil and paper to draw with. Instead Pam began to write poems that bore some resemblance to the style of A. A. Milne. By the end of the year, she had written enough poetry for her father to gather the poems into a private collection called *Tea by the Garden Wall*. It was her first published book.

Throughout her school years she continued writing—love poems and stories about girls who sacrificed dearly for what they believed. After studying dance at the High School of Performing Arts in New York City, Conrad studied at Hofstra University. Before she earned a degree, she married, on June 25, 1967, and left for various parts of the United States with her military husband, Robert R. Conrad. During her travels, she only wrote boring notations in her diary and upbeat letters home. The Conrads lived in Colorado, Texas, and Nebraska, which later became the setting for her first novel, *Prairie Songs*.

It wasn't until Conrad returned to New York, when her daughters were in school, that Conrad turned to writing. She met Johanna Hurwitz (author of many children's books) at the 1981 Hofstra Writer's Conference. The two became friends, and Hurwitz encouraged Conrad to write for publication. Conrad tried everything from magazine articles to romance novels. In 1982, the Conrads divorced. Their daughters, Johanna and Sarah, were 10 and 7 respectively. Pam continued her college studies and earned an undergraduate degree from the New School of Social Research in 1984. Johanna Hurwitz continued to encourage Conrad. A year before graduation, a children's book, *I Don't Live Here* (Dutton, 1984), was published. It was, however, her first young adult book, *Prairie Songs*, that caught the attention of readers when it was published in 1985.

Prairie Songs was Conrad's first historical novel. Explaining how she came to write about a woman who moved from New York to Nebraska, Conrad said that she "did not do research for it." However, when she was growing up, she read all the Little House books. During junior high, she read Willa Cather's books and lived "out West" when she was married and moving around the country with her Air Force husband. During those times, she also read many journals written by pioneer women. However, Conrad explained, "I never thought I was doing research. I thought I was reading what I loved to read."

Conrad began her writing with historical novels. She attended writing conferences and took courses. She knew that she wanted to make a living through her writing. The first book sold was "an imitation of a

Beverly Cleary book." But there was another story that she felt she had to write. The story was about a prairie woman who lived in the late 1800s. She loved the prairie and the story. Her editor asked her to write another Nebraska book, but she had nothing more to write.

For a time she tried to write contemporary fiction. One day, before she went to her desk to write, the words "just began to come to me" while showering. She jumped out of the shower, wrote them down, went back into the shower, and jumped out again. She said, "It was as if something was speaking to me." Those words resulted in the book *My Daniel* (Harper, 1989), the story of twelve-year-old Julia Creath and her sixteen-year-old brother, Daniel, who had found a "treasure that would help bring money to the family." The story of the treasure, a gigantic brontosaurus, and the summer Daniel died for it, is told by eighty-year-old Julia when she returns to Nebraska to take her grandchildren to the museum to see the dinosaur. Later, Conrad penned another prairie book, *Prairie Visions: The Life and Times of Solomon Butcher* (Harper, 1991). Conrad's biography of the photographer Solomon Butcher, who had a significant role in the recording of Nebraska history, is interesting and humorous. The stories told to Butcher by Nebraska settlers include "The Jack Nolan Escape," "Grasshopper Storm," and "Restless Night."

Kent Brown, Conrad's friend, suggested the idea for *Pedro's Journal: A Voyage with Christopher Columbus, August 3, 1492–February 14, 1493* (Caroline House, 1991), a story of the ship's boy on the *Santa Maria*. Brown, an editor associated with the Highlights Foundation and Boyds Mills Press, often appeared on the same panels with Conrad at the International Reading Association's annual conference. Both also participated in the Highlights Foundation Workshops for writing. Brown knew that Conrad loved boats and sailing and inquired if Conrad was interested in creating captions for a book he had in mind. The picture book was to be a sketch book of the ship's boy on the *Santa Maria*. At first Conrad responded with an "Ugh!" Columbus brought back memories of third-grade bulletin boards and reports. She was not really interested. Later, Brown sent her *Admiral of the Ocean Sea: A Life of Christopher Columbus* by Samuel Morrison (Little, Brown, 1991; 1942). Morrison had recounted the journey through Columbus's log. Conrad found the book immensely interesting and soon agreed to Brown's suggestion. *Pedro's Journal* resulted.

Bits and pieces of Conrad's life have made their way into her books. The Pug dog in *Stonewords* (Harper, 1990) is named Oscar. In real life,

Oscar was Conrad's Pug, Balki. An episode in *Pedro's Journal*, where Pedro gets his pants caught on one of the boat's cleats while he attempts to take his first swim off of the boat, describes a similar incident that occurred to Conrad. She, too, got caught on a boat cleat and hung over the edge like a fish, the description used to describe Pedro's predicament.

Conrad's fear of the prairie is much like Emmeline's in *Prairie Songs*. During her childhood, Conrad stuck gravel up her nose, risked her life on a wooden swing, and lived along the railroad tracks. Readers will recognize those actions from Darcie and Roman in Conrad's books.

Pam Conrad's writing awards included the International Reading Association Award (1986), the Cowboy Hall of Fame Award (1986), the Golden Kite Award (1986), the Edgar Allan Poe Award for the Best Juvenile Mystery (1991), and the Boston Globe-Horn Book Honor Award (1990).

Conrad died on January 22, 1996, after struggling for several years with breast cancer. Her friend Johanna Hurwitz was still there during her illness. Hurwitz helped establish a fund in 1995 to help Conrad pay her medical expenses for experimental treatments.

Zoe Rising (Harper, 1996), a sequel to *Stonewords*, was published the June following Conrad's death. *The Rooster's Gift*, a picture book, was released the following October. Additional titles, *Don't Go Near That Rabbit, Frank!*; *This Mess*; *Blue Willow*; and *Animal Lullabies*, were published in the following two years. At the time of her death, Conrad was living in Rockville Centre, Long Island, New York.

Books and Notes

Pam Conrad's writing included picture books, fiction, historical fiction (a blend of fact and fiction), and biography for middle-grade/middle-school readers.

Historical Fiction/Biographies

Pam Conrad's *Prairie Songs* catapulted her to success in 1985. Louisa Downing, a young woman, tells the story of two pioneer women, her mother, who survives, and Emmeline, the fragile wife of the prairie doctor, who moves from petulance to insanity. At the conclusion of the novel, the Downing children survey the work of Solomon Butcher, a photographer. Solomon Butcher was a real photographer, and Conrad also wrote his biography. Conrad's topics deal with the unearthing of a meteor, the history of a town, and Christopher Columbus's arrival in America.

Call Me Ahnighito. Illustrated by Richard Egielski. (Harper, 1995).

My Daniel (Harper, 1989).

Our House: The Stories of Levittown. Illustrated by Brian Selznick. (Harper, 1995).

Pedro's Journal: A Voyage with Christopher Columbus, August 3, 1492–February 14, 1493. Illustrated by Peter Koeppen. (Caroline House, 1991).

Prairie Songs. Illustrated by Darryl S. Zudeck. (Harper, 1985).

Prairie Visions: The Life and Times of Solomon Butcher (Harper, 1991).

Picture Books

Pam Conrad's picture books gained popularity when *The Tub People* was published in 1989. It was the story of seven little wooden Tub People—mother, father, grandmother, doctor, policeman, boy, and dog. When the tub child is sucked down the drain, the family begins an adventure ending in a new room with a rumpled quilt for climbing. Other stories feature a rooster who thought his gift was to raise the sun each morning, a doll giving a party, and a day filled with strawberries.

Animal Lingo. Illustrated by Barbara Bustetter Falk. (Harper, 1995).

Animal Lullabies. Illustrated by Richard Cowdrey. (Harper/Laura Geringer, 1997).

Doll Face Has a Party. Illustrated by Brian Selznick. (Harper, 1994).

Molly and the Strawberry Day. Illustrated by Mary Szilagyi. (Harper, 1993).

The Tub Grandfather. Illustrated by Richard Egielski. (Harper, 1993).

The Tub People. Illustrated by Richard Egielski. (Harper, 1989).

Mystery

In *Stonewords*, Zoe is left with her grandparents and is overjoyed when she finds a playmate already living there. As Zoe grows up, she becomes intrigued by Zoe Louise's strange behavior. *Zoe Rising* is a sequel to *Stonewords*.

Stonewords: A Ghost Story (Harper, 1990).

Zoe Rising (Harper, 1996).

Contemporary Realistic Fiction for Middle-Grade Readers

Read about Niki Bennett, a third-grader who doesn't like the house she lives in but manages to make life interesting anyway.

I Don't Live Here. Illustrated by Diane deGroat. (Dutton, 1984).

Seven Silly Circles. Illustrated by Mike Wimmer. (Harper, 1987).
Sequel to *I Don't Live Here.*

Staying Nine. Illustrated by Mike Wimmer. (Harper, 1988).

For More Information About/By the Author

Articles

Raymond, Allen. "Pam Conrad: She Said to Herself, 'Now What?' " *Teaching K–8* (November/December 1990): 38–40.

Scales, Pat. *A Teacher's Resource to Pam Conrad* (HarperCollins, 1994).
Includes notes about the author and suggestions for extension activities to accompany *Prairie Songs*, *My Daniel*, and *Prairie Visions*. Request guide from HarperCollins Children's Books, 10 East 53rd Street, New York, NY 10022.

Bruce Coville

◆ Fantasy

Syracuse, New York
May 16, 1950

- 📖 *The Monster's Ring*
- 📖 *Aliens Ate My Homework*
- 📖 *Goblins in the Castle*
- 📖 Magic Shop Series
- 📖 My Teacher Is an Alien Series
- 📖 Space Brat Series
- 📖 Anthologies (ghosts, unicorns, monsters)

About the Author
and the Author's Writing

Bruce Coville has written somewhat seriously from age 17, but did not publish until he was 28. In the interim he was a gravedigger, a toy maker, a magazine editor, and a door-to-door salesman. He has now written nearly fifty books for young readers, in addition to having written poems, plays, short stories, newspaper articles, hundreds of letters, and even more journal entries.

Bruce Coville was born in Syracuse, New York, and except for a year at Duke University in North Carolina lived in that area until 1990, when he moved to New York City. He returned to Syracuse two years later. His grandparents had a dairy farm three miles outside of Phoenix, a little town near Syracuse. He remembers two incidents that spurred his thinking about becoming a writer. First, his father introduced him to the original

Tom Swift book. A whole new world opened up. He loved *Mary Poppins* and *Dr. Doolittle*. He says, "I can remember getting up ahead of everyone else in the family when I was nine or ten, so I could huddle in a chair and read *The Voyages of Dr. Doolittle*. I also read lots of things that people consider junk literature (Nancy Drew, the Hardy Boys, Tom Swift, and zillions of comic books). It all goes into the hopper, it all becomes part of your own work later on."

The second incident was during sixth grade when Coville's teacher, Mrs. Crandall, abandoned her usual "creative writing" dictates and allowed the students to write whatever they wanted. He began to write seriously as a high school student.

He says he started writing children's books when his mother-in-law-to-be "handed me a copy of *Winnie-the-Pooh* to read. I had never read Pooh as a kid (I couldn't figure out where Christopher Robin lived and it confused me). But now I thought it was wonderful, and I knew this was the kind of thing I wanted to write. Not only that, but my wife-to-be was a brilliant artist, with a style that was just perfect for children's books. Her pictures made me want to write stories to go with them." For several years Coville wrote, but he did not sell his first book, *The Foolish Giant* (Lippincott, 1978), until he was 27. It was illustrated by his wife, Katherine (Kathy). They did another picture book called *Sarah's Unicorn* (Lippincott, 1979) and Kathy also created the pictures for *The Monster's Ring* (Pantheon, 1982).

Bruce Coville attended Duke University (North Carolina), the State University of New York at Binghamton, and the State University of New York at Oswego and earned and undergraduate degree in 1974. He taught elementary school for seven years. During this time he wrote *The Monster's Ring*. Originally it was a five-page short story called "Monster for a Day," and a warm-up exercise for a course in children's literature. The story, he says, "was a funny story. Yet, I was dissatisfied with it, because it didn't seem to have any point. So, I started thinking about what kind of kid *needed* to be a monster. I looked around my class and there was Russell, a basically good kid who was always being pushed around. I figured if anyone could make good use of the ability to turn into a monster, it would be him. So I rewrote the book, this time using Russell as my main character."

While he was a teacher, Coville read the story to his classes for Halloween. As a kid, he always wanted "a real Halloweeny story to read on Halloween night." He writes the kind of story he likes to read. "This isn't the 'perfect' Halloween book, which is just as well, because it means I get to go back and try again."

Several years after the success of *The Monster's Ring*, Coville returned to writing more stories about Mr. Elive's Magic Shop. Each story was to be about a different character, each of whom visits the Magic Shop and gets strange items that start an adventure. The stories were intended to be part of a book called *Tales from the Magic Shop*. He began by making a list of about a dozen ideas for stories. Then he began to write. But Coville soon discovered that he is more of a novelist than short story writer. Every time he would begin a story the idea and story got out of hand. "The Dragon's Egg" became much longer. For a time he thought it might be the anchor for a collection of magic stories, but the story "insisted on being a book." In the process, however, Coville wrote thirteen drafts. In the first drafts, Ti never got any bigger than a dog before she had to return, and there was no night flying for Jeremy. At the end of those versions, Jeremy left her in the front of the shop instead of insisting on going behind the counter. The book *Jeremy Thatcher, Dragon Hatcher* was published by Harcourt/Yolen in 1991. Other magic shop books include *Jennifer Murdley's Toad* (Harcourt, 1992) and *The Skull of Truth* (Harcourt, 1997). *Jennifer Murdley's Toad*, says Coville, "is one of the funniest things I've ever written." In *The Skull of Truth*, Charlie, a sixth-grader, often lies until he acquires a mysterious skull that forces him to tell the truth.

C. S. Lewis and Lloyd Alexander are among Coville's role models. He has always considered himself a fantasy writer.

When Coville wrote *The Monster's Ring* it included some events that were based on real life. Both Russell and Eddie are modeled on real students who were members of Coville's class. The stranger parts of the story are based on classroom visits from Coville's "half mad twin brother, Igor." Igor used to visit the class on Halloween, often jumping on desks to get away from excited class members. Igor actually did visit Coville's classroom, but the identity of Igor remains an official mystery. Igor was a featured character in *Goblins in the Castle* (Pocket Books, 1992). Coville wrote the story in the late 1970s but drastically rewrote the book for publication in 1992. The Toad-in-a-Cage castle is filled with secrets—hidden passages that lead to every room, a long stairway that winds down to the dungeon, the weird creature named Igor who lived there, and the mysterious night noises.

During his early years of writing, Coville often wrote in the middle of the night because it was the only time available. He says, "[I] did a lot of my best writing that way, thinking 'I can't wait until I don't have to have a regular job, so I can stop working this way.' "

His writing often follows an arc that begins very slowly and then moves very quickly to the conclusion. *My Teacher Flunked the Planet* (Minstrel, 1992) typifies this arc. He spent almost six months on the manuscript, and then wrote the last half (about 75 pages) in about three days.

His writing process begins with an outline, a step that allows him to submit the story idea to publishers. They contract for a completed book and pay a royalty advance. At first, Coville resisted an outline, feeling that it would constrict his creativity. He has found that there is still room for surprises as he writes, even with the outline. The outline simply helps the surprises take the right direction.

To assist with character development, Coville sometimes uses a chart copied and modified from an old issue of *Writer's Digest*. The chart consists of a list of questions that asks about each character. The questions include external, physical appearances and deeper issues. Coville says, "Often times stuff I put down on a list like this simply to fill in a space is seized upon by the subconscious and eventually becomes important, in one way or another, to the actual story."

Bruce Coville has written books of fantasy, collected stories about ghosts and monsters into anthologies that he edited, retold tales from Shakespeare (in picture book form) in prose, and written several titles for young adults. Whenever Coville has thoughts and ideas for books he keeps it in a thick folder called "IDEAS."

He usually writes on a computer. He writes at all times of the day. The wee hours of the morning "are very good for me—the interruptions are fewer, since anyone who could interrupt is asleep."

Bruce Coville has spent most of his life near Syracuse, New York. When he was nineteen he married Katherine Dietz. Katherine Dietz lived "right around the corner" from Coville. She was (and is) "a wonderful artist and we began trying to create books together." They sold their first book in 1977. Katherine and Bruce Coville are the parents of three children: a son, Orion (born in 1970); a daughter, Cara (born in 1975); and a son, Adam (born in 1981). Bruce lived in New York City for a couple of years but after he moved back to Syracuse, the couple moved into a brick house with their youngest son, three cats, and a dog named Booger. Coville disclaims any responsibility for the dog's name.

When he manages to get free time, he is involved in the theater: acting, directing, and writing. Musical theater is his favorite.

He tells young readers, "I wanted to be a writer from the time I was in sixth grade. I started trying to write professionally when I was seventeen years old. But I was twenty-seven before I finally sold a book, and thirty-six before I was able to make a living as an author. It was a long haul—but now I live the life I always dreamed of. The point? Believe in yourself, and *keep trying*. No matter what you want to do, no matter how many times you may fail. Good Luck!"

Books and Notes

Bruce Coville has a wide range of interests. He writes about mythical characters, aliens, dragons, and unicorns. He has collected stories about ghosts and monsters. His books are laced with humor and imaginative creatures juxtaposed with real-life characters. His books have been nominated for nearly 40 children's choice and state book awards.

Magic Shop Series

Each of these tales, although not sequels, begin in Mr. Elive's Magic Shop. Each of the main characters purchases an object that then takes them on adventures.

Jennifer Murdley's Toad. Illustrated by Gary A. Lippincott. (Harcourt, 1992).

Jeremy Thatcher, Dragon Hatcher. Illustrated by Gary A. Lippincott. (Harcourt/Yolen, 1991).

The Monster's Ring. Illustrated by Katherine Coville. (Pantheon, 1982).

The Skull of Truth. Illustrated by Gary A. Lippincott. (Harcourt, 1997).

Space Brat Series

The bratty Blork is introduced to readers as a tantrum-throwing character who is not able to save his pet Toonoobie when it is taken by the Big Pest Squad. In subsequent books, Blork creates his "evil twin" when he is pulled into a copy machine and later, bratty Blork and his friends Moomie Peevik, Appus Meko, and their pets are captured by the dread Squat and taken to his planet, Snarf.

Space Brat. Illustrated by Katherine Coville. (Pocket, 1992; Minstrel, 1992 [1993]).

Space Brat 2: Blork's Evil Twin. Illustrated by Katherine Coville. (Minstrel, 1993).

Space Brat 3: The Wrath of Squat. Illustrated by Katherine Coville. (Minstrel, 1994).

Space Brat 4: Planet of the Dips. Illustrated by Katherine Coville. (Pocket Books, 1995).

Prose Retellings of Shakespeare's Plays

Coville has retold, in prose, episodes from some of William Shakespeare's classic tales. Each of the tales is in picture book format.

William Shakespeare's MacBeth. Illustrated by Gary Kelley. (Dial, 1997).

William Shakespeare's A Midsummer Night's Dream. Illustrated by Dennis Nolan. (Dial, 1996).

William Shakespeare's The Tempest. Illustrated by Ruth Sanderson. (Delacorte, 1994).

Anthologies

Bruce Coville has gathered some of the most talented children's book writers and compiled their stories into collections about unicorns, monsters, and ghosts. Among the contributing authors are: Jane Yolen, Nancy Springer, Lawrence Watt-Evans, Neal Shusterman, Mel Gilden, Michael Stearns, Greg Cox, as well as a host of others.

Bruce Coville's Book of Ghosts: Tales to Haunt You. Compiled and edited by Bruce Coville, assisted by Lisa Meltzer. Illustrated by John Pierard. (Scholastic, 1994).

Bruce Coville's Book of Ghosts II: More Tales to Haunt You. Compiled and edited by Bruce Coville, assisted by Lisa Meltzer. Illustrated by John Pierard. (Scholastic, 1997).

Bruce Coville's Book of Monsters II: More Tales to Give You the Creeps. Compiled and edited by Bruce Coville, assisted by Lisa Meltzer. Illustrated by John Pierard. (Scholastic, 1996).

Bruce Coville's Book of Nightmares II: More Tales to Make You Scream. Compiled and edited by Bruce Coville, assisted by Lisa Meltzer. Illustrated by John Pierard. (Scholastic, 1997).

A Glory of Unicorns. Compiled and edited by Bruce Coville. (Scholastic, 1998).

My Teacher Is an Alien Series

My Teacher Is an Alien. Illustrated by Mike Wimmer. (Minstrel, 1989).

Other Titles

Aliens Ate My Homework. Illustrated by Katherine Coville. (Pocket, 1993).

Goblins in the Castle (Pocket, 1992).

How I Survived My Summer Vacation (Minstrel, 1988).

My Teacher Flunked the Planet. Illustrated by John Pierard. (Minstrel, 1992).

Oddly Enough. Short Story Collection. (Harcourt, 1994; Scholastic, 1996).

For More Information About/By the Author

Articles

"Authors & Illustrators: Bruce Coville." *Simon Says Kids.* URL: http://www.simonsays.com/kidzone/auth/bcoville.html (Accessed October 1997).

McElmeel, Sharron. "Author Profile: Bruce Coville." *Library Talk* 6, no. 1 (January/February 1993): 14–16.

Strickland, Brad. "Pinson Elementary Library: Our Breakfast with Bruce Coville." URL: http://www.bham.net/edu/pinson/bruce.html (Accessed October 1997).

Roald Dahl

**Llandaff, South Wales
September 13, 1916–
November 23, 1990**

📖 *James and the Giant Peach*
📖 *Danny, The Champion of the World*
📖 *Charlie and the Chocolate Factory*

About the Author
and the Author's Writing

Roald Dahl was born September 13, 1916, in South Wales, the son of Harold Dahl (who died when Roald was just four years of age) and Sofie Magdalene Hesselberg. Harold was a native of Norway and immigrated to England during the turn of the century. When his first wife died, leaving him with a son and daughter to raise, Harold returned to Norway to search for a spouse to help him raise his children. He married Sofie in 1911 and together they had five more children. Roald's older sister died of appendicitis in 1920 and his father died a few months later. Roald's mother was left with a sizable estate and instructions to send their children to English schools. At the age of nine, Roald was sent off to Llandaff Cathedral School and two years later to St. Peter's School in

Weston-Super-Mare. During his boarding school years, according to his memoir, *Boy: Tales of Childhood* (Farrar, 1984), he was often flogged. He graduated from the Repton Public School in Derby in 1934. He soon accepted a position with the Shell Oil Company in London. After working for five years for Shell (part of the time in East Africa), Dahl joined the Royal Air Force as a pilot. Despite attending English schools, the children developed and retained a deep awareness of their Norwegian heritage. Sofie spoke Norwegian at home and read Norse myths to them. The family also made yearly trips to Norway to visit relatives.

By 1942, after flying missions over Africa and being stationed in Greece, Dahl was assigned to work at the British Embassy in Washington, D.C. He met the writer C. S. Forester, who asked to interview him about his war experiences over lunch. Forester found that he could not take notes and eat at the same time, so Dahl offered to jot down some notes and send them later. Forester submitted them to the *Saturday Evening Post* without changing a word. They accepted Dahl's story "A Piece of Cake," and paid him $1,000. Dahl says that he lost most of that money to Senator Harry Truman during a poker game in Washington.

Soon Dahl was publishing in some of the same periodicals as J. D. Salinger and James Thurber. The *Post* accepted eleven other wartime stories from Dahl. The first were realistic accounts, but the later stories were a mixture of realism and imagination. His first children's book, *The Gremlins* (Random), was published in 1943, although many mark the beginning of his children's writing with *James and the Giant Peach* (Knopf) in 1961. *The Gremlins* tells about vicious, mischievous little men who live in fighter aircraft and cause them to crash—something usually attributed to enemy gunfire. Some say Dahl coined the term *gremlins* in this story. Disney Studios illustrated this now extremely rare book and were, at one time, planning to make the story into a full-length cartoon. The book's success is said to have garnered an invitation for Dahl to the White House, where he met Franklin and Eleanor Roosevelt. He became good friends with the Roosevelts.

An extremely successful writer, Dahl won Edgar Awards from the Mystery Writers of America in 1954 and 1959. Alfred Hitchcock bought some of Dahl's stories for his television show.

Meanwhile, Dahl returned home and married actress Patricia Neal on July 2, 1945. They settled in a farmhouse in Great Missenden, England. They had five children: Olivia Twenty (born April 20, 1954); Tessa (born April 11, 1957); Theo Matthew Roald (born July 30, 1960);

Ophelia Magdalena (born May 12, 1964); and Lucy Neal (born August 4, 1965). Several tragedies befell the family. Dahl suffered chronic crippling back pains from a plane-crash injury in 1940 in Libya. Over a period of years he had eight major operations. Their daughter Olivia died from complications of measles at the age of seven in 1962, and their only son, Theo was seriously brain-damaged when a Manhattan taxi hit his baby carriage. Dahl's wife, Patricia, a well-known actress, suffered three strokes, one massive in 1965—just six months before their daughter Lucy Neal was born. Despite these tragedies, Dahl is said to have maintained a wry sense of humor and a positive outlook on life. Many gave credit to Dahl for nursing Patricia Neal back to health. He encouraged her to continue therapy and pushed her to make an acting comeback. Others, such as his unofficial biographer, Jeremy Treglown, describe his encouragement as bullying. He states that Neal and others often called Dahl "Roald the Rotten" because he was so intolerant and cruel. He also describes Dahl's tantrum when his publisher did not supply the exact brand of pencil he wanted.

Dahl attributed his writing success to his children, often saying, "If I had not had children of my own, I would not have most likely begun to write books for children, and, if I had, the books would not have been nearly so successful." In 1960, after more than fifteen years of writing for adults, Dahl turned to children's books. *James and the Giant Peach* and his next book, *Charlie and the Chocolate Factory* (Knopf, 1963), are still among his most popular titles.

He wrote in a brick building separated from the main house, Gipsy House, at Great Missenden. The floor was littered with leaves, paper, and even a few goat droppings. The walls were lined with ill-fitting sheets of Styrofoam—yellowed from age and pipe smoke. The dilapidated hut was nestled among the trees in the Dahls' apple orchard. There Dahl, a six-foot-five-inch man, sat in a old dusty armchair, wrapping himself in an old sleeping bag, with his feet propped up on an old suitcase. A paraffin stove and electrical heater suspended from the ceiling helped to heat the hut. Even so, his hands were often numb with cold. He wrote longhand, saying he could not type. An occasional visit from his daughter's pony or a magpie pecking on the window were the only interruptions of his writing time. For more than thirty years he settled in that writing chair, for the most part oblivious to what was (and wasn't) around him. His writing desk was a lapboard covered with green billiard cloth, and he brushed eraser particles with a shoe brush recycled from his boarding school days.

A small table near his chair was cluttered with memorabilia, photos, fossils, mineral samples, and a ball of foil—the wrappings from Cadbury's Milk Chocolate Bars that were his favorite since his days with Shell Oil Company. He also kept the ball-joint end of his femur (both of his hip joints had been replaced) and some of the bone chips from his many back operations on the table. He considered himself "an old man full of metal."

Each day from 6 to 8 PM he drank whiskey, and the better part of a bottle of wine with his meal. He had 4,000 or more bottles of wine, mostly Bordeaux, maturing in his wine cellar. In contrast to the motley hut where Dahl wrote, the main house was museum quality. The house was furnished with a Norwegian Cottage Chair, sketches by Henry Moore (an old friend), Oscars, photographs of famous authors in Neal's study, and a stunning collection of art and furniture.

The family weathered Theo's accident, Patricia's stroke, and their eldest daughter's death. In the midst of all of this, Dahl formed a relationship with Felicity Crosland in 1979, which changed in 1983 when Patricia and Roald's marriage ended. The three, Roald, Patricia, and Felicity, according to Patricia, were often together on holidays. Patricia did not know the extent of the relationship until much later. In 1983 Patricia Neal divorced Dahl, and he married Felicity on December 15, 1983. That was also the year he earned one of Britain's most prestigious awards in children's books, the Whitbread Award.

In a letter written to Trumpet Book Club members, Felicity (Liccy) Dahl describes their day as beginning with a breakfast of tea and grapefruit, the morning paper, and the mail. The day would often include a "treat" among the boring mundane chores—a special meal, a surprise visit to children at a school, or a hospital visit to a sick child. Roald's favorite treat, however, was a trip to London to play Blackjack with his cronies.

Dahl spent two hours in the morning and often two hours in the afternoon writing. He felt the time limit was four hours—after that, one could not be creative.

Dahl could not identify a "favorite" among his titles, but he acknowledged the popularity of *Charlie and the Chocolate Factory* and *James and the Giant Peach*. He thought *The BFG* (Farrar, Straus & Giroux, 1982) might come to be considered his best work. He slipped a reference to *The BFG* into *Danny, The Champion of the World* (Knopf, 1975).

Danny's father told him the story while Danny was sick in bed in the gypsy caravan.

More than half of Dahl's career was spent writing children's books. One of his books, *Roald Dahl's Revolting Rhymes* (Knopf, 1982), featured his wacky versions of well-known English folktales. Even after his death that book spawned a spin-off title, *Roald Dahl's Revolting Recipes* (Viking, 1994), a book by his wife Felicity Dahl and Josie Fison. The book contains recipes for such wonderful concoctions as "Willy Wonka's Nutty Crunch Surprise," "George's Marvelous Medicine," and "Stink Bugs' Eggs."

James and the Giant Peach, originally illustrated by Michel Siméon, was made into a movie by Disney. A book titled *James and the Giant Peach: The Book and Movie Scrapbook* (Disney, 1996), written by Dahl's youngest daughter, Lucy Dahl, has been published with her photographs. A book version of the movie, *Disney's James and the Giant Peach,* with illustrations by Lane Smith, was published by Disney Press in 1996, as well.

In 1988 Puffin Books in the United States published six titles in paperback, each released with new cover illustrations by Richard Egielski, Robert Barrett, Bill Bell, Tony Ross, and Chris Van Allsburg. Dahl seemed to gain popularity in the late 1980s, and the movies released in the late 1990s enticed a new group of readers for Dahl's work.

Dahl's books have not been without controversy. Joseph Schindelman's illustrations for *Charlie and the Chocolate Factory*, drew complaints of stereotypical portrayals and the book was withdrawn in several places. It was re-illustrated and the book again gained a devoted audience. By 1977 *Charlie and the Chocolate Factory* and *Charlie and the Great Glass Elevator* (Knopf, 1972) had sold over 1 million hardcover copies in the United States alone. *James and the Giant Peach* had sold over 350,000 copies.

In a *Publishers Weekly* article for which Dahl was interviewed, Sarah Critchton wrote, "[There is] a sect of American librarians and teachers who find the books too nasty and macabre for the impressionable child. 'Must the peach *squash* Aunt Sponge and Aunt Spiker? Must the aunts *crunch* when it rolls over them?' " Dahl replied, "Of course, they deserve it." In a *New York Times* interview Willa Petschek reported that Dahl said, "Some librarians order 40 copies of my books, but there's a certain bunch of American lady librarians who flay me for what they consider the violence in my children's stories. [They] have no sense of humor."

In *Boy: Tales of Childhood* and *Going Solo* (Farrar, 1986) Dahl told about his summer visits to his grandparents, Bestemama and Bestepapa, on an island in Norway. Readers of his autobiographical titles will recognize several episodes in *The Witches* (Farrar, 1983; Puffin, 1985) and *Danny, The Champion of the World*.

Other members of Dahl's family joined the ranks of children's writers. In addition to books authored by Dahl's widow, Felicity, and the scrapbook created by Lucy Dahl, Tessa Dahl, who lives in England, has authored *Gwenda and the Animals* (Puffin, 1992) and *School Can Wait* (Puffin, 1992).

Roald Dahl died of leukemia at the age of 74 on November 23, 1990. His books continue to be best-sellers and his paperbacks have sold over 17 million copies.

Felicity Dahl is searching for a suitable place to display his personal memorabilia. Some manuscripts and related materials have been auctioned to benefit the Roald Dahl Foundation. In 1996 the Roald Dahl Children's Gallery at the Buckinghamshire County Museum on Church Street in Aylesbury, UK, opened for visitors. The gallery can handle up to 85 visitors per hour. Visitors can explore Willy Wonka's inventions and go inside the Giant Peach, crawl along Fantastic Mr. Fox's tunnel, and ride in the Glass Elevator.

Books and Notes

Dahl created his children protagonists with great imagination, which they used to ace either monsters or evil adults, coming up with preposterous ideas that always seemed to turn out wonderfully. Dahl's books are full of grotesque people, sinister events, and subversive lessons.

The BFG. Illustrated by Quentin Blake. (Farrar, Straus & Giroux, 1982).

Charlie and the Chocolate Factory. Illustrated by Joseph Schindelman. (Knopf, 1963).

Charlie and the Great Glass Elevator. Illustrated by Joseph Schindelman. (Knopf, 1972).

Danny, The Champion of the World. Illustrated by Jill Bennett. (Knopf, 1975).

Fantastic Mr. Fox. Illustrated by Donald Chaffin. (Knopf, 1970).

George's Marvelous Medicine. Illustrated by Quentin Blake. (Knopf, 1981).

James and the Giant Peach. Illustrated by Michel Siméon. (Knopf, 1961). Reissued in 1996 with illustrations by Lane Smith.

Matilda. Illustrated by Quentin Blake. (Viking, 1988).

Roald Dahl's Revolting Rhymes. Illustrated by Quentin Blake. (Bantam, 1986).

The Witches. Illustrated by Quentin Blake. (Farrar, 1983; Puffin, 1985).

For More Information About/By the Author

Articles

Guthmann, Edward. " 'Matilda' Is Smart to the Goony Adult World." *San Francisco Chronicle* (Friday, August 2, 1996): D3.

Hamlin, Jesse. "What Makes a Successful Family Film: 'House Arrest,' 'Matilda,' 'Jack' Are Latest Bids." *San Francisco Chronicle* (Sunday, August 4, 1996): 33.

Stack, Peter. " 'Peach'—Fruit of Imagination Roald Dahl Tale Turned Into Offbeat Film Fantasy." (Friday, April 12, 1996): D1.

Books

Meeks, Christopher. *Roald Dahl: Kids Love His Stories*. Illustrated by Robin Richesson. (Rourke, 1993).

Powling, Chris. *Roald Dahl* (Carolrhoda, 1998).

Shavick, Andrea. *Roald Dahl: The Champion Storyteller*. Illustrated by Alan Marks. (Oxford University Press, 1998).

Treglown, Jeremy. *Roald Dahl: A Biography* (Farrar, 1994).

Warren, Alan. *Roald Dahl: From the Gremlins to the Chocolate Factory*. Edited by Dale Salwak and Daryl F. Mallett. (Borgo Press, 1994).

Museum/Books

Aleph-Bet Books, Inc. URL: http://www.clark.net/pub/alephbet (Accessed October 1997).

Information about rare editions of Dahl's books. Helen & Marc Younger, Rare & Collectible Children's and Illustrated Books, 218 Waters Edge, Valley Cottage, NY 10989.

Roald Dahl Gallery. URL: http://www.nd.edu/~khoward1/Dahl/Museum.html (Accessed October 1997).

Paula Danziger

Contemporary Realistic Fiction ◆ Humorous Stories

Washington, D.C.
August 18, 1944

📖 *Amber Brown Is Not a Crayon*
📖 *The Cat Ate My Gymsuit*
📖 *Remember Me to Harold Square*

About the Author
and the Author's Writing

Once you have met Paula Danziger and become familiar with her books, you will immediately know why many readers praise her enthusiastically. Meeting Danziger once, however, will not ensure that you will recognize her again. She might have short brown hair, but the next time it might be long and very curly. Another time it might be as blond as the sunshine. Her clothing ranges from conventional to long caftans with split skirts and gathered tops. She is anything but conventional. For example, when asked to pose for a picture with three preteenage boys she orchestrated a "stick-the-tongue out" pose as the picture was clicked.

She has a passion for old-time beaded purses and adores electronic games, and is known to frequent antique shops in search of the purses and to carry a small electronic game in her pocket or purse. She is quick to share her love of reading.

While visiting a Hopi reservation in Arizona, Danziger replied to a young six-year-old's question, "If you tell me what you want to be when you grow up. I'll tell you what I want to be when I grow up."

The little girl looked up at Danziger and said, "But you are up." Danziger's publisher often refers to her as a "teenager at heart," but she prefers to think of herself as a "human being at heart."

Danziger was born in Washington, D.C., and grew up in Virginia and New Jersey. She lived on a farm in Holidaysburg, Pennsylvania, for three years. She enjoyed art, loved reading and writing, telling stories, and especially comedy. From the time she was a second-grader she knew that she wanted to be a writer. As a college student she was a baby-sitter for John Ciardi's children. His interest in her writing encouraged her. Ciardi and his wife took Danziger to literary conferences, and he became her mentor, helping her understand the necessary mix for a successful book. He suggested that she take a poem, underline the serious lines in blue, the funny ones in red, and ones that contain both serious and humorous tones in purple. That is the mix she strives for now.

After receiving a degree in English, Paula Danziger taught junior high students. Then she was involved in two car accidents. First a police patrol car collided with a car in which she was a passenger. She suffered whiplash. Later, her mother took her to a doctor for the whiplash, and a drunk driver hit their car head on. She was wearing a seat belt, yet her head hit the windshield, and she lost the ability to read and write for a long period of time. Danziger spent months in the hospital. After a long recovery, she returned to school to earn a masters degree in reading, wanting to help children with disabilities learn to read.

Danziger began to write seriously during graduate school. She felt "out of control" because of the accident. The main character, Marcy Lewis, in her first book, *The Cat Ate My Gymsuit* (Delacorte, 1974), is much like Paula might have been at that age, a little chubby and hating gym. Danziger took three years to write that book in longhand. *The Pistachio Prescription* (Delacorte, 1978) followed. It's the story of Cassandra Stephens, whose mousy brown hair makes her doubt her status in her family. She eats pistachios whenever she gets nervous, but her red fingers always give her away.

Danziger was teaching junior high again while completing *Can You Sue Your Parents for Malpractice?* (Delacorte, 1979). After that, Danziger decided to write full-time. She enjoyed teaching; however, she also had low points—finding her grade book, bells ringing during the middle of great discussions about books and writing. Like Marcy in *The Cat Ate My Gymsuit*, Danziger felt she had to come to terms with who she was. She had to find her strengths and weaknesses. So, she wrote a sequel to *The Cat Ate My Gymsuit*. Marcy explores the same questions Danziger was asking in *There's a Bat in Bunk Five* (Delacorte, 1980).

In 1978 Danziger decided to write a book about divorce. She was living in Woodstock, New York, and often took the train to New York City. On Friday afternoons the train would be filled with young children traveling to see one parent in New York City and Sunday evenings returning to the other. In the book, *The Divorce Express* (Delacorte, 1982), Phoebe's mother lives in New York City with her wardrobe of alligator and swan patterns. Her father wears message T-shirts and lives in Woodstock. Meanwhile Rosie, Phoebe's newfound friend, lives in Woodstock with her mother, Mindy, a white Jewish woman. Rosie's father, an African American Christian man, lives in New York City with his new wife. Phoebe's mother is planning to marry Duane—and Phoebe can't stand him. He is a stuffed shirt and says things like, "Make out your Christmas list. Those things your father can't afford, we'll buy."

Many incidents from Danziger's life have found their way into her books. Her brother was a lot like Marcy's brother in *The Cat Ate My Gymsuit* and *There's a Bat in Bunk Five*. The fathers in her earlier books yell a lot—just like her father. Ms. Finney, the teacher in her first two books, is similar to Danziger as a junior high school teacher. *The Cat Ate My Gymsuit* recounts Danziger's growing up. At 12 she was put on tranquilizers, and she says, "I should have gotten help." "My father was a very unhappy person, very sarcastic, and my mother was very nervous and worried about what people thought. It wasn't a happy childhood." Her often quoted quip about her family is, "Now our family would be dysfunctional; but back then we were just Danzigers."

Danziger's sense of humor comes through in all of her writing. Her characters carry the last name of many of her favorite comedians—Marcy *Lewis*, Phoebe *Brooks*, Jerry *Martin*, Cassandra *Stephens*, Lauren *Allen*. Marcy's father's name, Martin Lewis, was reminiscent of the partnership between comedians Dean Martin and Jerry Lewis.

Her then seven-year-old niece, Cassie, inspired her series of books about Amber Brown. Cassie was completely freaked out about a pizza party at school for her best friend, Danny. Paula used that conversation in the first of her successful series about Amber Brown, books written for that age group. *Amber Brown Is Not a Crayon* (Putnam, 1994) deals with Amber and her best friend, Justin, who is about to move. Amber's name and the title of the first book is a joke as well. Danziger told her friends, Marc and Laurie Brown, the creators of many books, including Arthur the Aardvard, to name their baby Amber. Then everyone would call her Crayola Face. The Browns named their daughter Eliza, and she receives advance review copies of all the Amber Brown books. Danziger promised Cassie that she would not write about her after sixth grade.

Danziger now has a house in Bearsville, New York; an apartment in New York City; and a flat in London, England, where she takes time to host a monthly literary segment for the British Broadcasting Corporation (BBC) children's show *Live and Kicking*. She was nominated for the British Book Award for Children.

Many of her earlier books were written for intermediate and middle-school readers, while her Amber Brown series focuses on a somewhat younger reading audience, second- through fourth-graders. While living in Woodstock and New York, many titles were set in those locations. For example, *Remember Me to Harold Square* (Delacorte, 1987) was set in summertime in New York City. In *The Divorce Express* children travel on the train between Woodstock and New York City. Now in London, Paula Danziger has used the city as the setting for at least two titles. Amber plans a trip to London and Paris in *You Can't Eat Your Chicken Pox, Amber Brown* (Putnam, 1995) until she contracts chicken pox. In *Thames Doesn't Rhyme with James* (Putnam, 1994) Kendra spends Christmas in London with her family, her boyfriend, and the boyfriend's family.

When asked where she gets her ideas for her books, Danziger answers cleverly, "from a store called 'Ideas R Us.' " She is not married and has no children. Her nephews Sam, Ben, and Josh often provide her with many ideas. Her niece, Cassie, is the model for the character Amber.

Although Danziger would have liked to have been a comedian, if she weren't a writer, some people think she has managed to become both. Her books are filled with jokes and humor. Her sense of humor is evident during conversations with her young admirers. When children ask for a recipe, she responds with sushi as her favorite food. Sushi has no real recipe, so we are left to wonder if Danziger just wants to avoid providing a recipe. Danziger likes to read, write, shop, hang out with her friends, and talk on the phone.

Books and Notes

Paula Danziger writes books about teenagers and their friendships. Her characters are strong, the writing is full of zany humor, and the episodes could be happening right here. Her first book in 1974 began an eighteen-year publishing relationship with Delacorte. Since 1992 her books have been published by Putnam, including a sequel to one of her Delacorte titles. One recent book Danziger coauthored with popular Scholastic author Ann M. Martin. Together they produced *P.S. Longer Letter Later* (Scholastic, 1998). Her recent series featuring Amber Brown is written for the primary early intermediate reader, while earlier titles attract late intermediate/middle-school readers.

Books for Late Intermediate/ Middle-School Readers

The Cat Ate My Gymsuit (Delacorte, 1974; Dell).

The Divorce Express (Delacorte, 1982).

It's an Aardvark-Eat-Turtle World (Delacorte, 1985).
Sequel to *The Divorce Express.*

Make Like a Tree and Leave (Delacorte, 1990).

P.S. Longer Letter Later. With Ann M. Martin. (Scholastic, 1998).

Remember Me to Harold Square (Delacorte, 1987).

Thames Doesn't Rhyme with James (Putnam, 1994).
Sequel to *Remember Me to Harold Square.*

Books for Primary/ Early Intermediate Readers

Amber Brown Goes Fourth. Illustrated by Tony Ross. (Putnam, 1995; Scholastic).

Amber Brown Is Not a Crayon. Illustrated by Tony Ross. (Putnam, 1994; Scholastic).

Amber Brown Sees Red. Illustrated by Tony Ross. (Putnam, 1997; Scholastic).

Amber Brown Wants Extra Credit. Illustrated by Tony Ross. (Putnam, 1996; Scholastic).

Forever Amber Brown. Illustrated by Tony Ross. (Putnam, 1996; Scholastic).

You Can't Eat Your Chicken Pox, Amber Brown. Illustrated by Tony Ross. (Putnam, 1995; Scholastic).

For More Information About/By the Author

Articles

Freeland, Dennis. "A Conversation with Paula Danziger." *Writing* (November 1988): 18–21.

"Paula Danziger." *Putnam/Berkley.* URL: http://www.mca.com/putnam/authors/paula_danziger/author.html (Accessed October 1997).

"Paula Danziger School Visits." *Putnam/Berkeley.* 1997. URL: http://www.mca.com/putnam/kids/author_appearances/paula_danziger_sv.html (Accessed October 1997).
Site includes presentation/travel requirements.

Books

Krull, Kathleen. *Presenting Paula Danziger* (Twayne, 1995).

Judy Delton

Contemporary Realistic Fiction ◆ Humorous Stories

**St. Paul, Minnesota
May 6, 1931**

📖 *Kitty in the Middle*
📖 *Angel in Charge*
📖 Pee Wee Scouts Series
📖 Lucky Lottery Series

About the Author
and the Author's Writing

After a number of years writing articles and books for middle-grade readers, Judy Delton hit it big in the late 1980s with the Pee Wee Scouts series for five- to eight-year-old readers.

Judy Delton found herself with a writing career in the middle of her "mid-life crisis." She had four children, was separated from a husband who couldn't hold a job, and felt like she was having a nervous breakdown. She needed an outlet and to support those four children. Up to that time, 1971, she "never wrote anything more than a note to the milkman." There were no other writers in Tomah, Wisconsin, where the family was living. Consequently, there was no one around who might tell her that she needed improvement—after all, no one else knew more about writing than she did. Her mother encouraged her to return to a more secure teaching career. In her first two years she published 160 articles, mostly personal essays about her children and day-to-day events. Finally, in 1974, she turned her mother into a duck and entered children's literature with a short book titled *Two Good Friends* (Crown, 1974), a story about a bear who loves to cook, but has a messy house, and a duck who keeps an immaculate house, but doesn't like to cook. Delton was the messy bear. Her mother appeared in *Penny-Wise, Fun-Foolish* (Crown, 1977) as an ostrich who collects coupons, and again in *Rabbit's New Rug* (Dutton, 1980) as the rabbit who wouldn't let anyone walk on its new rug. Everything her children said became story material. Her son's comment, "Boy you sure are crabby in winter," became the inspiration for *My Mom Hates Me in January* (Albert Whitman, 1977). Her son's name, Jamie, appeared in a picture book, *It Happened on Thursday* (Whitman, 1978). The story tells Jamie's theory that Thursdays are magical—a theory that falls apart when his mother becomes ill.

Judy Delton has lived most of her life in St. Paul, and attended as well as taught in parochial (Catholic) schools in the area. When she began writing about Kitty, she attended a parochial school. Delton has said, "I am Kitty." Writing books is "the cheapest form of therapy there is." Delton says, "I didn't realize that my grandfather hadn't liked me until Kitty told me." The Kitty books are about growing up Catholic in the 1940s. One episode in *Kitty in the Middle* (Houghton, 1979) is from one of Delton's daughters. As an elementary-age child, Delton's daughter Jina and a young Lutheran friend discovered that the wedding receptions at the nearby Catholic Church often had interesting foods, little sandwiches, mints, and so forth. The girls found that they could be "guests" at the reception and eat the fancy foods. That made its way into the books.

Only Jody (Houghton, 1982) was based on her son Jamie's life, and many incidents in her Angel books come from her daughters—including the profile of the character herself. Delton's daughter Jennifer seldom smiled before she was five. That image helped Delton create Angel. But once Angel was in a story, "things began to happen, she became a person of her own." A friend's Thanksgiving catastrophe became Delton's idea to turn the party ham of Angel's family green. In the story, Rudy saves the day by turning the party into a St. Patrick's Day event. Angel's displeasure with her haircut is from Delton having cut her daughter's hair too short.

In June 1988, Delton launched the Pee Wee Scouts series. Delton was signing books at an educators' conference, and George Nicholson, then the director of children's books at Dell, indicated he was looking for a series of books about scouts for the five- to eight-year-old reader. Delton agreed to submit a manuscript. Her editor at Dell, Lori Mack, read the submission and told Delton that the story "did not have enough 'sparkle.' " Delton thought that was the end of the series. But Delton woke up one night with an idea for the "sparkle." The next morning she rewrote the manuscript and sent it off to Mack. She contracted to produce 12 Pee Wee Scout books. The first was *Cookies and Crutches* (Dell, 1988). The Boy Scouts and Girl Scouts of America were unhappy with the word *scouts* in the series. By the nineteenth title, *Piles of Pets* (Dell, 1993), the organizations had filed suit stating that the publisher (and Delton's series) gave the false impression that the organizations had authorized or sponsored the series. According to an article in *Publishers Weekly* (January 25, 1993), a Federal District Court Judge ruling stated that the organizations "cannot restrict defendant's rights to author and publish books on a particular organization," and that doing so would "obviously conflict with basic First Amendment principles. . . . As a general rule, one may write fiction about virtually any topic involving any public or private organization, corporation, or person." By the time the decision was reached, the series had already sold more than 3.5 million books.

Spring Sprouts (Dell, 1990) was inspired by her then eighteen-year-old daughter's decision to have a garden with carrots. Because they were not growing like she thought they should, she began pulling them up. When she discovered where the carrots were growing, she said, "Why, I thought they grew on the branches."

Delton penned another series for Dell, Condo Kids, aimed at readers in the fourth to sixth grades, about children living in a suburban development called Huckleberry Heights. A third series, for Hyperion, dealt with the luck of winning: Lottery Luck begins with *Winning Ticket!* (Hyperion, 1995). Daisy Green and one younger brother convince another brother to buy a lottery ticket. When the ticket is a winner, the Green family become millionaires. Subsequent titles follow the Green family as they travel to England, take a cruise, travel to Washington, D.C., to solve a mystery, find adventures at an aunt's lake cottage, and suffer the pangs of moving from their crowded apartment into a spacious new house. The settings come from Delton's love of England, trips to a lakeside cabin, and her surroundings in the St. Paul area.

In 1958 Delton married, and during the 1960s she became the parent of four children, Jina, Jennifer, Julie, and Jamie. In the 1970s she was raising the children as a single parent and had begun her writing career.

She was firmly established as a children's book author with the phenomenal success of her Pee Wee Scouts series. Two of her daughters have also published books. Julie Delton authored *My Uncle Nikos* (Crowell, 1983), a picture book about Helena's special relationship with her Uncle Nikos, an uncle who lives in the mountains of Greece in a small house surrounded by a large garden. Jina penned a novel, *Two Blocks Down* (Harper, 1981), about a high school girl torn between friends.

Meanwhile, Judy Delton continues her prolific career. Watch for more series titles and new adventures of Angel. Delton now writes from a well-outfitted office in an elegant Victorian home. She says of her residence/office, "This is the house that books bought." And so it is.

Books and Notes

Judy Delton has written successful series for the early primary and intermediate readers. Popular characters include ten-year-old Angel; Kitty, a preteenager attending a parochial school; the Scouts; suburban children who live in Huckleberry Heights; and other children who have experiences much like her readers' do. Humor is a critical element in each of her books. The following lists include selected titles.

Pee Wee Scouts Series

All Dads on Deck. Illustrated by Alan Tiegreen. (Dell, 1994).

Blue Skies, French Fries. Illustrated by Alan Tiegreen. (Dell, 1988).

Eggs with Legs. Illustrated by Alan Tiegreen. (Dell, 1996).

Fishy Wishes. Illustrated by Alan Tiegreen. (Dell, 1993).

Moans and Groans and Dinosaur Bones. Illustrated by Alan Tiegreen. (Dell, 1997).

Pee Wees on First. Illustrated by Alan Tiegreen. (Dell, 1995).

Stage Frightened. Illustrated by Alan Tiegreen. (Dell, 1997).

Stories About Angel

Angel in Charge. Illustrated by Leslie Morrill. (Houghton, 1985).

Angel's Mother's Baby. Illustrated by Margot Apple. (Houghton, 1989).

Angel's Mother's Boyfriend. Illustrated by Margot Apple. (Houghton, 1986).

Angel's Mother's Wedding. Illustrated by Margot Apple. (Houghton, 1987).

Back Yard Angel. Illustrated by Leslie Morrill. (Houghton, 1983).

Stories About Kitty

The first book in the series begins with Kitty in the third grade and ends when Kitty becomes a freshman at a Catholic high school in St. Paul during World War II.

Kitty from the Start (Houghton, 1987).

Kitty in the High School (Houghton, 1984).

Kitty in the Middle (Houghton, 1979).

Lottery Luck Series

Next Stop, the White House! Illustrated by S. D. Schindler. (Hyperion, 1995).

Royal Escapade. Illustrated by S. D. Schindler. (Hyperion, 1995).

Ten's a Crowd. Illustrated by S. D. Schindler. (Hyperion, 1995).

Winning Ticket! Illustrated by S. D. Schindler. (Hyperion, 1995).

Condo Kids Series

Huckleberry Hash. Illustrated by Alan Tiegreen. (Dell, 1990).

Miscellaneous Titles

The Mystery of the Haunted Cabin (Houghton, 1986).

Only Jody (Houghton, 1982).

Writing Advice

The 29 Most Common Writing Mistakes and How to Avoid Them (Writer's Digest Books, 1985).

For More Information About/By the Author

Articles

Delton, Judy. "Eliminating Trivial Pursuits." *Writer's Digest* 71, no. 10 (October 1991): 26–27.

Delton, Judy. "Writing for Today's Child." *Once Upon a Time* (Spring 1995): 16–23.

Delton, Judy. "Writing for Today's Child." *Publishing Research Quarterly* 7, no. 3 (February 1991): 55.

Lois Duncan

Philadelphia, Pennsylvania
April 28, 1934

📖 *Don't Look Behind You*
📖 *Gallows Hill*
📖 *Killing Mr. Griffin*

About the Author
and the Author's Writing

Known for her mystery and suspense novels, many with psychic elements, Lois Duncan writes picture books, early chapter books, and occasional nonfiction pieces.

Lois Duncan was born in Philadelphia, the daughter of Joseph and Lois Steinmetz, internationally known magazine photographers. Her father spent years with the Ringling Brothers Circus, which wintered in Sarasota, Florida. Many of her childhood years were spent there. At the age of ten she began to submit stories to magazines. She sold her first story to a magazine at age thirteen, but not before collecting her share of rejections. She even sold home economics reports for $50. Entering a writing contest sponsored by *Seventeen Magazine* at the age of sixteen, she won second place, at seventeen she came in third, but at eighteen she garnered first place. She said, "I used the money to get married, but should have bought a car. It would have lasted longer." She continued to write and had three children, Robin, Kerry, and Brett. When she and her husband divorced, magazine writing did not provide enough money to support herself and children, so she turned to the more lucrative romance/confession field. That area provided needed family income, while she continued to publish young adult novels. Soon she was also writing and speaking at conferences across the United States.

In the 1960s she met and married an electrical engineer, Donald Wayne Arquette. They moved their family to Albuquerque, New Mexico, where Arquette had a job. Duncan taught in the journalism department at the University of New Mexico, even though at the time she did not have a college degree. She had two more children, Donald Jr. and Kait. When Kait was in kindergarten, Duncan started working toward her own degree, graduating from the university with honors in English in 1977. She was elected to Phi Beta Kappa.

Duncan became known for her mysteries and suspense titles having psychic elements, including ESP (extrasensory perception). Her photography hobby provided illustrations for an inspirational book of verse for children, *From Spring to Spring* (Westminister, 1984). In 1988 she began contributing to an early chapter book series for younger intermediate readers. The series, Springboard Books, is intended to provide a bridge from picture books to chapter books. Her first title was *Wonder Kid Meets the Evil Lunch Snatcher* (Little, Brown, 1988). The story involved a band of lunch-snatching bullies who torment Brian and his friends.

Readers found Duncan's books suspenseful and filled with psychic drama. Her heroines struggle with supernatural powers in *Down a Dark Hall* (Little, Brown, 1974); plot a joke that turns deadly in *Killing Mr. Griffin* (Little, Brown, 1978); discover a stranger identical to themselves in *Stranger with My Face* (Little, Brown, 1981); practice witchcraft in *Summer of Four* (Little, Brown, 1976); and help to solve a baby-snatching mystery in *The Third Eye* (Little, Brown, 1984). One book turned painfully real in the summer of 1989. *Don't Look Behind You* (Delacorte, 1989) had been released in June. The heroine, April, was based on the personality of Duncan's youngest daughter, Kait. In the book, a murder contract was put out on April's family, who were under the witness protection program, because April's father had testified against interstate drug dealers. April was chased by a hitman in a Camaro. In July of 1989, Kait, Duncan's eighteen-year-old daughter, was chased and shot to death on the way home from a friend's house in Albuquerque. Witnesses say the man who killed Kait was driving a Camaro. During an interview in the fall of 1989 (just a couple of months after Kait's murder), Duncan said that she and her family had found themselves "living a horror much more frightening than anything [she] could have written." She found her books "rushing back into her life." After 40 years of writing fiction, Lois Duncan wanted to be able to rewrite Kait's story, to revise the chapter in which Kait decides to go out, put her car on a different street, have the killer's gun misfire. Duncan wishes desperately to be able to rewrite the ending of the chapter but she realizes that "everyone's story is programmed to end with good-bye."

Duncan had always been able to change the outcome of her mysteries, but she could not control this outcome. Her daughter's death was regarded as a random shooting by the Albuquerque police. But the family and others feel that Kait was targeted because she knew too much about an Asian criminal ring operating from the Albuquerque area and as far as Orange County, California. Many coincidences surfaced—details surrounding Kait's murder that were reflected (or foreshadowed) in some episodes of Duncan's books. A heroine's boyfriend in one novel, Michael Gallagher, shared his name with an investigative reporter, Mike Gallagher, who would not let the police ignore the case. He wrote an article pointing out discrepancies in the police investigation. A psychic's sketch of the suspect resembled the picture of a hit man drawn on a foreign edition of one of Duncan's books. Coincidences piled up. Devastated by her beloved daughter's death, Duncan laid out the details of their investigation and the family's real-life experience with psychics in the book *Who Killed My Daughter?* (Delacorte, 1992). Although the book was written for adults, it was named a *School Library Journal* "Best Book of the Year" and named to the American Library Association's "Best Book for Young Adults." A synopsis of the Duncan-Arquette version of Kait's story was published in *Woman's Day* (June 2, 1992).

Since Kait's murder, Duncan has spent much of her time trying to solve the mystery of her daughter's death. Her oldest daughter, Robin, consulted a psychic. The family believes that the information they have received through the psychics could only have come from Kait. Three psychics over several years have provided information that later proved to be true. At first Duncan was "annoyed at Robin for consulting a psychic." She viewed the psychics as opportunists. But, when none of them would accept money, and when their information began to pan out,

Duncan changed her view of them and the information that they were providing.

"*The Third Eye*, a story about a teenage psychic, was dedicated to Kait. At the time I wrote the book, I had never met a psychic and wasn't even sure that I really believed in them. Today I've had first-hand experience working with a psychic and am a true believer."

At the time of Kait's death Duncan had a contract for some mystery books. For a number of years she could not bring herself to write them. In 1989, two picture books were released, but those had been written before Kait's death. Her first book after Kait's death was *Who Killed My Daughter?* That year, 1992, was also when Duncan was presented the Margaret A. Edwards Award, presented by the *School Library Journal* and the Young Adult Services Association to honor a living author for a distinguished body of adolescent literature. Still unable to return to her mystery/suspense fiction, Duncan wrote a book about the circus, featuring photographs taken by her father, Joseph Janney Steinmetz. She also retold, in picture book format, a Navajo tale, *The Magic of Spider Woman* (Scholastic, 1996). That same year a book of stories, *Night Terrors: Stories of Shadow and Substance* (Simon, 1996), edited by Duncan, was published. The collection contained stories written by notable writers in the mystery/suspense genre, Alane Ferguson, Joan Lowery Nixon, Norma Fox Mazer, Harry Mazer, Richard Peck, and others. Nine years after Kait's murder, Duncan published *Gallows Hill* (Delacorte, 1997), the story of seventeen-year-old Sarah, who works at a fortune-telling booth at a school carnival. During the carnival, Sarah finds that she really *can* see the future in the crystal ball—a talent that makes some of her fellow classmates regard her as a witch. Duncan edited a 1998 collection of stories, *Trapped!* (Simon), about individuals who are "trapped" in some way—emotionally, physically, or mentally.

Lois Duncan Arquette and Donald Arquette moved from the Albuquerque area, but their presence is still felt by the Albuquerque police, who continue to be pressured by the family to investigate leads found by the family. Robin, their oldest daughter, continues to be involved in media productions, and Brett, their eldest son, is a "computer whiz" who is a sometime contributor to technical periodicals. The family keeps a low profile and does not publicize their whereabouts because of the yet-to-be found suspects in Kait's murder.

Books and Notes

Lois Duncan began her career by writing in the lucrative romance magazine field, but recognition came when she became a successful writer of mystery and suspense tales for the intermediate and older reading audience. She also has written picture books and nonfiction titles.

Mystery

Don't Look Behind You (Delacorte, 1989).

Death threats to April's father forces the family into the federal government's witness protection program. April's actions lead a hired killer to her family's new location.

Down a Dark Hall (Little, Brown, 1974).

The atmosphere in Kit's new boarding school is unsettling, but she doesn't know why—at least not at first.

Gallows Hill (Delacorte, 1997).

When Sarah's work at a fortune-telling booth unveils her psychic powers, she is suspected of being a witch.

Killing Mr. Griffin (Little, Brown, 1978).

A teenage prank turns deadly.

Locked in Time (Little, Brown, 1985).

Nore begins to sense an aura of evil and mystery around her new family and her stepmother's Louisiana plantation.

Stranger with My Face (Little, Brown, 1981).

Laurie's parents cannot tell her and a stranger apart. Who is this person—a person with her face?

The Third Eye (Little, Brown, 1984).

Karen worries that her psychic powers will make her seem different from other people, but when she is asked to help locate missing children, she realizes that she must use her power regardless of what others might come to think of her.

Nonfiction Titles

The Circus Comes Home: When the Greatest Show on Earth Rode the Rails. Photographs by Joseph Janney Steinmetz. (Doubleday, 1993).

Photographs and text tell the story of the Ringling Brothers Circus, which toured the United States until 1956. Information includes descriptions of acts such as the Flying Wallendas and the Elephant Ballet.

Psychic Connections: A Journey Into the Mysterious World of PSI (Delacorte, 1995).

Written in collaboration with William Roll, Ph.D., project director for the Psychical Research Foundation. The text is based on laboratory research and documented case histories. Topics include astral projection, near-death experiences, apparitions and hauntings, poltergeists, clairvoyance, telepathy, and practical applications of ESP.

Who Killed My Daughter? (Delacorte, 1992).

A true account (to date) of the Duncan-Arquette family's efforts to investigate and solve the murder of Kaitlyn Clare Arquette (1970–1989).

Story Collections
(edited by Lois Duncan)

Night Terrors: Stories of Shadow and Substance (Simon, 1996).

Eleven tales of terror from outstanding writers including Joan Aiken, Alane Ferguson, Madge Harrah, Theodore Taylor, and others.

Trapped! (Simon, 1998).

Different writers share stories across genres. Each story features a young protagonist who is trapped in some way—emotionally, physically, or mentally.

Picture Books

The Birthday Moon. Illustrated by Susan Davis. (Viking, 1989).

Shares, in rhyme, the wonderful things one can do with the perfect birthday present, the moon.

Songs from Dreamland: Original Lullabies. Illustrated by Kay Chorao. (Knopf, 1989).

Chorao's soft, dreamlike illustrations accompany this collection of lullabies and poems about sleep.

For More Information About/By the Author

Articles

The Lois Duncan Home Page. URL: http://www.iag.net/~barq/lois.html (Accessed October 1997).

McElmeel, Sharron. "Author! Author! Lois Duncan." In *Educator's Companion to Children's Literature, Volume 1: Mysteries, Animal Tales, Books of Humor, Adventure Stories, and Historical Fiction* (Libraries Unlimited, 1995): 27–29.

Eleanor Estes

Contemporary Realistic Fiction ◆ Humorous Stories

West Haven, Connecticut
May 9, 1906–July 15, 1988

📖 *The Hundred Dresses*

📖 *The Moffats*

📖 *Ginger Pye*

About the Author
and the Author's Writing

Born May 9, 1906, in West Haven, Connecticut, Eleanor Rosenfeld Estes seemed to have had an idyllic childhood. Her hometown, Cranbury, became the setting for many of her books. At the time Estes was growing up in West Haven, the town had open fields, woods, and a lot of open spaces—a typical New England small town. Now, the town is a large suburb of New Haven. The brooks and streams are gone. Only the Green remained by the time Estes wrote about the Moffats and Ginger Pye.

Her father, Louis Rosenfeld, and mother, Caroline Gewecke Rosenfeld, were book lovers. Her mother could quote Tennyson, Shakespeare, and Heine. Estes particularly recalled the way her mother told "Great Claus and Little Claus." Her father was a mathematician who could add, in his head, a column of numbers a mile long and a mile wide.

Eleanor Rosenfeld graduated from high school in West Haven and began working in the New Haven Free Public Library. By 1928 she was head of the library, and, in 1931, was given a Caroline M. Hewins scholarship for children's librarians. She went to New York to study at the Pratt Institute Library School. The following year she met and married fellow student Rice Estes. She continued her work as a children's librarian at the New York Public Library. Her husband became director of the Pratt Institute Library.

From the time she was very young she wanted to be a writer. In 1941 Estes was successful in getting her first book published, *The Moffats* (Harcourt), the first of several books about the Moffat family. The books were translated into Dutch, French, Italian, and Norwegian. Her book *The Hundred Dresses* (Harcourt, 1944) was translated into Turkish.

Many incidents in her books come from her life. *Ginger Pye* (Harcourt, 1951) is a story about the Pye family and their very smart dog. After her success with the Moffats, Estes decided that she wanted to write a book about the dog, Ginger, she and her brothers had as children. When only a puppy, the dog ran away on Thanksgiving day and did not return until May. By then, Ginger was grown. At first Estes thought that Ginger would become part of the Moffat family, but instead she invented the Pye family. The Pyes lived in Cranbury, just as the Moffats did. A second book, *Pinky Pye* (Harcourt, 1976), focuses on an abandoned black kitten who can type.

For three consecutive years her books were named Newbery Honor Books—*The Middle Moffat* (1943), *Rufus M.* (1944), and *The Hundred Dresses* (1945). Seven years later, in 1952, she was awarded the Newbery for *Ginger Pye*. However, *The Hundred Dresses* is the one that has endured. Objections were made against the book for its use of the word *Polack* to refer to the members of Wanda Petronski's family. Wanda, a Polish girl from a poor, motherless family, insists that she "owns" 100 dresses. It is only when she moves away that children in her class realize how their behavior affected her. The book has become must reading for all children.

For many years the Estes family lived in Brooklyn in a small faculty house on the campus of Pratt Institute. In the early 1970s the family moved to New Haven. Most of the incidents in the stories came from Eleanor Estes's childhood memories, but Estes's daughter, Helena, also showed up in many of her books, under various names. The stories in *The Witch Family* (Harcourt, 1960) are stories Eleanor told Helena when she was young. Helena followed in her mother's footsteps, working in a public library on Long Island while attending library school.

Eleanor Estes was a fan of the theater, opera, museums, and most artistic performances. She loved the ocean, and the birds and beaches associated with the location. Travel, pets, and cooking were also among her favorite things. Eleanor Estes was eighty-two when she died on July 15, 1988.

Books and Notes

The Moffat Family

The Moffat family first appeared in *The Moffats*. The stories are set in the New England Town of Cranbury just before and during World War I. The family consists of Mama, a widowed dressmaker, and her four children, Sylvia, Joey, Jane, and Rufus.

The Middle Moffat. Illustrated by Louis Slobodkin. (Harcourt, 1942).

The Moffat Museum. Illustrated by Eleanor Estes. (Harcourt, 1983).

The Moffats. Illustrated by Louis Slobodkin. (Harcourt, 1941).

Rufus M. Illustrated by Louis Slobodkin. (Harcourt, 1943).

The Pye Family

Ginger Pye. Illustrated by Eleanor Estes. (Harcourt, 1951).

Pinky Pye. Illustrated by Eleanor Estes. (Harcourt, 1958).

Other Titles

The Coat-Hanger Christmas Tree. Illustrated by Susanne Suba. (Atheneum, 1973).

The Hundred Dresses. Illustrated by Eleanor Estes. (Harcourt, 1944).

The Lost Umbrella of Kim Chu. Illustrated by Jacqueline Ayer. (Atheneum, 1978).

For More Information About/By the Author

Articles

Obituary. *Current Biography* 49, no. 9 (September 1988): 57.

Aileen Fisher

◆ Poetry

**Iron River, Michigan
September 9, 1906**

📖 *The Coffee-Pot Face*
📖 *Rabbits, Rabbits*
📖 *When It Comes to Bugs*

About the Author
and the Author's Writing

Aileen Fisher was born shortly after the turn of the century in Iron River, Michigan. Her family pioneered in the Iron River area. Her parents were N. E. Fisher and Lucia Riker. Fisher's father and uncle were both early storekeepers in Iron River. Her father took up a homestead in 1888 and began clerking in a grocery and provisions store owned by P. N. Minckler. Fisher considers herself a lucky child. When she was five years old, her father was advised to give up his business and move to the country, where life would be less stressful. The family built a big white house on the bank above a river, two miles west of town. They called their home "High Banks" because it overlooked the river, always red from the water pumped from the iron mines. The river provided many days of wading, swimming, fishing, and skating. There were always pets—cats and dogs especially. The horses always knew how to twitch and turn to chase away the flies, and the cows knew how to turn green grass into white milk and yellow cream. Chickens provided eggs, which Aileen gathered each evening. When she was eight a sister was born, and six years later, another sister was born.

Aileen attended the University of Chicago from 1923 to 1925, and graduated from the University of Missouri with a degree in journalism in 1927. Returning to Chicago to work, in a job placement bureau, she also began to write verse. She became friends with Olive Rabe, one of Chicago's first female lawyers. When Rabe's health began to fail due to low blood pressure, the friends looked around for a place with a higher altitude. They eventually moved to Boulder, Colorado. Their first day in town, they purchased a car for $100 and moved into an unheated four-room house on Fifth Avenue (now called Evergreen Avenue). They spent hours hiking into the mountains, where they would often write surrounded by nature. The two friends collaborated on many prose pieces, for example, auto insurance articles and a biography of Emily Dickinson, *We Dickinsons: The Life of Emily Dickinson as Seen Through the Eyes of Her Brother Austin* (Atheneum, 1965), and a title about Louisa May Alcott, *We Alcotts: The Story of Louisa M. Alcott's Family as Seen Through the Eyes of "Marmee," Mother of Little Women* (Atheneum, 1968). Fisher also continued to write poetry. Her first title, *The Coffee-Pot Face*, was published by McBride Company in 1933 with Fisher's own illustrations. Her childhood surroundings provided inspiration for many of her poems. No one had taught her Haiku or other verse forms, but reading helped her to know how different writers used words to make things happen or emphasize some thought or feeling. Writing, though, took practice. To become a writer, "You practice patiently."

Eventually, in 1938, Fisher and Rabe bought a 200-acre parcel of land in the foothills west of Boulder. The ranch had rocky meadows, pine trees, and a view of the Arapahoe Glacier and snow-covered Bald Mountains. The two designed and built a cabin with a high beamed ceiling and a fireplace—but with no electricity, central heat, or running water. They rented the land for Brahma cattle, and built their own furniture and raised peacocks.

They preferred books and the unspoiled countryside, not gadgets. For years the two friends traipsed around the mountain trails, hiking, working with wood, and gardening. In 1968 Olive Rabe died. This was forty years after doctors had given up on her. A couple of years after her friend's death, Fisher donated her ranch to the American Friend's

Service Committee and moved into Boulder at the foot of Flagstaff Mountain. In addition to two studies, her home has a guest room for frequent visitors and bookshelves that overflow with first editions of her many books and wind-weathered wood sculptures collected over years of mountain climbing. Although in the city, her house is set back from the street and is close to the homes of many small animals and some deer, the subject of many of her poems. And even though it has been thirty years since she lived on the ranch, Fisher still misses the peace, quiet, and the close contact with nature.

Her most lucrative writing was published in the 1970s by Bowmar as the Bowmar Nature series, used for many years in classrooms and libraries across the nation. The income from these books prompted Fisher to begin to study investment strategies.

Once writing consumed much of Fisher's time—she wrote four hours a day from 8 AM to noon. She wrote with pencil or pen and never tried her poetry out on children, only on herself. In the 1980s she belonged to the Boulder Writers Club, but spent more time on reprint requests and on investments than on writing. She became known to her friends as a renowned poet and a good investor. She donated to many causes, one of her favorites being the Cousteau Society, founded by the late Jacques Cousteau.

In her eighties, Fisher was still enjoying the city lights at night and took daily hikes with her German shepherd, Gretchen. Now, past ninety, Fisher writes little but is active managing her own affairs. Many of Fisher's books are being reissued, or individual poems are being reprinted in collections or magazines. Some poems have been reprinted more than fifty times. Her poems have been translated into many languages, including Norwegian and Japanese.

Aileen Fisher still lives in her home in Boulder, still enjoys the animals and nature around her, and is keenly aware of her success as a published writer. She still receives many, many letters from children, most of whom, she says, seem to be third-graders. It seems "that third grader teachers like my poetry best."

Books and Notes

Aileen Fisher's poetry is included in many collections. Several poems are included in *Talking Like the Rain: A First Book of Poems* by X. J. Kennedy and Dorothy M. Kennedy (Little, Brown, 1992); *The Random Book of Poetry for Children* by Jack Prelutsky, illustrated by Arnold Lobel (Random, 1983); and *Read-Aloud Rhymes for the Very Young* by Jack Prelutsky, illustrated by Marc Brown (Knopf, 1986). Her own volumes of poetry include the following.

Always Wondering: Some Favorite Poems of Aileen Fisher. Illustrated by Joan Sandin. (Harper, 1991).

The House of a Mouse. Illustrated by Joan Sandin. (Harper, 1988).

I Stood Upon a Mountain. Illustrated by Blair Lent. (Crowell, 1979).

Like Nothing at All. Illustrated by Leonard Weisgard. (Crowell, 1969).

Listen, Rabbit. Illustrated by Symeon Shimin. (Crowell, 1964).

Out in the Dark and Daylight. Illustrated by Gail Owens. (Harper, 1980).

Rabbits, Rabbits. Illustrated by Gail Niemann. (Harper, 1983).

The Story of Easter. Illustrated by Stefano Vitale. (Harper, 1997).

When It Comes to Bugs. Illustrated by Chris Degen and Bruce Degen. (Harper, 1986).

For More Information About/By the Author

Articles

"Poetry Place: Jack Prelutsky Chats with Aileen Fisher." *Instructor* 103, no. 3 (October 1993): 70.

"Workshop Named for Author." *Past-Present Prints: News Bulletin of Iron County Historical Museum Society, Museum Site: Caspian Michigan* 1, no. 13 (April 1980): 1.

Louise Fitzhugh

◆ Contemporary Realistic Fiction

Memphis, Tennessee
October 5, 1928–November 19, 1974

📖 *Harriet the Spy*
📖 *The Long Secret*

About the Author
and the Author's Writing

Cited as "one of the funniest and most original children's books of the day," *Harriet the Spy* (Harper, 1964) signaled the beginning of an era in which the old assumptions about parental infallibility disappeared and the highly individualized child character appeared. Authors began to develop the character's personalities with little regard for what a proper child might do. Harriet M. Welsch, the character developed by Louise Fitzhugh, is an eleven-year-old living in Manhattan whose goal is to become a famous writer. So each day she writes observations in her notebook—observations she makes on her "spy route." Eventually her notebook falls into the hands of one of her classmates and, when her classmates read the notes she has made about them she becomes very unpopular. Harriet, however, does not seem to be motivated by malice. It is her honesty and dedication that make her notes seem so ruthless. By creating this indisputably determined and forthright character, Fitzhugh changed the direction of children's literature.

Louise Fitzhugh was born in Tennessee in 1928. Her father, Millsaps Fitzhugh, was an attorney. Her mother was Louise Perkins

139

Fitzhugh. She grew up in Memphis, where she attended the Hutchison School and Southwestern College. Later, she also attended Bard College and New York University as a literature major, stopping six months short of obtaining her degree. She enrolled in the Art Students League and later in Cooper Union in New York. In 1954 she spent part of a year in France, and, three years later, returned to Europe to spend a year in Italy. She also lived in Washington, D.C., before returning to live in New York City and on the North Shore of Long Island. Later she moved to Bridgewater, Connecticut.

As an eleven-year-old, Louise Fitzhugh wrote and knew she would become a writer and an artist. For the next twenty-two years she worked at both crafts. By 1961 her first book illustrations appeared in *Suzuki Beane* (Doubleday), which she also coauthored with Sandra Scoppettone. In 1963 Fitzhugh had a one-person show of her paintings at the Banfer Gallery in New York City. The next year, 1964, Fitzhugh's most popular title, *Harriet the Spy*, was published and selected by the *New York Times Book Review* as one of sixteen year's best juvenile books. The book also won the Oklahoma Sequoyah Children's Book Award in 1967. Her third book, *The Long Secret* (Harper, 1965), was a sequel to *Harriet the Spy*. Her fourth book, *Bang, Bang, You're Dead* (Harper, 1969), an antiwar book, was another collaboration with Scoppettone. That book was selected by the Brooklyn Museum and the Brooklyn Public Library for the Brooklyn Art Books for Children citation.

At the time of her unexpected death in 1974, she was working on the text and illustrations for *I Am Five* (Delacourt, 1978), an uncompleted series. The book and its companion titles were published posthumously in 1978, 1979, and 1982, as well as a book titled *Nobody's Family Is Going to Change* (Farrar, 1974). The book featured a black, middle-class, New York family. The family has a maid and two children, Emma and Willie, both of whom attend private schools. The children fail to meet their parents' expectations. Emma's goal is to become a lawyer, and Willie plans to become a professional dancer. Their parents disapprove of female lawyers and of male dancers.

Louise Fitzhugh died unexpectedly November 19, 1974, of an aneurysm in New Milford, Connecticut. While she was living she enjoyed the theater, tennis, and playing the flute. Her book *Nobody's Family Is Going to Change* was adapted in 1978 as a television movie titled *The Tap Dance Kid*, and in 1983 became a play debuting at the

Broadhurst Theater in New York. The play won two Tony Awards—one going to Hinton Battle for Best Featured Actor in a Musical.

Thirty-two years after its publication, *Harriet the Spy* was produced as a movie starring Rosie O'Donnell as Ole Golly, the nanny who keeps tabs on Harriet, and Robert Joy as Harriet's harried father. Reviewers, for the most part, did not think that the movie matched the book's engaging plot and dialogue. The director, Canadian Bronwen Hughes, resorted to creating a "Harriet," played by Michelle Trachtenberg, that was too emoting to be believable. Eartha Kitt's cameo appearance as Agatha K. Plummer was not notable. Nevertheless, the movie attests that the book remains one of the best children's novels ever written.

Books and Notes

Louise Fitzhugh's writings were all for children and self-illustrated. Several titles were published posthumously. *Harriet the Spy* was criticized for its "disagreeable people and situations." Yet a reviewer noted that "many adult readers appreciating the sophistication of the book will find it funny and penetrating. Children, however, do not enjoy cynicism." The reviewer doubted if the book would "appeal to many of them." Several years later another reviewer noted that "none of the reviewers . . . truly looked at what Louise Fitzhugh had so brilliantly done." By then the book had become a favorite title with children.

Harriet the Spy. Illustrated by Louise Fitzhugh. (Harper, 1964).

The Long Secret. Illustrated by Louise Fitzhugh. (Harper, 1965).
Sequel to *Harriet the Spy*.

Books Authored
with Sandra Scoppettone

Bang, Bang, You're Dead. Illustrated by Louise Fitzhugh. (Harper, 1969).

Suzuki Beane. Illustrated by Louise Fitzhugh. (Doubleday, 1961).

Other Titles

I Am Three. Illustrated by Susanna Natti. (Delacorte, 1982).

I Am Four. Illustrated by Susan Bonners. (Delacorte, 1982).

I Am Five. Illustrated by Louise Fitzhugh. (Delacorte, 1978).

I Know Everything About John and He Knows Everything About Me. Illustrated by Lillian Hoban. (Doubleday, 1993).

Sport. Illustrated by Louise Fitzhugh. (Delacorte, 1979).

For More Information
About/By The Author

Articles

Stahl, J. D. "Satire and the Evolution of Perspective in Children's Literature: Mark Twain, E. B. White, and Louise Fitzhugh." *Children's Literature Association Quarterly* 15, no. 3 (Fall 1990): 119+.

Books

Wolf, Virginia. *Louise Fitzhugh* (Twayne, 1991).

John D. Fitzgerald

Historical Fiction   ◆   Humorous Stories

Price, Utah
1907–May 21, 1988

 📖 The Great Brain Series

 📖 *The Great Brain*

 📖 *The Great Brain Does It Again*

About the Author
and the Author's Writing

    John Dennis Fitzgerald was born in Price, Utah, in 1907, but the exact date is unknown. His mother was Tena Neilsen, a devoted Mormon, and his father was Thomas D. Fitzgerald, a devoted Catholic. The Fitzgerald family included three sons, Sweyn Dennis, Thomas Dennis, and John Dennis, and a daughter, Katie. An adopted brother, Earnie, also lived with the family. Each of the sons had "Dennis" as a middle name as a reminder of the cowardly Irish ancestor. Thomas D. Fitzgerald owned a newspaper, *The Advocate*, which reported the news in the Utah Territory. When the elder Fitzgerald died, he was so loved by the community that a Catholic funeral mass was held in the St. George Latter Day Saints (LDS) Tabernacle.

    After his father's death John D. Fitzgerald decided not to return to college and asked the purchaser of his father's newspaper to give him a job. Fitzgerald worked as a journalist for *The Advocate* before moving to Denver, Colorado. He was a jazz musician, a drummer; a publicity agent for MGM; a reporter; and for four years a foreign correspondent for United Press in Europe, Asia, and Australia. When he returned he became a short story writer. Fitzgerald published more than 300 short stories and essays, before the short story market collapsed, and the Fitzgeralds found themselves eating a Thanksgiving dinner of pancakes—with no syrup. John Fitzgerald hocked his typewriter and got a job in a bank.

His wife, however, never lost faith in her husband's writing abilities or career. One Christmas in the early 1950s, Fitzgerald's wife purchased a new typewriter for him, and he began writing again. She suggested a novel. Fitzgerald wrote three memoirs, two books for professional writers, and one book of historical fiction for young readers before beginning writing children's books. His first book, *Papa Married a Mormon* (Prentice-Hall, 1955), became a best-seller, a selection of two book clubs, and was published in seven foreign countries. The same characters and relationships later became the subject of Fitzgerald's children's books. *Papa Married a Mormon* is based on the true story of Tom and Tena Fitzgerald and their relationship from the late 1800s to about 1930 in the Silverlode area near St. George. The couple's home is occupied by their four children, one adopted son, and a Methodist widow, who resides with the family declaring that a mining town is unsuitable for a single woman. Aunt Bertha took no wages while living with the family and stayed until she died at the age of seventy-nine. Tom's sister, Cathie, came West to educate the children, hoping to influence them to embrace Catholicism. Ironically, her brand of religion actually turned John's older brother, Thomas D., toward the Mormon church. Thomas's independence and escapades were always the subject of discussion. As an adult John D. Fitzgerald often told his friends and spouse about his older brother and his "Great Brain." "The Great Brain and I had so many adventures together that I guess I could never really run out of stories to tell." They grew up together in Utah at a time with no radio, television, or movies. Fitzgerald's wife enjoyed his stories about his conniving older brother, and encouraged him to write them down. He wrote seven books about his childhood and a couple of adult titles about his family and childhood. The books are Tom's story told from the younger brother's (John D.'s) point of view. "My memories of Tom are very graphic, because he swindled me so many times when I was a boy." Hundreds of letters arrived asking what happened to the Great Brain at the Catholic Academy in Salt Lake City. Those letters resulted in *The Great Brain at the Academy* (Dial, 1972).

At the time of his death after a long illness, on May 21, 1988, John D. Fitzgerald was living in Titusville, Florida.

Books and Notes

Before writing children's books Fitzgerald wrote three memoirs, two books for professional writers, and one book of historical fiction. His children's books tell of his childhood and of his older brother, Thomas Dennis Fitzgerald, otherwise known as "the Great Brain."

The Great Brain Series

The Great Brain. Illustrated by Mercer Mayer. (Dial, 1967).
Book One. Begins the story of Thomas D. Fitzgerald, age 10, told from his younger brother's viewpoint. Mr. Standish is the "mean" schoolmaster. The Jensen kids get lost in a cave. Other characters in the tales include Thomas's brothers Sweyn, J. D. (the narrator), Basil (the "Greek kid"), and Andy (who loses a leg).

More Adventures of the Great Brain. Illustrated by Mercer Mayer. (Dial, 1969).
Book Two. Continues the story of Thomas D.'s swindling ways.

Me and My Little Brain. Illustrated by Mercer Mayer. (Dial, 1971).
Book Three. Tom leaves for school in Salt Lake City, so Tom's favorite swindle victim, J. D., takes Tom's place as the town hustler. Outlaws kidnap J. D. and his four-year-old adopted brother, Earnie.

The Great Brain at the Academy. Illustrated by Mercer Mayer. (Dial, 1972).
Book Four. Thomas's life at the academy includes setting up an illegal candy-selling scheme and episodes with the newfangled sport of basketball.

The Great Brain Reforms. Illustrated by Mercer Mayer. (Dial, 1973).
Book Five. Thomas D. is at home on vacation in Adenville, Utah. His scheming ways manage to endanger the life of two friends, and Thomas finds that he must reform.

The Return of the Great Brain. Illustrated by Mercer Mayer. (Dial, 1974).
Book Six. In an effort to encourage Thomas to remain reformed, his friends threaten to ostracize him if he pulls one more swindle. The "promise" to reform serves only to refine, not inhibit, the ingenious workings of this "conman's mind."

The Great Brain Does It Again. Illustrated by Mercer Mayer. (Dial, 1975).
Book Seven. The last and final episodes in the life of conartist Thomas D. Fitzgerald and his brothers and sister.

Historical Fiction

Brave Buffalo Fighter. Illustrated by John Livesay. (Independence Press, 1973).
A story based on the diary of Susan Parker as her family journeyed west to Fort Laramie.

Memoirs and Other Writings

Although these books are for adults, the stories are about the same characters and relationships as in the Great Brain series and, thus, might provide some interesting details that could be shared with young readers.

Mamma's Boarding House (Prentice-Hall, 1958).

Papa Married a Mormon (Prentice-Hall, 1955).

Uncle Will and the Fitzgerald Curse. With Robert C. Meredith. (Bobbs-Merrill, 1961).

Books for Professional Writers

The Professional Story Writer and His Art (Crowell, 1963).

Structuring Your Novel: From Basic Idea to Finished Manuscript. With Robert C. Meredith. (Barnes & Noble, 1972).

For More Information About/By the Author

Articles

Reading the memoirs listed above will provide much information about Fitzgerald's family during his childhood. Articles about his adult life seem to be nonexistent. An obituary did appear in *Publishers Weekly* on August 26, 1988.

Paul Fleischman

**Monterey, California
September 5, 1952**

📖 *Bull Run*
📖 *Seedfolks*
📖 *Joyful Noise:
    Poems for Two Voices*

About the Author
and the Author's Writing

Paul Fleischman might list the number 2 as a lucky number in his life. Paul Fleischman was the second child of Albert Sidney "Sid" and Betty Fleischman, and became the author of the second book of poetry to win the Newbery Award. Paul and his wife, Becky, have two sons.

Paul Fleischman was born September 5, 1952, in Monterey, California. His father, Sid Fleischman, was a children's book author. As a child Paul watched his father researching, writing in notebooks, improvising, and reading aloud from his writing.

Paul was intelligent in school, and even though he had homework, he often "threw it off the school bus." He began piano lessons in elementary school and quit after finishing the elementary grades. Later, as an eleventh-grade student, he rediscovered classical music. He ditched school and spent hours in the public library reading and steeping himself in the music of Brahms, Berlioz, Schubert, Chopin, and Beethoven. For a time he played saxophone and taught himself to play the recorder. At this time, writing books held no appeal to Fleischman, but he was interested in writing music. He was "racing through the newly appeared record collection in the Santa Monica, California, public library."

For the first two years after high school, Paul Fleischman attended the University of California at Berkeley. After leaving the university, he rode a bicycle up the coast to Vancouver, traveled by train across Canada, and settled down in the woods near Bradford, New Hampshire. He had neglected to outfit himself with winter clothing suitable for the climate. He had "no winter coat, no gloves, no scarf, and no long underwear," but he had brought his recorder. When he found a college in the nearby town of Henniker that sponsored a recorder consort he joined the group. He found that playing music with other people was "infinitely more enjoyable than playing alone. It was glorious fun . . . and the seed for *Joyful Noise* [Harper, 1988] was planted." He began to realize that playing music was a lot like writing prose. Every sentence seemed to have a rhythm like a musical phrase.

At age twenty-five Fleischman returned to college, this time to the University of New Mexico. He graduated in 1977 and turned to writing. His first book, *The Birthday Tree* (Harper, 1979), was pounded out on a hand-me-down Olympia typewriter during a winter holiday in 1977. With some reluctance, he showed the story to his father. "I've written a story, if you'd like to read it." His father liked it, and so did the editor at Harper.

Paul Fleischman has described the voices that contributed to his writing success. The first was his father, Sid. Paul grew up in Santa Monica/Los Angeles, where he, his older sister Jane, and his younger sister Anne were often called into the family living room to hear the newest chapter from a book their father was writing. He once suggested that Mr. Mysterious and his family get lost; the suggestion was incorporated into a chapter in the book *Mr. Mysterious & Company* (Little, Brown, 1961). His father read his books to the children throughout Paul's high school years. "Hearing my father read was my introduction to writing. Every sentence had its own arc—the most important word was the last word, which gave a sense of ending."

The second voice was that of a neighbor who asked Paul as a fifth-grader to pose for a toy catalog. As payment for posing, Paul chose a short-wave radio kit. The kit required assembly, but once the radio was constructed he "heard the 'music' of the many languages that came into the house. I especially liked the Arabic stations." Paul would often turn off the lights and just listen to the sounds. Short-wave users were often requested to send a little card telling others how the station was reached. Paul felt like he was part of history.

The third voice belonged to Vince Scully, the voice of the Los Angeles Dodgers. Paul grew up in the Santa Monica/Los Angeles area, and listened to Vince Scully announcing baseball, while setting type for his namecard business.

The fourth voice was silence. He got that from Malamud's *The Fixer*. In prison the code for communicating when the second man was taken away was silence.

The fifth voice was his alto recorder that his parents started him playing. When he quit college and traveled across Canada, settling in New Hampshire, his traveling companion was his recorder.

Folk dancing brought forward a sixth voice. "Folk dancing was like dancing on your short wave radio." His favorites include Sweet Honey and a black rock group, The Bobs.

Prairie Home Companion inspired bringing the spoken word into focus, giving Fleischman his seventh voice. Garrison Keillor is a spellbinding storyteller. Fleischman first heard Keillor in Nebraska while his wife was attending nursing school. Fleischman says, "Keillor was like theater."

Other voices came from favorite books, such as Julia Cummingham's *Drop Dead*, Leon Garfield's *Night of the Comet*, and works by Isaac Singer and Richard Kennedy.

Paul, as did his father, fills notebooks with information from his reading and research. He often looks for historical events, an object, or a memorable character to provide a focus point on which to build a story or a poem. He wrote *I Am Phoenix: Poems for Two Voices* (Harper, 1985) out of his love of music and birds. Its success lead him to think about writing a second poetry book for two voices, but he dismissed the idea. He wanted to move into something different, rather than repeat something from past successes. So instead of another book of poetry for two voices, he wrote a book of twelve voices. Each narrator presents her or his thoughts evoked by Beethoven's *Rondo in C*. The book, *Rondo in C* (Harper, 1988), was a picture book. But he kept the idea for another book in two voices.

New voices kept appearing. He had already authored *I Am Phoenix: Poems for Two Voices* was working on a novel. A number of circumstances led to the subject of insects for his second book of poetry for two voices. He had no electricity (although his friends did) in the woods in New Hampshire and he had watched the moths flutter around the light. During his train journey, years before, across Canada, he had purchased a book, *Beyond Your Doorstep* (Knopf) by Hal Borland. Borland often mentioned another writer, Edwin Way Teale. Fleischman had read many of Teale's books. Some years later Fleischman was browsing in an old bookstore when he noticed the name "Teale" on a book's spine. The book, *The Strange Lives of Familiar Insects* (Dodd), inspired the theme of his first poem, "The Moth's Serenade." Dissatisfied with the results he turned back to the novel. Later that autumn, he scrapped the beginnings of two novels and salvaged his first two poems, "Requiem" and "The Moth's Serenade." Twelve more poems resulted in *Joyful Noise: Poems for Two Voices.* This book won the 1989 Newbery Award, and was the second book of poetry awarded the Newbery. His father, Sid Fleischman, had also won the Newbery, in 1987 for *The Whipping Boy* (Greenwillow, 1986). Paul celebrated by buying a piano for his Pacific Grove home.

The following year his novel *Saturnalia* (Harper, 1990) was published. Since college Fleischman had wanted to create a story about Saturnalia, a Roman festival—a time when a master would exchange places with his slave. The idea for featuring the exchange between slave and master was intriguing, but he could not find the right setting. One day, while looking for a copy of the play "What the Butler Saw," he discovered a reference book with the same title, Ernest Sackville Turner's *What the Butler Saw: Two Hundred and Fifty Years of the Servant Problem* (St Martin's Press, 1962). Fleischman feels "It was like destiny calling." He was able to read about the Puritans who tried to educate the Indians to be their servants after King Phillip's War.

Fleischman connected the festival and the role of the Indians and Puritans in his novel *Saturnalia*. The book is filled with contrasting elements: dark and light, good and evil. The contrasts recalled images from his childhood. For example, a judge's wife had been murdered in the neighborhood when he was a child. The woman often walked at night through the alleys. Paul walked those same alleys during the day. The contrast of the dark and light, innocent and dangerous, fascinated Fleischman in a way that inspired the novel's contrasts. Events during the day are uplifting and even comical, while night events are full of mystery and darkness. The manuscript was finished within less than a year and required little revision.

One of Fleischman's poems in his earlier book, *I Am Phoenix*, was titled "Warbler." He later wrote *Townsend's Warbler* (Harper, 1992), a book telling the story of this special type of warbler and the bird's discovery and documentation in 1834 during John Townsend's transcontinental exploration to find exotic plant and animal life. The warbler is named for Townsend, who identified the fragile black and yellow striped warbler. In *Townsend's Warbler*, Fleischman included information about Townsend's journey and the warbler's migrations, as well as excerpts from Townsend's journal.

In 1993 Harper published *Bull Run*. Sixteen people headed for the battle at Bull Run, the first major battle of the Civil War. Their voices elude the excitement, loathing, and apprehension about the battle. Several are convinced that it will be the *only* battle in the Civil War. Among the voices are a war-fevered boy, a disillusioned doctor, a slave woman, a sketch artist, a lover of horses, and a black man who wants to shoulder a gun more than anything. Each of the sixteen tell their story in a chapter, some adding a second chapter to their story.

Fleischman wrote an account of the Trojan War in *Dateline: Troy* (Candlewick, 1996). The story is clear and considerably shorter than the *Iliad*, but it includes all the important details and is very accessible to readers who would struggle with the complexity of the *Iliad*. Wonderful newspaper collages juxtapose events in Troy with the present day.

Book ideas come from many places, often involving libraries or reading. A few years ago, while lunching at a bagelry, Fleischman discovered that there was no issue of the *San Francisco Chronicle* to read. He resorted to reading a copy of a free New Age newspaper. On page 2 he found an article about a psychotherapist who uses gardening as therapy. Ancient Egyptian doctors often prescribed walking through a garden as a cure for the insane. Fleischman immediately made other connections. There was the time his mother spent working at the Veterans Hospital's therapeutic garden in Los Angeles. There was his friend who had helped establish one of Boston's many community gardens, and another who had worked at the Homeless Garden Project in Santa Cruz. All of these voices and points of view came together. Fleischman had found an idea that would allow him to use a multiple-point-of-view approach as he had in *Bull Run*. Unlike *Bull Run*, *Seedfolks* (Harper, 1997) was set in the present. Their accounts would be more like short stories and open-ended. His Boston friend inspired the story of a gardener who had a strong capitalistic interest and sold his produce, even though it was against the rules. He became Virgil's father. Maricela's chapter came from his wife's work with pregnant teenagers. Gonzalo's character came from Fleischman's work with a middleschool English as a Second Language (ESL) class. His efforts to initiate conversations mirrors those of Sam's in the book. The characters are old, young, Korean, Hispanic, tough, haunted, and hopeful.

In the end, thirteen voices tell their stories in *Seedfolks*, and the stories vary as much as the flowers that grow from a packet of mixed wild-flower seeds.

Like his father, Paul Fleischman loves to research and uncover the past. "I am especially drawn to the out-of-the-way corners of History." Paul Fleischman and his wife, Becky, live in an old house near the ocean, approximately 100 miles south of San Francisco, in Pacific Grove, California. His wife is a nurse, and his sons, Dana and Seth, are usual children. Paul still plays the recorder and spends time walking and jogging. For many years he has written with a pencil and notebook at a public library. Even though his writing is slow and laborious, when finished, the manuscript seldom needs much revision. He has written several novels and books of poetry. Among his favorite things are the color Prussian blue, reading, birds, and music.

Books and Notes

Paul Fleischman has written several novels, historical fiction, and books of poetry. His book's dedications give his sense of family and friends. *Rondo in C* is dedicated to his son Dana, *Joyful Noise: Poems for Two Voices* is dedicated to his son Seth, and *Saturnalia* is dedicated to his good friend, writer Ivy Ruckman. Many of his books reflect voices from his reading and life experience. Multiple voices and viewpoints dominate his writing in both prose and poetry. Novels, such as *Bull Run* and *Seedfolks*, represent the voices of multiple characters. The titles listed in the book lists that follow are representative of his total body of work.

Historical Fiction

Paul Fleischman's interest in the "out-of-the-way corners of History" have resulted in several books that reflect the emotions and events of historical periods.

The Borning Room (Harper, 1991).
Georgina recounts the personal effects of the Civil War and the Underground Railroad during accounts of the many turns in her life that took place in the borning room next to the family kitchen.

Bull Run. Illustrated by David Frampton. (Harper, 1993).
Sixteen views of the first battle of the Civil War.

Dateline: Troy. Illustrated by Gwen Frankfeldt and Glenn Morrow. (Candlewick, 1996).
An uncomplicated view of events in the ancient history of Troy.

Path of the Pale Horse (Harper, 1983).
Lep, a fourteen-year-old boy living in Philadelphia during the rage of yellow fever (1793), longs to be a doctor. His mentor, Dr. Peale, allows Lep to accompany him to the city, where Lep learns about the ideology, science, and myths of medicine in the late 1700s.

Saturnalia (Harper, 1990).
The experiences of William, a Narraganset Indian apprentice to a printer,

exemplify early American colonial life for less fortunate individuals.

Poetry

Fleischman's first book of poetry, *I Am Phoenix: Poems for Two Voices*, was illustrated by Ken Nutt. Although the title page for his second volume, *Joyful Noise: Poems for Two Voices*, lists the illustrator as Eric Beddows, they are in fact the same person. Ken Nutt sometimes uses the pseudonym Eric Beddows.

I Am Phoenix: Poems for Two Voices. Illustrated by Ken Nutt. (Harper, 1985).

Joyful Noise: Poems for Two Voices. Illustrated by Eric Beddows. (Harper, 1988).

Ghosts' Grace: A Poem of Praise for Four Voices. Illustrated by Cary Austin. (Harper, 1996).

Other Titles

Rondo in C. Illustrated by Janet Wentworth. (Harper, 1988).

When a young piano student plays Beethoven's piece, each audience member has their own response. Listeners remember images of flying geese, Mama's old house on West Twelfth, a downhill run, a morning's first squint of sunlight, pounding rain, a train's departure, concerts and balls in Vienna, swirling snow, a past romance, and riding a horse at dusk.

Seedfolks. Illustrated by Judy Pedersen. (Harper, 1997).

Thirteen people's lives are reflected in their stories involving gardens and gardening.

Shadow Play: A Story. Illustrated by Eric Beddows. (Harper, 1990).

A true collaboration between the author and illustrator, who created shadow illustrations to depict Fleischman's retelling of "Beauty and the Beast." The illustrations depict a shadow puppet play and reveal at the end that all the beasts are really creations of the puppeteer. Picture book format.

Time Train. Illustrated by Claire Ewart. (Harper, 1991).

The Rocky Mountain Un Limited takes Miss Pym's class back through time when dinosaurs roamed the earth. Along the way the clothes, buildings, carriages, automobiles, uniforms, animals, and surroundings provide readers with clues to the time period, through which the children pass.

Townsend's Warbler (Harper, 1992).

An account of John Townsend and his identification and documented sighting of the warbler that is now named for him.

Whirligig (H. Holt, 1998).

Sixteen-year-old Brian finds forgiveness and atonement as he travels the country building a whirligig in honor of the girl whose death he caused.

For More Information About/By the Author

Articles

Fleischman, Paul. "Newbery Medal Acceptance." *Horn Book* 65, no. 4 (July/August 1989): 442–51.

Fleischman, Paul. "Sound and Sense." *Horn Book* 62, no. 5 (September/ October 1986): 551–55.

Irwin, Jennifer Brown. "The Fictive Voice in Science." *New Advocate* 5, no. 1 (Winter 1992): 23–30.

Sid Fleischman

Contemporary Realistic Fiction ◆ Humorous Stories ◆ Historical Fiction

Brooklyn, New York
March 16, 1920

📖 *The Whipping Boy*
📖 *The Midnight Horse*
📖 The Bloodhound Gang Series
📖 The McBroom Series

About the Author and the Author's Writing

Albert Sidney Fleischman was born in Brooklyn, New York, but grew up in San Diego, California. He spent his high school years perfecting his sleight-of-hand magic, and, before he was seventeen, he was traveling nationwide as a vaudeville magician. His original sleight-of-hand tricks were included in a book he published for magicians. By the time he was in his early 20s, talking pictures and radio brought about the decline of vaudeville. Fleischman joined the U.S. Navy reserve and found himself assigned to a destroyer escort. "I went to the war as a magician and by some hocus-pocus came out a writer." When he returned from the war, he entered San Diego State College and graduated in 1949. By graduation he had married Betty Taylor, and together they had become the parents of Jane and Paul. Another child, Anne, was born later.

Sid Fleischman became a reporter for the San Diego *Daily Journal*, and turned to writing fiction when the paper folded in 1950. His first novels were suspense and mystery thrillers. Some were purchased for motion pictures, and Fleischman had the opportunity to write screenplays.

During the 1960s, Fleischman was drawn to writing books for children. His first book, *Mr. Mysterious & Company* (Little, Brown, 1961), was written for his children. The first books were written very quickly, but as his skills developed, the time it took for him to write a book increased. At the peak of his writing career, it took three months to write a book, sometimes longer if his character gets into some difficulty. Fleischman says, "Every novel I write is an adventure into the unknown. I never know the endings in advance. I write to find out 'what happens next' and how it all ends." He is always anxious to get to his desk to see what will happen. The writing desk is cluttered with pieces of his work—story ideas, library books, research, letters, notes, pens, pencils, and a typewriter.

Fleischman's first book for his children included his interest in magic. Other life experiences contributed to his books. For example, when he was traveling with the vaudeville magic show, he tried unsuccessfully to pan for gold in the California gold territory. That experience was incorporated into *By the Great Horned Spoon* (Little, Brown, 1963), the basis for Walt Disney's film *The Adventures of Bullwhip Griffin*.

Chance led him to listen to a folk storytelling of those born at the stroke of midnight, who have the power of ghosts. That led to *The Ghost of the Noonday Sun* (Little, Brown, 1965). Fleischman explored the tall tale genre in *Chancy and the Grand Rascal* (Little, Brown, 1966). A one-page tall tale cut from that book became the basis for *McBroom Tells the Truth* (Little, Brown, 1966), which anchored his soon-to-come series about the popular McBroom.

Fleischman continued to write his humorous tales, while moving into longer and more serious novels. *The Whipping Boy* (Greenwillow, 1986) not only brought Fleischman the 1986 Newbery Award, but gave readers a glimpse into life from a past time, when a member of a royal household could keep a "whipping boy" to take punishment for an errant royal child.

His friend, writer Sue Alexander, asked Fleischman to create a magic trick for her *Witch, Goblin, and Ghost's Book of Things to Do* (Pantheon, 1982); she included the trick in "Goblin's Magic Trick." The illustration of "Mr. Mysterious" in the story bears a strong resemblance to Sid

Fleischman. Sid Fleischman says, "Personal bits and pieces are all over my novels. . . . *The 13th Floor* developed from the discovery that my late wife was descended from a woman tried as a witch in 17th century New England."

In 1996 Greenwillow published an autobiography of Fleischman's life, *The Abracadabra Kid: A Writer's Life.*

Sid Fleischman still lives in the old-fashioned two-story home, full of creaks and character, that he and his late wife, Betty, shared for over 40 years in Santa Monica, California. This home, near the Pacific Ocean, is where all three of their children grew up. His writing has been divided between children's books and writing films. And now he says, "[I] spend a great deal of my free time in my other world of magic and magicians. I keep in practice."

Books and Notes

Sid Fleischman wrote first of magicians and humorous tall tale characters such as McBroom. Other books explored historical settings and different localities. His villains were uncovered by magic, trickery, and wits.

The McBroom Series

McBroom is a tall tale character invented by Sid Fleischman. The first book was *McBroom Tells the Truth*. The series now includes a dozen titles. Over the years many publishers have produced Fleischman's wacky tales of McBroom. Little, Brown republished several earlier titles with newly created illustrations. Fleischman's most recent books featuring McBroom are collections of three tales published by Greenwillow.

Here Comes McBroom: Three More Tall Tales. Illustrated by Quentin Blake. (Greenwillow, 1992).

McBroom and the Beanstalk. Illustrated by Walter Lorraine. (Little, Brown, 1978).

McBroom and the Big Wind. Illustrated by Walter Lorraine. (Little, Brown, 1982 [1967]).

McBroom and the Great Race. Illustrated by Walter Lorraine. (Little, Brown, 1980).

McBroom and the Rainmaker. Illustrated by Walter Lorraine. (Little, Brown, 1982).

McBroom Tells a Lie. Illustrated by Walter Lorraine. (Little, Brown, 1976).

McBroom Tells the Truth. Illustrated by Walter Lorraine. (Little, Brown, 1981 [1966]).

McBroom's Almanac. Illustrated by Walter Lorraine. (Little, Brown, 1984).

McBroom's Ear. Illustrated by Walter Lorraine. (Little, Brown, 1982 [1969]).

McBroom's Ghost. Illustrated by Robert Frankenberg. (Little, Brown, 1981 [1971]).

McBroom's Wonderful One-Acre Farm: Three Tall Tales. Illustrated by Quentin Blake. (Greenwillow, 1992).

McBroom's Zoo. Illustrated by Walter Lorraine. (Little, Brown, 1982 [1972]).

The Bloodhound Gang Series

This series features a "gang" of children who set out to solve mysteries befalling themselves and their friends. The series was relatively short-lived but produced five titles, all published in the early 1980s. Many of today's young readers are familiar with the tales from the PBS series *3-2-1 Contact*.

The Bloodhound Gang in the Case of the Cackling Ghost. Illustrated by Anthony Rao. (Random, 1981).

The Bloodhound Gang in the Case of the Flying Clock. Illustrated by William Harmuth. (Random, 1981).

The Bloodhound Gang in the Case of the Secret Message. Illustrated by William Harmuth. (Random, 1981).

The Bloodhound Gang in the Case of the 264-Pound Burglar. Illustrated by William Harmuth. (Random, 1982).

The Bloodhound Gang's Secret Code Book: With Five Stories. Illustrated by Bill Morrison. (Random, 1983).

Historical Fiction

Settings come from Fleischman's travel experiences, for example panning for gold in California, and from his reading. It is true that "royal households *did* keep whipping boys to suffer the punishments due a misbehaving prince" (one of his historical themes).

Bandit's Moon. Illustrated by Joseph A. Smith. (Greenwillow, 1998).
Annyrose, a twelve-year-old, relates her adventures with Joaquãin Murieta and his band of outlaws in the California gold-mining region during the mid-1800s.

The Whipping Boy. Illustrated by Peter Sis. (Greenwillow, 1986).

The tale of a royal prince that demands his "whipping boy" accompany him when he runs away. The two become friends when they both fall into the hands of two unsavory villains.

Other Titles

The Ghost on Saturday Night. Illustrated by Laura Cornell. (Greenwillow, 1997).
When Professor Pepper gives tickets to Opie for a ghost-raising, instead of a nickel payment for guiding him through the dense fog, Opie manages to earn money anyway when he helps to thwart a bank robbery. (Originally published by Little, Brown, 1974, with illustrations by Eric Von Schmidt.)

The Scarebird. Illustrated by Peter Sis. (Greenwillow, 1988; Mulberry, 1994).
The value of human friendship becomes apparent to a lonely old farmer when a young man comes to help him and his scarecrow with their farm.

The 13th Floor: A Ghost Story. Illustrated by Peter Sis. (Greenwillow, 1995).
Twelve-year-old Buddy Stebbins follows his missing sister back in time and finds himself aboard a seventeenth-century pirate ship captained by a distant relative.

For More Information About/By the Author

Articles

Fleischman, Paul. "Sid Fleischman." *Horn Book* 63, no. 4 (July/August 1987): 429–32.

Books

Fleischman, Sid. *The Abracadabra Kid: A Writer's Life* (Greenwillow, 1996).

Paula Fox

Contemporary Realistic Fiction ◆ Historical Fiction

New York, New York
April 22, 1923

📖 *The Slave Dancer*

📖 *Monkey Island*

📖 *One-Eyed Cat*

About the Author
and the Author's Writing

"I had always wanted to be a writer." But before devoting herself to writing, she was a European reporter for a news agency, a professor of English literature, and even a machinist.

Paula Fox was born in New York. Her mother was of aristocratic Spanish/Cuban descent. Her father was Irish/English, a playwright, and a Hollywood scriptwriter. Her very young mother was not able to accept responsibility for a child, so Paula was sent to live in a minister's home in upstate New York. He taught her to read, but her maternal grandmother "rescued" her from his home and took her back to New York. When she was eight years old, they went to Cuba. There, her grandmother was a companion to an elderly relative who owned a plantation. Paula became fluent in Spanish and became friends with the village children. She became the only girl on the baseball team. Her memories include the noises of guinea fowl and monkeys.

When Batiste came to power in Cuba in 1934, twelve-year-old Paula was sent back to the United States. In the United States she became a "traveling child," seldom seeing her parents and moving from school to school, attending nine by the time she was 12. Her salvation seemed to be the quite solace in the public libraries. "Wherever I went, except in Cuba, there was a library. Even though my schools changed, I'd always find a library." Recently she said, "As a child, reading was everything to me. Stories were a kind of magic that could take you anywhere and everywhere."

She was forced to leave school at the age of 16 to support herself. Although writing was always at the edge of her life, she did not even consider making a living with her writing. Her father, although she seldom saw him, was a writer. Instead of writing she worked as a model, a sales clerk, and a machinist at Bethlehem Steel. She was in San Francisco when she and three young Mexican Americans worked to assist 600 Mexican families stranded when the railroad terminated their jobs. She was particularly interested in protecting the children from exploitation by the very agencies that were supposed to help—police departments, courts, and social workers.

In London she worked as a reader for a movie company and later for a British publisher. In 1946 she worked for an English news agency and was assigned to Paris and Warsaw. She was just 23. Returning to New York City she worked in a public relations agency and married Richard Sigerson, the father of her two sons, Adam and Gabriel. At the age of 30 she was divorced and needed to support her children. She had to wait to write full-time until she "could type without dogs or kids in my lap." She studied at Columbia University and began to work with emotionally disturbed children in Dobbs Ferry, New York. She worked teaching English to Spanish-speaking children and taught fifth grade at the Ethical Culture Schools in New York City. During this time she began to write seriously.

In 1962 Paula Fox was remarried to Martin Greenberg. At the time, he was a professor of English at C. W. Post College. Fox wrote a TV script and it was accepted. Two short stories were published in *Negro Digest*. Her husband was awarded a Guggenheim Fellowship, and the family headed for a six-month stay in Greece. The family's experience was "golden." Adam, then twelve, worked for a carpenter; Gabe, at ten, worked for a cobbler; and Paula finally had the time to write uninterrupted. She wrote *Poor George* (Harcourt, 1967) at this time. She was teaching fifth grade when she got a call from an editor at Harcourt Brace accepting the book. Shortly after, Richard Jackson, then at Macmillan, bought *Maurice's Room* (Macmillan, 1966). Harcourt Brace published three novels, but then, because of reorganization, did not buy her next books. They were picked up by Dutton, North Point, and Godine. Most recently she has followed her longtime editor to Dorling Kindersley, which has published her 1997 title *Radiance Descending* under the DK INK imprint.

A few years ago she said, "Writing fiction, I believe, is not a kind of literal transferring of the writer's life. It is reflection and imagination directed toward what a writer has felt and seen." And recently she elaborated, "All stories are woven out of the stuff of one's life, whether actual or one's imagined life. *Lily and the Lost Boy* [Orchard, 1987] is based on six breath-taking months on the Greek Island of Thasos. *Western Wind* [Orchard, 1993] draws on memories of Maine and the islands, ocean, and seashore, which I loved as a girl. *Monkey Island* [Orchard, 1991] is the fearful imagining of poverty and abandonment, things so near at hand in cities. One winter I fed a one-eyed cat that took shelter in the litter of a neighbor's back yard; the rest of *One-Eyed Cat* [Bradbury, 1984] is imagined. You look at a child with Down syndrome and wonder and marvel—*Radiance Descending* came from that."

Paula Fox and her husband, Martin Greenberg, a literary critic and retired professor of English literature, live in a Brooklyn brownstone built in 1860. "The vivid garden in the back is a blessing in the midst of stone and concrete." Of her family she says, "I have a daughter and two sons, and lots of grandchildren, scattered all about the country from Oregon to Connecticut. One son is very far away indeed, in Madagascar, as Technical Advisor to the National Zoological Park."

When she has time Fox plays the piano; she says that "reading is still my best pleasure, carrying me off to other places and into other souls."

Books and Notes

Paula Fox has written novels of contemporary realistic fiction, historical fiction, and retold folktales. Her themes vary, each focusing on a unique individual whose story she tells with respect. Her books often deal with isolation, especially the lack of communication and understanding between generations. A sampling of her titles is listed here.

Contemporary Realistic Fiction

A Likely Place. Illustrated by Edward Ardizzone. (Simon, 1997).

A little boy feels he can never please his parents, and he can't spell. He spends a week with a kooky baby-sitter and makes a special friend.

Lily and the Lost Boy (Orchard, 1987).

The theme of Greek tragedy plays out as Fox explores the life of a young American girl and boy during their family's stay on the Greek island of Thasos.

Monkey Island (Orchard, 1991).

An eleven-year-old boy finds himself alone and homeless in New York City.

Moonlight Man (Bradbury, 1986).

Explores a teenager's developing relationship with a father she has barely known.

Radiance Descending (DK INK, 1997).

Eleven-year-old Paul struggles with his feelings toward his younger brother, who has Down syndrome. All the attention neighbors and friends give his brother causes Paul to question his own worth.

Western Wind (Orchard, 1993).

Elizabeth Benedict is sent to live in a primitive Maine island cottage with her grandmother the summer after a new baby brother is born. She questions her own role and value in the family, and finds, instead, an answer to the value of her grandmother and her family.

Historical Fiction

The Slave Dancer. Illustrated by Eros Keith. (Bradbury, 1973).

Thirteen-year-old Jessie must play his fife aboard a slave ship so the captured slaves will dance to keep their muscles strong, drawing a higher price when the ships land in America. Newbery Award 1974.

Retold Tales

Amzat and His Brothers: Three Italian Tales. (Orchard, 1993). Tales remembered by Floriano Vecchi and retold by Paula Fox. Illustrated by Emily Arnold McCully.

For More Information About/By the Author

Articles

Fox, Paula. "About Language." *The Ohio Review* 52 (1995): 7.

Fox, Paula. "Critical Revisions." *Dissent* 42, no. 2 (Winter 1995): 259+.

Fox, Paula. "On Language." *School Library Journal* 41, no. 3 (March 1995): 122+.

Fox, Paula. "To Write Simply." *Horn Book* 67 no. 5 (September 1991): 552+.

Fox, Paula. "The Village by the Sea: Acceptance Speech for the Boston Globe-Horn Award for Fiction." *Horn Book* 66, no. 1 (January 1990): 22+.

Random House. "Paula Fox." URL: http://www.randomhouse.com/teachersbdd/pfox.html (Accessed December 1998).

Russell Freedman

**San Francisco, California
October 11, 1929**

📖 *Eleanor Roosevelt: A Life of Discovery*
📖 *An Indian Winter*
📖 *Louis Braille*

About the Author
and the Author's Writing

Russell Freedman's parents met in a bookstore, and their first conversation was over a stack of best-sellers. Perhaps it was destiny that Freedman would become a writer. Born October 11, 1929, in San Francisco, Freedman grew up in a house filled with books and frequented by visiting authors. Freedman's father was the manager of the San Francisco office of Macmillan publishing. He was the first publishing representative to call on librarians and knew every librarian west of the Rockies. Russell would often accompany his father on his calls.

Russell Freedman graduated from the University of California and served with the U.S. Army during the Korean War. For a time he was a reporter, and later an editor, with the Associated Press. His first book was inspired by an article Freedman read in the *New York Times* about a sixteen-year-old blind boy who invented a braille typewriter. While investigating the story's background, Freedman found that another sixteen-year-old boy, Louis Braille, had invented the braille system itself. More research uncovered several other teenagers who earned notable places in history. The information became the basis for his first book, *Teenagers Who Made History* (Holiday, 1961). Freedman continued to write nonfiction at first, and later biographies. Subjects ranged from American history to animal behavior.

Eventually he turned to biography. In 1987 Holiday published his collective biography, *Indian Chiefs*, which included the life stories of six chiefs who led their nations in moments of crisis and decision. Usually these decisions included whether to fight or cooperate with encroaching white pioneers. The book came about when James Giblin, a well-known author of nonfiction and at the time an editor at Clarion, suggested to Freedman that he write a biography of a famous American. Together they settled on Lincoln. Because Lincoln was one of the first presidents to be highly photographed, they decided on a photo essay format. Freedman set out to do the background research for the book, attempting to do as much firsthand research as possible.

Describing his research, Freedman said, "While writing my biography of Abraham Lincoln, I visited all the important historical sites, from his log-cabin birthplace in Kentucky to Ford's Theatre in Washington, D.C. The biggest thrill was stepping into a temperature-controlled bank vault at the Illinois State Historical Library in Springfield in the company of Tom Schwartz, Curator of the Lincoln Collection. Tom showed me original documents written in Lincoln's own hand—letters to his wife, drafts of speeches, notes scrawled on scraps of paper during long-ago trials in country courthouses. Each document had been treated with a special preservative that removed all traces of acid from the paper. Pointing to one of Lincoln's courtroom notes, Tom said, 'This will last a thousand years.' I'll never forget that afternoon. I already knew a great deal about Lincoln, yet there's something magical about being able to lay your eyes on the real thing. Looking at those original documents, I could feel Lincoln's presence as never before—almost as though he had reached out to shake hands."

Lincoln: A Photobiography (Clarion, 1987) earned Freedman the Newbery Award in 1988, one of the few works of nonfiction so honored by the American Library Association. Many children who have read the book send letters to Freedman. One of his favorites was from a young boy from Indiana who wrote: "Dear Mr. Freedman: I read your book about Abraham

Lincoln and I liked it very much. Did you take the photographs yourself? I'm a photographer myself."

Freedman says, "Truth is often stranger than fiction," and that historians are really storytellers, sharing epic poems. The person writing history must view him- or herself as "a storyteller—one who does not make up things. They must have a pact with readers to stick to the fact. Non-fiction writers must construct their manuscripts based on research, but that does not rule out art and imagination." The successful writer will find the narrative line and will evoke picture scenes in the reader's mind, creating a narrative framework that will keep the reader turning the pages. Scenes are dramatized but factual.

The characterization brought to the writing must include real glimpses of the person. For example, Lincoln often said "Howdy" and "stay a spell." He wore carpet slippers even when he greeted great dignitaries. He referred to his wife as "mother" even at a White House reception. Lincoln's spectacles were in a velvet case in his pocket when he was assassinated, along with a hanky with "A. Lincoln" stitched in red, a brown leather wallet (with red silk lining), a five-dollar Confederate bill, and a newspaper clipping praising his job as president.

Freedman uncovered other information that helped personalize the public man. William Hearne noted that when Lincoln's young sons accompanied him to his law offices, the children "were absolutely unrestrained in their amusement." And Lincoln's wife Mary said, "Mr. Lincoln was exceedingly indulgent with his children." Good anecdotes bring the character to life.

Research for Franklin Delano Roosevelt's biography uncovered anecdotes about FDR's childhood. When he did not want to practice the piano he would complain of pain in his hand. Headaches were used as excuses for not attending church. And, once, in the middle of the night, he released the horses in a hotel's stable. One of the most charming anecdotes Freedman uncovered about Franklin D. Roosevelt involved an exchange with Roosevelt's wife, Eleanor. In 1928, seven years after FDR contracted polio, he was asked to run for governor. FDR commented to Eleanor, "It's not that I'm afraid to run it's that I'm afraid to run and fail."

Eleanor's response: "Then don't."

"Don't Run?"

"No," said Eleanor, "Then don't fail."

On-location research and library research are important to all of Freedman's books, but serendipity has also played a part in several of his books. When Freedman was working on the FDR biography he was making a routine visit to his attorney and coincidentally discovered that one of FDR's grandsons, Curtis D. Roosevelt, was the attorney's client. Curtis was the son of FDR's daughter Anna. He shared information about growing up with his grandparents in the White House and tumbling around on the bed. Another time he was at his doctor's for a routine physical when the topic of his current work came up. The doctor had an 80-year-old patient who was a young naval doctor who attended FDR at Hot Springs. Yet a third chance encounter occurred after the book was published. During a book signing in Cincinnati, an elderly gentleman approached him with a book, saying, "I'd like you to sign this book, I'm in it." Sure enough, on page 167 there is a news photograph of FDR and Churchill at Yalta in a jeep, along with a member of the Secret Service. The gentleman was the Secret Service agent pictured in the photograph. Freedman asked him, "Did you realize how ill Roosevelt was." The man replied that many had noted Roosevelt's "hacking cough" and that he had commented, "That's no cough, that's a death rattle." A day after that comment, FDR died. As Freedman left the library, the former Secret Service agent was signing Freedman's books on page 167.

Freedman usually begins his research about a subject by reading the most recent relevant books, and creating a bibliography. Following the reading, he does field research, as much as possible, and collects photographs. Over 1,000 photographs have to be culled down to 90 or 100 that might be used to illustrate the manuscript. If possible, he interviews subjects themselves or those who had some association with them.

However, some subjects do not lend themselves to some forms of research. Interviews were not used for *Indian Chiefs*, because the topic is from the nineteenth century. He researched that book entirely in the library. He become acquainted with over 300 watercolors by a Swiss artist, Karl Bodmer, who recorded a winter with the Mandan Indians in North Dakota in 1833–34. The village was wiped out by a small pox epidemic and has not been inhabited since 1837. The tribe lived in dome-shaped huts built from earth. The only things remaining are the circular ridges marking the location of every house and the medicine lodge in the village. Those paintings became the inspiration for *An Indian Winter* (Holiday, 1992). Freedman traveled to Ft. Berthold, North Dakota, where he saw descendants of the people in the paintings.

Freedman often works on more than one project at a time. He focuses on one title, but is often working on others. For example, during 1991 he was working on the manuscript for *Eleanor Roosevelt: A Life of Discovery* (Clarion, 1993), checking out research details for *An Indian Winter*, and beginning the initial stages of collecting material for another book, about Lewis Hines, a photographer who documented the plight of child labor in America. Yet to come is a biography about Babe Didrickson Zaharias.

"One of the best things about my work as a writer of non-fiction is the chance it gives me to travel widely in search of material for my books. Recent trips have taken me to Louis Braille's birthplace in the French Village of Couporay, to Yunnan Province in China, where I witnessed ancient tribal dances that inspired Martha Graham, and to the Little Bighorn Battlefield in Montana where Crazy Horse and his warriors confronted George Armstrong Custer and the men of the Seventh Cavalry Regiment.

"Of course, I do plenty of reading and library research while I'm working on a book, but nothing can take the place of first-hand, eyewitness impressions. There's something special, something magic, about seeing the real thing with your own eyes. When I return from a trip and sit down in my study to write about events that may have happened long ago, I can often picture the scenes in my mind's eye with clarity and feeling—because I have been there myself."

Russell Freedman's large Manhattan apartment is filled with books, plants, and many visiting relatives and friends. "Writing is my full-time job. Every morning I retire to my study, where I spend most of the day working on my latest project. If I am working against a deadline, which I often am, I work after dinner too, sometimes quite late." When he is not writing, he enjoys walking through Riverside Park or through the busy streets of his neighborhood, the Upper West Side, and savoring the incredible variety of films, plays, concerts, restaurants, and street life that New York offers. He travels a great deal to do research for his books and to see the world.

Books and Notes

Topics from American history, animals, children, and people who made a mark on our society have all become topics for well-researched books by Russell Freedman. Every detail is carefully researched and presented in a narrative that weaves facts into a readable and intriguing text for young readers. Photographs are often from the National Archives or historical documents of the times. The Wright Brothers' own photographs documenting their development of the plane illustrate their biography. Photographs by Lewis Hine illustrate the text discussing his crusade against child labor. Period paintings and drawings illuminate other manuscripts. Just as important as the writing is the choice of illustrations. Unless otherwise noted, the books listed are illustrated with photographs that Freedman selected from various sources, most often public archives.

Buffalo Hunt (Holiday, 1988).

Eleanor Roosevelt: A Life of Discovery (Clarion, 1993).

Franklin Delano Roosevelt (Clarion, 1990).

Indian Chiefs (Holiday, 1987).

An Indian Winter. Illustrated with paintings and drawings by Karl Bodmer. (Holiday, 1992).

Kids at Work: Lewis Hines and the Crusade Against Child Labor. Illustrated with photographs by Lewis Hine. (Clarion, 1994).

The Life and Death of Crazy Horse. Illustrated by Amos Bad Heart Bull. (Holiday, 1996).

Lincoln: A Photobiography (Clarion, 1987).

Martha Graham, a Dancer's Life (Clarion, 1998).

Out of Darkness: The Story of Louis Braille. Illustrated by Kate Kiesler. (Clarion, 1997).

The Wright Brothers: How They Invented the Airplane. Illustrated with photographs by Orville and Wilbur Wright. (Holiday, 1991).

For More Information About/By the Author

Articles

Freedman, Russell. "Bring 'Em Back Alive: Writing History and Biography for Young People." *School Library Journal* 40, no. 3 (March 1994): 138–41.

Freedman, Russell. "Eleanor Roosevelt." *Horn Book* 71, no. 1 (January 1995): 33+.

Freedman, Russell. "Message from Beijing." *Horn Book* 68, no. 6 (November 1992): 688+.

Freedman, Russell. "Newbery Medal Acceptance." *Horn Book* 64, no. 4 (July/August 1988): 444–51; also *Journal of Youth Services in Libraries* 1, no. 4 (Summer 1988): 421–28.

Freedman, Russell. "Pursuing the Pleasure." *Horn Book* 62, no. 1 (January/February 1986): 27–32.

McElmeel, Sharron. "Author! Author! Russell Freedman." In *Educator's Companion to Children's Literature, Volume 2: Folklore, Contemporary Realistic Fiction, Fantasy, Biographies, and Tales from Here and There* (Libraries Unlimited, 1996): 109–12.

Jean Fritz

**Hankow, China
November 16, 1915**

- 📖 *Homesick: My Own Story*
- 📖 *What's the Big Idea, Ben Franklin?*
- 📖 *You Want Women to Vote, Lizzie Stanton?*

About the Author and the Author's Writing

Jean Fritz's parents were YMCA missionaries living in Hankow, China, when Jean (Guttery) was born November 16, 1915. She spoke Chinese before English. Her first 12 years were spent in China, where she encountered so many people of different cultures that she "began early to try to figure out what her life would be like if she were someone else." Ever since, she has been exploring other lives by writing biographies and historical books.

The family lived in a big house with high ceilings, filled with storybook characters brought there by Jean's imagination. One family story that was often told was about her great-great-grandmother, Ann Hamilton, who had eaten dinner with George Washington. An entry in George Washington's diary records that indeed he had "bated" one night at the Hamiltons. Years later Jean Fritz would use that story as the basis for *The Cabin Faced West* (Coward, 1958).

In China she attended a school along with many English children who seemed intent on continuing the American Revolution and effecting a different outcome. Jean developed an interest in that period of history and extensive research for her children's books provided an opportunity to learn about it in splendid detail. Her detail and accuracy have become a benchmark for other biographers.

Jean and her parents returned to the United States and settled in Connecticut when Jean was in her early teens. She had longed to be "home," although she had never been in the United States. She was often referred to as "that kid who was born in China." As an adult she turned to writing American history for children, in part, she believes, to "find my roots." Her first book *The Cabin Faced West*, retells about Washington's overnight stay in her family's cabin. "*The Cabin Faced West* was drawn from family history, but the loneliness of Ann, the central character, reflects the loneliness I experienced as a child."

Later Fritz turned to biography. She enjoyed researching and authenticating details about each subject. She begins by reading books about the person. She also seeks out old newspapers and original letters and diaries that she locates in libraries and historic societies. She enjoys the role of detective, treasure hunter, puzzle solver, and eavesdropper. And she has been all of those. Fritz writes about people who are no longer living because one doesn't "know the full story of a person who is still alive and doing things."

Fritz likes subjects that have interesting and complex stories to tell. For example, a recent biography of Stonewall Jackson shows him to have been a flamboyant show-off, struggling for approval. No dialogue is included unless she can substantiate the conversations or dialogue. If she makes a supposition that makes sense according to other evidence, but which she cannot positively authenticate, she qualifies the statement with the phrases, "must have," "perhaps," or "may have." It is never given as fact.

She is steadfast in her efforts to keep details correct. For example, when she could not locate the name of Paul Revere's horse, she did not include one. Then, several weeks after the book was published, she located the name, Brown Beauty. Had she known that fact when Margot Tomes created the jacket illustration, it would not have shown the horse as a dapple gray.

Serendipity still plays a part in her writing. For example, when Fritz was in Texas researching material for *Make Way for Sam Houston* (Putnam, 1986), she went to Independence, where Sam Houston had been baptized in his sixties. Fritz was visiting the church where the baptism had taken place and talking with the present-day minister, who also was interested in Sam Houston's story. The minister showed her a letter written by a college student who had been baptized along with Houston. The letter to the student's mother described the event. Fritz was not expecting this information. During a visit to China before writing *China Homecoming* (Putnam, 1985), Fritz wanted to visit the foreign cemetery where her infant sister had been buried. She was shown an area that is now a children's playground. For some reason Fritz walked around the edges looking at the grass and she found parts of a gravestone. Then she discovered that the benches were overturned gravestones. She found Russian, American, and German names, but did not find her sister's. She said, "I did find myself . . . a whole part of my history." The book became a record of her memories of her youth and a witness to the historical and social changes that had taken place since she left China in 1928.

Her first books about American heroes profiled six revolutionary characters that were part of the founding of the United States, including presidents and other notables. In 1981, while being interviewed by Elaine Edelman for *Publishers Weekly* (July 24, 1981, p. 77), Fritz was asked why she did not write any books featuring women. She replied that she was "not a sociologist." By 1992 she was writing about women. *George Washington's Mother* (Putnam, 1992), *Harriet Beecher Stowe and the Beecher Preachers* (Putnam, 1994), and *You Want Women to Vote, Lizzie Stanton?* (Putnam, 1995) were added to her published works. When she wrote the books about Lizzie Stanton and Harriet Beecher Stowe, Fritz commented, "[I] certainly identified with the frustration of being a girl in a world which favors men."

While many of her books seek to preserve a view of U.S. history, in *Homesick, My Own Story* (Putnam, 1982) she sought to preserve her own. After her father died, she realized that she had no one to talk to in Chinese and no one to ask, "Do you remember when?" The book recalls her childhood years in China, a time so different and so cut off from the rest of her life that she wanted to preserve it.

For more than 40 years the Fritz home has been in Dobbs Ferry, New York. Her involvement with the library during those early years is what first convinced Jean Fritz to write books for children. She and her husband, Michael, often travel to locations of Fritz's stories and enjoy vacations in the Caribbean. When they traveled, the manuscript Fritz was working on stayed behind in the refrigerator—the safest place she could think of.

In July 1995 Fritz's husband, Michael, died. Jean Fritz says, "We were always a close-knit family, exploring new parts of the country at every vacation, and making big productions of Christmas and birthdays. I am now living alone and am dependent on either a walker or wheelchair because a surgeon made a mistake on my back, killing the nerves in my left leg. I continue to give speeches around the country and continue to write." Jean and Michael Fritz raised two children, David and Andrea. David is married to Carmela, and they are the parents of Jean's only two grandchildren, Dan and Michael Scott. Andrea and her husband, Frank Pfleger, live on a lake in New York state with their house and barn cats. Andrea took most of the photographs for Fritz's autobiography, *Surprising Myself* (R. C. Owen, 1992). When she is not writing, says Fritz, "I read a great deal and love to travel, and have always liked being near the ocean."

In the fall of 1997, Fritz was working on a biography of Lafayette. One of her trips to do on-location research took her to Lafayette, North Carolina, the first town named for Lafayette, where she helped celebrate his birthday on September 6. "I like to go to the homes of people I write about. Once I brought back a souvenir. John Hancock's house in Boston is now the state house, and, while there, I saw workmen digging at the foundation when I asked if they'd found anything. They said they had unearthed some bricks which turned out to be bricks from Hancock's own house. I was given a brick and it sits proudly beside my fireplace."

Books and Notes

Historical Fiction

The Cabin Faced West (Coward, 1958).

Homesick: My Own Story. Illustrated by Margot Tomes. (Putnam, 1982).

Revolutionary Biographies

Can't You Make Them Behave, King George? Illustrated by Tomie de-Paola. (Coward, 1977).

What's the Big Idea, Ben Franklin? Illustrated by Margot Tomes. (Coward, 1976).

Where Was Patrick Henry on the 29th of May? Illustrated by Margot Tomes. (Coward, 1975).

Why Don't You Get a Horse, Sam Adams? Illustrated by Trina Schart Hyman. (Coward, 1974).

Will You Sign Here, John Hancock? Illustrated by Trina Schart Hyman. (Coward, 1976).

Biographies of Other Historic People

The Great Adventure of Christopher Columbus: A Pop-up Book. Illustrated by Tomie dePaola. (Putnam, 1992).

Harriet Beecher Stowe and the Beecher Preachers (Putnam, 1994).

Stonewall. Illustrated by Stephen Gammell. (Putnam, 1997 [1989]).

Traitor, the Case of Benedict Arnold (Putnam, 1997 [1981]).

You Want Women to Vote, Lizzie Stanton? Illustrated by DyAnne DiSalvo-Ryan. (Putnam, 1995).

Miscellaneous Titles

Around the World in a Hundred Years: From Henry the Navigator to Magellan. Illustrated by Anthony Bacon Venti. (Putnam, 1994).

George Washington's Mother. Illustrated by DyAnne DiSalvo-Ryan. (Putnam, 1992).

Just a Few Words, Mr. Lincoln: The Story of the Gettysburg Address. Illustrated by Charles Robinson. (Grosset, 1993).

The Man Who Loved Books. Illustrated by Trina Schart Hyman. (Putnam, 1981).

For More Information About/By the Author

Articles

"Author Profile: An Interview with Jean Fritz." *The Book Report* 7, no. 4 (January/February 1989): 28–31.

Fritz, Jean. "Biography: Readability Plus Responsibility." *Horn Book* 64, no. 6 (November/December 1988): 759–60.

Fritz, Jean. "Turning History Inside Out." *Horn Book* 61, no. 1 (January/February 1985): 29+.
Boston Globe-Horn Book Award—1984.

Girard, Linda. "The Truth with Some Stretchers (Jean Fritz Biographies for Children)." *Horn Book* 64, no. 4 (July/August 1988): 464+.

McElmeel, Sharron. "Author! Author! Jean Fritz." In *Educator's Companion to Children's Literature, Volume 2: Folklore, Contemporary Realistic Fiction, Fantasy, Biographies, and Tales from Here and There* (Libraries Unlimited, 1996): 113–16.

Books/Videos

Fritz, Jean. *Surprising Myself.* Photographs by Michael Fritz. (R. C. Owen, 1992).

A Visit with Jean Fritz. [Video: VHS; 25 minutes]. (Putnam, 1987).

Jean Craighead George

Contemporary Realistic Fiction ◆ Nonfiction, Nature

Washington, D.C.
July 2, 1919

- 📖 *Julie of the Wolves*
- 📖 *My Side of the Mountain*
- 📖 *The Cry of the Crow*

About the Author
and the Author's Writing

From the beginning Jean Craighead George was destined to become a writer and an observer of animals and nature. She was one of three children in the family of Frank C. and Carolyn Craighead. "I was born in a family of naturalists in Washington, D.C. My father was an entomologist for the United States Forest Service and took my brothers and me outdoors every weekend and vacation. He taught us the animals and plants, the wild edible plants, and how to make fishing lines and lean-tos." Jean's mother was an entomologist for a short time. Her brothers, Frank C. Jr. and John (twins), earned undergraduate degrees in science and graduate degrees in ecology and wildlife management. "My brothers were two of the first falconers in the United States and gave me a falcon to train when I was thirteen. We collected wild flowers, insects and wild pets like owls, frogs, possums, skunks, and vultures. Ours was a remarkable childhood."

The children spent their summers on Frank Craighead's family land that John Craighead had settled in Southern Pennsylvania in 1742. The area became known as "Craighead" and family members have lived there ever since. The family home was filled with pets. Any wild thing the children wanted to ask questions about was allowed in the house. About her father Jean says, "He would become so enthusiastic about the life history of the spider we could not avoid being fascinated, ourselves." Jean's first pet was a "stick." But when the pet got up and walked away, she realized it was an insect—a walking stick. In addition to the falcon her brothers gave her, Jean also had a pet turkey vulture and a possum that hid in the basement. From third grade she wanted to write. "At 8 years old I began writing poetry and letters. I kept a diary and wrote many stories." Her third-grade teacher sent her to do a math problem and instead, "I wrote a poem." She says the easiest thing for anyone to write is what goes on around you.

"With this rich background, I went on to Penn State University to study science and English, learn more about zoology, and write about my experiences. After college I was a newspaper reporter until I married, then I began to write nature books. They came easily to me as they sprung from my childhood."

Jean George began her nature writing as a coauthor with her husband, John L. George. Their first book was *Vulpes the Red Fox* (Dutton, 1948) and the last book they wrote together appeared in 1956 when they coauthored *Dipper of Copper Creek* (Dutton). She developed her own sense as an author and soon was writing alone. Some of her earliest works were periodical articles and short nonfiction books about animals. Her first solo book, *Hole in the Tree* (Dutton, 1957), appeared the next year. Within three years her popular *My Side of the Mountain* (Dutton, 1959) appeared.

The Georges became parents to three children, Carolyn Laura "Twig," John Craighead "Craig," and Thomas Lothar "Luke." In 1963 the Georges divorced. Jean continued her writing career. While the children were growing up, Jean brought home a fox, raccoons, weasels, turtles, owls, and skunks. Snakes also made their way into her home—boa constrictors, garter snakes, milk snakes, and even poisonous ones. When she was researching *One Day in the Prairie* (Crowell, 1986) she even brought home a tarantula.

"One day my children counted them [the animals]. The menagerie totaled 173. *The Tarantula in My Purse: And 172 Other Wild Pets* [Harper, 1996] is a recent telling of these tales." *My Side of the Mountain* comes from experiences in her teenage years when she was given a falcon to train. She knew that if she ever became a writer, she would use the experiences in a story.

One of her favorite stories involves her crow, Crow-Bar. Crow-Bar was knocked from his nest in a storm, and one of her sons brought the crow home. Eventually the bird spent nights in the apple tree near the family's front porch. When the children fixed scrambled eggs, the bird knocked on the window and invited himself for breakfast. The bird would walk with the children to the bus stop and then come back to knock at the window. For a time the family attempted to teach the bird to say "hello." After two months they gave up. Then one day a delivery man came to the door and was surprised when George answered the door, "I just heard you in the apple tree saying 'hello.' " George went outside and looked up in the tree. There was Crow-Bar saying "hello, hello." The bird even knew what to do with his new skill. He flew down to picnic tables and said "hello," scaring people away and eating their food. He also learned to say "hiya babe."

At first George refused to write a book about a crow "because no one would believe it." While visiting a school George made the same comment when telling the crow's story. One little girl said, without hesitation, "I would." *The Cry of the Crow* (Harper, 1980) recounts experiences with Crow-Bar as Mandy views herself and family in a different light when they care for an abandoned crow.

George's writing style changes often because of boredom. The demands of nonfiction totally saturate George. Writing a novel requires a different focus—one that provides a welcome change. Sometimes her nonfiction shows up in strange ways in her fiction. For example, when she wrote *River Rats, Inc.* (Dutton, 1979) she named the chief protagonists Joe Zero and Crowbar Flood. *River Rats, Inc.* was an adventure/ mystery set on the Colorado River. There was not a crow in sight—only Crowbar.

George subscribes to many scientific journals, and an article in one of them about wolves fostered George's interest in animal communication. She visited a research center in the Northwest and flew to the Arctic Research Lab in Alaska. There she met Gordon Haber, who was studying wild wolves in McKinley National Park. She discovered that wolves do have a language of communication. They pass messages silently, and she even came to believe that "wolves can grin." She let her son Luke play with the wolves' puppies. During observation, George also noted the hierarchy in the wolves' community. There were alpha leaders, the beta (or second) leader, and the lowest of the pack, the omega, which stayed at home with puppies. She was supposed to be researching an article for *Reader's Digest*, but the article was not published. Instead, George used the information to create *Julie of the Wolves* (Harper, 1972) and the book's sequels, *Julie* (Harper, 1994) and *Julie's Wolf Pack* (Harper, 1997).

Later George wrote a book about animal communication, *How to Talk to Your Animals* (Harcourt, 1985), and specific books about talking to dogs and cats. For thirty years George's parents lived in the Florida Everglades. Visits and canoe trips through the Everglades provided information for *The Talking Earth* (Harper, 1983).

A trip to Barrow, Alaska, to participate in a whale watch organized by her son Craig inspired another book. George examines the importance of whaling to Eskimo culture, the dependence they have on whales for food and shelter. George was originally apprehensive about going to Barrow. It was several years after *Julie of the Wolves* had been written and she was returning to the same area where that book had been set. What if the Eskimos felt that she had portrayed them inaccurately? However, when her plane was landing, she saw that the students from the school had been let out to greet her at the airport. The vice principal introduced the children and the community to George. Many had copies of *Julie of the Wolves* for autographing. George went to a whaling site by snowmobile. Her son provided her with multilayered clothing, wool pants, long underwear, and so forth. To reach the whaling camp, she traveled on a five-mile stretch of ice. They had tents for sleeping and triple-weight sleeping bags. The whaling crew used seal-skin covered boats propelled through the icy water by crew members using a harpoon paddle. It seemed all Eskimos had citizen band (CB) radios, and, when a whale was taken, the signal went out over the CBs, "Gloria, Gloria, hallelujah—a whale has been taken." Everyone went to the scene and helped with the harvest. Every part of the whale was used and everyone shared the bounty. The book, tentatively titled *Whale of Barrow* during its prepublication stage, was published as *Water Sky* (Harper, 1987).

In talking about the research necessary for her books, George says, "I do a great deal of reading and also talking and listening to scientists." While she was researching Rocky Mountain goats, George read all she could about the subject and contacted a young man, Doug Chadwick, who was an acknowledged expert. George and her son Luke spent several weeks camping with Chadwick and his wife, Beth, above timberline. They were able to observe and record the behavior and interaction of the goats. *Going to the Sun* (Harper, 1976) told the story of a secretly married couple who spent a summer tracking a herd of Rocky Mountain goats, concluding that the goats should not be hunted.

George considers herself a nature writer. She says, "Thoreau was one, Edwin Wax, Anne Schwindler, John Boroughs, Edward Abbey. I like to be called a nature writer—both naturalist and writer." She considers being an author of children's books her greatest accomplishment. Her writing style takes readers along on her expeditions to observe animals and nature. She carefully describes the setting as it might be viewed from the reader's vantage point, then she skillfully moves the point of view to the animal.

Jean Craighead George has lived in Chappaqua, New York, for many years. Her home is an old-fashioned brown shingle house surrounded by wetlands (they were there even before it was fashionable to be involved with the preservation of wetlands). The house is filled with paintings, drawings, collages, and sculptures—most created by George herself, her family, or her friends. A large fountain bubbles in the center of an indoor pond surrounded by plants. The pond, a focal point in the foyer, is stocked with fish. Twig has two daughters, Craig is a biologist, and Luke is an orthinologist. Craig has worked in Alaska and Luke has worked extensively in the Sea of Cortez in Baja California.

Of her current activities, she says, "Most of my activities are connected with my work. I hike, canoe, swim, camp in the back country, and paint animals and scenery. But I also love the theater, musicals, modern dance concerts, music and collaborating with composer, Chris Kubie. We laughed and sang as we worked on our children's musical *One Day in the Woods*. And we are laughing and singing now as we work on children's songs for a movie.

"My dearest memories of writing are sitting at my typewriter in my office on the sun porch on the back of our old brown shingle house in Chappaqua. I could work and watch my three children play with the pets—gulls, robins, crows, raccoons, etc. I could be interrupted in those days and get right back to my thoughts; and, oh, how worthwhile those interruptions were—a complaint about a crow who flew off with the toys, a prideful call from a tree where a raccoon had climbed to join Twig,

Craig, and Luke, laughter from the year where the goose and the duck were splashing under the hose with the neighborhood kids. It was my children and their animals who really wrote the books."

Books and Notes

Ecological Mysteries

George creates natural settings through the use of highly descriptive language. A sense of drama is achieved by having the action conveyed through the animal's senses.

The Case of the Missing Cutthroats: An Ecological Mystery (Harper, 1996).

Who Really Killed Cock Robin? An Ecological Mystery (Harper, 1991).

Julie Trilogy

Set in the North Slope of Alaska, this series's main character is Julie, a thirteen-year-old Eskimo who runs away from her father's home to escape an unwanted marriage. She is befriended by a wolf pack that helps her survive in the icy north. In the second book Julie returns to her father's Eskimo village struggling to find a way to save her beloved wolves from the threat of a changing Arctic. In the process she meets and falls in love with a Siberian man. *Julie's Wolf Pack* continues the story, in which Kapu (the alpha male) must protect his pack from famine and disease while attempting to unite the pack under his leadership.

Julie of the Wolves. Book 1. Illustrated by John Schoenherr. (Harper, 1972).

Julie. Book 2. Illustrated by Wendell Minor. (Harper, 1994).

Julie's Wolf Pack. Book 3. Illustrated by Wendell Minor. (Harper, 1997).

Nature Novels

Jean Craighead George's writing weaves a narrative through information about animals and locations. Readers can glean information about the setting and animals from the novels, and get direct information through the nonfiction titles.

The Cry of the Crow (Harper, 1980).
Crow.

The Missing 'Gator of Gumbo Limbo: An Ecological Mystery (Harper, 1992).
Southern Florida; alligator.

My Side of the Mountain (Dutton, 1977).
Peregrine falcon; survival in the wilderness.

On the Far Side of the Mountain (Harper, 1990).
Sequel to *My Side of the Mountain*. Peregrine falcon.

The Talking Earth (Harper, 1983).
Florida Everglades.

The Tarantula in My Purse: And 172 Other Wild Pets (Harper, 1996).

Thirteen Moons Series

Each of the thirteen titles explores the relationship between an animal and its environment. George writes about the daily lives of each animal. Illustrations help illuminate the animal's actions and visualize the flora and fauna of the setting. Animals featured in her titles include bears, chickarees, fox pups, gray wolves, moles, monarch butterflies, salamanders, wild pigs, and winter birds, in addition to the alligator, deer, owl, and mountain lion featured in the titles below.

The titles were originally published by Crowell in the 1960s and rereleased with new illustrations in the 1990s.

The Moon of the Alligators. Illustrated by Michael Rothman. (Harper, 1991).

The Moon of the Deer. Illustrated by Sal Catalano. (Harper, 1992).
Deer; Connecticut.

The Moon of the Mountain Lions. Illustrated by Ron Parker. (Harper, 1991).
Mount Olympus—Washington state.

The Moon of the Owls. Illustrated by Wendell Minor. (Harper, 1993).
Great-horned owl; Catskill Mountains.

Picture Books

In addition to novels and nonfiction books, George has written some picture books. She weaves the story of wildlife and the out-of-doors.

Dear Rebecca, Winter Is Here (Harper, 1993).
Written in the form of a letter from a grandmother to her granddaughter, Rebecca.

The Grizzly Bear with the Golden Ears. Illustrated by Tom Catania. (Harper, 1982).
A mother grizzly bear swipes food from other bears, and finally learns her lesson.

The Wounded Wolf. Illustrated by John Schoenerr. (Harper, 1978).
A wolf's struggle to stay alive in the cold and barren Alaskan landscape.

For More Information About/By the Author

Articles

Hopkins, Lee Bennett. "Jean Craighead George." *Elementary English* 50, no. 7 (1973): 1049–53.

Jean Craighead George. URL: http://www.avicom.net/ceri/jcg/ (Accessed November 1997).

McElmeel, Sharron. "Author! Author! Jean Craighead George." In *Educator's Companion to Children's Literature, Volume 1: Mysteries, Animal Tales, Books of Humor, Adventure Stories, and Historical Fiction* (Libraries Unlimited, 1995): 57–61.

Books/Videos

Cary, Alice. *Jean Craighead George* (Learning Works, 1996).

Podell, Thomas. *Good Conversation! A Talk with Jean Craighead George*. [Video]. (Podell Productions, 1991).

Patricia Reilly Giff

Contemporary Realistic Fiction ◆ Biographies

Brooklyn, New York
April 26, 1935

- 📖 *Fourth-Grade Celebrity*
- 📖 *Laura Ingalls Wilder: Growing Up in the Little House*
- 📖 *Watch Out, Ronald Morgan*
- 📖 Polk Street School Series
- 📖 The Lincoln Lions Band Series

About the Author
and the Author's Writing

As a child Patricia Reilly Giff was a reader. She read with her father, shared books from her mother's childhood, and was a regular visitor to the public library. The library was in her hometown of St. Albans, New York. The library was tiny, somewhat dusty, and filled with books spilling from the shelves, resting on the tables, and piled on chairs. The librarian, Miss Bailey, often piled books in Patricia's arms. Patricia read every minute she could, often ignoring her homework. She says, "I learned to read by listening to my father read the classics aloud, and by reading the books my mother loved. One of my favorite books was *Little Women*." She earned a college degree in English and then a masters degree in history. For several years before marrying Jim Giff in 1959, she taught elementary school. She eventually returned to college to earn a second masters degree, this one in reading. She became a reading teacher and consultant, mostly for the Elmont Public Schools in Elmont, New York, where the family lived. She juggled teaching and family responsibilities. Her family included her husband, Jim, and three children, James, William, and Alice. After twenty years of teaching, Giff realized that even though she had always wanted to write she had never tried to write a story and she was forty years old. She set a goal of writing each day for a year. At the end of the year she continued writing. Her husband combined two adjacent kitchen closets in their apartment to create a writing area for Giff. He encouraged her and suggested she write about some of her students—and their struggles. Every morning, with a cup of hot tea close by, she wrote for an hour or two and then would go off to teach school.

Her first book was *Today Was a Terrible Day* (Viking, 1979). When she finished the manuscript, she went to the library and found a copy of *Writer's Market*. The third submission came back with a letter from George Nicholson stating, "We want to publish your book." Her first books were published in 1979. Then she began writing chapter books, and the books became a series, The Kids of Polk Street School. Within a year they had sold over 1.5 million copies. "Later, I became obsessed with writing real books for young readers." Six years later the series had grown to 12 titles and had sold more than 15 million copies. The popular series focuses on classroom experiences and features children, much like the children Giff taught during her years at Elmont. "My characters are often based on people I know—children I worked with, teachers, friends. Ms. Rooney is probably the teacher I was and Mrs. Paris the teacher I wanted to be—understanding, wonderful with children, wise, and perfect."

One of the children Giff met while on cafeteria duty became the inspiration for Ronald Morgan. It was raining and she was trying to put down the window, and he offered to help. He was wearing a yellow rain slicker. When she asked why he didn't leave his coat in his room he responded, "It's new." When he had finished helping he sat down to eat and before long, before anyone else was finished, he had a ring of tomato soup around his mouth and cracker crumbs down his T-shirt. He confessed he really wasn't the window monitor, his job was the wastebaskets. He raced out of the cafeteria but not before Giff got his name— R O N A L D. Ronald Morgan was born that day. Giff just knew he "was a kid to write a book about."

After Giff's books began to be published regularly, she found that balancing family, teaching, and writing was overwhelming, so she retired from teaching. Her husband, Jim, retired from the New York City police force, and the family moved to a rural wooded area in the northeast corner of Westport, Connecticut, in 1985. The long, winding road leading to the home is tree-lined and sprinkled with old farmhouses and new homes cozily positioned among trees, streams, and ponds. For a time the couple maintained an apartment in New York's Greenwich Village. They now have a summer cottage on the west branch of the Delaware River near Hancock, New York.

Wherever she is, Giff writes. She wrote *Rat Teeth* (Delacorte, 1984) while wearing her robe when it snowed outside. She drank hot chocolate, ate candy, and sneaked out of doing the evening dishes as often as she could. "Rat Teeth" was a character in another book, *Left-Handed Shortstop* (Delacorte, 1980). He was the subject of so much mail, Giff finally realized she must give the character his own book. Children wanted to know what happened to him.

Other books include bits and pieces from her or her family's life. Her series of detective stories, *The Polka-Dot Private Eye*, draws heavily on the experiences of her husband, a retired detective, and those of her father who was an inspector in the New York police department. A librarian at a meeting in Philadelphia suggested the series. Giff's husband inspired the character of Detective Garcia in *Have You Seen Hyacinth MaCaw?* (Delacorte, 1981).

Many characters and incidents in Giff's Polk Street School books come from her association with children. Giff's daughter, Alice "Ali," is Emily Arrow, and she really did save a worm's life once. That inspired the opening scene of *Fish Face* (Dell, 1984), where Emily Arrow, "Beast," and Jill Simon find a worm covered with ants and save its life. Giff herself is Casey in *Fourth-Grade Celebrity* (Delacorte, 1979), and she is Grace in *The Gift of the Pirate Queen* (Delacorte, 1982). A boy, named Richard, suggested she write a story about a boy named Beast. She knew a girl who said "Snaggle Doodles," and she herself was afraid to climb the gym ropes. Polk Street School is much like Elmont School, where Giff taught for many years. Giff often includes her daughter's and sons' names in her books. Look for Jimmy, Ali, and Billy. She has also included the names of her cats, Bonnie and J. R. Fiddle, in some books.

Giff says she has three major sources for ideas. The first is her children: Jim, Bill, and Alice. "Alice spent her days being tortured by her two brothers." The boys would hang Alice's Holly Hobby doll and make a cemetery gravestone with "Holly" on the stone. Giff's second source is her twenty years of working with school children. The first year she worked with gifted students; the rest were spent working with students who had reading problems. In her second year of teaching, she had 40 fourth-graders, several who had only first-grade reading skills. Those students often appear in her books. Four of those students, however, were among the children who could not read by the end of the year. One ended up as an alcoholic, two received life sentences for murder, and the fourth spaced out on drugs. As a reading teacher she said, "If I taught them skills, it took so long that I had turned them off to reading."

Giff receives many letters about her characters and books. One boy wrote, "My name is Matthew. Please do not use my name in your book again. I don't wet the bed and everyone is teasing me." In the next book, Matthew became everyone's best friend, especially Beast's.

Patricia Reilly Giff has been associated as an educational consultant with Dell Yearling Books. They publish her Polk Street School series and the Lincoln Lions Band series. In addition, she continues to write and travels to speak with children and teachers about reading and writing.

Her husband, Jim, often travels with her to classrooms or teachers' conferences. Children from Eskimo villages in the Bering Strait to the country schools in County Longford, Ireland, love to meet someone who writes. Giff says, "I love to see what they're reading. . . . Whole language is not restricted to the United States. Classrooms all over the world are boasting of the books they're reading every day."

In addition to Giff's Polk Street School series (The Kids of the Polk Street School and The New Kids at the Polk Street School), Giff has also created the Lincoln Lions Band series, all for Dell. She has also created books for the Adventures of Casey Valentine and Her Friends series and Meet Abby Jones, Junior Detective. Recently she has written series books for Viking Penguin. The Ballet Slippers series feature Rosie, her friends, and Rosie's ballet class. One of her most popular series features Ronald Morgan.

Dell published Lily's Crossing in 1997. Giff says that story is "really about my childhood . . . which took place during the Second World War, in Rockaway, New York." The Reilly family had a cabin at Rockaway and though they didn't sleep there, they spent almost every day there in the summertime. Patricia was awkward on land but loved being in the water swimming and being around the boats. "I always felt good about it, so I thought one day that I would write Lily." It took Giff about four years to write the book. Giff says, "I am Lily; I am the grandmother. The bakery really existed, but it was in St. Albans, where I grew up. Albert was a little bit of many boys I knew when I was growing up." The bakery did have signs that said things like "loose lips sink ships." And Giff's mother put stars on the ceiling when Giff's younger sister, Anne, was born. When the glue holding the stars dried out, a star or two fell, and, occasionally, the girls called them "falling stars," thinking they were very special, maybe even magic.

Those who have read Giff's humorous titles will find *Lily* much different. It will make readers cry.

Patricia Reilly Giff lives with her husband, Jim, and three cats in Weston, Connecticut. Their children, Ali, Jim, and Bill, are grown, and there are four grandchildren. The first grandchild was named "Jimmy," the third James in the family. When she is not reading in the bathtub or sitting on the beach, Giff is probably writing or overseeing her bookstore, The Dinosaur's Paw, which she and her family opened in Fairfield, Connecticut. The store is part of Giff's efforts to bring children and books together. Among her favorite foods are baked potatoes and chocolate candy. Favorite colors include yellow and sometimes red. Of a favorite book, Giff says: "Impossible to choose; there are so many to love."

Books and Notes

Ballet Slippers

This series of short chapter books, published by Viking, features Rosie, who has all kinds of experiences involving her ballet lessons, performances, and other such things.

Dance with Rosie. Illustrated by Julie Durrell. (Viking, 1996).

Not-So-Perfect Rosie. Illustrated by Julie Durrell. (Viking, 1997).

Starring Rosie. Illustrated by Julie Durrell. (Viking, 1997).

Biographies

Diana: Twentieth-Century Princess. Illustrated by Michele Laporte. (Viking, 1991; Puffin, 1992).
Originally published by Viking as *Princess Diana*. Women of Our Times series.

Laura Ingalls Wilder: Growing Up in the Little House. Illustrated by Eileen McKeating. (Viking Kestrel, 1987).

Mother Teresa, Sister to the Poor. Illustrated by Ted Lewin. (Viking, 1986).

Casey, Tracy & Company

Love, from the Fifth Grade Celebrity. Illustrated by Leslie Morrill. (Delacorte, 1986).

Friends and Amigos Series

In these books Sarah visits New York and loses her dog, writes to a pen pal in South America, learns Spanish when her friend Anna Ortiz is away at camp, and then is too embarrassed to speak Spanish in front of her friends until Anna's cousin explains her own secret fears. Benjamin is another major character. He saves a fiesta and finds that the Christmas spirit is only what you make it.

Adios, Anna. Illustrated by DyAnne DiSalvo-Ryan. (Dell, 1995).

Good Dog, Bonita. Illustrated by DyAnne DiSalvo-Ryan. (Dell, 1996).

Happy Birthday, Anna, Sorpresa. Illustrated by DyAnne DiSalvo-Ryan. (Dell, 1996).

Ho, Ho, Benjamin, Feliz Navidad. Illustrated by DyAnne DiSalvo-Ryan. (Dell, 1995).

It's a Fiesta, Benjamin. Illustrated by DyAnne DiSalvo-Ryan. (Dell, 1996).

Say Hola, Sarah. Illustrated by DyAnne DiSalvo-Ryan. (Dell, 1996).

The Kids of the Polk Street School

Ms. Rooney's class has several interesting students, including Richard Best "Beast" and Emily Arrow. Each month brings more incidents from their classroom. Both Ms. Rooney and Patricia Reilly Giff like candy corn and have "puffy brown hair." It is really Giff's husband, Jim, who cleans up in Polk Street School.

The Beast in Ms. Rooney's Room. Illustrated by Blanche Sims. (Delacorte, 1984).

In the Dinosaur's Paw. Illustrated by Blanche Sims. (Delacorte, 1985).

Pickle Puss. Illustrated by Blanche Sims. (Delacorte, 1986).

Snaggle Doodles. Illustrated by Blanche Sims. (Delacorte, 1985).

Sunny-side Up. Illustrated by Blanche Sims. (Delacorte, 1986).

The Lincoln Lions Band

The Great Shamrock Disaster. Illustrated by Emily Arnold McCully. (Dell, 1993).

Meet the Lincoln Lions Band. Illustrated by Emily Arnold McCully. (Dell, 1992).

Yankee Doodle Drumsticks. Illustrated by Emily Arnold McCully. (Dell, 1992).

Abby Jones, Junior Detective

Have You Seen Hyacinth MaCaw? Illustrated by Anthony Kramer. (Delacorte, 1981).

Loretta P. Sweeny, Where Are You? Illustrated by Anthony Kramer. (Delacorte, 1983).

Tootsie Tanner, Why Don't You Talk? Illustrated by Anthony Kramer. (Delacorte, 1987).

New Kids at the Polk Street School

The early primary-age siblings of The Kids of the Polk Street School series share their school experiences. Stacy, Emily Arrow's younger sister, is one of the stars.

All About Stacy. Illustrated by Blanche Sims. (Dell, 1988).

Fancy Feet. Illustrated by Blanche Sims. (Dell, 1988).

Spectacular Stone Soup. Illustrated by Blanche Sims. (Dell, 1989).

The Polka-Dot Private Eye Series

Dawn Tiffanie Bosco was a character in The Kids of the Polk Street School series. She popped up in this series when her Noni, her grandmother, gave her a polka-dot detective box.

The Case of the Cool-Itch Kid. Illustrated by Blanche Sims. (Dell, 1994).

The Clue at the Zoo. Illustrated by Blanche Sims. (Dell, 1990).

The Mystery of the Blue Ring. Illustrated by Blanche Sims. (Dell, 1987).

The Powder Puff Puzzle. Illustrated by Blanche Sims. (Dell, 1987).

The Riddle of the Red Purse. Illustrated by Blanche Sims. (Dell, 1987).

The Secret at the Polk Street School. Illustrated by Blanche Sims. (Dell, 1987).

Ronald Morgan

Ronald Morgan is a second-grade boy who has all sorts of humorous and identifiable dilemmas. He has trouble training his dog, and finds out what he is good at when he gets a surprise medal at camp.

Good Luck, Ronald Morgan. Illustrated by Susanna Natti. (Viking, 1996).

Ronald Morgan Goes to Bat. Illustrated by Susanna Natti. (Viking, 1988).

Ronald Morgan Goes to Camp. Illustrated by Susanna Natti. (Viking, 1995).

Other Titles

The Gift of the Pirate Queen. Illustrated by Jenny Rutherford. (Delacorte, 1982).

Sixth-grader Grace has lost her mother and discovered that her sister has diabetes. She learns to be brave like the pirate queen Grace O'Malley, whom her Irish cousin says she resembles.

Lily's Crossing (Delacorte, 1997).

Historical fiction set at Rockaway Beach in 1944 during World War II. Lily's friendship with a young Hungarian refugee helps her view the war with a more reasoned perspective. (Novel.)

Next Year I'll Be Special. Illustrated by Marylin Hafner. (Doubleday, 1993).

Marilyn just knows next year will be better in second grade. (Picture book.)

Shark in School. Illustrated by Blanche Sims. (Delacorte, 1994).

Matthew is concerned that everyone at his new school will find out that he is a terrible reader. (Novel.)

The War Began at Supper: Letters to Miss Loria. Illustrated by Betsy Lewin. (Delacorte, 1991).

Children in Mrs. Clark's class write letters to their former student teacher in the Persian Gulf during that crisis.

For More Information About/By the Author

Articles

Lodge, Sally. "The Author as Bookseller: Patricia Reilly Giff's Career Comes Full Circle." *Publishers Weekly* 241, no. 16 (April 18, 1994): 26–27.

"Patricia Reilly Giff: A Writer Who Believes in Reading." *Teaching K–8* (April 1987): 34–36.

Jamie Gilson

Beardstown, Illinois
July 4, 1933

📖 *Soccer Circus*
📖 *Hello, My Name Is Scrambled Eggs*
📖 *Thirteen Ways to Sink a Sub*
📖 Itchy Richard Series

About the Author
and the Author's Writing

In the late 1970s, Jamie Gilson took the challenge of a local librarian who asked her to write a book, because "aside from sports stories, there just aren't enough good books for eight- to twelve-year-old boys." Since that challenge Gilson become a popular writer by creating novels and true-to-life narrators like Harvey, Mitch, Sam, and more recently "Itchy Richard." Gilson first observed her own sons, then eleven and twelve years old, and concluded that what interested them and their peers most (after hockey) was collecting beer cans. She taped interviews with several collectors before creating Harvey for *Harvey, the Beer Can King* (Lothrop, 1978). It was not by accident that Harvey and his family's story took place in Pittsfield, Illinois, the town where Gilson had lived as a twelve-year-old.

Gilson was born in Beardstown, Illinois, and spent her early years in several small midwestern towns, where her father worked as a flour miller. At the age of nineteen she entered a recipe contest and won a trip to New York. Scraps from that bake-off inspired one of her narrators, natural food whiz Mitch McDandel, who makes his appearance in *Dial, Leroi Rupert, DJ* (Lothrop, 1979). Mitch became the star and bake-off contestant in the sequel, *Can't Catch Me, I'm the Gingerbread Man* (Lothrop, 1981).

Jamie Gilson has long thought of herself as a social historian, going out to find what children are doing. Her earliest writing, just out of college, was for educational radio and television. "I didn't begin to write books, though, until my children were seven, eleven, and twelve years old."

Her first four books featured sixth-graders, while her fifth book, *Thirteen Ways to Sink a Sub* (Lothrop, 1982), and its sequel, *4B Goes Wild* (Lothrop, 1983), featured fourth-graders. She visited classrooms and took notes, noticing boys against girls much of the time. *Hello, My Name Is Scrambled Eggs* (Lothrop, 1985) came from her involvement with refugees. A Chicago area administrator told her that although there were many novels of immigrants at the turn of the twentieth century, there were few if any books about today's refugees. At about that time Alison Jacobs, a teacher of English as a second language, urged Gilson to mention needlework made by Hmong women from Laos in her monthly *Chicago Magazine* column.

Jacobs who introduced Jamie Gilson to Hmong women and other Loatians, as well as Cambodian and Vietnamese refugees. She decided to write about a Vietnamese family, began collecting stories, talking to a lot of people, including many children, and listening to their experiences. One woman was given a hair dryer on her first night in America and thought it was a gun. That incident is included in *Hello, My Name Is Scrambled Eggs*.

A woman who had come to the United States just after the fall of Saigon helped Gilson understand the importance of small-town life to refugees. On this woman's first day in America she had been at a baton-twirling contest and an ice cream social. Jamie Gilson decided this story should include Harvey and his hometown of Pittsfield. "I began to wonder how Harvey would deal with a new kid in his community—a stranger to such things as hot dogs, Halloween, and snow . . . I did not know in the beginning that Tuan would come to live with Harvey. I had notebooks full of stories before the plot for *Scrambled Eggs* came together. Finally I knew that the setting should be a small town and that Tuan's family would be sponsored by a church group."

Jamie Gilson does extensive research for all of her writing and always has people check her books. In *Scrambled Eggs* a Wilmette boy, originally from Vietnam, a family sponsor, the teacher Alison Jacobs, and Lien Du, a woman who left Saigon several years before the book was written, all checked the book's manuscript for accuracy.

"Sometimes," says Gilson, "I get ideas by chance, as when a Texas boy told me that his class was studying meal worms and his teacher decided that she wanted everyone to see what the worms looked like 'big.' She [the teacher] put them on the overhead projector and, it got really hot, they fried." *Bug in a Rug* (Clarion, 1998) is in the Itchy Richard series.

Gilson feels that it is important for the reader to like the person telling the story, the narrator, because readers will be loyal to a character they like. Harvey is bumbling and makes mistakes, but children stick with him because they know that he is basically a good guy.

Other readers identify with Sam. They say even though they are not dyslexic, they understand his feelings in *Do Bananas Chew Gum?* (Lothrop, 1980). Food plays an important part in Gilson's books, so it is no surprise that another narrator, Mitch McDandel, is a food whiz. People often tell Gilson that they make the banana tofu milkshake from *Can't Catch Me, I'm the Gingerbread Man.*

Gilson says, "One of the joys of writing children's books is the opportunity of talking with them about themselves and about writing. I often visit schools and fill my notebook with story ideas. A fifth-grade class helped me learn soccer to write *Soccer Circus* [Lothrop, 1993]. One boy told me that the best game is played in the mud. I used that. I later spent two weeks with another group of fifth graders before beginning *Wagon Train 911* [Lothrop, 1996] in which a group of kids are working on a big Oregon Trail project. I also note what the boys and girls are saying to and about each other, how they're standing and sitting, and what they're wearing."

The Gilsons live on a curve of Lake Michigan in a suburb of Chicago, Wilmette, where she does most of her research. Sometimes Gilson travels to research, going to an archeological dig in southern Illinois, a bake-off in Miami Beach, or an Outdoor Education camp with a group of fifth-graders in Wisconsin. Gilson has gone to a trike-a-thon that benefited a local nursery school, and has visited schools to check the contents of school lockers and compile lists of things that are in the backs of desks—old notes, an orange eraser with pencil caves in it, a cracked neon-pink water gun, and folded stars that shoot like Frisbees.

Jamie married Jerome Gilson, a trademark lawyer. All three of their children, Thomas, Matthew, and Anne, have earned college degrees and are living in their own homes. Gilson loves to ride her bicycle, cross-country ski, and, of course, sink into a cozy chair and read.

Books and Notes

Itchy Richard Series

Seven-year-old Richard is first introduced to readers when he finds that he has lice in his hair. Later he is embarrassed to wear the purple pants his aunt and uncle give him, but he's more embarrassed when his uncle comes to school. A new boy in class and a science experiment about bats give Richard some new concerns.

Bug in a Rug (Clarion, 1998).

It Goes Eeeeeeeeeeeee! Illustrated by Diane deGroat. (Clarion, 1994).

Itchy Richard. Illustrated by Diane deGroat. (Clarion, 1991).

Other Titles

In Gilson's books she consistently creates characters that readers care about and includes zippy dialogue and plenty of humor. While her narrators for the most part are male (her goal to begin with was to create books for boys), the books include interesting female characters. Her major narrators are Sam Mott, Mitch McDandel, and Hobie Hanson. The list below has been grouped by narrator. Two additional books feature Harvey from *Harvey, the Beer Can King*, and others include new groups of school children.

Hobie Hanson Titles

Double Dog Dare. Illustrated by Elise Primavera. (Lothrop, 1988).

4B Goes Wild. Illustrated by Linda Strauss Edwards. (Lothrop, 1983).

Hobie Hanson, Greatest Hero of the Mall. Illustrated by Anita Riggio. (Lothrop, 1989).

Hobie Hanson, You're Weird. Illustrated by Elise Primavera. (Lothrop, 1987).

Soccer Circus. Illustrated by Dee DeRosa. (Lothrop, 1993).

Sticks and Stones and Skeleton Bones. Illustrated by Dee DeRosa. (Lothrop, 1991).

Thirteen Ways to Sink a Sub. Illustrated by Linda Strauss Edwards. (Lothrop, 1982).

Mitch McDandel Titles

Can't Catch Me, I'm the Gingerbread Man (Lothrop, 1981).

Dial, Leroi Rupert, DJ. Illustrated by John Wallner. (Lothrop, 1979).

Sam Mott Titles

Do Bananas Chew Gum? (Lothrop, 1980).

Harvey Titles

Harvey, the Beer Can King. Illustrated by John Wallner. (Lothrop, 1978).

Hello, My Name Is Scrambled Eggs. Illustrated by John Wallner. (Lothrop, 1985).

Other Titles

Wagon Train 911 (Lothrop, 1996).

You Cheat! Illustrated by Maxie Chambliss. (Bradbury, 1992).

For More Information About/By the Author

Articles

Edmister, Pat. "Teacher's Guide to Jamie Gilson." *Simon Says Kids*. URL: http://www.simonsays.com/kids/teachers/index.cfm (Accessed December 1998).

Includes lesson plans for extension activities for several of Gilson's books.

Carol Gorman

**Iowa City, Iowa
February 16, 1952**

📖 *The Miraculous Makeover
of Lizard Flanagan*

📖 *Chelsey and
the Green-Haired Kid*

📖 *Jennifer-the-Jerk Is Missing*

About the Author
and the Author's Writing

After writing two novels that did not sell, Carol Gorman's third novel, *Chelsey and the Green-Haired Kid* (Houghton, 1988), sold well. Her first published piece was an article called "The Mayberry Method," which was about parenting techniques from the *Andy Griffith Show*. That article was accepted on its first submission, making her think that writing was going to be easy. When rejection letters started coming in she discovered that it was not going to be as easy as she had thought, but by then she was determined to write full-time.

Carol Maxwell Gorman was born in Iowa City, Iowa, and grew up there with a sister and two brothers. Her father was a pediatrician, and her mother took care of the home. During college Gorman studied drama and played Maria in *West Side Story*. For that role Gorman had to dye her hair dark. The next year she played Peter Pan and had to cut off her hair. Gorman says, "The same man who set up the apparatus to fly Sandy

Duncan on Broadway came to Iowa City and brought the equipment that allowed me to fly as Peter Pan. It was wonderful." By the time Gorman earned her college degree, she had established her own family in Iowa. Because there was little opportunity for an actress in Iowa, she became a language arts teacher and taught seventh graders for seven years. After marrying Ed Gorman, she began her writing career. Two of her first books were nonfiction. One was a report titled *Pornography* (Watts, 1988) that raised basic questions about morality, sexuality, and our rights as a free people. An earlier book examined events concerning the farm crisis in the early 1980s, *America's Farm Crisis* (Watt, 1987). The New York Public Library named this book as one of the best nonfiction books of the year for junior and older readers.

Her writing quickly turned to mystery and suspense tales, perhaps because her mother often entertained her with mysteries to solve. Gorman often imagined her own mysteries as well. "Our house was set near a deep ravine. At night it was filled with darkness. One of my best friends lived on the other side of the ravine. We used flashlights to send secret messages back and forth."

She wrote two novels that did not sell well, but her third manuscript, *Chelsey and the Green-Haired Kid*, her first published mystery novel, was cited as an outstanding book for the reluctant reader by the American Library Association. It also earned the Ethical Culture Book Award, and was nominated for three state awards. Gorman says Chelsey's wheelchair confinement was incidental to the story. But Chelsey and her friend Jack (because of his green hair) *are* a little on the edge of the mainstream, bringing the two of them together. Chelsey's wheelchair contributes one of the most chilling episodes of the book. Chelsey and Jack are being chased by the criminals. When they get to "Suicide Hill" Jack hops on Chelsey's wheelchair and both of them sail down the hill. The wheelchair character was inspired by Gorman's experience working at the University of Iowa Children's Hospital. There she saw children and teenagers maneuvering through life in wheelchairs, observed the reactions of others to them, and recognized the same hopes, dreams, and interests as those who were not physically challenged. It seemed natural to have a character in a wheelchair and provided a unique means of escaping the villains. That steep hill in *Chelsey and the Green-Haired Kid* was modeled after a hill in downtown Iowa City. It wasn't called Suicide Hill, but it was steep and dangerous, just as Gorman describes it.

Gorman wrote a number of other titles. *T.J. and the Pirate Who Wouldn't Go Home* (Scholastic, 1990) is the story about a fourteen-year-old boy, and eccentric uncle, and a time machine. When T.J.'s Uncle Ainsley manages to build a time machine, he accidentally transports a pirate from the 1690s to the present. Captain Billy enjoys eating Big Macs, watching game shows, burglarizing stores, and pick-pocketing people—behavior one might expect of a pirate. However, Uncle Ainsley and T.J. are anxious to send him back. Undoubtedly some inspiration for the plot came from Gorman's childhood love of "anything written by Madeleine L'Engle." She also loved Nancy Drew and Trixie Belden.

Gorman's main characters often "have a lot of me in them." Some characters, like Chelsey, have more nerve than Gorman, but there are many other similarities.

Gorman writes four to five pages a day on a computer. She researches extensively before writing. Once she got an idea while eating in a restaurant with her son. The restaurant employs many hearing-impaired individuals, and one young employee was staring at her while he was clearing tables. At least ten times during the meal he caught her eye and smiled. "I never did find out why I received so much of his attention that day, but I turned that incident into the beginning of a manuscript. The young man had witnessed a murder, and the woman having lunch is a TV reporter. He attempts to ask her for help." The idea germinated for years, before Gorman began writing the story. Her research included taking classes in American Sign Language, visiting classrooms with deaf students, and attending a church that held services in sign language. Eventually she changed the story to have Jill's best friend, Valerie, killed by a hit-and-run driver. The only witness was Jill's seven-year-old deaf sister, and when the killer realizes there was a witness, Jill's sister becomes a target.

Another story involves a young woman who is offered money for her education if she spends a year with an Amish family. The idea is that if the rebellious teenager can stay the year, she will be worthy of this investment in her future. Gorman began by reading books about the Amish, then she investigated the Old Order Amish community near her hometown, staying with a family for several days. She attended an Amish wedding, an Amish "sewing" or quilting, and helped can garden produce. She also helped prepare chickens for eating by plucking the feathers, washing, gutting, and cutting them up for cooking. She read by lamp light and shared meals in their homes.

Gorman often weaves bits and pieces of her life into the books. Sometimes a favorite meal (fried chicken and mashed potatoes) shows up in a book. She used the tunnels under her alma mater, West High School in Iowa City, in *Graveyard Moon* (Avon, 1993). At other times it's a character, a name, or an event. "I keep a name file. When I am visiting a school and readers ask me to autograph books, I take notice of interesting first and last names. I enter them into my file and then use those names in the book. Not the same person's first and last names, but an interesting first name with another last name. I also gather names from newspaper and magazine articles."

A two-story house in her hometown and a another large stately-looking house with a half-circle driveway became some of the settings in *Jennifer-the-Jerk Is Missing* (Simon, 1994) and *The Miraculous Makeover of Lizard Flanagan* (Harper, 1994). Gorman and her husband later bought the two-story house.

Gorman writes seven days a week and sets up a demanding schedule. When she is not writing, she enjoys trips to New York to meet with editors and her agent. "I love reading, gardening, having dinner with friends, and going to my aerobics classes." Gorman also spends a lot of time visiting schools. "While I am at schools I look at what the students are wearing, listen to their conversations, and, if I have the chance, talk with them about school and life." All of this, she says, "helps me stay current and in tune with what my readers are experiencing."

Now that her son has graduated from the University of Maryland and is beginning his career in the Midwest, Carol and Ed Gorman share their home in Iowa with several cats.

Books and Notes

Chelsey and the Green-Haired Kid (Houghton, 1988).
 Two unlikely friends, a spunky wheelchair-bound Chelsey, and Jack, a green-haired kid, witness an "accident" and then set out to convince the police that it was no accident.

Die for Me (Avon, 1992).
 A group of friends seem to be targeted to die, one by one, and the person responsible seems to be one of them.

Graveyard Moon (Avon, 1993).
 Kelly's horror begins the night her initiation takes place in a graveyard. She is not sure which of her friends she can trust.

Jennifer-the-Jerk Is Missing (Simon, 1994).
 Malcolm's witnessing of a kidnapping is not believed because he has a reputation for telling stories. His sitter finally believes him, and together they set out to find the kidnappers.

Lizard Flanagan: Supermodel? (Harper, 1998).

A sequel to *The Miraculous Makeover of Lizard Flanagan*. This time "Lizard" is beginning to realize that maybe things are different. Or are they?

The Miraculous Makeover of Lizard Flanagan (Harper, 1994).

"Lizard" wonders what has happened to her friends between last year and this year. They used to like sports just like Lizard did. Now her friends like boys.

T.J. and the Pirate Who Wouldn't Go Home (Scholastic, 1990).

T.J.'s eccentric uncle builds a time machine that transports a pirate into the twentieth century.

For More Information About/By the Author

Articles

Carol Gorman's Web Site. URL: http://www.geocities.com/Athens/Delphi/6765/ (Accessed November 1997).

"Harrison Elementary Visiting Authors: Carol Gorman." URL: http://www.cedar-rapids.k12.ia.us/Harrison/CarolG.html (Accessed November 1997).

McElmeel, Sharron L. "Author Profile: Carol Gorman." *The Book Report* 14, no. 5 (March/April 1996): 22–25.

Mary Downing Hahn

Ghost Stories ◆ Historical Fiction ◆ Contemporary Realistic Fiction

**Washington, D.C.
December 9, 1937**

- 📖 *Anna All Year Round*
- 📖 *Daphne's Book*
- 📖 *The Dead Man in Indian Creek*
- 📖 *Time for Andrew*

About the Author and the Author's Writing

Mary Downing Hahn was the oldest of three children born to Kenneth Ernest and Anna Elisabeth Downing. When she was five her first sibling, a sister Connie, was born. When she was nine her brother, Jack, was born. Their mother taught in the local elementary school, just a few blocks from the family's home. Everyone in College Park (their hometown) knew her and her children. "So whenever we got into trouble our mother almost always found out about it. As a result of Mother's spy network, my brother and I spent much of our childhood under house arrest. My sister behaved herself." As a child Mary was a voracious reader. Her "first and favorites were Milne's Pooh books, followed by Mary Poppins, the Moffat books by Estes, the Nancy Drew books, Albert Payson Terhune's collie stories, *Lassie, Come Home* (which I read at least five times), fairy tales, Dickens' novels, especially *Oliver Twist*, Stevenson's

Treasure Island, Kidnapped and *The Black Arrow*, Edgar Allan Poe, Sherlock Holmes stories—in short, almost anything I could get my hands on."

Hahn attended school in College Park, received and undergraduate degree from the University of Maryland, College Park, in 1960. In 1969 she received a masters degree from the same university. From 1970 to 1974, she returned to the University of Maryland, College Park, to work on a Ph.D. in English literature.

For a time she taught art, worked as a freelance artist, and, finally, while working on her Ph.D., she taught college English courses. In 1975 she became a children's librarian in Prince County, Maryland. She enjoyed using puppets to tell stories, did reference work, and visited schools as a librarian and an author. In 1992 she became a full-time writer.

She was asked about her favorite books and authors while she was a librarian. At the time she said, "The best thing about working in a library is that they pay you to read." She continued, "The children's writers I like best are Betsy Byars, Katherine Paterson, Helen Cresswell, Diane Jones, Joan Aiken, Roald Dahl, Lois Lowry, and, yes, Judy Blume." She said, "I was given a long list of books to read and by the time I had finished I was convinced I could write one of my own. Of course, it turned out to be harder than I thought, but I kept at it until I succeeded."

Hahn's first book, *The Sara Summer* (Clarion, 1979), deals with peer acceptance. The narrator, Emily, is a tall, skinny, shy girl, very unsure of herself and quite self-conscious—just as Hahn was at 12 years of age. "Like Emily, I wasn't as grown up as my friends and often was teased about my height and daydreaming." One of the incidents in the story happened to Hahn. "I once raced a friend home, turned to see if I was winning, and ran into the door, splitting my head open and bleeding all over the rug as a result."

Ideas for Hahn's books come from her memory or observations of her own daughters' experiences. Hahn remembers herself as shy and awkward, loving to read and daydream. She observed the behavior of some of her daughters' friends, and, in *Daphne's Book* (Clarion, 1983), Hahn attempted to address the subject of peer pressure again. When her younger daughter, Beth, read the book when she was sixteen, she immediately recognized her two worst enemies from seventh grade, Sherry and Michelle. " 'You could have at least changed their names, Mom.' Even though Sherry and Michelle had both moved far from Columbia, Maryland, I think Beth was afraid she'd leave high school one afternoon and find the two of them waiting for her, threatening to beat her up because they didn't like the things I'd put in the book about them." But Hahn says, it was worse "when Beth's friends read the book and said that she had been just like Jessica in the seventh grade." Beth considered Jessica quite "wimpy," and was rather annoyed with the situation. She even threatened to sue her mother if Hahn put any more of her life in a book. Her final retort was, "I want to be a writer when I grow up so how am I supposed to write about my life if you've put all the best parts in your books?"

Daphne's Book gave Hahn another opportunity to explore the theme of peer acceptance, a theme of *The Sara Summer* also. "It [the theme in *The Sara Summer*] was rather superficial, and I wanted to explore the problem in more depth. Sara was unacceptable because of her own hostility, and she brought problems on herself. Daphne is victimized for no fault of her own. Her imagination and artistic nature set her apart, as well as her home situation." Hahn dealt with a similar theme in *The Jellyfish Season* (Clarion, 1985). In that book the narrator feels that she is unable to cope with her older cousin.

The rest of Hahn's books might not draw so blatantly on her daughters' lives, but she does say, "In one way or another, every book I write is autobiographical." Settings tend to be places she knows well—the Maryland suburbs, Chesapeake Bay, and West Virginia. "All writers draw on their own experiences, but we exaggerate them, change them, and make them more interesting than they really were. That's why we write fiction!"

Memories of time spent on the Chesapeake Bay beach and a summer sharing a house with relatives inspired *The Jellyfish Season*. "Although the narrator, Kathleen, is the most like me, my younger self resembled Patsy (I could be a real brat!), and my teenage self resembled Fay (I once had a secret sailor boyfriend very much like Joe and got into a lot of trouble with my parents as a result)." Hahn's dog Binky got a role in *Time for Andrew: A Ghost Story* (Clarion, 1994), and she included her childhood friend's prowess at marbles.

"*The Gentleman Outlaw and Me, Eli: A Story of the Old West* [Clarion, 1996] represents my childhood fantasy of running away disguised as a boy. I used to watch the trains rumble past and dream of riding one way out West. Though the wild outlaw days were long gone by then I yearned to have the sort of adventures I watched so avidly at the movies.

Writing about Eliza gave me the chance to act out my never forgotten daydreams." The book, set in 1887, tells the story of Eliza, who disguises herself as a boy and travels toward Colorado in search of her missing father. Before she reaches her father, she falls in with a gentleman outlaw and joins him in his illegal schemes.

Stepping on the Cracks (Clarion, 1991) is set in Hahn's hometown, College Park. She thinly disguised the town as "College Hill." "I lived in Margaret's house, and my best friend Ann lived next door in Elizabeth's house. Passing trains shook my bed at night, the woods and university farm were off limits, the Trolley Stop Shop supplied us with candy, bubble gum, and sodas. As I wrote, it all came back—the bullies I feared, my egregiously unfair sixth grade teacher, my uncle's heroic death in the war, the radio shows I loved, the stars in my grandmother's window, the fatty taste of stew and Spam, shouting 'Step on a crack, break Hitler's back' all the way home from school." The book is set in 1944, and Margaret's brother is fighting in the war. Margaret gains a new perspective of the school bully, Gordy, when she discovers that Gordy is hiding his own brother, an army deserter. Gordy's story continues in *Following My Own Footsteps* (Clarion, 1996). The year is 1945, and, after Gordy's abusive father is arrested, Gordy's grandmother takes the family into her North Carolina home. Gordy has just begun to respond to his grandmother's discipline when his father returns. A third title, *As Ever, Gordy* (Clarion, 1998), describes Gordy and his sister's residence with their older brother after their grandmother dies. Thirteen-year-old Gordy finds himself between the bully he was and the boy his grandmother was helping him become.

A 1997 manuscript explored the Baltimore of 1914 through recollections of Hahn's mother. *Anna All Year Around* will be a chapter book for younger readers. The book gave Hahn the opportunity to " 'know' my mother's father. Ira Plumley Sherwood died when my mother was just 13 years old, a loss she still feels. As a child, it saddened me that I had never known my other grandfather. When I wrote *Anna All Year Round*, however, my mother's father came to life. As a result, I now feel close to a man who died years before I was born."

Mary Downing Hahn and her husband, Norman Jacob, live in Columbia, a planned city, halfway between Baltimore and Washington, D.C. It has a lot of open space and many footpaths. Hahn's two daughters are grown and have both completed art school. Kate graduated from the Chicago Art Institute and works for a nonprofit urban renewal group in Los Angeles. Kate lives in Santa Monica, and, in addition to working, is taking graphic design coursework and learning about computer-generated art. Beth graduated from the Pennsylvania Academy of Fine Arts and now is the academy's website coordinator. Because Beth is just two hours away by train, Hahn sees her more than Kate, but she keeps in touch with both by e-mail and phone.

In addition to her two daughters, Hahn has five nieces, one nephew, and one great-niece, ranging in age from 11 to 30. Her brother's daughter, Meredith, is a lot like Hahn was at age 11. She is a voracious reader. Perhaps Hahn has a whole new generation of subjects for her books.

Hahn's husband, Norman Jacob, manages a large public library in Bowie, Maryland. He often listens when Hahn has a "problem with a book." He proofreads, as well. Sometimes he even accompanies Hahn when she speaks at schools. Students at one school "all wanted his autograph as well as mine. He got a big kick out of that!" When Hahn is not writing she is reading, walking, or traveling. And, "Like most people, I also grocery shop, cook, clean the house, do the laundry, and other boring adult things. I never iron, however. And, to be perfectly honest, I'd rather eat out than cook."

Writing takes up much of her time and she does not draw, paint, or sew as much as she used to. She has thought that she might create a picture book and get back to making puppets and dolls. She does paint pictures of magical creatures for sale at fantasy and science fiction conventions. She and her husband enjoy shopping for antiques, visiting museums, attending concerts and the ballet, as well as hiking and exploring the Maryland countryside.

Books and Notes

While Hahn uses settings, characters, and incidents from her life to create stories for middle-grade readers, she produces many genres—ghost stories, historical fiction, and contemporary realistic fiction. Her books have received a multitude of awards, including three William Allen White Awards. *Time for Andrew* was named the 1997 award winner. The book also received the 1996 California Young Reader Medal, the 1997 Georgia Children's Book Award, the 1996 Texas Bluebonnet Award, the 1996 Utah Children's Book Award, and the 1996 Dorothy Canfield Fisher Children's Book Award (Vermont). The International Reading Association/Children's Book Council Joint Committee selected *Time for Andrew* for "Children's Choices for 1995." *The Doll in the Garden: A Ghost Story* received the 1992 William Allen White Children's Book Award, and *Daphne's Book* received the 1986 White Award. *December Stillness* was selected for the 1990–1991 White Award Master List. *Stepping on the Cracks* was chosen for the 1993–1994 White Award Master List. Selected titles are listed below.

Contemporary Realistic Fiction

Daphne's Book (Clarion, 1983).

The Dead Man in Indian Creek (Clarion, 1990).

December Stillness (Clarion, 1988).

Following the Mystery Man (Clarion, 1988).

The Jellyfish Season (Clarion, 1985).

The Sara Summer (Clarion, 1979).

The Spanish Kidnapping Disaster (Clarion, 1991).

Tallahassee Higgins (Clarion, 1987).

The Wind Blows Backward (Clarion, 1993).

Ghost/Witch Stories

The Doll in the Garden: A Ghost Story (Clarion, 1989).

Look for Me by Moonlight (Clarion, 1995).

Time for Andrew: A Ghost Story (Clarion, 1994).

The Time of the Witch (Clarion, 1982).

Wait Till Helen Comes: A Ghost Story (Clarion, 1986).

Historical Fiction

As Ever, Gordy (Clarion, 1998).

Following My Own Footsteps (Clarion, 1996).

The Gentleman Outlaw and Me, Eli: A Story of the Old West (Clarion, 1996).

Stepping on the Cracks (Clarion, 1991).

For More Information About/By the Author

Articles

"Hahn Wins 1991 Scott O'Dell Award." *Publishers Weekly* 239, no. 6 (January 27, 1992): 23.

"Mary Downing Hahn Biography." URL: http://www.carr.lib.md.us/authco/hahn.htm (Accessed November 1997).

Lynn Hall

Animal Tales ◆ Humorous Stories ◆ Mystery

Lombard, Illinois
November 9, 1937

📖 *Danza*
📖 *Tin Can Tucker*
📖 *Dagmar Schultz and the Angel Edna*
📖 *Here Comes Zelda Claus, and Other Holiday Disasters*

About the Author and the Author's Writing

At the age of seven Lynn Hall ran away from home to join a pony-ride concession. She stayed the afternoon. Unsuccessful at running away, she returned home to spend her preteen and teen years cleaning horse stalls at a local riding stable, hoping to earn an occasional ride. Years later, a love of horses and dogs and a dull office job brought Lynn Hall into a world where she could join the pony-ride concessions, the horse show circuit, endurance races, and enjoy as many exciting adventures with animals as she could imagine. She entered the world of children's books.

As a child, some of her closest "friends" were books, yet the possibility of becoming a writer never occurred to her. She often read library books by flashlight after her bedtime. She thought little about those who created the books, but when she did, she envisioned them as brilliant creatures. She thought of herself as an ordinary offspring in a family of farmers, teachers, and Methodist ministers. Hall's parents used to tell her, "If you aren't good, you're going to grow up and be like the Goat Lady and live in a shack with a bunch of animals."

Her parents were correct. Although her home is far from a "shack," she did grow up to live with a bunch of animals. In 1975 a friend helped translate her sketches into a plan for the house of her dreams. A builder roughed out the home and Hall finished the interior and brick exterior. The result is a stone house built on twenty-five wooded acres overlooking the Volga River Valley near Elkader, Iowa, and it has been her home ever since. She named it "Touchwood" and shares it with her animals. At one time she spent a her leisure time designing and building stables. She had an Arab-Morgan mare, Star, and bred Paso Fino horses for show. It was a Paso Fino stallion that became the subject of her book *Danza* (Scribner, 1981). At first her novels were best characterized as animal stories; however, in later years that focus turned to human relationships and family interactions. *The Horse Trader* (Scribner, 1981), *Tin Can Tucker* (Scribner, 1982), *Half the Battle* (Scribner, 1983), and *Denison's Daughter* (Scribner, 1983) are just a few titles that reflect family relationships themes.

Lynn Hall was born November 9, 1937, in Lombard, Illinois. Her parents, Ray Hall and Alice Seeds Hall, had grown up in Iowa but met in Chicago. The Halls had three daughters, Jan, Lynn, and Lois, the youngest. When Lynn was nine, the family moved to West Des Moines, Iowa. Their house had been the town's first library and later a funeral home. When the Halls moved in, there were still jars of embalming fluid in the basement, escape routes out a window and onto a porch, and a secret room behind the furnace in the crawl space under the front room, where the library had been. While riding along with her dad delivering bulk gas, Lynn found a "seedy riding stable that tolerated kids hanging around." Once discovered, Lynn spent as much time as she could at the stable. In exchange for chores, she was given free riding time. Hall was thirteen when the family moved again, this time to Webster City, Iowa. She babysat, earning 25¢ per hour, and amassed $100 in one year. The money bought her first horse, a little brown mare. Lynn and her best friend, Ann, rode their horses and camped in tents on summer nights. They rode their horses to a bean field to watch a movie—over the fence at the drive-in theater. The two girls and their horses were inseparable. Not long after, the family decided to move back to West Des Moines. The house was smaller and there were no escape routes.

Lynn Hall graduated from Valley High School in West Des Moines. She moved to Colorado and by the mid-1950s Lynn Hall was living in Fort Worth, Texas, working as a secretary. She returned to Des Moines in 1957 and worked as an assistant in a veterinarian's office long enough to know that she did not want to be a veterinarian. On May 1, 1960, she married Dean W. Green. They divorced in September the following year. Prior to her marriage, she had wandered from state to state and job to job figuring she was "just filling in my time until I got married. I guess I probably was looking for a husband, and I found one." When the marriage ended, Hall sat down to think. She did not have a college education, and didn't know if she could provide herself with a good life. She worked in Kentucky, Wisconsin, raising chinchillas and painting pet portraits. She also worked at a number of clerical jobs, none with any real future.

One day, walking past a bookstore near Drake University, she saw a children's book about horses. Hall read that book, not believing all of the mistakes. She knew that she could do better.

She started writing at nights, on weekends, and during vacations. She ignored a few friends who attempted to discourage her by telling her that she would not be able to make a living by writing. She saved enough money from her job and chinchilla venture to quit working for six months, and wrote two books. The first was patterned after the books she had loved from her childhood. Her mentor, Henry Felsen, a local author, told her it was good enough to break into the market twenty years earlier, but she'd have to do better now. She returned to work before any book was accepted for publication but continued to write nights and weekends. Her second book, *The Shy Ones* (Follett, 1967), was her first published book. She received a $400 advance on that book. That day she quit her job. She later joined an advertising agency in Des Moines, and during the next four years wrote radio commercials and pounded out six more books on her typewriter.

There was enough money to give her an escape. She started looking for a place to live, investigating the Ozarks (her parents retired to Arkansas), the Rockies, and Connecticut. She decided to stay in Iowa, living for a time in Clayton, Garnavillo, and Masonville before she found the acreage near the Volga River. She bought a 100-year-old farmhouse in the forest. She began remodeling with her earnings from book royalties. Later she designed and built a new "cottage." It was finally considered finished in 1983. It is made of stone, has stone floors, and has a kennel connected to the house. The design is reminiscent of the European houses where farmers quartered the animals under the house roof. For almost eight years the house had been a hobby. She had nailed floorboards, shingled the roof, and worked alongside the local carpenter, Sox, and his friend Peter. Together they built her dream house. When she moved in, the house was a concrete shell with open joists. She showered with a garden hose and cooked in the fireplace until the stove was installed. She built walls, cupboards, and shelves, laid slate tile on the concrete floor, and, the following year, built the stone exterior and a stone fence around the front lawn. Then she began to buy horses.

During the time Hall was working alongside Sox and Peter, she was also working on the manuscript for a mystery title, *The Tormentors* (Harcourt, 1990). In that book she names the chief protagonist, Sox—no doubt after the carpenter. Sox has a beloved German shepherd that vanishes and sets out to find the thief, becoming involved with a ring of dangerous dog trainers who kidnap animals for illegal profit.

She has lived a solitary life for many years at "Touchwood," raising Paso Fino horses and English Cocker Spaniels. She ran Touchwood Kennels, breeding and showing English Cocker Spaniels that she had trained. Her Collies were also well known. For more than twenty-five years she was a full-time writer, one of those few writers who can earn complete support with their writing. Her leisure time was filled with dog shows, cross-country skiing, riding, swimming, and playing the piano—and of course, reading.

Then in the late 1980s, Lynn Hall decided that she would not deal with big-town publishers anymore. She was getting rejected because "her books were not typical Lynn Hall books." She turned to the dog shows and self-published books that she could sell at the dog shows. By March of 1991, Lynn Hall wrote, "the business [was] seriously foundering, financially, and probably wouldn't last more than another few months." She said she would "continue to write, but only when I want to, maybe an average of a book a year." However, by the mid-1990s it seemed she had stopped writing altogether.

When she first began writing best-selling books, they concerned interpersonal relationships—often between people and their animals, often dogs or horses. One of Lynn Hall's most popular books is *Sticks and Stones* (Follett, 1972), a story that deals with the hurt caused by vicious rumors in a small Iowa town. It was one of the first adolescent books to deal with homosexuality. The setting was Buck Creek, Iowa, a fictional town. She wrote the book while living in Clayton, Iowa, and coincidentally shared some of the same characteristics as a real small town named Buck Creek. The book was nominated for the prestigious Newbery Award. In 1977 it won the Silver Quill Award given in Denmark.

Her horse stories began with the first of a trilogy, *A Horse Called Dragon* (Follett, 1971). The book was rejected three times because publishers felt her style switched when she moved from focusing on the wild horse, Dragon, to people. She rewrote the book three times, finally cutting the book in half. Her publisher bought the revised manuscript, and the book earned the publisher's Charles W. Follett Award. A $3,000 stipend accompanied the award, and it was the first time an animal story had received the award.

About the same time, Hall penned a historical novel about the outstanding St. Bernards. The monks of the St. Bernard hospice in the Swiss Alps trained these dogs, named after the hospice, for snow rescue work. The book *Barry, the Bravest St. Bernard* (Garrard, 1973) was sent to the one of the largest family movie producers for consideration as a made-for-television movie. The company kept the book for two years and then sent it back as not suitable. A few months later the company aired their TV movie about Barry, but Hall did not receive a penny. In 1992 the book was republished by Random House with new illustrations as a book in their Step Into Reading series.

A real-life drama inspired her story *Danza*. While she was researching Danza's story, she encountered a blind stable boy who also worked on his brother's fishing boat. Hall was intrigued. She decided that she would make up the character, because most would not believe the real story. She used the stable boy as a prototype blind character in *Half the Battle*. The story is about two brothers, one blind and one sighted, who prepare for a 100-mile horse endurance race in New Mexico. Her editor said, "A good title is 'half the battle,' " so she decided to use that title for this story.

In 1987 Hall launched a humor and fantasy series with Scribner and produced several mysteries. When asked "how a writer goes from animal stories to mysteries," Hall responded, "It was a pleasant change of pace. . . . I'd always loved reading mysteries and it was simply fun to write them. For one thing, books based on plot are easier to write than books based on less tangible things, like character development, personal relationships, etc." The best-received of Hall's mysteries was probably a young adult novel, *The Killing Freeze* (Morrow, 1988), and for younger readers, *The Mystery of Pony Hollow* (Random, 1992).

Lynn Hall wrote books for children because she wanted to do something interesting, that would give her independence and security. Others could write children's books, but none could write her stories, influenced by her work with and love of animals. That sensitivity shines through in her books about human relationships, as well.

Books and Notes

Animal Tales

Barry, the Bravest St. Bernard. Illustrated by Antonio Castro. (Random, 1992).
Originally published by Garrard in 1973 and republished by Random House as a title in it's Step Into Reading series. Step 4.

The Soul of the Silver Dog (Harcourt, 1992).

Windsong (Scribner, 1992).

Dagmar Schultz Series

Dagmar Schultz and the Angel Edna (Scribner, 1989; Aladdin, 1992).

Dagmar Schultz and the Green-Eyed Monster (Scribner, 1991).

Dagmar Schultz and the Power of Darkness (Scribner, 1989; Aladdin, 1992).

The Secret Life of Dagmar Schultz (Scribner, 1988; Aladdin, 1991).

Dragon Trilogy

A Horse Called Dragon. Illustrated by J. Cellini. (Follett, 1971).
Book 1. Published in paperback by Scholastic, 1976, with the title *Wild Mustang*.

New Day for Dragon. Illustrated by J. Cellini. (Follett, 1975).
Book 2.

Dragon Defiant. Illustrated by J. Cellini. (Follett, 1977).
Book 3.

Mystery

Murder in a Pig's Eye (Harcourt, 1990).

The Mystery of Pony Hollow. Illustrated by Ruth Sanderson. (Random, 1992).

The Mystery of the Phantom Pony. Illustrated by Marie DeJohn. (Random, 1993).

Ride a Dark Horse. (Morrow, 1987).
A "Gusty" McCaw Mystery.

Shadows. Illustrated by Dave Henderson. (Random, 1992).

The Tormentors (Harcourt, 1990).

Other Stories

Fair Maiden (Scribner, 1990).

Flying Changes (Harcourt, 1991).

For More Information About/By the Author

Articles

"Face-to-Face with Lynn Hall." *The Follett Forum* (Fall 1989): 1–3.

Monson, Valerie. "She Writes for Youths Because There's Still Lots of Kid in Her." *Des Moines Register* (April 5, 1983): T-1.

Quimby, Mildred. "East Iowa Author Claims Disney Goof." *Cedar Rapids Gazette* (February 8, 1977): 4.

Schrader, Ann. "Authoress Hall: Creative Urge Isn't Nuisance." *Cedar Rapids Gazette* (January 19, 1975): 5B.

Tanner, Larry. "To Publish: Right Book, Editor." *Cedar Rapids Gazette* (April 17, 1977): 17A.

Wallace, Christie. "She Likes the Challenge of Writing Books for a Living." *Cedar Rapids Gazette* (April 19, 1978): 10B.

Books

Stan, Susan. *Presenting Lynn Hall*. (Twayne, 1996).

Virginia Hamilton

Contemporary Realistic Fiction ◆ Historical Fiction ◆ Fantasy

---
Yellow Springs, Ohio
March 12, 1936

- 📖 *Zeely*
- 📖 *M. C. Higgins, the Great*
- 📖 *The House of Dies Drear*

About the Author
and the Author's Writing

Virginia Hamilton was the fifth child in a family living in Yellow Springs, Ohio. The village had been a station on the Underground Railroad, just seventy miles from the Ohio River and home to Antioch College and the descendants of abolitionists and fugitive slaves. Virginia Hamilton's mother, Etta Belle (Perry) Hamilton, was the oldest daughter of a fugitive slave. Virginia's father, Kenneth James Hamilton, was a musician and an "outlander" who ran gambling halls in mining towns. The family was very poor when Virginia was born during the days of the Depression. Her parents managed to turn the rich soil of the Miami Valley, where their village was situated, into a working farm with plenty of food for the family, and extra to sell by the bushel to other villagers.

She was the "baby" of the family, and, because she was bright and sensitive, she was left to explore. The Perrys were warm-hearted and very private people. They were caring to the sick and to those who were landless. They were also storytellers; her mother was among the best.

Virginia Hamilton still remembers the first story she ever heard. She sat riveted as her mother told her the true tale of her grandfather's escape from slavery when he was a boy. Although he made it to the Underground Railroad and won his freedom, his mother was forced by her owner to go back to the plantation.

Virginia's father, a descendant from a Creole family, was a storyteller too. His family had come from Illinois, Iowa, and many places west. They had wandered far and wide in the United States and Canada. He always fancied himself as a traveling man. Her father knew Jack London and Lemon Jefferson. He, himself, was an exceptional mandolinist. As a young musician he had been rejected for membership in the musician's union simply because he was black. Kenneth Perry often played his mandolin in the dark of night, a comfort to Virginia, who did not like the darkness.

Virginia Hamilton began to write from the time she was seven years old. She said, "I'm a writer, I think, nearly by birth." Her childhood was spent near the Perry Clan in Yellow Springs, Ohio. As she prepared to enter college, she chose Antioch College, the college in her hometown.

Virginia attended Antioch College on a full scholarship. Because she didn't have much money, she couldn't afford the NAL Classic hard covers, which cost $1.50 each, that she loved to read. Learning of her plight, the Antioch college-store manager gave many of the books to her, telling her to pay later and assuring her that there was no hurry—a gesture that endeared her to book-sellers.

Eventually she attended Ohio State University and then, at age 19, moved to New York City. She met Dixieland musicians and began to sing. And it was here that she met poet and anthologist Arnold Adoff. The two met at a party, he a native New Yorker and substitute teacher in Harlem, and she a struggling writer from a small town in Ohio. They married March 19, 1960. Her father, Kenneth Hamilton, died that same year. In 1967 Virginia Hamilton's first book, *Zeely* (Macmillan), was published. Later, Arnold Adoff and Virginia Hamilton built a redwood home in Yellow Springs, Ohio, next to her mother's home on Perry family land. The land, a stone's throw from Antioch College, is part of the family land of Levi Perry, a fugitive slave from Virginia. In the late 1850s, his mother, Mary Cloud, a Potawatomi Indian, brought Levi to Jamestown, Ohio. As a young man, he moved slightly west to Yellow Springs, bought a farm, and raised 10 children. His eldest daughter, Etta Belle, gave birth to a girl named Virginia. Virginia Hamilton and Arnold

Adoff raised a daughter, Leigh Hamilton, and a son, Jaime Leigh, in Yellow Springs as well.

As a college student Hamilton kept a card file on Africa—countries, governments, populations, climates, tribal mores, and languages. Wherever she traveled the file went with her. It was a hobby of sorts. She has said that "the novel *Zeely* came out of my study and writings on Africa." One of her college friends, who was working at Macmillan, recalled a short story Hamilton had written during their college years. Hamilton has said, "I had forgotten about the story, but when she reminded me of the story and suggested that I develop it into a children's book, I took a look at the eighteen pages." The novel did not evolve overnight. It took a long time, but eventually *Zeely* emerged. Hamilton said that she "never really decided to write for children. It just happened, a happy accident." She had thought she might become an athletic instructor, or a singer. She definitely did not want to continue her part-time work bookkeeping or accounting.

Zeely made connections for Hamilton, connections that made becoming a writer possible. The book is the chilling story of 11-year-old Elizabeth "Geeder" Perry and her brother John "Toeboy" Perry. One summer, while visiting their Uncle Ross's farm, Geeder finds a picture of a Watusi queen who resembles Zeely. Zeely is the grown daughter of Mr. Nat Tayber, who rents a corner of their uncle's land. Geeder feels that Zeely *must* be a queen and becomes infatuated with her fantasies—until Zeely brings her back to reality. In reality, Uncle Ross resembles Hamilton's Uncle Lee, a collector of antiques and stray cats. Geeder and Toeboy are much like Hamilton and one of her brothers, acting and sleeping outside in much the same way. However, Hamilton says of Zeely's character, "I never knew anyone like her."

Hamilton's second book, *The House of Dies Drear* (Macmillan, 1967), is a dramatized history of the Underground Railroad in Ohio from a contemporary perspective. The book is a mystery filled with excitement, black history, and strong black family members. Hamilton felt that this book was part of her return to all of her wonderful relatives, honoring them and showing the importance of the black church to her and her family. She also tried to balance the pros and cons of small-town life.

Her third book was a modern fable, *The Time-Ago Tales of Jahdu* (Macmillan, 1969). The story, set in Harlem, is told by Mama Luka, an old woman who cares for Lee Edward after school while his mother is at work. She followed this title with a second Jahdu book, *Time-Ago Lost:*

More Tales of Jahdu (Macmillan, 1973). Hamilton said these books are the "toughest to write." They contain impish heroes and magic.

When asked how her books get started, Hamilton responds, "I just go to the typewriter and the cobwebs vanish."

The Planet of Junior Brown (Macmillan, 1971) was Hamilton's fourth book. Junior Brown is a 262-pound musical prodigy who is over-protected by his neurotic mother. Other characters include a loner, Buddy Clark, and Mr. Pool, a teacher-turned-janitor. This book was selected as a Newbery Honor Book in 1972.

Virginia Hamilton is currently one of the outstanding fiction writers for children and young adults. She has received every major award and honor given to writers of books for young readers. In 1975 she was the winner of the Newbery Medal for *M. C. Higgins, the Great* (Macmillan, 1974). She made history by being the first black woman and writer to receive the award. In addition, she has received the Newbery Honor Book designation for *The Planet of Junior Brown* and *Sweet Whispers, Brother Rush* (Philomel, 1982). She has twice been honored by the International Board on Books for Young People (IBBY).

Hamilton's writing has garnered dozens of awards, including the Newbery Award, the Hans Christian Andersen Award for the body of her work (1992), and the Laura Ingalls Wilder Award and the very prestigious John D. and Catherine C. MacArthur Fellowship, both in 1995. The fellowship is commonly called the "genius award," and Hamilton became the first author of children's books to receive the fellowship, which carries a generous cash stipend for several years. In 1997 Hamilton was the recipient of the Ohioana Book Award in the juvenile category.

Virginia Hamilton and Arnold Adoff continue to live in Yellow Springs on land where Hamilton grew up. Other family members live nearby, some still living on Grandpa Perry's farm, the original Perry settlement.

Hamilton and Adoff spend time on their favorite island, Culebra Island, Puerto Rico. According to Adoff, the island, which is close to St. Thomas, is "populated with people of all colors—white, brown, black, and everything in between." They have black hair, brown hair, and blond hair, but red hair is unusual. Once when he did see a red-haired girl on the island, she inspired his book *Flamboyan* (Harcourt, 1988). Hamilton describes her husband as "a whirlwind; he keeps everything stirred up and crazy." In addition to their frequent trips to Culebra, Hamilton and Adoff spend time in New York City, where they have space in their son and daughter's shared apartment. Leigh is an opera singer, and Jaime, a songwriter, is into pop rock. Adoff and Hamilton do not give out their New York or Culebra Island addresses or phone numbers; those are places where they can get away from intrusions to write, read, attend the opera, and dig in sandy beaches.

Books and Notes

Liberation Literature

In her collections, Hamilton relates "stories told by African Americans in the plantation era." She has gathered the stories and recast them in a colloquial way. "I'm trying to show this liberation literature to a present day audience," she observed. "The oppressed had only their imagination to set themselves free." Hamilton wrote *Her Stories* in honor of her mother, Etta Belle Perry Hamilton, who died in 1990 at the age of 97.

Her Stories: African American Folktales, Fairy Tales, and True Tales. Illustrated by Leo Dillon and Diane Dillon. (Blue Sky, 1995).

Many Thousands Gone: African Americans from Slavery to Freedom. Illustrated by Leo Dillon and Diane Dillon. (Knopf, 1993).

Animal Tales

Early in her career Hamilton retold the *Tales of Jahdu* in several titles, and, more recently, she has retold folktales from the African American culture, especially those featuring tricksters and traditional animal characters.

The All Jahdu Storybook. Illustrated by Barry Moser. (Harcourt, 1991).
A collection of old and new adventures of Jahdu, the trickster.

The Dark Way: Stories from the Spirit World. Illustrated by Lambert Davis. (Harcourt, 1990).

A collection of folktales, legends, and myths involving the supernatural.

Jaguarundi. Illustrated by Floyd Cooper. (Blue Sky, 1995).
Speaks of the threat of extinction facing animals of the rain forest.

A Ring of Twisters: Animal Tales of America, the West Indies, and Africa. Illustrated by Barry Moser. (Blue Sky, 1997).
Twelve trickster tales that show the migration of African culture to America via the West Indies.

When Birds Could Talk and Bats Could Sing: The Adventures of Bruh Sparrow, Sis Wren, and Their Friends. Illustrated by Barry Moser. (Blue Sky, 1996).
Birds populate this collection of stories originally written down by Martha Young on her father's plantation in Alabama in the late 1840s.

Contemporary Realistic Fiction

The Bells of Christmas. Illustrated by Lambert Davis. (Harcourt, 1989).
Describes a family Christmas in 1890 in Springfield, Ohio.

Cousins (Philomel, 1990).
Cammy feels she will be prepared when her grandmother dies, but is unprepared when another relative dies accidentally.

Drysolong. Illustrated by Jerry Pinkney. (Harcourt, 1992).
A young man, Drysolong, relieves the stress of a family living on a drought-ridden farm.

Plain City (Blue Sky, 1993).

Twelve-year-old Buhlaire, a "mixed" child, searches for her roots—a place in her community. In the process she gradually discovers more about her long-absent father.

Fantasy

Dustland (Harcourt [1989], c1980).

Four children are projected into the future to a bleak region called Dustland. Sequel to *Justice and Her Brothers*.

The Gathering (Harcourt [1989], c1981).

Justice and her brothers return to Dustland to destroy the force that threatens the development of their advanced civilization.

Justice and Her Brothers (Harcourt [1989], c1978).

An eleven-year-old and her twin brothers attempt to understand their extrasensory powers.

Other Titles

In the Beginning: Creation Stories from Around the World. Illustrated by Barry Moser. (Harcourt, 1988).

Twenty-five myths about the creation of the world.

The Mystery of Drear House: The Conclusion of the Dies Drear Chronicles (Macmillan, 1988).

A black family, living in the house of Dies Drear (now long-dead), must decide what to do with his stupendous treasure.

For More Information About/By the Author

Articles

Bishop, Rudine Sims. "Virginia Hamilton." *Horn Book* 71, no. 4 (July/August 1995): 442–46.

Cefali, Leslie. "Living History with Virginia Hamilton: Meet the Author's Teachers Guide." *Instructor* 103, no. 6 (February 1994): 64.

Coles, Yolanda Robinson. "Talking with Virginia Hamilton." *American Visions* 10, no. 6 (December/January 1995): 31.

Goldner, Diane. "A Family of Storytellers: Children's Book Author Virginia Hamilton." *Good Housekeeping* 222, no. 2 (February 1996): 22.

Hamilton, Virginia. "Anthony Burns: Acceptance Speech for 1988—Boston Globe-Horn Book Award for Nonfiction." *Horn Book* 65 (March/April 1989): 183–86.

Hamilton, Virginia. "Boston Globe—Horn Book Award Acceptance." *Horn Book* 60 (February 1984): 24–29.

Hamilton, Virginia. "Newbery Award Acceptance." *Horn Book* (August 1975): 337–43.

Speech given at the American Library Association's meeting in San Francisco, California, on July 1, 1975.

Hamilton, Virginia. "Writing the Source: In Other Words." *Horn Book* 54 (December 1978): 609–19.

Hein, Paul. "Virginia Hamilton." *Horn Book* 51 (August 1975): 344–48.

Hopkins, Lee Bennett. "Virginia Hamilton." *Horn Book* 51 (August 1975): 563–69.

"Virginia Hamilton." URL: http://www.virginiahamilton.com/pages/signatureeditions.html (Accessed January 1998).

Marguerite Henry

◆ Animal Tales

Milwaukee, Wisconsin
April 13, 1902–November 26, 1997

📖 *Misty of Chincoteague*
📖 *King of the Wind*

About the Author
and the Author's Writing

For dozens of years the words *horse stories* were synonymous with Marguerite Henry. Her well-researched books have become classics and touchstones for other children's book authors who write in the genre.

Marguerite Henry was born Marguerite Breithaupt on April 13, 1902, in Milwaukee, Wisconsin, the daughter of Louis and Anna Breithaupt. As a child, her three older sisters and one brother doted on her. Birthdays and holidays became occasions for reading original poems and participating in home-written and -produced plays.

Her already grown sister, Marie, made her dresses. Elsie, a young nurse, taught Marguerite the door-knob method of pulling teeth. Fred, her grown brother, would hold her hand and run with her until she flew through space. Her family had one horse, Bonnie. Because Bonnie had a habit of biting Marguerite's older brother, Fred, in the britches, Bonnie was sold. Gertrude, the sister nearest Marguerite's age, became Marguerite's confidant. Printer's ink got in her blood when her father allowed

Marguerite to read proofs in her father's print shop—a shop that yielded a treasure of big fat tablets and bundles of pencils that wrote in big black swathes. Marguerite attended Milwaukee's Teaching College and after graduating met and married Sidney Crocker Henry. They settled into an apartment in Chicago and Marguerite Henry began writing for publications such as *The Nation's Business* and *Saturday Evening Post*. Soon the Henrys moved to a little cottage in Freeport, Illinois. Their cook, Beda, and Beda's husband, Effendi, became the subject of Henry's first book, *Anno and Tauna* (A. Whitman, 1940). Henry collected their tales of Finland. *Dilly Dally Sally* was also published that same year (Saalfield, 1940). The Henrys left their cottage and moved to a two-acre plot with a weathered cottage near Wayne, Illinois, called "Mole Meadow."

Henry began writing horse stories in 1945 after receiving a letter about the legend of the Spanish Moor ponies. It is said that the ponies were washed into the sea centuries ago, when a Spanish galleon was wrecked in a hidden reef. The descendants of these horses ran wild on Assateague Island. One day a year, the oyster men and clam diggers on the island turn cowboy and round up the wild ponies, drive them into the sea, and swim them to their own island, Chincoteague Island, to be sold at a big auction during Pony Penning Days. Wesley Dennis, an illustrator, and Henry went to Pony Penning Days, returning with a story and one of the ponies. Henry named the pony Misty. That was the beginning of *Misty of Chincoteague* (Rand, 1947). The story centers around Paul and Maureen Beebe, who have their hearts set on buying Phantom at Pony Penning Days. They are delighted when they learn they can purchase Phantom's colt, Misty, also. Through Misty, the Beebes are able to calm Phantom and win an exciting race. Phantom escapes back to the island, but Misty remains with the Beebes. Henry flew to Chincoteague Island many times to immerse herself in the quaint and special vocabulary of the area.

In reality, Misty remained at Mole Meadow in the Henrys' pasture. In the spring of 1957, Misty was sent back to Chincoteague. Her farewell fodder was a combination of oats and lumps of sugar. Henry's publisher sent $20 worth of carrots. In addition to Misty, the Henry pasture was home to Friday, a Morgan horse, a western burro (the model for Brighty), three fox cubs for *Cinnabar*, assorted families of cats and kittens, and a lively dachshund named Alex.

Readers wrote begging Henry to write a sequel to *Misty* (Rand, 1947), but a story was not in the making. That is, not until Henry was in Austria researching material for *White Stallion of Lipizza* (Aladdin, 1994). A tidal storm swept over the islands of Chincoteague and Assateague, and one sentence in a New York newspaper threw Henry into a panic: "Misty, the pony of story book fame, has been brought into the kitchen of the Beebe family to await the birth of her foal." Twenty-four hours later Henry was there. Misty and her colt, Stormy, were doing fine. The once beautiful island, now mauled by the sea, provided the story. She had her sequel, *Stormy Misty's Foal*. Misty's second foal was named Wisp O'Mist. In 1961 a film based on *Misty of Chincoteague* was produced by Twentieth Century Fox. Three different horses played the role of Misty.

Life Magazine carried three picture stories about Misty (June 10, 1957; May 23, 1960; May 25, 1961). *National Geographic* carried a story about Misty and Stormy in their December 1962 issue. According to a newspaper article in the *Cedar Rapids Gazette* (Wednesday, October 18, 1972), Misty died on October 16, 1972, at the age of twenty-six. Ralph Beebe said at the time that the brown and white pony "will be mounted by a taxidermist and placed in her stall on his ranch." The Beebes had Misty with them for fifteen years.

Henry's other books came from the same diligent research as the books about Misty. *King of the Wind* (Rand, 1948) tells the story of an Arabian horse befriended by the Earl of Godolphin, who recognizes the small horse for its true value. This Newbery Award story is more than a horse story. It is the tale of the devotion of a young deaf mute boy and his lifelong relationship with the horse. Henry searched old books and yellowed manuscripts about Morocco, France, and England to trace the life story of the Godolphin Arabian who had rubbed shoulders with sultans and kings. She researched the origin of Morgan horses for her book *Justin Morgan Had a Horse* (Rand, 1954). And Annie Bronn Johnston was the inspiration for *Mustang, Wild Spirit of the West* (Rand, 1966), a story of the fight to protect the wild horses of the west. Horse lovers of all ages joined with "Wild Horse Annie" to convince federal legislators to pass a bill giving congressional protection for the mustangs. *Brighty of the Grand Canyon* (Rand, 1963) required many trips to the Grand Canyon. Henry spent weeks there riding up and down the dangerous trails first pounded out by Brighty's hoofs. When she researched *Gaudenzia, Pride of the Palio* (Rand, 1960) she made three trips to Italy to sample the flavor of the old walled city of Siena and the ancient customs of the famous Palio race. The book was republished with the title *The Wildest Horse Race in the World* (Rand, 1976). Several other titles, including

Sire of Champions (Checkerboard, 1988), and *The Rescue of Sham* (Checkerboard, 1988) have been excerpted from Henry's *King of the Wind* and adapted for younger readers. The short books, 24 pages each, are meant for the late primary reader.

Henry was inspired to write *San Domingo* (Rand, 1972) when she received a letter one December from a fourth-grade boy. The letter, accompanied by one from his teacher, told of an abused boy who had a much-loved horse that his father sold while the boy was in school. The boy became a model for the character, but to protect the boy's identity, Henry changed the setting to the Old West and created a character who worked for the Pony Express. She went to great lengths so there would be no repercussions on Andy by his father. San Marino's Huntington Library was renowned for its collection of diaries for the period she had chosen. One handwritten ledger gave Henry the character of the boy's father, Hugh Glass, a dauntless frontiersman, whom she named Jethro Lundy. She and her artist traveled the Oregon Trail through the Nevada Territory, through Utah, and through the vast territory of Nebraska, to the starting point of St. Joseph, Missouri. Rand McNally later published the story as *Peter Lundy and the Medicine Hat Stallion* (Rand, 1976).

In addition to the movie about Misty, *King of the Wind*, *Brighty of the Grand Canyon*, and *Justin Morgan Had a Horse* were made into movies.

Henry choose to write about horses because "it is exciting." The fact that horses, as heavy as a full ton, can be trained to be led by a piece of string intrigued her. She said, "This to me is a constant source of wonder and challenge." Henry's writing brought hundreds of fan letters. For a time her publisher answered the questions her readers asked in a newsletter. Many of the questions and answers were incorporated into a book, *Dear Readers and Riders* (Rand, 1969). The book answered many questions about what was real and what was fiction in her books. Wesley Dennis illustrated all her earlier books, and after his death, Henry established a collaboration with Robert Lougheed. Their illustrations became as much of a trademark for Henry's books as her fluid narratives. In later years, a variety of illustrators have contributed to Henry's published writings.

Marguerite Henry's youngest sister, Gertrude Breithaupt Judd, lived all her life in the Milwaukee area and often read Henry's manuscripts. Henry is often quoted as saying, "Editors could be wrong, but not Gertrude." Gertrude also assisted Henry by dealing with correspondence and responding to requests for permissions and interviews.

In the early 1970s, the Henrys moved to Rancho Santa Fe, California, where at the time she said, "there are more horses than people." The Henrys had no children of their own, but she often took suggestions for writing from her nieces, nephews, and neighborhood children. In 1989 the last parcel of the Beebe land on the islands was offered for sale in a Washington, D.C., newspaper. Henry immediately called friends in Virginia and together they established the Misty Foundation, dedicated to preserving part of the land and legend of the real Misty and Stormy. Henry was named honorary president. For more than seven years, the foundation raised funds and eventually established a memorial on six-tenths of an acre in an area known as "The Thicket"—an area where Misty had roamed. On July 29, 1997, a life-size statue of Misty, created by equine master sculptor Brian Maughan, was unveiled. An equine museum and education center is also planned. Wesley Dennis's son, Morgan Dennis; representatives of the foundation; and descendants of Grandma and Grandpa Beebe were present at the unveiling. Marguerite Henry was the foundation's honorary president until her death in November 1997. Pennsylvania resident Kendy Allen, owner of Misty II (the great-granddaughter of the original Misty), serves as honorary spokeswoman and ambassador, and chairs the Chincoteague Benefit Auction. Paul Newman's salad dressing company, Newman's Own, and thousands of other donors support the foundation.

Marguerite Henry died in her home in Rancho Santa Fe on November 26, 1997. She had suffered several strokes in the mid-1990s, and a family friend, Susan Foster Ambrose, cared for her. Henry died of complications from those strokes. At the time of her death she had written 59 books, which had been translated into 12 languages.

Books and Notes

Rand McNally originally published the majority of Marguerite Henry's books. Simon and Schuster, Aladdin (paperbacks), Checkerboard Press, and Macmillan publish many titles. For the most part, in the narrative above, the original Rand McNally publication date is used. In the book lists below, current editions are cited.

Album of Horses. Illustrated by Wesley Dennis. (Aladdin, 1993).
Originally published by Rand McNally in 1951. Describes breeds of horses.

Brown Sunshine of Sawdust Valley. Illustrated by Bonnie Shields. (Simon, 1996).
Molly wants a horse of her own, but when her father's mare gives birth to a mule, Molly decides to keep the mule as her own.

Marguerite Henry's Album of Horses: A Pop-up Book. Illustrated by Ezra N. Tucker. (Aladdin, 1993).
A toy moveable book.

Misty of Chincoteague. Illustrated by Wesley Dennis. (Checkerboard, 1988).

Misty's Twilight. Illustrated by Karen Jaus Grandpre. (Macmillan, 1992; Aladdin, 1996).
Captivated by the story of "Misty of Chincoteague," a woman with a horse farm in Florida raises one of Misty's descendants to become a champion show horse.

Our First Pony. Illustrated by Rich Rudish. (Aladdin, 1997).
Justin and Joey, twins, buy and raise a pony. When the pony foals, the boys find they are responsible for a whole new pony family.

San Domingo: The Medicine Hat Stallion. Illustrated by Robert Lougheed. (Aladdin, 1992).
Pre–Civil War story of a boy and his hostile father, who trades the boy's beloved horse to the Pony Express.

White Stallion of Lipizza. Illustrated by Wesley Dennis. (Macmillan, 1994).
The story of the dancing white horses that entertained royalty. The breed survives today.

For More Information About/By the Author

Articles

Henry, Marguerite. "A Weft of Truth and a Warp of Fiction." *Elementary English* 51 (October 1974): 920–25.
Tells of the beginnings and research of the story *San Domingo*.

Misty of Chincoteague Foundation, Inc. URL: http://www.modelhorses.com/mcf/mcf.html (Accessed December 1997).

Information About the Misty of Chincoteague Foundation, Inc.

Attn: Foundation Secretary, Misty of Chincoteague Foundation, P.O. Box 212, Chincoteague, VA 23336.

Clifford B. Hicks

Marshalltown, Iowa
August 10, 1920

📖 *Alvin Fernald, Foreign Trader*
📖 *Alvin's Secret Code*

About the Author
and the Author's Writing

Clifford B. Hicks was born in 1920 in Marshalltown, Iowa, the son of Nathan LeRoy and Kathryn Marie (Carson) Hicks. He attended Northwestern University, living in Pearson Hall from 1940 to 1942. According to Northwestern's June 13, 1942, commencement program, Clifford Bryon Hicks obtained an undergraduate degree in science and graduated with honors. During World War II he served in the U.S. Marine Corps. As a lieutenant serving in the South Pacific, he was involved with the battle at Bougainville, September 16, 1944. When members of his unit were wounded, he returned to help. For his bravery, he was awarded a Silver Star. He returned in 1945 and married Rachel Reimer. He began writing for the *Des Moines Register and Tribune*, a daily newspaper in Des Moines, Iowa, and for a number of years was an associate editor of *Popular Mechanics* magazine. One of his first published works was a book for adults, *Popular Mechanics Do-It-Yourself Materials Guide* (Popular Mechanics, 1955). Four years later, his first children's book, *First Boy on the Moon* (Winston, 1959), was published, and a year later the first of the Alvin Fernald books was published. *The Marvelous Inventions of Alvin Fernald* (Winston, 1960) included information about Alvin's inventions, including Supersecret Eavesdropper, the One-Jerk Bed Maker, and the Automatic Man Trap.

Alvin, a 12-year-old boy, was the most well known kid in Riverton, Indiana, because of his numerous scrapes and adventures. He had short blond hair, like his police sergeant father, and more freckles on one side of his face than the other. Alvin is said to have been based on a composite of Hicks's three sons, David, Douglas, and Gary.

In *Alvin Fernald, Superweasel* (Holt, 1974), Alvin mounts a campaign against pollution in Riverton, Indiana. He wears a unique costume and leaves messages signed "Superweasel." His campaign is going great until an impostor appears and begins committing destructive acts. Another book sparked readers' interest in codes and ciphers. In *Alvin's Secret Code* (Holt, 1963) Hicks uses codes and ciphers to create critical elements of the plot. At the beginning of the story, Alvin finds a mysterious message on a scrap of paper. Alvin takes it to a former U.S. spy to find out its meaning. In the book Mr. Link helps Alvin understand the difference between codes and ciphers, and, in the process, Alvin learns that his discovery is not a secret message from a Russian spy. Information about codes and ciphers comes in handy as Alvin uses his cryptography knowledge to help his dad save money on a stereo, to rescue Mr. Link, and to find a hidden treasure.

Alvin's best friend was Shoie, the best athlete in Roosevelt School, although he didn't always like that role. At times he seemed to trip over his own limbs. He was the star of Roosevelt football and basketball teams, and he could throw a baseball farther than anyone else.

Alvin's younger sister, Daphne, was nicknamed "The Pest." The Pest idolized Alvin and always managed to elude his Foolproof Burglar Alarm to join the action. The Pest wore Alvin's outgrown jeans rather than dresses, and carried a football or baseball wherever she went.

Hicks's character Peter Potts starred in three titles, but never had the popularity that Alvin Fernald gained. The popularity of books about Alvin Fernald have spanned two decades. As recent as 1992, one of the books, *Alvin Fernald, Mayor for a Day* (S. French, 1992), was adapted as a play by S. French Publishers. The series has been translated into three foreign languages, and some of Alvin's scrapes led him onto episodes of "The Wonderful World of Disney." Few if any of the books authored by Hicks have been available for purchase during the last few years. Where they are available in libraries, they continue to be read with interest. Clifford B. Hicks has retired and now lives in Brevard, North Carolina.

Books and Notes

Alvin Fernald, Foreign Trader (Holt, 1966).

Alvin Fernald, Master of a Thousand Disguises. Illustrated by Eileen Christelow. (Holt, 1986).

Alvin Fernald, Mayor for a Day: A Juvenile Play in Two Acts (S. French, 1992).

Alvin Fernald, Superweasel. Illustrated by Bill Sokol. (Holt, 1974).

Alvin Fernald, TV Anchorman. Illustrated by Laura Hartman. (Holt, 1980).

Alvin's Secret Code (Holt, 1963).

Alvin's Swap Shop. Illustrated by Bill Sokol. (Holt, 1976).

First Boy on the Moon (Winston, 1959).

The Peter Potts Book of World Records: A True Account of the Astounding Feats of Peter Potts and Joey Gootz, as Witnessed and Sworn to by Me, Peter Potts. Illustrated by Kathleen Collins Howell. (Holt, 1987).

Pop and Peter Potts. Illustrated by Jim Spence. (Holt, 1984).

The Wacky World of Alvin Fernald. Illustrated by Laura Hartman. (Holt, 1981).

World Above (Holt, 1965).

For More Information About/By the Author

Articles

About the Author–Clifford B. Hicks. URL: http://members.xoom.com/AlvinFernald/author.htm (Accessed December 1998).

Lee Bennett Hopkins

◆ Poetry

**Scranton, Pennsylvania
April 13, 1938**

- 📖 *Been to Yesterdays:
  Poems of a Life*
- 📖 *Side by Side*
- 📖 *Hand in Hand: An American
  History Through Poetry*

About the Author
and the Author's Writing

Lee Bennett Hopkins was teaching in New Jersey when he found a slim volume of poetry by Myra Cohn Livingston, *Whispers and Other Poems* (Harcourt, 1958). He searched for more poetry, reading and sharing the poetry of such notables as David McCord, John Ciardi, and Eve Merriam. He became a poetry addict.

After six years at Fair Lawn Elementary, Hopkins went to work for Bank Street College of Education in New York City. One day, he was searching for poems by Langston Hughes to share with his students. He managed to find just one volume, *The Dream Keeper and Other Poems* (Knopf, 1932), an outdated volume with stereotypical illustrations. The day after Langston Hughes died (May 22, 1967), he called Virginie Fowler Elbert, an editor at Knopf, to protest the lack of a newer book of

Hughes's poetry. Elbert invited him to lunch and then asked Hopkins to compile a new collection. *Don't You Turn Back: Poems by Langston Hughes* (Knopf, 1969) became the first book of poetry Lee Bennett Hopkins compiled. Ann Grifalconi illustrated that new edition. It was named a 1969 ALA Notable Book. (In 1994 Knopf published a new edition of *The Dream Keeper* with illustrations by Brian Pinkney. Lee Bennett Hopkins wrote the introduction.)

Lee Bennett Hopkins spent his first ten years at 806 Philo Street in Scranton, Pennsylvania, where he was born April 13, 1938. All three of the Hopkins children were born there—Lee Bennett in 1938, Donald George in 1941, and Donna Lea in 1947. His father was a police officer and his mother a homemaker. They were the typical nuclear family. In the late 1940s the family decided to move to Newark, New Jersey. The rest of his childhood was not idyllic. The family moved in with an aunt and uncle and their three children. With both of Hopkins's parents, a brother, and a sister, there were ten people living in a small apartment. Eventually Hopkins's family located an affordable basement apartment in an inner-urban area in the Seth Boyden Project. By the time Hopkins was thirteen, they had moved to a railroad flat in another section of Newark. A year later his father left the family, and they did not see him again for thirty-six years. His mother took up housework to keep the family together. Lee often stayed home to take care of his sister, Donna Lea.

He was out of school a great deal. A teacher, Mrs. Ethel Kite McLaughlin, introduced Lee to two things, reading and the theater. Both gave him hope and direction. Hopkins did manage to finish school and worked his way through college, becoming an elementary teacher. His first teaching assignment was at a modern, well-provisioned school in New Jersey, where the principal, Mrs. Haenechen, took an interest in his career. She became his mentor and eventually arranged for a scholarship for him to the Bank Street School of Education. He continued to teach so that he could use part of his meager salary to send his sister to a private school. He taught disadvantaged children in programs that he was designing while teaching at Bank Street College in New York City. During his teaching years he continued to spend much time reading to his students. One of the first books he read was Maurice Sendak's *Where the Wild Things Are*—still one of his favorites.

He also read poetry, finding that it often appealed to those who were difficult to motivate. He was always searching for new poets and poetry for his students. After his Langston Hughes poetry anthology, Hopkins proposed a series of holiday poetry collections to Harcourt Brace Jovanovich. They were interested. Hopkins sifted through literally thousands of poems each time he created one of his anthologies. Eventually, he identified twenty or so poems for the collection. Within each thematic collection he seeks a balance of voices—no more than three poems by any one poet. He also attempts to create a progression and flow within each volume. His first selection identifies approximately 200 poems, and then he begins to reread to make a final cut. He looks for poems where the last word of one poem will lead into the next. He also seeks to arrange the poems in a logical content sequence. For example, when Hopkins compiled the poems for *My Mane Catches the Wind: Poems About Horses* (Harcourt, 1979) he began with a poem about a foal and ended with a poem about the death of an old mare. Thus, in addition to being a thematic-based collection it also dealt with the life cycle. Hopkins also attempts to balance the collection between well-known poets, such as Aileen Fisher and David McCord, and new poets. Given a choice, he favors contemporary poets and poetry. Not only does Hopkins search original books of poetry for suitable poems, he solicits new poems from his "take-out" poets from around the country. He says, "I write to them and tell them what theme I'm working on. Often they respond with a wonderful poem that ends up in my collection." Because most poetry he uses is not in the public domain, he must pay republishing fees to the poets whose poems he uses. For that reason, his books cost "a lot of money to produce." But, Hopkins says, "I would rather pay the high fees and have a better book than fill them up with all that public domain poetry. There are good poems in the public domain; the point being that poems should not be used just because they are free for the using."

In fact, for ten years the idea of compiling a book of poems about dinosaurs was in Hopkins's files. He imagined that there would be a lot of poems about dinosaurs, but he was wrong. When he finally began locating the poems, he decided to focus on nonfiction aspects of dinosaurs rather than collecting humorous poems. Many poems (eight out of the eighteen in the book) were commissioned.

In the early 1980s Hopkins was asked to compile a poetry book for early readers. In addition to his own criteria, he was asked to confine the poems he selected to those that were no longer than thirteen lines including the title, and contained no lines longer than thirty-eight characters. He worked for over two years on the first "I Can Read" volume.

Surprises was published by Harper in 1984. A second volume, *More Surprises* (Harper, 1987), was published three years later.

Hopkins normally does not repeat poems from one collection to another. However, in 1985, the Children's Book Council asked him to create a poem for National Book Week—a poem that would fit on a bookmark. He created a poem titled "Good Books, Good Times!" Later, because it fit the criteria, he included the poem in *More Surprises*. He had been thinking of creating a collection of poems about the joys of reading. In 1990 the book *Good Books, Good Times!* (Harper) was published. Five years later, twenty-one of his own poems were published in *Good Rhymes, Good Times* (Harper, 1995). Those poems focused on the good times of childhood, from favorite pastimes to the quiet magic of seasons.

Hopkins created three more "I Can Read" volumes of poetry—*Blast Off! Poems About Space* (Harper, 1995), *Questions* (Harper, 1992), and *Weather* (Harper, 1994). Lee Bennett Hopkins has said, "Poetry is my passion. I love both reading and writing poems. So much can be said with few words and lines. The power of poetry forever mystifies me."

He has used his writing and anthologies to share his life. Grace Clarke of Simon and Schuster arranged a lunch meeting between Hopkins and Hilary Knight, an illustrator, to discuss the possibility of working together on a 96-page, full-color volume of poetry. Hopkins and Knight liked each other from the beginning and their friendship resulted in a wonderful collection of poems, *Side by Side* (Simon, 1988). Hopkins included many of his favorite poems, classics side by side with contemporary voices and thoughts. A favorite or two of Knight's were also included. Knight placed a boyhood picture of Hopkins in front of the house where he was born in Scranton, Pennsylvania. On that same page (80), Knight placed himself as a child on the right side. Hopkins's novels *Mama* (Knopf, 1977; Simon, 1992) and *Mama and Her Boys* (Harper, 1981; Simon, 1993) share much of the struggles Hopkins, his mother, and his siblings endured during those years in Newark, New Jersey. In 1995 *Been to Yesterdays: Poems of a Life* (Wordsong/Boyds Mills, 1995) was published. The poems share the span and depth of Hopkins's life from childhood to present.

Lee Bennett Hopkins is the recipient of the University of Southern Mississippi Medallion for "lasting contributions to children's literature." Five of his books have been honored with a Notable Books designation of the American Library Association. He has served on the board of directors of the National Council of Teachers of English (NCTE) and has twice chaired the NCTE Poetry Award Committee, first in 1978 and again in 1991. To encourage the recognition of poetry, he has established and created two major awards. In 1993 he established and funded the Lee Bennett Hopkins Poetry Award, presented annually since 1993 by the Children's Literature Council of Pennsylvania. In 1995 he established and funded the Lee Bennett Hopkins/International Reading Association (IRA) Promising Poet Award. That award is presented every three years.

He believes that poetry "should flow freely in the lives of children; it should come to them as naturally as breathing." And for himself, he says, "Every day is Poetry Time."

From a child in the projects, whose family struggled for existence, Lee Bennett Hopkins has emerged as "Mr. Poetry." Everything he writes, everything he does professionally, seems to aim toward bringing poetry into the lives of children. After living in New Jersey, then New York, Hopkins finally moved to a home in Westchester County, New York, where he has a glorious view of the magnificent Hudson River. He had always been a "city boy," and now he is surrounded by nature. The new setting gives him another perspective. He works there and in a garden apartment in a nineteenth-century brownstone building in New York's Greenwich Village. Wherever he is, he is gathering ideas for his writing. His beloved Cavalier King Charles Spaniel, Royal Dude, is always at his side.

Books and Notes

"I Can Read" Poetry

Blast Off! Poems About Space. Illustrated by Melissa Sweet. (Harper, 1995).

More Surprises. Illustrated by Megan Lloyd. (Harper, 1987).

Questions. Illustrated by Carolyn Croll. (Harper, 1992).

Surprises. Illustrated by Megan Lloyd. (Harper, 1984).

Weather. Illustrated by Melanie Hall. (Harper, 1994).

Other Anthologies

All God's Children: A Book of Prayers. Illustrated by Amanda Schaffer. (Harcourt, 1998).

April, Bubbles, Chocolate: An ABC of Poetry. Illustrated by Barrett Root. (Simon, 1994).

Been to Yesterdays: Poems of a Life. Illustrated by Charlene Rendeiro. (Wordsong/Boyds Mill, 1995).

Climb Into My Lap: Poems to Read Together. Illustrated by Kathryn Brown. (Simon, 1998).

Extra Innings: Baseball Poems. Illustrated by Scott Medlock. (Harcourt, 1993).

Flit, Flutter, Fly: Poems About Bugs and Other Crawly Creatures. Illustrated by Peter Palagonia. (Doubleday, 1992).

Good Books, Good Times! Illustrated by Harvey Stevenson. (Harper, 1990).

Good Rhymes, Good Times: Original Poems. Illustrated by Franc Lessac. (Harper, 1995).

Hand in Hand: An American History Through Poetry. Illustrated by Peter M. Fiore. (Simon, 1994).

Happy Birthday: Poems. Illustrated by Hilary Knight. (Simon, 1991).

It's About Time: Poems. Illustrated by Matt Novak. (Simon, 1993).

Let Them Be Themselves (Harper, 1992).

Marvelous Math: A Book of Poems. Illustrated by Karen Barbour. (Simon, 1997).

On the Farm. Illustrated by Laurel Molk. (Little, Brown, 1991).

Opening Days: Sports Poems. Illustrated by Scott Medlock. (Harcourt, 1996).

Pterodactyls and Pizza: A Trumpet Club Book of Poetry. Illustrated by Nadine Bernard Westcott. (Trumpet, 1992).

School Supplies: A Book of Poems. Illustrated by Renee Flower. (Simon, 1996).

Small Talk: A Book of Short Poems. Illustrated by Susan Gaber. (Harcourt, 1995).

Song and Dance: Poems. Illustrated by Cheryl Munro Taylor. (Simon, 1997).

Through Our Eyes: Poems and Pictures About Growing Up. Illustrated by Jeffrey Dunn. (Little, Brown, 1992).

Weather: Poems. Illustrated by Melanie Hall. (Harper, 1994).

Novels

Mama. Illustrated by Stephen Marchesi. (Simon, 1992).

Mama and Her Boys. Illustrated by Stephen Marchesi. (Simon, 1993).

For More Information About/By the Author

Articles

Phelan, Carolyn. "Two Poets." *Booklinks* (July 1994): 41–45.

Stan, Susan. "Conversations: Lee Bennett Hopkins." *The Five Owls* (March/April 1996): 81–82.

Books

Hopkins, Lee Bennett. *The Writing Bug*. Illustrated by Diane Rubinger. (R. C. Owen, 1993).

Langston Hughes

◆ Poetry

Joplin, Missouri
February 1, 1902–May 22, 1967

📖 *The Dream Keeper and Other Poems*
📖 *Don't You Turn Back: Poems by Langston Hughes*
📖 *The Sweet and Sour Animal Book*

About the Author
and the Author's Writing

Langston Hughes became "The Poet Laureate of Harlem." He was very involved in writing about black culture, dealing with the suffering of blacks in America and Africa. He was one of the earliest black activists, and his writing and stories were ahead of his time. He published works in all forms of literature, but became best known for his poetry and his sketches about a black man, Jesse B. Simple. During his lifetime Langston Hughes become one of the dominant voices in American literature, and many thought he was *the* most influential black poet.

Langston Hughes was born in Joplin, Missouri, on February 1, 1902, but spent most of his childhood, between the years of 1903 and 1915, in Lawrence, Kansas. He was named James Langston Hughes but was known as Langston Hughes throughout his life. His parents, Carrie Langston Hughes and James Hughes, separated shortly after he was born. Carrie Langston Hughes took her son to her mother's home at 732

Alabama Street in Lawrence, Kansas. Langston's father went to Mexico to avoid the racism he encountered in the United States. During first grade Langston attended school in Topeka, Kansas, where his mother had a job. By the beginning of second grade, Hughes had returned to his grandmother's home. Langston's mother went to live in Detroit and later Cleveland. Langston entered second grade at Pinckney School at 801 West 6th Street in Lawrence. At Pinckney all the black children at the primary level were segregated into one room and taught by a black teacher.

Periodically Mary Langston would rent out her home, and she and Hughes would move in with her friends, the Reeds, at 731 New York Street. Hughes called the Reeds "Auntie" and "Uncle" even though they were not blood relatives. It was his Auntie Mary Reed, the Sunday School superintendent for many years at the Saint Luke's AME (African Methodist Episcopal) church, who influenced Langston to attend church, if somewhat reluctantly. Later he said that the rhythm in those churches influenced his poetry. While Langston and his grandmother lived at the Reeds, he attended the New York School. He was remembered as a bright and independent thinking student.

By the time Langston Hughes entered the eighth grade at Central School, he began to protest the racism he was subjected to. At Central he was taught by Ida Lyons, who moved all the black children to what Langston called the "Jim Crow" row. The protest by Langston and his friends resulted in their suspension. Their reinstatement came only after a prominent African American physician, Dr. Grant Harvey, intervened. That was the year that Langston Hughes began to write poetry. His writing was influenced by the work of Paul Laurence Dunbar and Carl Sandburg. He was selected class poet.

Langston Hughes joined his mother in Cleveland and attended high school there. After graduation, he went to Mexico where he spent the next fifteen months with his father. Despite this time together, Hughes has said that his relationship with his father was never very strong. On the other hand, his mother was very supportive of his writing, especially his poetry. After returning to the United States, Langston Hughes entered Columbia University. He studied engineering, but left after only one year to pursue writing. By 1923 he was a member of the crew of *SS Malone* bound for Africa, where the ship visited thirty or more ports. Before returning to New York City, Hughes lived in Paris, Venice, and Genoa.

Hughes later continued his college career after receiving a scholarship to Lincoln University in Pennsylvania. He was a prolific writer, devoting more than 40 years to writing and lecturing. Some have written that Hughes was "discovered" in 1925 by white poet Vachel Lindsey while Hughes was working as a busboy. The truth is, however, that Hughes had already established himself as a "bright young star of the Black Renaissance by then." His poems had already been published in several collections and publications. Over a period of years he wrote 16 books of poems, two novels, three collections of short stories, four volumes of "editorial" and "documentary" fiction, 20 plays, children's poetry, three autobiographies, and a dozen radio and television scripts.

A critical turning point in Hughes's life was when he discovered New York, Harlem, the cultural life, and the literary circle of other black writers: Countee Cullen, Arna Bontemps, Wallace Thurman, Zora Neal Hurston, and Eric Walrond. Hughes immersed himself in the Harlem experience—the language, the music, the people. He began to integrate the spirituals, blues, and jazz into the rhythm of his poems. His friends were quoted as saying, "No one enjoyed being a Negro as much as Langston Hughes." His writings spoke to the human experience while expressing himself with humor, wit, and endurance. Langston Hughes is remembered as a famous member of the Black Renaissance in the 1920s, surviving the Great Depression because he was such a great writer.

Langston Hughes died May 22, 1967. In 1991 when the Pinckney School in Lawrence, Kansas, was replaced, the school renamed its library "The Langston Hughes Library." *The Collected Poems of Langston Hughes* was published in 1994 by Knopf and several selected volumes have been published for children.

Books and Notes

Black Misery. Illustrated by Arouni. Introduction by Jesse Jackson and afterword by Robert G. O'Mealley. (Oxford, 1994).

This edition is part of the Iona and Peter Opie Library of Children's Literature. Originally published by Eriksson in 1969.

The Block: Poems. Selected by Lowery S. Sims and Daisy Murray Voigt. Illustrated by Romare Bearden. (Viking, 1995).

Includes thirteen Langston Hughes poems.

Carol of the Brown King: Nativity Poems. Selected and illustrated by Ashley Bryan. (Atheneum, 1998).

Includes five poems by Langston Hughes and one anonymous poem presenting the story of the first Christmas from different perspectives.

Don't You Turn Back: Poems by Langston Hughes. Selected by Lee Bennett Hopkins. Illustrated by Ann Grifalconi. (Knopf, 1969).
Includes 45 poems.

The Dream Keeper and Other Poems. Illustrated by Brian Pinkney. (Knopf, 1994).
Includes the 59 poems originally selected for this title by the author and seven additional poems. First published by Knopf in 1932 (and republished in 1986) with illustrations by Helen Sewall.

The Sweet and Sour Animal Book. Illustrated by students from the Harlem School of the Arts. Introduction by Ben Vereen and afterword by George P. Cunningham. (Oxford, 1994).

This edition is part of the Iona and Peter Opie Library of Children's Literature. Includes 26 short poems.

For More Information About/By the Author

Articles

Black History at Piedmont Area Journal. URL: http://www.members.tripod. com/~blackhistory/blackhistory.htm (Accessed November 1997).

Books

Cooper, Floyd. *Coming Home: From the Life of Langston Hughes* (Philomel, 1994).

Irene Hunt

◆ Historical Fiction

Pontiac, Illinois
May 18, 1907

📖 *Across Five Aprils*
📖 *Up a Road Slowly*

About the Author
and the Author's Writing

In 1964 after more than 30 years teaching, 57-year-old Irene Hunt published her first novel, *Across Five Aprils* (Follett). It won the Newbery Award in 1965. It was the saga of an Illinois farm family during the Civil War. The well-researched novel took a personal look at the war and included many historical details about Union and Confederate generals, President Lincoln, and monumental battles.

Irene Hunt was born May 18, 1907, near Pontiac in southwestern Illinois. Although some biographical accounts state that she was born near Newton, Illinois, according to the de Grummond Collection archives at the University of Southern Mississippi, that doesn't seem to be the case. Her parents, Franklin P. and Sarah (Land) Hunt, did move to a family farm near Newton when Hunt was less than one year old, remaining in the area throughout her childhood. When Irene Hunt was seven years old her father died. His death left a lasting mark.

After high school, Hunt attended the University of Illinois. She began teaching French and English in the public schools in Oak Park, Illinois, in 1930 while she continued to work toward her undergraduate degree, received in 1939. After six more years of teaching she attended the graduate college at the University of Minnesota, where she earned a masters degree in 1946. She moved to South Dakota that same year, accepting a position as a psychology instructor at the University of South Dakota. Hunt also completed some advanced graduate work at the University of Colorado at Denver. By 1950 she had returned to Illinois and was teaching French and English to high school students in the Cicero Schools.

During her years of teaching Hunt spent long hours, often late into the night, at her kitchen table typing out her stories. She accumulated rejection slips, but also learned with each manuscript. Her first novel was finally accepted and published in 1964. The following year, 1965, the book received a Newbery Honor Award. The story, *Across Five Aprils*, was set on the family farm where she had grown up. She had researched the history and rechecked every detail. The story featured the fictional Creighton family, with many of the incidents based on family letters and records, and stories her grandfather told. Hunt's grandfather had been nine years old when the war broke out. He remembered the war clearly and recounted the pain, sorrows, and happy moments of the times. The book was dedicated to her grandfather's great-grandchildren.

In 1965, after fifteen years of teaching, she became Director of Language Arts in the Cicero Schools. As an educator, she focused on bringing great books to students and teachers alike. She felt strongly that books not only enlighten but also bring confidence to young readers. She continued to write, and two years later her book *Up a Road Slowly* (Follett, 1966) was published. In 1967 that book was named the Newbery Award winner. After four years as director she retired to write full-time.

Up a Road Slowly opens with a scene from her life. When her father died another little girl had told Hunt that she wasn't going to live there anymore. Hunt's grief over her father's death and her bewilderment about what would happen caused her to hide in a closet. In the book, however, it is Julie's mother who has died. The book is a mix of childhood memories and fiction.

For many years, Irene Hunt lived in North Riverside, Illinois. When she was not writing or traveling, she enjoyed refinishing furniture and cooking. By the early 1970s she had moved to St. Petersburg, Florida.

Books and Notes

Across Five Aprils (Follett, 1964; Silver Burdett, 1993).

A Newbery Honor Book. The Creighton family in southern Illinois is torn apart by the Civil War.

The Everlasting Hills (Scribner, 1985).

Jeremy Tyding is learning-disabled and his father cannot accept Jeremy or his handicap. When Jeremy wanders into the mountain wilderness, he finds a stranger who shows him the love and understanding his father seems unable to show.

The Lottery Rose (Scribner, 1976).

Georgie suffers abuse from infancy. When he is placed in a home with other boys, he finds that acceptance and learning to love come with difficulty.

Up a Road Slowly (Follett, 1966; Silver Burdett, 1993).

Newbery Award winner. Gleaned from Hunt's own childhood memories. Julie grows from a bratty seven-year-old to a mature and loving seventeen-year-old while living with her stern aunt.

William: A Novel (Scribner, 1977).

Three orphaned African American children establish a loving family group with a white teenage girl.

For More Information About/By the Author

Articles

"Irene Hunt Papers." *de Grummond Collection Web Site*. URL: http://www.lib.usm.edu/~degrum/findaids/hunt.htm (Accessed November 1997).

Johanna Hurwitz

Contemporary Realistic Fiction ◆ Biographies

New York, New York
October 9, 1937

📖 *Baseball Fever*
📖 *Aldo Applesauce*
📖 *Astrid Lindgren: Storyteller to the World*

About the Author
and the Author's Writing

One hot day in June, Johanna Hurwitz sent her daughter off to school. Later in the day the phone rang and Hurwitz found out that the school wanted her to bring clean clothes and a can of paint remover. When Hurwitz arrived at school, she found out that a painter had been working in the school and had left a can of paint. A boy came by and picked up the paint, the lid fell off the can, and green paint spilled all over Hurwitz's daughter, Nomi. Nomi was sent to the nurse, but the nurse had never dealt with a case of green paint. Nomi was then taken to the school custodian for suggestions. The custodian suggested putting Nomi in the school shower, but during the shower there was a fire drill, so the nurse found an old raincoat in the lost and found. The bell was just ringing when Hurwitz arrived. Before they got Nomi cleaned up, Hurwitz had made three more trips home for items such as a hair comb and sneakers. The young man who dumped the paint probably was being punished enough just worrying about what would happen. In fact, they thought "he might not even paint his own house when he grew up."

The Law of Gravity (Morrow, 1978) retells a similar incident. Episodes such as this from Hurwitz's life and those around her are inspiration for her writing. In 1998 Hurwitz's fiftieth book was published. Her first book was *Busybody Nora* (Morrow, 1976). Her parents told her that writers "must have another way to make a living."

Johanna Hurwitz was born October 9, 1937, in New York City. Her childhood was spent in an apartment in the Bronx, now an urban wasteland. The apartments are gone, and the close-knit ethnic neighborhood is in serious decay. When Hurwitz was growing up, her family's two-bedroom apartment brimmed with laughter and books. Johanna read books at home and frequently visited the nearby library. It became a second home for Hurwitz. From the time she was very young, she aspired to be a librarian and, "For as long as I can remember, I wanted to become a children's book author. I suspect that had I never married, or if I'd married someone else, or if I'd had different children, I still would have managed to write books."

As an adult she worked part-time in college libraries while she earned her degrees from Queens College and Columbia University. She earned a degree in library science, and, for a time, she worked at the New York Public Library. She also was a librarian in a school where Aliki Brandenberg had two children enrolled. Hurwitz liked to imagine that she would read her stories and say, "Oh, Johanna, I love these stories. I'd love to illustrate them and I'll send them to my publisher." However, it wasn't that easy. She worked on stories for the early primary child. Her characters were age five (Nora) and three (Teddy). Because Morrow Junior Books had published the Ramona books, she thought she would try sending to them. Ramona was a little sister living in the suburbs in a rather middle-class house. Nora was the big sister living in an urban apartment building. Morrow liked them, and she ended up writing several books about Nora and Teddy, and more books about their neighbor, Russell, and his little sister, Elisa.

Hurwitz is always on the lookout for ideas and details to include in her stories. Russell is a little boy who lived in her neighborhood, and Elisa is his little sister. During her time as a New York City public librarian, a coworker regularly brought a hard-boiled egg for lunch, once discovering that the egg was raw. A similar incident showed up in *Aldo Applesauce* (Morrow, 1979).

Hurwitz says, "The books I have written have all been influenced directly or indirectly by my family. From my first book, *Busybody Nora*, which was based on our everyday experiences living in a New York City apartment building, to *Baseball Fever* [Morrow, 1981], which grew out of my childrens' passion for a sport that makes no sense to their father, to *Yellow Blue Jay* [Morrow, 1986], which grew out of our summer vacations to Vermont, to *Much Ado About Aldo* [Morrow, 1978], which features my family's cats, there is little about my family life that doesn't become a source of inspiration."

Johanna Hurwitz tells about the beginning of *New Shoes for Silvia* (Morrow, 1993), a picture book illustrated by Jerry Pinkney. "When my daughter graduated from college, she spent a year working as a liaison for a Sister City in Nicaragua. It took three weeks for her letters to arrive home and like any mother, I worried about her wellbeing. So I went to visit. My daughter wrote asking me to bring clothing, which she could give to people she knew. I arrived in Managua with a huge suitcase filled with clothing for other people. Among the clothes was a pair of bright red shoes. We gave the shoes to a little girl, but they were too big for her small feet. She walked around hugging the shoes to herself, afraid they would be taken away and given to someone else. 'How could she use the shoes right now?' I asked myself. And suddenly, I had an idea for a picture book."

In addition to books of realistic fiction filled with humor, Hurwitz has written several biographies. Her interest in biography began when David A. Adler, who was working part-time for the Jewish Publication Society, asked her if she would be interested in writing a biography of Anne Frank for young readers. Hurwitz considered it, partially because her own birth name had been Frank. *Anne Frank: Life in Hiding* was published by the Jewish Publication Society in 1988. The following year Hurwitz's biography about author Astrid Lindgren, *Astrid Lindgren: Storyteller to the World* (Viking, 1989), was published. It was her love of music that brought her to write a biography of Leonard Bernstein, *Leonard Bernstein: A Passion for Music* (Jewish Publication Society, 1993). She had already used Bernstein's last name for her popular Ali Baba character (she had also used Puccini and Vivaldi as characters' last names).

Most of her books take place in large urban areas such as New York City or Washington, D.C., but places Hurwitz visits or vacations provide other locations. *Faraway Summer* (Morrow, 1998) takes place in Vermont, where the Hurwitzs often spend summers. That story, which takes place in 1910, tells of the experiences of a Russian immigrant from New York City during two weeks with a Vermont farm family.

When Hurwitz is not writing, her favorite activity is "browsing in second-hand bookstores. I am forever discovering old books that I never heard of but which look fascinating. So I buy them and take them home to read. One such second-hand book, a collection of stories by many different authors all using the same plot, was the inspiration for the anthology I put together, *Birthday Surprises* [Morrow, 1995]." *Birthday Surprises* includes stories by Richard Peck, Ann M. Martin, Jane Yolen, David A. Adler, Barbara Ann Porte, Pam Conrad, Karla Kuskin, James Howe, Ellen Conford, and herself. Inspiration comes from her family, friends, and surroundings. She is always vigilant for story ideas. Undoubtedly her new grandchild will provide some fresh story inspirations. Johanna and Uri Hurwitz live in Great Neck, New Jersey.

Books and Notes

Fiction

Most of Hurwitz's fiction is humorous and deals with contemporary events. *Faraway Summer*, which is historical, seems to be a departure from her usual fiction fare. Most of her titles deal with children involved with family or school relationships. She has written for a variety of reading levels, from primary to middle school.

The Down & Up Fall. Illustrated by Gail Owens. (Morrow, 1996).

Elisa in the Middle. Illustrated by Lillian Hoban. (Morrow, 1995).

Even Stephen. Illustrated by Michael Dooling. (Morrow, 1996).

Ever-Clever Elsie. Illustrated by Lillian Hoban. (Morrow, 1997).

Faraway Summer. Illustrated by Mary Azarian. (Morrow, 1998).

A Llama in the Family. Illustrated by Mark Graham. (Morrow, 1994).

Make Room for Elisa. Illustrated by Lillian Hoban. (Morrow, 1993).

New Shoes for Silvia. Illustrated by Jerry Pinkney. (Morrow, 1993).

Ozzie on His Own. Illustrated by Eileen McKeating. (Morrow, 1995).

School Spirit. Illustrated by Karen Dugan. (Morrow, 1994).

Spring Break. Illustrated by Karen Dugan. (Morrow, 1997).

Biography

Anne Frank: Life in Hiding (Jewish Publication Society, 1988; Beech Tree, 1993).

Helen Keller: Courage in the Dark. Illustrated by Neverne Covington. (Random, 1997).
A Step Into Reading, Step 3 book.

Leonard Bernstein: A Passion for Music. Illustrated by Sonio O. Lisker. (Jewish Publication Society, 1993).

Other

A Word to the Wise, and Other Proverbs. Illustrated by Robert Rayevsky. (Morrow, 1994).

For More Information About/By the Author

Articles

"Johanna Hurwitz . . . A Talent for Caring." *Early Years: Teaching PreK–8* (August/September 1986): 50–52.

McElmeel, Sharron. "Author! Author! Johanna Hurwitz." In *Educator's Companion to Children's Literature, Volume 1: Mysteries, Animal Tales, Books of Humor, Adventure Stories, and Historical Fiction* (Libraries Unlimited, 1995): 79–83.

"Meet Author: Johanna Hurwitz." *Frank Schaffer's Classmate* (April/May/June 1989): 42–43.

Paul B. Janeczko

Passaic, New Jersey
July 25, 1945

📖 *Poetspeak*
📖 *That Sweet Diamond: Baseball Poems*
📖 *The Place My Words Are Looking For:*
What Poets Say About and Through
Their Work

About the Author
and the Author's Writing

Paul B. Janeczko was like most other kids. He collected and traded baseball cards, gambling for the best of the lot. Before long, he wasn't only collecting them, he was looking for all the possibilities of the information on the back. During evenings when he was supposed to be studying his catechism (he attended Our Lady of the Assumption School), or doing his homework, he pushed everything aside and dragged out his "Keds" box to study all his baseball cards. He organized them according to teams, then he organized a group of those players born in New Jersey. Later he organized an "Alphabet Team" with each position fielded by a player whose last name started with a different letter of the alphabet. At other times he arranged the cards to make up a team of all Polish players, and so forth.

At this time he showed little promise for becoming a writer. He was more interested in baseball cards and his bike than he was in school. He had two major goals: to survive one more year of delivering newspapers (without being attacked by the mad dog at the top of the hill), and to become more than a third string player on the Little League Team. He did not reach either goal, but by the time he was in fifth grade, his mother made him read 20 minutes a day. At first he resented the time spent reading, but soon began to enjoy it. During junior high school he wanted to be a top 40 disk jockey, an Edsel salesman, or a bullpen catcher.

Then he discovered poetry. He became a poetry junkie, reading poetry the way some people watch soap operas or follow their favorite sports team. He read poems almost every day, while eating breakfast, during an April blizzard, or while waiting to have a molar drilled and filled. He read poems from any source. Years after his baseball-card collecting days, he graduated from college with a degree in English and began to teach. His studies not only helped him recognize and understand good poetry, but also to write some poetry. His first poems were published in the school's literary magazine.

He found himself dissatisfied with the poetry anthologies that he was expected to use for teaching high school English. He took it upon himself to find poems he enjoyed using and those that appealed to his students. He mimeographed them and used them in his classes. Those efforts at collecting poems began his first anthology.

In creating his anthologies, he says, "I look for poems that strike me. These are the ones I save." His files are filled with poems he reads over and over. But the files alone do not make an anthology. When he begins to select, he looks for connections, not necessarily the obvious ones. Each book of poems requires time to read, select, reread, and gather the poetry into groups that flow from one connection to another. How long does it take? "The tinkering and experimenting with poems and placement takes months, but reading, looking for the right ones is an ongoing process."

He was the first recipient of the Lupine Award in 1989 for his collection *Brickyard Summer: Poems* (Orchard, 1989). The Lupine Award is given each year to an outstanding book about Maine or by a Maine author by the Children's and Young Adult Services Section of the Maine Library Association.

Like collecting baseball cards, poems aren't meant to be kept in a shoebox. They are meant to be traded—to be passed on and shared.

Paul B. Janeczko no longer teaches in a classroom. He is a full-time writer living in Hebron, Maine.

Books and Notes

Paul B. Janeczko, a former high school teacher, has achieved success as an anthologist. Many of his collections are geared toward the young adult, but are accessible to intermediate and middle-school readers as well. He has found a niche introducing contemporary poets to young readers. In two of his volumes, *Poetspeak* and *The Place My Words Are Looking For*, he includes notes from each poet telling how they came to write the particular work included. His collection *That Sweet Diamond: Baseball Poems* combines his early love of baseball and his ongoing love of poetry.

Brickyard Summer: Poems. Illustrated by Ken Rush. (Orchard, 1989).

Home on the Range: Cowboy Poetry. Illustrated by Bernie Fuchs. (Dial, 1997).

I Feel a Little Jumpy About You: A Book of Her Poems & His Poems Collected in Pairs. With Naomi Shihab Nye. (Simon, 1996).

Looking for Your Name: A Collection of Contemporary Poems (Orchard, 1993).

The Music of What Happens: Poems That Tell Stories (Orchard, 1988).

The Place My Words Are Looking For: What Poets Say About and Through Their Work (Bradbury, 1990).

Poetry from A to Z: A Guide for Young Writers. Illustrated by Cathy Bobak. (Bradbury, 1994).

Poetspeak: In Their Work, About Their Work: A Selection (Collier, 1991).

Preposterous: Poems of Youth (Orchard, 1993).

Stardust Hotel: Poems. Illustrated by Dorothy Leech. (Orchard, 1993).

That Sweet Diamond: Baseball Poems. Illustrated by Carole Katchen. (Atheneum, 1998).

Wherever Home Begins: 100 Contemporary Poems (Orchard, 1995).

For More Information About/By the Author

Articles

Janeczko, Paul B. "Eight Things I've Learned About Kids and Poetry." *Publishing Research Quarterly* 8, no. 1 (Spring 1992): 55.

Janeczko, Paul B. "Enhance Writing Skills with Poems That Transform." *Instructor* 107, no. 1 (August 1997): 25–27.

Janeczko, Paul B. "Explore Rhythm and Rhyme with Limericks (Teaching Rhythm and Rhyme to Students)." *Instructor* 107, no. 2 (September 1997): 30–32.

Janeczko, Paul B. "Growing Minds: On Becoming a Teacher." *NEA Today* 3 (October 1984): 28.

Janeczko, Paul B., and Kim Mathews. "Don't Chuck Huck: An Individualized Approach to the Classics." *English Journal* 79, no. 4 (April 1990): 41.

"Paul Janeczko." *Penguin Books USA Inc. Web Site*. ©1997. URL: http://www.penguin.com/usa/childrens/authors/appreg/janeczpa01.html (Accessed December 1997). Site includes current appearance fee and full description of presentation.

Romano, Tom. "Authors' Insights: Turning Teenagers Into Readers and Writers." *English Journal* 81, no. 7 (November 1992): 96–98.

Rudyard Kipling

Bombay, India
December 30, 1865–January 17, 1936

📖 *The Jungle Book*
📖 *Just So Stories*

About the Author
and the Author's Writing

Rudyard Kipling, an English short-story writer, poet, and novelist, was the first English writer to receive the Nobel Prize for Literature (in 1907). Kipling is best known for his writing about his two homelands (England and India), and their ties to one another. For a time Kipling lived in the United States, where he wrote *The Jungle Book*, perhaps his most enduring work.

Joseph Rudyard Kipling was born to English parents December 30, 1865, in Bombay, India, where his father, John Lockwood Kipling, was teaching in the Bombay School of Art. During the day, Indian servants took care of young Rudyard and taught him the Hindu language.

It was the custom of English parents living in India to remove their children from India by the time they were five to avoid the deadly diseases of the colony, diseases the child might contract if they attended school there. Rudyard was sent to Southsea, England, and placed in the care of foster parents. Kipling would later describe his feelings during those years as being deserted.

By the time Kipling was 12 years old he was enrolled at the United Services College, established to provide an economical education for the sons of Army officers. Kipling was an eager reader and soon became editor of the school journal. Some friendships he made at this school would last a lifetime. Family finances prohibited him from going to a university after graduation, so he returned to India and joined the staff of a newspaper in the northwestern city of Lahore. He honed his journalistic skills during these years. By 1887 Kipling moved to a newspaper in Allahabad and wrote many stories about his travels in northern India.

In 1889 Kipling returned to England. His writing soon attracted attention in both England and the United States. During this time his writing was geared toward adults. Soon after Kipling returned to England, he became acquainted with an American literary agent, Wolcott Balesteir. Balesteir collaborated with Kipling on his second novel. In January of 1892, Kipling married Balesteir's sister, Carrie Balesteir, in London, and they soon moved to the United States. When Kipling arrived in Vermont on February 17, 1892, he was bundled in hairy goatskin and buffalo lap robes. He first toured Vermont in a horse-drawn sleigh on that snowy night. That summer, the couple moved to Brattleboro, Vermont, living in a rented cottage for a year. They built a home near Brattleboro, in Dummerston, Vermont, and named it "Naulahka," Hindu for "something of great value."

In addition to other tales, he wrote *The Jungle Book* (1894) and *The Second Jungle Book* (1895). These stories tell of Mowgli, an Indian child who is raised by a family of wolves. In a letter to his friend Charles Eliot Norton, Kipling said, "Those four years in America will be blessed unto me for all my life. . . . It's an uncivilized land (I still maintain it), but how the deuce has it wound itself around my heartstrings in the way it has." Kipling made little effort to fit into the social climate in his American home. "Me and the aborigines are excellent friends, but they can't understand why I don't come to chicken suppers and church sociables and turkey sprees." Kipling stayed close to Naulahka, where he did much of his work. When the Kiplings' first child was born, the couple hired an English nurse as Kipling said, "No good to defile her speech at the very outset with the Yank peacock cry." Kipling did however make friends in Vermont with James Conland. It was Conland's tales about his work on fishing boats that inspired Kipling's famous novel *Captains Courageous*.

In 1896 the Kiplings returned to England, where he wrote poems for the *London Times*. The Kiplings' daughter, Josephine, died of pneumonia in 1899. Shortly after, in 1902, a collection of stories that presents humorous explanations for how animals got a specific attribute, *Just So Stories*, was published. Their son, John, was killed in 1915 at the Battle of Loos during World War I. The deaths of his children, as well as his own failing health (a bleeding ulcer not discovered for years), are thought to have clouded Kipling's view of the world and his writing. He wrote no more children's stories, and his adult writings revealed a darkened view of life. Rudyard Kipling died in 1936.

Books and Notes

Many publishers have published editions of Rudyard Kipling's children's stories. A Walt Disney production created a worldwide audience for Kipling's *The Jungle Book*. While the Disney versions are under copyright, the Kipling stories are in the public domain, so many authors/illustrators have retold and reillustrated his stories.

The Jungle Book. Illustrated by William Dempster. (Classic, 1968).

The Jungle Book: Based on the Mowgli Tales from "The Jungle Book." Retold by Tony Oliver. Illustrated by Animation Cottage, Thomas Cheney, and Richard Kriegler. (Saban, 1990).

Just So Stories: For Little Children (Oxford, 1995).

Mowgli Stories from "The Jungle Book." Illustrated by Thea Kliros. (Dover, 1994).

For More Information About/By the Author

Articles

Allen, Anne Wallace. "A Victorian in Vermont." *The Gazette* (Cedar Rapids, IA: Sunday, January 18, 1998): 1F, 4F.

Books

Kamen, Gloria. *Kipling* (Atheneum, 1985).

Murray, Stuart. *Rudyard Kipling in Vermont: Birthplace of the Jungle Books* (Images from the Past, 1997).

James Arthur Kjelgaard

**New York, New York
December 5, 1910–July 12, 1959**

📖 *Fire-Hunter*
📖 *Big Red*
📖 *Snow Dog*

About the Author
and the Author's Writing

James Arthur Kjelgaard, better known as Jim, was the fourth son in a family of seven children. Jim had three older brothers, one younger brother, and a sister. His father practiced medicine in New York, but discontinued the practice and moved the family to a farm in the Pennsylvania mountains when Jim was still a toddler. The farm was over 700 acres, filled with horses, dairy cattle, sheep, dogs, and chickens.

The boys in the family kept the cattle where they were supposed to be. The cows often got out of the pasture and into the apple orchards, where they would get sick from eating too many apples. The boys had a difficult job keeping the cows out of the orchard, because few of the pastures were fenced.

The farming enterprise did not last. Eventually Kjelgaard's father sold the farm and moved the family to nearby Galeton, Pennsylvania, where he established another medical practice. Within one-half mile of their home, the boys found good hunting, fishing, and trapping. Between attending school they checked their trap lines, hunted for deer, and fished for trout. Kjelgaard and his brothers spent many icy nights on hunting or trapping trips in abandoned cabins on the top of mountains in the woods outside of Galeton. Some nights they would wake up to find that the water in the buckets (inside the cabin) had frozen while they slept.

Their sister, Betty, became a writer. One of the brothers became a forest ranger. Others went their own ways. Jim held a number of jobs, including laborer, factory worker, plumber's apprentice, and surveyor's assistant.

He turned to writing as an avocation and began to get his stories and articles published. By 1951 Jim Kjelgaard was married and the father of a daughter, Karen. He also had authored numerous stories and "four books for boys." He lived just eight more years, dying July 12, 1959, in Milwaukee, Wisconsin. During his lifetime he authored 39 books.

Books and Notes

Big Red (Holiday, 1945).

The Black Fawn (Dodd, 1958).

Desert Dog (Holiday, 1956).

Fire-Hunter (Holiday, 1951).

Hidden Trail (Holiday, 1992).

Irish Red, Son of Big Red (Holiday, 1951).

Outlaw Red, Son of Big Red (Holiday, 1953).

Rescue Dog of the High Pass. Illustrated by Edward Shenton. (Dodd, 1958).

Snow Dog (Holiday, 1948).

Stormy (Holiday, 1959).

Swamp Cat. Illustrated by Edward Shenton. (Dodd, 1957).

For More Information About/By the Author

Limited information is available on some book flaps of his books. Check general reference sources.

Suzy Kline

**Berkeley, California
August 27, 1943**

- *Herbie Jones and the Dark Attic*
- *Orp*
- *Mary Marony and the Chocolate Surprise*
- *Song Lee in Room 2B*
- *Horrible Harry and the Dungeon*

About the Author
and the Author's Writing

Suzy Kline was born in Berkeley, California, and spent her childhood in northern California. As an eight-year-old she felt that her grandfather in Indiana must miss his son (her father) very much, so she began to write weekly letters to him. Suzy's aunt told her that the letters "helped him live a little longer, which made me feel really good about writing." She also kept a diary and wrote poems in a notebook. However, she spent more time playing sports than reading. She loved playing kickball, baseball, basketball, and chase. Later at Albany High School, she developed a love of reading, inspired by Mr. Ruebman's passion for literature. After graduation Kline attended the University of California at Berkeley and California State University at Hayward, where she earned her undergraduate degree and teaching credentials. She married Rufus Kline in the late 1960s, and eventually the couple moved to Torrington, Connecticut, where they raised their two daughters, Emily and Jennifer. Suzy Kline began teaching elementary school in the mid-1970s.

For more than twenty years Suzy Kline has taught elementary school. After 17 years as a second-grade teacher, she "looped" with her students. Looping is when a teacher moves with her students into the next grade. She says, "I love reading aloud to my students and encouraging them to write stories about their everyday experiences." For five years she was the drama director of the school and wrote plays.

She began writing in 1981—in the morning, on weekends, and during the summer. She collected 127 rejection slips before Putnam agreed to publish her first book. The Horrible Harry books are a montage of the classes and children that have been in her classrooms in Torrington, Connecticut. She says, "Many of the activities that happen in Room 2B really happened in my classroom." When she writes she says she "[tries] to imagine what Horrible Harry and Doug and Sidney and Song Lee would do if they were really in my room. Then I let them do it."

As with most authors, the ideas for her books come from her memories of childhood and all the facets of her present life in her classroom and family. For example, when Kline "looped" with her second-grade students into third grade, so did Harry. He "loops" with Miss Mackle in third grade. And, like her own childhood practice of keeping a diary and a notebook, the character Herbie Jones also keeps a notebook. Her experiences writing school plays as drama director motivated her to write *The Herbie Jones Reader's Theater* (Putnam, 1992).

Suzy Kline often visits schools to talk about writing and her books. She takes along her mailbag of rejection letters and shares the galleys and enlarged pictures. She also brings along objects that have inspired her writing. For example, she brings an old diary, Green Slime, a Monster Ball, and a lightbulb necklace.

When Kline is not teaching or writing books about Herbie Jones, Song Lee, or her many other primary-aged characters, she finds much to do. She writes in her notebook, reads nonfiction, enjoys sports, musicals, and movies. She often browses in bookstores, collects coffee mugs, dances, paints, and takes weekend trips with her family. The Klines' two daughters are grown and both married. Jennifer went to Wellesley College and studied economics at the University of Connecticut at Storrs. She is now a computer consultant and lives in New Hampshire. Emily attended Dartmouth College, where she studied English. She teaches in Connecticut.

The Klines share their Connecticut home with four cats, Giz, Tux, Zeeb, and Teeter. Rufus Kline teaches sociology at the University of Connecticut and writes for the *Litchfield County Times*. He also wrote a picture book of his own, *Watch Out for These Weirdos* (Viking, 1990). Suzy continues to teach in the Torrington, Connecticut, schools and writes whenever she can find the time. During school breaks or vacations she visits schools to talk about her books.

Books and Notes

Reviewers have cited Kline's books as being "funny and true-to-life," and they are often mentioned on lists for those just beginning to read chapter books. Her Song Lee titles have also appeared on several lists focusing on contemporary fiction that features Korean characters. Her strength is her ability to characterize the boys and girls who inhabit her books in such a way that readers identify with them and their problems. And, her books are filled with humor. The series of titles featuring Orp and his sister, Chloe, are well suited to the preteen reader. Her books have been listed in the International Reading Association's Children's Choice selections; nominated for regional/state awards in Indiana, West Virginia, and the Pacific Northwest; and have received starred reviews in several publications.

Herbie Jones and the Dark Attic (Putnam, 1992).

The Herbie Jones Reader's Theater (Putnam, 1992).

Horrible Harry and the Drop of Doom. Illustrated by Frank Remkiewicz. (Viking, 1998).

Horrible Harry and the Dungeon. Illustrated by Frank Remkiewicz. (Viking, 1996).

Horrible Harry and the Purple People. Illustrated by Frank Remkiewicz. (Viking, 1997).

Marvin and the Mean Words. Illustrated by Blanche Sims. (Putnam, 1997).

Mary Marony and the Chocolate Surprise. Illustrated by Blanche Sims. (Putnam, 1995).

Mary Marony and the Mummy Girl. Illustrated by Blanche Sims. (Putnam, 1994).

Mary Marony Hides Out. Illustrated by Blanche Sims. (Putnam, 1993).

Orp and the Chop Suey Burgers (Putnam, 1990).

Orp and the FBI (Putnam, 1995).

Song Lee and Leech Man. Illustrated by Frank Remkiewicz. (Viking, 1995).

Song Lee and the Hamster Hunt. Illustrated by Frank Remkiewicz. (Viking, 1994).

Who's Orp's Girlfriend? (Putnam, 1993).

For More Information About/By the Author

Articles

None located. Check standard biographical sources.

E. L. Konigsburg

♦ Contemporary Realistic Fiction

New York, New York
February 10, 1930

📖 *Jennifer, Hecate, Macbeth, William McKinley, and Me, Elizabeth*

📖 *From the Mixed-Up Files of Mrs. Basil E. Frankweiler*

📖 *The View from Saturday*

About the Author
and the Author's Writing

Elaine Lobl (E. L.) Konigsburg was born Elaine Lobl in New York City February 10, 1930, but shortly thereafter, while still an infant, the family moved to Pennsylvania. Her childhood years were spent in several small mill towns. She was the second of three sisters. After graduating as valedictorian from Farrell Senior High School in Farrell, Pennsylvania, she found a job in 1947 as a bookkeeper in a wholesale meat market—the Shenago Valley Provision Company. A brother of one of the owners, David Konigsburg, sometimes visited the office. Soon she had saved enough money to enter college, wanting to become a chemist. David Konigsburg was a graduate student in the psychology department.

Elaine was a test subject for several tests he had to practice giving. She graduated in 1952 with honors, and she and David Konigsburg were married.

She worked as a chemist while doing graduate work at the University of Pittsburgh from 1952 to 1954. After graduate school, David received his doctorate and the family moved to Jacksonville, Florida. For a time she taught biology and science at a private girls school, the Bartram School. She began to think that perhaps she was not suited for teaching chemistry. She left teaching a few weeks before their first child, Paul, was born. Two more children Laurie and Ross, followed. She returned to teaching part-time in 1962, but only briefly. The family moved to the New York area, first settling in New Jersey and later in Westchester. On Saturdays Konigsburg took art lessons at the Arts Students League. After they moved to Westchester and Ross entered kindergarten, Konigsburg began to write. She wanted to write something about suburban children. Ideas came from observing people and from reading. The idea for *Jennifer, Hecate, Macbeth, William McKinley, and Me, Elizabeth* (Atheneum, 1967) came from experiences as newcomers in an apartment building.

The idea for *From the Mixed-Up Files of Mrs. Basil E. Frankweiler* (Atheneum, 1967) came from a story in the *New York Times* about the acquisition of a statue for $225. No one knew who had sculpted the statue, but some felt that the statue had come from the Italian Renaissance period and was perhaps sculpted by someone famous. Another story that she read was in a book that told about some children kidnapped by pirates who lost all sense of civilization over a period of time. The third element that brought this story together was a family excursion to Yellowstone National Park. They decided to have a picnic and bought supplies at a grocery. Not finding any picnic tables, they looked for a clearing and set out their meal. The children were caught up in the discomforts of warmish chocolate milk, ants invading their picnic area, and melting cupcake icing. She brought the two readings and the picnic together, parlaying the incidents into a scenario where two upper-suburban children run away from home. Because they still want some of the comforts of home, they consider living in the Metropolitan Museum of Art with its stately beds, and all the elegance of the surroundings. During their days and nights in the Metropolitan Museum of Art, the two children find themselves involved in a mystery.

Eventually she had two books under consideration by publishers, and it was actually her second book that was the published first. She was also working on the manuscript for *About the B'nai Bagels* (Atheneum, 1969). Both *Jennifer, Hecate, Macbeth, William McKinley, and Me, Elizabeth* and *From the Mixed-Up Files of Mrs. Basil E. Frankweiler* were published by Atheneum in 1967. Interestingly enough, *Jennifer, Hecate, Macbeth, William McKinley, and Me, Elizabeth* was named a Newbery Honor Book and *From the Mixed-Up Files of Mrs. Basil E. Frankweiler* was named a Newbery Award Medal Winner. Both were named to the American Library Association's (ALA) Notable Children's Book list.

The Konigsburgs left the New York area and on the day that they were moving into a new home in Jacksonville, Florida, Konigsburg got the call that *From the Mixed-Up Files of Mrs. Basil E. Frankweiler* had been named the 1968 Newbery Winner and that *Jennifer, Hecate, Macbeth, William McKinley, and Me, Elizabeth* had been cited as a Newbery Honor Book. She was the first author, in the history of the awards, to have a first place and a runner-up book in the same year.

About the B'nai Bagels was published in 1969 by Atheneum, which continued to publish her other titles. She wrote about a wacky camel-keeper who spends his summer with his father, the amusing life of Eleanor of Aquitaine, and about Leonardo da Vinci in *The Second Mrs. Giaconda* (Atheneum, 1975).

Many of her books have been self-illustrated, including both of her Newbery Award books. Her sons and daughter have posed for the illustrations. Laurie was Claudia and Ross was Jamie in *The Mixed-Up Files of Mrs. Basil E. Frankweiler*. Paul was Benjamin Dickinson Carr in *(George)* (Atheneum, 1970).

The first Newbery Medal gave her the courage to continue to place the settings of her books in unusual places with unusual people. She says, "Children from all over the world let me know that they liked books that take them to unusual places. . . . That gave me the courage to write about Eleanor of Aquitaine . . . and about Leonard da Vinci." "They let me know that they like books that had more to them than what meets the eye." In *The View from Saturday* (Atheneum, 1996) she created four short stories inside the longer novel. The idea "was the most natural thing in the world." At first she wrote about a strangely dressed young man boarding the school bus and taking a seat alongside Ethan. After

Konigsburg walked along the beach to think about what she had written, she began connecting ideas to stories that she had in her "mixed-up files." Before she had finished her walk she realized that all those short stories' themes were tied together. *The View from Saturday* earned Konigsburg her second Newbery Award, 19 years after her first.

Elaine and David Konigsburg's daughter and two sons are grown and there are five grandchildren, four girls and one boy. Two have been the title character in their own books. Samuel Todd, the eldest grandchild, is the star of *Samuel Todd's Book of Great Colors* (Simon, 1990) and *Samuel Todd's Book of Great Inventions* (Simon, 1991). Amy Elizabeth stars in *Amy Elizabeth Explores Bloomingdales* (Simon, 1992). The other three grandchildren, Anna, Sarah, and Meg, do not have their own books—yet.

The Konigsburgs reside in Ponte Verde Beach, Florida. When she is not writing, she loves to draw, paint, read, and walk along the beach. She also loves movies.

Books and Notes

Some of Konigsburg's titles are as long as complete sentences and others are just one word. Each title is unique and seems to reflect Konigsburg's sense of logic and experimentation.

About the B'nai Bagels. Illustrated by E. L. Konigsburg. (Atheneum, 1969).

Amy Elizabeth Explores Bloomingdales. Illustrated by E. L. Konigsburg. (Simon, 1992).

The Dragon in the Ghetto Caper. Illustrated by E. L. Konigsburg. (Atheneum, 1974).

From the Mixed-Up Files of Mrs. Basil E. Frankweiler. Illustrated by E. L. Konigsburg. (Atheneum, 1967).

(George). Illustrated by E. L. Konigsburg. (Atheneum, 1970).

Jennifer, Hecate, Macbeth, William McKinley, and Me, Elizabeth. Illustrated by E. L. Konigsburg. (Atheneum, 1967).

A Proud Taste for Scarlet and Miniver. Illustrated by E. L. Konigsburg. (Atheneum, 1973).

Samuel Todd's Book of Great Colors. Illustrated by E. L. Konigsburg. (Simon, 1990).

Samuel Todd's Book of Great Inventions. Illustrated by E. L. Konigsburg. (Simon, 1991).

The Second Mrs. Giaconda (Atheneum, 1975).

T-Backs, T-Shirts, Coat, and Suit. Illustrated by E. L. Konigsburg. (Atheneum, 1993).

The View from Saturday. Illustrated by E. L. Konigsburg. (Atheneum, 1996).

For More Information About/By the Author

Articles

Hanks, D. Thomas. "The Wit of E. L. Konigsburg: To 'One Dog Squatting' from the Metropolitan Museum of Art." *Studies in American Humor* 5, no. 4 (Winter 1986): 243.

Books/Videos

Good Conversation! A Talk with E. L. Konigsburg. [Video]. (Tom Podell Productions, 1995).

Hanks, Dorrell Thomas, Jr. *E. L. Konigsburg* (Twayne, 1992).

Konigsburg, E. L. *Talktalk: A Children's Book Author Speaks to Grown-Ups* (Atheneum, 1995).

Madeleine L'Engle

◆ Science Fiction

New York, New York
November 29, 1918

📖 *A Wrinkle in Time*
📖 *The Young Unicorns*
📖 *A Circle of Quiet*
📖 *A Wind in the Door*

About the Author
and the Author's Writing

Madeleine Camp was born November 29, 1918 in New York City on a snowy night. She spent her first twelve years there before moving to Europe with her parents, Charles Wadsworth Camp (a writer) and Madeleine Hall Barnett Camp (a pianist). The family lived mostly in France and Switzerland. Madeleine was sent to a boarding school in Switzerland, and her father died while she was there. Later, she attended school for four years at Ashley Hall in Charleston, South Carolina, and spent four years at Smith College. She graduated in 1941 with an undergraduate degree (with honors).

After graduating from Smith College she attended the New School for Social Research in New York for a year. She moved into an apartment in Greenwich Village with three other women. Two women were attempting to start acting careers. Madeleine knew she wanted to be a writer, but she was the one who got a job in a theater and looked toward becoming a playwright. She met Hugh Franklin, an actor in Chekhov's *The Cherry Orchard*. They married a year later. By 1952 both of them had retired from the theater and moved into an old white farmhouse, Crosswicks, in Goshen, a small village in northwestern Connecticut. They took over a failing general store and pitched into life in the small village. During this time Madeleine worked at writing as well, always using a family name from her mother's side, "L'Engle." During this ten year period, little of L'Engle's writing was published. Three children joined the family, Josephine, Maria, and Bion. She received many rejection slips for *Meet the Austins* (Vanguard, 1960; Farrar, 1997) and other manuscripts. The Franklins' venture was very successful but "suddenly the fun and challenge was gone." After nine years the Franklins decided to move back to the "quiet of New York." Before settling down in New York City, however, the Franklins took their three children and headed off across the continent on a ten-week camping trip. During that trip L'Engle got the idea for *A Wrinkle in Time* (Farrar, 1962). They found that life in New York and around the theater was much more exciting and peaceful than village life in Connecticut. The family continued to spend summers at Crosswicks. Hugh Franklin returned to acting and eventually became well known for playing Dr. Charles Tyler in the soap opera *All My Children*. Meanwhile from 1960 to 1961, L'Engle studied in graduate school at Columbia University. During the next decade, L'Engle served on the summer faculty of the University of Indiana in Bloomington, was writer-in-residence at Ohio State University, Columbus, and at the University of Rochester in New York. For more than three decades she has been the writer-in-residence/librarian at the Cathedral Church of St. John the Divine in New York City. She has also been a lecturer at Wheaton College, Illinois.

She also amassed rejection slips. She had had six books published by the time she tried to sell *A Wrinkle in Time*. It was rejected by virtually every major publisher. They said, "It's too strange and much too difficult for children." Finally, at a party, a friend introduced her to John Farrar. He invited her to send the manuscript, and the book was published in 1962. It was awarded the Newbery Medal in 1963 and earned the Sequoyah and the Lewis Carroll Shelf Awards in 1965. It is Farrar's all-time best-seller. The *Chicago Tribune* wrote that the book was "exciting and beautifully written." *The New York Times* called the book "wholly absorbing—for in her highly accelerated spin through space, L'Engle never loses sight of human needs and emotions." About the book, the awards, and positive reviews, L'Engle said, "Since it was the book no-body wanted, it felt kind of nice."

In some circles, Madeleine L'Engle is referred to as the "female C. S. Lewis." So it is rather fitting that both Lewis and L'Engle have many of their literary papers at Wheaton College in Wheaton, Illinois. L'Engle has also donated papers to the de Grummond Children's Literature Collection at the University of Southern Mississippi. She received the University of Southern Mississippi's Medallion in 1978.

When the Franklins settled in New York City, it was in a rambling eight-room apartment in New York's Upper West Side on the ninth floor, facing the Hudson River. It is quiet and peaceful among the hustle and bustle of the city. Hugh Franklin died in 1986, and L'Engle continued to live in the apartment they had shared. The walls are filled with floor-to-ceiling bookshelves filled to capacity with hardbacks. Any wall space left is filled with photographs of L'Engle and her late husband, with others such as John F. Kennedy and Lyndon Johnson. L'Engle shares her home with cats and dogs. Various children, grandchildren, and friends show up from time to time. She divides the time she has "at home" between her New York City apartment, her Connecticut home, and the Cathedral. However, she is often traveling and speaking across the country and overseas. In a recent year she was scheduled for lectures in Japan and Russia, two weeks at Oxford in England, and one-day presentations in the United States.

Even though she has entered her eighth decade, she continues to write. Her talents include children's books, science fiction, coming-of-age novels, suspense and mystery novels, mainstream adult novels, poetry, plays, journals, and religious tomes.

Books and Notes

L'Engle's writings examine the Einsteinian concept of time and space, telepathic communication, injustice, evil, war, the environment, and personal and religious love. Although she never consciously writes for children, many of her books are designated by her publisher as "juvenile." Often one finds a blend of science fiction, fantasy, and moral issues in her work.

The Arm of the Starfish (Ariel, 1965).

A Circle of Quiet (Farrar, 1972).

Dragons in the Waters (Farrar, 1976).

The Journey with Jonah. Illustrated by Leonard Everett Fisher. (Farrar, 1967).

Meet the Austins (Vanguard, 1960; Farrar, 1997).

The Summer of the Great-Grandmother (Farrar, 1974).

A Wind in the Door (Farrar, 1973).

A Wrinkle in Time (Farrar, 1962).

For More Information About/By the Author

Articles

de Grummond Children's Literature Collection Web Site. URL: http://ocean.st. usm.edu/~dajones/findaids/l'engle. htm (Accessed December 1997).

Horowitz, Shel. "Madeleine L'Engle: Faith During Adversity." URL: http:// www.frugalfun.com/l'engle.html (Accessed December 1997).

"An Interview with Madeleine L'Engle." *Writing* (March 1987): 11–13.

Raymond, Allen. "Madeleine L'Engle: Getting the Last Laugh." *Teaching PreK–8* (May 1991): 34–36.

Wheaton College Web Site. URL: gopher:// gopher.wheaton.edu:70/00/Wheaton_ Archives/SC/findaids/sc03/leng2. txt (Accessed December 1997).

Books

Gonzales, Doreen. *Madeleine L'Engle: Author of a Wrinkle in Time* (Dillon, 1991).

Hettinga, Donald R. *Presenting Madeleine L'Engle.* Twayne's Young Adult Authors Series, no. 622. (Twayne, 1993).

Shaw, Luci, ed. *The Swiftly Tilting Worlds of Madeleine L'Engle: Essays in Her Honor* (Harold Shaw, 1998).

Robert Lawson

Historical Fantasy ◆ Contemporary Realistic Fiction

New York, New York
October 4, 1892–May 26, 1957

📖 *The Story of Ferdinand*

📖 *They Were Strong and Good*

📖 *Rabbit Hill*

About the Author
and the Author's Writing

Ferdinand, the flower-loving bull, is an icon throughout the world, although the character's creator is little known outside the realm of children's books. Robert Lawson was born October 4, 1892, in a New York City suburb. His ancestors were Scotch, Irish, and Dutch. Readers can discover them in his Caldecott Award Book, *They Were Strong and Good* (Viking, 1940). Lawson grew up in Monclair, New Jersey, where he read books and enjoyed football, baseball, and skating.

He once won a one-dollar bill in high school as a prize in a poster contest, and this sparked an interest in art. However, he thought he ought to have some skills for making a living. For a time he thought he was interested in construction engineering, but his lack of interest in mathematics curtailed that possibility. At the age of 20 he entered the New York School of Fine and Applied Art. By 1914 he had completed his studies and had moved into Greenwich Village. He became a freelance illustrator and worked on scenery illustrations for the theater. Eventually he sold drawings to magazines such as *Vogue* and *Harper's Weekly*. During World War I, he spent almost two years painting camouflage scenes in France for the "40th Engineers."

After the war, Lawson returned to the United States and spent the next ten years attempting to make a living with his freelance artwork—commercial art and greeting card designs. By 1922 Lawson had married a fellow artist, Marie Abrams. The two settled in a sprawling house in Westport, Connecticut. Eventually they built another home, near their first, high on a hill—Rabbit Hill. They planned to spend the rest of their lives in that house. The Lawsons' goal was to pay off the large mortgage as soon as possible. Because greeting card work was good steady pay, they each resolved to create one design a day until the house was free of debt. It took just three years, and the mortgage was paid.

Soon Lawson was concentrating on advertising. His sense of fantasy helped him to create some unique advertisements featuring gnomes, which lead to an invitation in 1930 to illustrate a book by Arthur Mason, *The Wee Men of Ballywooden* (Doubleday, 1930). His gnomes looked thousands of years old. He later illustrated a second book for Mason. The following year Lawson took up etching, leading to a commission for a series of plates. By 1936 Lawson was asked to collaborate on a book with Munro Leaf. Leaf intended to write a story that incorporated gnomes, as Lawson was so good at illustrating gnomes. However, when the story was finished it turned out to be *The Story of Ferdinand* (Viking, 1936). It was the bull, Ferdinand, smelling the flowers that became the internationally recognized icon, and the model for the drawings Walt Disney cartoonists used to create the animated cartoon of the book. People often approached Lawson who were only aware of that one book and its classic illustrations.

Lawson continued to illustrate many books by other authors, including titles for John E. Brewton, Richard and Florence Atwater, Ruth Barnes, and Carl Sandburg, in addition to more titles by Munro Leaf. The first book Lawson both authored and illustrated was *Ben and Me* (Little, 1939). It was a book of historical fiction dealing with the life and inventions of Benjamin Franklin. The story was written as if told by the spunky mouse (Amos) that lived in Ben's hat. Walt Disney used that book as the basis for a movie.

In 1940, in addition to illustrating another title by John E. Brewton, Lawson wrote and illustrated his second book, *They Were Strong and*

Good, for which Lawson earned the coveted Caldecott Award in 1941. The book chronicled the life of his ancestors, who were neither rich nor famous but were "strong and good." He wanted to give children a sense of pride in their own ancestors. Toward the end of 1943 Lawson completed a manuscript of the story *Rabbit Hill* (Viking, 1944). The book was so well promoted that it was in its second printing even before publication.

Other book topics by Lawson included rabbits who wanted a different tail, *Robbut: A Tale of Tails* (Viking, 1948); a prep-school boy who had a nose as talented as a bloodhound, *Smeller Martin* (Viking, 1950); and a professor who rode across the United States on a bicycle, a bicycle that rode in mid-air, *McWhinney's Jaunt* (Little, 1951).

In *Mr. Revere and I* (Little, 1953) the narrator was Sherry, Paul Revere's horse. The next year a sequel to *Rabbit Hill*, *The Tough Winter* (Viking, 1954), was published. The tale described "rugged times on the hill." Lawson's final tale from an animal's perspective was *Captain Kidd's Cat* (Little, 1956).

Maria Lawson died in 1956, and a year later Robert Lawson died. Shortly before his death *The Great Wheel* (Viking, 1957), an idealized history of the Ferris wheel, was published and he had completed the text for *Why Bats Are* (unpublished). He was working on the illustrations. Many of Lawson's books have remained relatively obscure, but the classic titles are still very popular in many libraries.

Books and Notes

Lawson illustrated all kinds of books written by other authors. He wrote and illustrated historical fantasy, perspectives on daily life, and animal fantasies.

Books Illustrated by Robert Lawson

Atwater, Richard, and Florence Atwater. *Mr. Popper's Penguins* (Little, 1938).

Brewton, John E., comp. *Gaily We Parade: A Collection of Poems About People, Here, There and Everywhere* (Macmillan, 1940; 1967).

Brewton, John E., comp. *Under the Tent of the Sky: A Collection of Poems About Animals Large and Small* (Macmillan, 1937).

Leaf, Munro. *Aesop's Fables* (Heritage Press, 1941).

Leaf, Munro. *The Story of Ferdinand* (Viking, 1936).

Leaf, Munro. *The Story of Simpson and Sampson* (Viking, 1941).

Leaf, Munro. *Wee Gillis* (Viking, 1938).

Books Written and Illustrated by Robert Lawson

Ben and Me; A New and Astonishing Life of Benjamin Franklin, as Written by His Good Mouse Amos, Lately Discovered, Edited and Illustrated by Robert Lawson (Little, 1939).

Dick Whittington and His Cat (Limited Editions Club, 1949).

The Great Wheel (Viking, 1957).

Mr. Revere and I (Little, 1953).

Rabbit Hill (Viking, 1944).

Robbut: A Tale of Tails (Viking, 1948).

They Were Strong and Good (Viking, 1940).

The Tough Winter (Viking, 1954).

For More Information About/By the Author

Articles

Fish, Helen Dean. "Robert Lawson, Illustrator in the Great Tradition." *The Horn Book Magazine* 16 (January/February 1940): 16–26.

Lawson, Robert. "The Newbery Medal Acceptance." *The Horn Book Magazine* 21 (July/August 1945): 233.

Books

Schmidt, Gary D. *Robert Lawson* (Twayne, 1997).

C. S. Lewis

◆ Fantasy

**Belfast, Ireland
November 29, 1898–November 22, 1963**

📖 The Chronicles of Narnia

About the Author
and the Author's Writing

Clive Staples (C. S. "Jack") Lewis was born in Belfast, Ireland, November 29, 1898. His father, Albert James Lewis, a solicitor, and his mother, Florence Augusta Hamilton Lewis, moved the family to the edge of town in 1905. It was in this home that Lewis wrote his first children's book about Animal-land.

His mother died of cancer in 1908, and Lewis was sent to Wynard School in Hertfordshire. Over the next few years he attended Campbell College in Belfast and Cherbourg School in Malvern, Worchestershire. It is at Cherbourg that "Lewis loses his Christian faith."

During the next decade Lewis went to Oxford and joined a cadet battalion as an officer, ending up in France during World War I. He was wounded in 1918, came home, and in 1919 returned to Oxford. He met Owen Barfield soon after. They would become lifelong friends. Lewis earned an undergraduate degree in 1922, and two years later began a one-year appointment in philosophy at Oxford. In 1924 he established a home with Jane Moore, a mother of a slain war-buddy, and her daughter Maureen. He thought of Moore as his foster mother. By this time he had written a couple books using the pseudonym of Clive Hamilton, met J. R. R. Tolkein, and had begun assessing his religious (or nonreligious) beliefs.

His father died of cancer in 1928 and the following year Lewis converted, on philosophical grounds, from atheism to theism. In 1931 Lewis had discussions with Hugo Dyson and Tolkein regarding Christianity as "myth come true." Before year's end Lewis is said to have "accepted Christ while riding in the sidecar of his brother's motorcycle on the way to Whipsnade Zoo." From that time (1931) until the end of his life, Lewis wrote and lectured. He became well known for the Chronicles of Narnia, his classic children's books, and for his works of Christian thought and moral philosophy. During the last years of Lewis's life, he spent his time tutoring, lecturing, and writing. In the 1930s Lewis and his brother went on annual walking tours during academic vacations.

In 1950 the first of the Chronicles of Narnia, *The Lion, the Witch and the Wardrobe*, appeared. The following year *Prince Caspian* was published. That was the same year his foster mother, Janie Moore, died. Each year from 1953 to 1956 saw the publication of another book in the Narnia series. In 1956 he married Joy Davidman Gresham in a ceremony in the Oxford registry office. He said this marriage was because of friendship. The following year he remarried Joy in a religious ceremony—this time for love. They married just three years before Joy died of cancer in 1960. Three years later C. S. Lewis died on November 22.

Books and Notes

In addition to his writing on religion and philosophy, Lewis is well known for his seven volumes comprising the Chronicles of Narnia. Narnia was a country with many provinces, and to the west lay a wild land of big mountains covered with dark forests or with snow and ice. The area was called the "Western Wild." The Narnia River flowed from a thundering waterfall and a pool of water, running all the way to the sea. On the east side of the Western Wild was an area known as Lantern Waste. This area is where the children, Peter, Edmund, Susan, and Lucy Pevensie, first enter Narnia and where Jadis, the White Witch, has her kingdom. The four English school children find their way through the back of a wardrobe into the magic land of Narnia and assist Aslan, the golden lion, to triumph over the White Witch, who has cursed the land with eternal winter.

The Chronicles of Narnia

The Lion, the Witch and the Wardrobe. Illustrated by Pauline Baynes. (Macmillan, 1950). Book 1.

Prince Caspian, the Return to Narnia. Illustrated by Pauline Baynes. (Macmillan, 1951).
Book 2.

The Voyage of the Dawn Treader. Illustrated by Pauline Baynes. (Macmillan, 1952).
Book 3.

The Silver Chair. Illustrated by Pauline Baynes. (Macmillan, 1953).
Book 4.

The Horse and His Boy. Illustrated by Pauline Baynes. (Macmillan, 1954).
Book 5.

The Magician's Nephew. Illustrated by Pauline Baynes. (Macmillan, 1955).
Book 6.

The Last Battle. Illustrated by Pauline Baynes. (Macmillan, 1956).
Book 7.

For More Information About/By the Author

Articles

Bredvold, Louis I. "The Achievement of C. S. Lewis." *The Intercollegiate Review* 4, no. 2–3 (January–March 1968): 116–22.

Into the Wardrobe: The C. S. Lewis Web Site. URL: http://cslewis.DrZeus.net/ (Accessed December 1998).

Books

Christopher, Joe R. *C. S. Lewis.* Twayne's English Author Series, no. 442. (Twayne, 1987).

Astrid Lindgren

◆ Humor

**Vimmerby, Sweden
November 14, 1907**

📖 *Pippi Longstocking*

📖 *Pippi in the South Seas*

📖 *The Children of Noisy Village*

About the Author
and the Author's Writing

Astrid Anna Emilia Ericsson was born November 14, 1907, in Vimmerby, Sweden. Her parents were Samuel August and Hanna Ericsson. Astrid was the oldest daughter of four children. She had an older brother, Gunnar, and two younger sisters, Stina and Ingegerd. The children grew up in an old red house surrounded by apple trees. Their farm was called Näs, near the town of Astrid's birth. She has described her childhood as "happy and filled with security and freedom." By age six she was learning how to thin fodder beets and cut nettles for the poultry. Astrid and her brother and sisters used to run through the forest, visiting a group of small villages populated by social outcasts—paupers, vagabonds, orphans, and other misfits. Sundays were reserved for church and Sunday school, and Astrid was forced to wear "freshly washed coarse black wool stockings." The Ericsson home did not have electricity until Astrid was seven years old, and even then they had no television, radio, telephone, or car.

Astrid and her siblings learned to love animals as they explored the fields of the family farm. During her childhood, there were no public libraries and no children's bookstores nearby. One of her teachers found a catalog of children's books and allowed each child to choose a gift. Astrid Ericsson's first book was *Snow White*. For years she treasured and kept that book. Eventually she read *Robinson Crusoe*, *Tom Sawyer*, and *Huckleberry Finn*. Her friends all thought she would grow up to be a writer, but she didn't. She felt it would be better not to write a book at all than to write a bad one.

In 1923 Astrid finished school and soon began working for the Vimmerby newspaper. When she was 19, she moved to Stockholm to attend a secretarial school. On April 4, 1931, Astrid Ericsson married Sture Lindgren, and in 1934 their daughter, Karin, was born. Lars, Astrid's son, was eight years older than Karin. It was Karin who inspired her mother's storytelling. One day Karin was ill and asked her mother to tell her a story. The story Astrid told her was about an outrageous little girl named Pippi Longstocking. The story was published in Sweden and became very popular. Eventually the story was translated into English and fifty other languages. Friedrich Oetinger, a Hamburg publisher, traveled to Stockholm to meet Lindgren and to acquire translation rights to *Pippi Longstocking* (Viking, 1950). Pippi Longstocking came to the United States in the 1950s, and at first, it did not seem that the books would be as popular as they were in Sweden. It has since become one of the most popular titles in the country. Many people know Lindgren because of her Pippi stories, but she also wrote many others. She wrote stories about the Noisy Village; about Ronia, the Robber's daughter; and about other interesting characters. While her books were being translated from Swedish into other languages, Astrid Lindgren was translating books published in the United States for her Swedish publishing house, Raben and Sjogren. The names she used as a translator were Anna Ericsson and Emilia Ericsson—names formed from her middle names and birth name.

In 1952 her husband, Sture Lindgren, died. Five years later, in 1957, Lindgren was given the Swedish State Award for Writers of High Literary Standard, the first children's literature author to receive this award. Just a year later Lindgren was the recipient of the Hans Christian Andersen Medal (International Children's Books Award). The next decade was eventful for Lindgren: She received several more awards; her mother, Hanna Ericsson, passed away in 1961; and her father, Samuel Ericsson, died in 1969. In 1967 the Swedish publishing house where Lindgren worked as a children's book editor established, with Friedrich Oetinger, the Astrid-Lindgren Award.

She retired from Raben and Sjogren after working there for twenty-four years. During that time, the publishing house had grown into the largest publisher of children's books in Sweden. Lindgren's writing has brought her worldwide recognition and many awards both for her writing and her translations. She received an honorary Ph.D. from the University in Sweden, the Lewis Carroll Shelf Award, and the German Bookseller's Peace Award (the first children's book author to ever receive the award). The Peace Award was accompanied by a large cash prize. She donated half of the prize money to German children and the other half to Swedish children.

Astrid Lindgren's son, Lars, and her friend, Friedrich Oetinger, both died in 1986. Later, Lindgren was named "Swede of the Year," and received awards from Sweden and Denmark. Lindgren founded "Solkatten" for disabled children.

Eventually Lindgren retired to the farm where she and her siblings grew up. The farm is a gathering place where her own children's children and their children come to visit. In her later years Astrid Lindgren became actively involved in animal rights, crusades for the better treatment of animals, and protests against high Swedish tax rates. Streets in Vimmerby, Sweden, are named for her books. In 1996 the first Astrid Lindgren statue was unveiled in Stockholm's Tenerlunden park (a bronze statue by Majalisa Alexanderson).

Books and Notes

Among Lindgren's most popular books are her titles about Pippi Longstocking. Pippi is a very curious nine-year-old with carrot-color hair worn in two tight braids. Pippi gets her last name from wearing one black and one brown stocking with black shoes that are twice as big as her feet. She lives alone, as her mother died when Pippi was very young and is now "an angel . . . up in Heaven." Her father, a sea captain, has been blown overboard in a storm. Pippi lives in a ramshackle house called Villa Villekulla. Pippi's friends are Tommy and Annika and her monkey, Mr. Nilsson. Lindgren's other books involve children who live in a village, Noisy Village, much like those villages that were near Lindgren's childhood farm home.

The Children of Noisy Village. Translated by Florence Lamborn. (Viking, 1962).

Pippi Goes on Board. Translated by Florence Lamborn. (Viking, 1957).

Pippi in the South Seas. Translated by Gerry Bothmer. (Viking, 1959).

Pippi Longstocking. Translated by Florence Lamborn. (Viking, 1950).

Ronia, the Robber's Daughter. Translated by Patricia Crampton. (Viking, 1983).

For More Information About/By the Author

Articles

Cott, Jonathan. "Profiles." *New Yorker* 59 (February 28, 1983): 46–48+.

Foo, Jane. *Astrid Lindgren*. URL: http://www.interlog.com/~wings/jane/a_lindgren/a_lindgren.html (Accessed December 1997).

Includes excerpts from several books, a bibliography of children's books, important dates, and other facts.

Books

Hurwitz, Johanna. *Astrid Lindgren: Storyteller to the World*. Illustrated by Michael Dooling. Women of Our Times series. (Viking, 1989).

Myra Cohn Livingston

◆ Poetry

Omaha, Nebraska
August 17, 1926–August 23, 1996

📖 *O Frabjous Day! Poetry for Holidays and Special Occasions*
📖 *Poems for Brothers, Poems for Sisters*
📖 *Celebrations*

About the Author and the Author's Writing

For the first eleven years of her life, Myra Cohn Livingston lived in Omaha, Nebraska, where she was born August 17, 1926. Despite the Depression, Livingston described her childhood as idyllic, surrounded by aunts, uncles, grandparents, cousins, and friends.

In 1937 the family moved to Los Angeles, California. There Myra began to play the French horn, and within two years she became a professional musician. She wrote for her school newspaper and composed poetry and plays for herself. She became so accomplished musically, that at the age of 16 she was invited to play with the Los Angeles Philharmonic Orchestra. After graduating from high school, she headed for Bronxville, New York, where she entered Sarah Lawrence College. The college did not have many opportunities for musical performance so she began to concentrate on writing. That first year she published poetry in a children's magazine and wrote about her idyllic childhood in a book titled *Whispers and Other Poems* (Harcourt, 1958). Many of the poems were published in magazines in the 1940s, but the book was not published until 1958.

When asked about the "bits and pieces of her life that readers could find in her writings," Livingston replied, "Almost everything I see turns up in a poem, whether it is something I find in my garden, an observation of a child playing or reacting, my pets, the moon in its various places, holidays observed; certainly my own childhood and feelings as a child are constantly being used in poems. I cannot imagine writing a poem without tracing it back to my own experiences and thoughts."

Livingston wrote in a journal every day. She would write in long-hand, on her Olympia typewriter, or on her Macintosh computer, even on old envelopes. She said, "Very often I will get an idea, maybe just a line or two, write it down and go back to it. One can spend hours over a single word at times, or forty years trying to write one particular poem ["The Dark" in *Worlds I Know and Other Poems* (McElderry, 1985)]. . . . Several poems in my book, *I Never Told You and Other Poems* [McElderry, 1992] are rewrites of poems I wrote at 18 and never seemed quite right to me before as they were in their first form."

Myra Cohn Livingston's writing career resulted in more than 40 books, including poetry for children and books for adults—one dealing with the subject of children as "authors" who "publish" books. She crusaded during her lifetime for an attitude of respect for legitimately published authors: "I feel that being an author is something one works for long and hard, and to give children the false impression that they can even write like authors do is erroneous." The elaboration of this idea is discussed further in *The Child as Poet: Myth or Reality* (Horn Book, 1985).

"In order to write one must learn the craft of writing poetry. Mere rhyme is not the answer, nor is prose arranged to look like poetry." During her lifetime Livingston taught thousands of children and formulated some very succinct ideas about the process of teaching the art of poetry writing. Her experiences are shared in *Poem-Making: Ways to Begin Writing Poetry* (Harper, 1991). The book discusses what makes a poem a poem—the use of meter, form, and rhyme to create the framework for the expression of observations and ideas.

Myra Cohn Livingston compiled several anthologies based on specific themes or subjects and wrote original poetry. For a time she taught at the University of California at Los Angeles (UCLA), and several of her students have published poetry.

Myra Cohn Livingston's husband, Richard Livingston, died in 1990. Her three children, Josh, Jonas, and Jennie, are all involved in creative ventures. Josh is a musicologist and a certified public accountant. Jonas is an executive with the Music Corporation of America. Jennie is a film-maker and artist. Livingston was very proud of her children. She said her daughter, Jennie, won "every major Film Critics Award for her documentary *Paris Is Burning.*"

During Livingston's life she lived in a villa built on three levels in the mountains near Santa Monica. She could look out across Beverly Hills down to the Pacific Ocean, and, if conditions were right, she could see all the way to Catalina Island. During her lifetime she enjoyed rare books, bookmarks, collecting books, the ocean, mountains, word games, bookbinding, friends, and family. Myra Cohn Livingston's collection of poetry books numbered around 10,000 volumes. She collected other types of books as well. Walls (not lined with books) were covered with photographs, art, and reprints of poems by her friends. A grand piano sat in her living room with more photographs of her sons and daughter. Myra Cohn Livingston died of cancer on August 23, 1996.

Books and Notes

Myra Cohn Livingston compiled several anthologies based on specific themes or subjects, as well as writing original poetry.

Abraham Lincoln: A Man for All the People: A Ballad. Illustrated by Samuel Byrd. (Holiday, 1993).

B Is for Baby: An Alphabet of Verses. Illustrated by Steel Stillman. (McElderry, 1996).

Call Down the Moon: Poems of Music (McElderry, 1995).

Cricket Never Does: A Collection of Haiku and Tanka. Illustrated by Kees de Kiefte. (McElderry, 1997).

Editor. *I Am Writing a Poem About—A Game of Poetry* (McElderry, 1997).

Festivals. Illustrated by Leonard Everett Fisher. (Holiday, 1996).

Keep on Singing: A Ballad of Marian Anderson. Illustrated by Samuel Byrd. (Holiday, 1994).

Let Freedom Ring: A Ballad of Martin Luther King, Jr. Illustrated by Samuel Byrd. (Holiday, 1992).

Riddle-me Rhymes. Illustrated by Rebecca Perry. (McElderry, 1994).

Roll Along: Poems on Wheels (Macmillan, 1993).

Selector. *Poems for Brothers, Poems for Sisters.* Illustrated by Jean Zallinger. (Holiday, 1991).

Selector. *Poems for Fathers.* Illustrated by Robert Casilla. (Holiday, 1989).

For More Information About/By the Author

Articles

Porter, E. Jane. "Profile: Myra Cohn Livingston." *Language Arts* (November/December 1980): 901–5.

Raymond, Allen. "A Poet—and Shaker of the Human Mind—Myra Cohn Livingston." *Early Years/K–8* (August/September 1964): 32–34.

Jack London

San Francisco, California
January 12, 1876–November 22, 1916

- 📖 *The Call of the Wild*
- 📖 *The Sea-Wolf*
- 📖 *White Fang*

About the Author
and the Author's Writing

Jack London became internationally famous for his book *The Call of the Wild* when he was only 29 years old. He was born in San Francisco in 1876 and grew up in Oakland. His mother, Flora Wellman, was a piano teacher and spirit-world medium. It is believed that his father was William Henry Chaney, Wellman's common-law husband. Chaney abandoned the family before Jack London was born, and, by the time he was eight months old, Wellman had married a widower, John London. John London was a struggling farmer, carpenter, and father of two young girls. Throughout Jack's childhood, he thought John London was his biological father.

When John London's health began to fail, Jack, at the age of fifteen, quit school to work in a cannery. However, he had already discovered the world of books at the Oakland Public Library. The work at the cannery was mindless, and Jack vowed that he would not stay in that "deadly" job. He borrowed money from his "Aunt Jennie," a woman who had been his childhood nurse. With that money he bought a sloop, *Razzle Dazzle*, and became a nighttime oyster pirate. As he raided the commercial oyster beds in San Francisco Bay, he had to avoid the patrol boats. But by the next year, at the age of sixteen, he had joined the California Fish Patrol and was working on the other side of the law. These adventures were the beginning of the accounts he would write in his books for young readers, *The Cruise of the Dazzler* (1902) and *Tales of the Fish Patrol* (1905). The next year, London joined a seal-hunting voyage traveling from Hawaii and Japan to the Bering Sea. This eight-month voyage became the story in his popular novel *The Sea-Wolf* (1904). Each of London's adventures, his trips to London, England's East End, his boxing days, and his journalist interests all became part of his books. The experience that yielded the most material was his trek to the Yukon during the Klondike gold rush days (1897–1898). The wealth of that experience, mixed with his vivid imagination, brought forth some of his most famous novels, *The Call of the Wild* (1903) and *White Fang* (1906). Many short stories from this period were collected in *The Son of the Wolf* (1900), *The God of His Fathers* (1901), *Children of the Frost* (1902), and *Smoke Bellew* (1912). Many of his stories were published in magazines, but it was his Klondike stories that caused a dramatic change in magazine fiction. The stories of human elements in combat and survival abandoned the strictly moral tales that were the usual fare of that time.

Jack London felt that his literary success was due to his own hard work. His routine included sitting down to write early each morning. His goal was to write 1,000 words each day. Between 1900 and 1916 he wrote more than 50 books, fiction and nonfiction, hundreds of short stories, and many articles on numerous topics. Many of his works are considered classics. In addition to his daily writing, Jack London lectured and regularly corresponded with many people. He received more than 10,000 letters each year and handled all of his own editing, negotiating with editors, and so forth. He also oversaw the construction of a custom-built sailing ship.

He settled on a ranch (farm) in the Sonoma Valley. It had a magnificent natural landscape and hundreds of trees—run-down but beautiful. It was a quiet place to write, surrounded by nature. At first he intended it to be a summer home, but then began to buy farm equipment and animals. Before long he knew he was there to stay. He built a new house and a new barn, and while the buildings were being constructed he took off to sail around the world to explore, write, adventure, and enjoy some great living. The trip gave him more material. He considered the sea a rich source for his stories. Jack and Charmian London's dream house on the ranch was nearly completed in 1913 when it caught fire and was destroyed. The fire crushed London financially and wrecked a long-cherished dream. For a time he was depressed, but finally forced himself to go back to work. He used an advance from *Cosmopolitan Magazine* to build a new study to their existing wood-frame ranch house. He continued to write and enjoyed sailing in the San Francisco Bay. In 1914 he went to Mexico as a war correspondent. During the next two years, Charmian convinced London to spend some time in Hawaii. The couple planned to rebuild Wolf House eventually, but had not done so by the time London died on November 22, 1916. He died of gastrointestinal uremic poisioning.

In 1919 Charmian London constructed a new house just a mile from Wolf House. She lived there until her death in 1955 at 84 years of age. At the time she specified that the house should be used as a memorial to Jack London and his writing. The Jack London State Historic Park is located a few miles off Highway 12, near the small town of Glen Ellen. The park was created in 1959 when a small portion, about 40 acres, of London's 1,400-acre Beauty Ranch was acquired by the state, partly through a gift from Irving Shepard, London's nephew and an heir to the London estate. The original park included London's grave, the ruins of Wolf House, and Charmian London's House of Happy Walls.

Additional acreage has been added over the years, so that today the park consists of more than 800 acres, including many of the ranch buildings and the cottage where London wrote much of his later work.

Books and Notes

Jack London's books have seen many editions and publishers. For example, London's *Call of the Wild* has no less than 280 separate entries in the Library of Congress catalog. Thus, it seemed more appropriate to provide the book's original publication date along with the title because publishers vary greatly depending on the year of printing.

The Son of the Wolf (1900).

The Cruise of the Dazzler (1902).

The Call of the Wild (1903).

The Sea-Wolf (1904).

White Fang (1906).

South Sea Tales (1911).

For More Information About/By the Author

Articles

Jack London State Historic Park. URL: http://parks.sonoma.net/JLPark.html (Accessed December 1997).

Books

Dyer, Daniel. *Jack London: A Biography* (Scholastic Press, 1997).

Lois Lowry

Fantasy ◆ Historical Fiction ◆ Humorous Stories

Honolulu, Hawaii
March 10, 1937

- 📖 *The Giver*
- 📖 Anastasia Series
- 📖 *Rabble Starkey*

About the Author
and the Author's Writing

In 1994 Lois Lowry received her second Newbery Medal, this time for *The Giver* (Houghton, 1993). During the summer award ceremony at the American Library Association's convention in Chicago, Lois Lowry met Allan Say. Say was the Caldecott Award winner for his *Grandfather's Journey* (Houghton, 1993). They thought they were meeting for the first time, but soon found out that they had probably played nearby or perhaps even on the same playground, in Japan more than forty years before. Both had been eleven-year-olds in Japan—Lois as the daughter of an Army dentist assigned to General MacArthur, Allan as a Japanese child living in Tokyo.

Lois Lowry was born March 10, 1937, to Robert and Katharine Hammersberg. The family moved all over the world during Lois's childhood. Lois spent the World War II years with her maternal grandparents in Pennsylvania. A move to postwar Japan brings back a flood of memories. At eleven she remembers packing away her Victorian dollhouse into a box as her family prepared to move from Pennsylvania to Tokyo to join her father. She cried as she watched the box marked "storage." The family often could not take all of their belongings on a move. She was allowed to take her favorite books. This time *The Yearling* accompanied her, as did *A Tree Grows in Brooklyn*, *Mary Poppins*, and *The Secret Garden*. The Bobbsey Twins and the Nancy Drew books stayed behind with the dollhouse and her bike. Years later, the house and street where she had lived in Pennsylvania became the setting for *Autumn Street* (Houghton, 1979).

She attended junior high school in Tokyo, high school in New York City, and entered Brown University in New Jersey in 1954. At that time her family was living in Washington, D.C. She studied at Brown for two years before leaving school to marry David Grey Lowry on June 11, 1956. Her high school yearbook described her as a future novelist, and it was a dream she kept on hold for over a decade while she accompanied her military husband around the country, from California to Connecticut, Florida, South Carolina, and finally settling in Cambridge, Massachusetts. David then entered law school. By the time the family moved to Maine, the Lowrys had four children, Alix, Grey, Kristin, and Benjamin, all under five years of age. In 1970, when her youngest child was seven, Lowry returned to school to finish her degree. She entered the University of Southern Maine and earned an undergraduate degree, continuing on in graduate school. During her graduate work she authored two textbooks, *Black American Literature* (J. Weston Walsh, 1973) and *Literature of the American Revolution* (J. Weston Walsh, 1974). An article she later wrote for a magazine caught the attention of an editor at Houghton Mifflin, who wrote to ask if she would consider writing a children's book.

At the age of forty, her life was changing. She had published two textbooks and had completed her college degree. Her marriage was also changing. In 1977 Lois Lowry says, "I left a marriage of 21 years, left a 12-room house (and a housekeeper!)." She moved from a spacious house in the country into a three-room furnished apartment "with tacky furniture" over a garage to start a new life as a writer. Her children, who were ages 19, 18, 17, and 14, stayed in Maine with their father. Her first children's book, *A Summer to Die* (Houghton, 1977), was published that same year. *A Summer to Die* is a fictionalized retelling of the death of Lowry's sister, Helen, and the effect of such a loss on a family. In the book she says, "Time goes on, and your life is still there, and you have to live it."

The book and the Helenium ("Helen's flowers," a memorial flower garden) were both created in memory of her sister, Helen, who died of cancer.

Since this modest beginning Lowry has had dozens of books published, has won two Newbery Awards, and has become one of the nation's premier writers of books for young readers. Most mornings, Lowry begins her writing day by 8 AM. She works until lunch and then, after a brief break, returns to writing until mid-afternoon. She writes novels, essays, and short stories, mostly for young readers.

She often draws on personal experiences for her books, and sometimes those experiences also influence what she *does not* write about. While writing *A Summer to Die*, Lowry decided to take a break and write a shorter, lighter story for a magazine. She created the character Anastasia Krupnik, based on her daughters, Alix and Kristin. Lowry liked Anastasia so much that she decided to dedicate a full-length book to her story. *Anastasia Krupnik* (Houghton, 1979) became the first book in a popular series. Anastasia is a composite of both daughters, both of whom are active, outgoing, and very independent. The time Anastasia answered her father's fan mail is similar to the time Kristin answered Lowry's mail. Many other incidents have come directly from her daughters' lives.

Her late son, Grey, and his love of airplanes gave Lowry the idea of having Sam interested in planes. Sam is Anastasia's little brother, who stars in *All About Sam* (Houghton, 1988).

Lowry has received all types of letters suggesting topics to include in the Anastasia series. Lowry's comments about some of the ideas give readers insight into Lowry's genius and her beliefs and life. One letter from a class in London included the following in their list of ideas for new Anastasia books:

- ✓ Anastasia's mother having twins (a boy/a girl).
- ✓ Anastasia's father falling downstairs after telling Anastasia off for getting drunk with her boyfriend.
- ✓ Sam entering a contest and winning $1 million. Mother picking up the room and finding the money in a pillow case.

The suggestions were interesting, especially because the son of a friend, Martin Small, had married three years before and had recently had twins. However, because the first Anastasia book had dealt with a new baby and the stepmother in another book, *Switcharound* (Houghton, 1985), and had a set of twins, Lowry decided against using the idea.

The second suggestion was discarded because Lowry felt that having Dad fall down the stairs did not really fit with the "tone of the books." Except for those with a morbid sense of humor, falling down stairs is not funny. However, Dad, a Harvard professor, is visited by his old girlfriend and finds that she is not at all what Dad remembers. Dad does have a humorous case of chicken pox in one of the books.

Anastasia being reprimanded for getting drunk is another idea that does not seem to fit the tone of the books. It was somewhat tempting for Lowry to include this message, however, because shortly before this suggestion Lowry's 29-year-old nephew had an automobile accident after drinking and ended up in a coma on a respirator.

Regarding Sam winning $1 million, Lowry recognized that a child winning that amount of money would not happen without a great deal of publicity, and besides, that amount of money would not fit into a pillowcase. Sam does have a winning situation, however: The gerbils have babies and eleven gerbils take over the house.

Lowry's award-winning book *Number the Stars* (Houghton, 1989) was based on the experiences of a childhood friend, Annelise. She used Annelise's story to bring the tragedies of the Holocaust to a slightly younger audience than might normally read about these events. The story centers on Annelise's experiences during the occupation of Denmark. In the book, Annemarie Johnansen is shown as a courageous child as she assists her family to help a Jewish family escape.

At the time that Lowry wrote *The Giver*, her father was in a nursing home suffering the loss of his long-term memory. One day while visiting, she realized that without long-term memory he had no concept of pain. She began to think about a society in which there was no knowledge of pain. Eventually the society portrayed in *The Giver* developed into a society where the need for personal and societal memory and for making connections with the past and with each other were not needed.

The Giver has become one of Lowry's most controversial books. Many find the ending too ambiguous, but Lowry crafted it so that readers could make their own connections (and endings). The book has also caught the eye of self-appointed censors—sometimes for being too Christian and sometimes for not being Christian enough, sometimes for being too American or too un-American. Others feel the book provides a dismal view of the world, while others think it is not dismal enough. The book requires the reader to examine their values and ideas about what direction societal values should go.

Lowry spent several years as a freelance writer and photographer. The photo on the cover of *The Giver* is hers. The manuscript for this book, and others, have been donated to the Kerlan Collection at the University of Minnesota.

The themes in Lowry's books center on saying good-bye, making connections, and belonging. Her characters come from every child she has ever known. Her own children (she had four), her grandchildren (two at last count), and even herself as a child, have brought bits and pieces of personalities and lives to Lowry's books. "Being a writer is what I love." Lowry says, "I love the people I meet—the children, writers, librarians, teachers. . . . I love the process of putting words on a page, rearranging them, making them work."

When she is not writing, she reads, gardens, and enjoys her dog, movies, and travel. She also spends time with her friends and grandchildren. Lowry's younger daughter, Kristin, is the mother of Lowry's first grandchild, James. Her older son, Grey, was a top-gun fighter pilot in the Air Force. In May of 1995, Grey was killed in a plane crash during a routine take-off in Germany. His widow, Margret, and their daughter, Nadine, live in Germany. Nadine was just one-and-a-half-years old when her father died. Alix, Lowry's other daughter, works with computers, and Lowry's son Ben writes very well and has a sports background.

To her friends, Lois Lowry is known as a fun person to be around. She is witty, clever, and interesting. In addition to her reading and gardening, she knits and plays bridge. Lois Lowry says she "lead[s] a pretty quiet life." While her life may be "quiet," her writing comes through loud and clear to her many readers.

Books and Notes

Anastasia Series

Anastasia Krupnik (Houghton, 1979).

Anastasia Again (Houghton, 1981).

Anastasia at Your Service (Houghton, 1982).

Anastasia Ask Your Analyst (Houghton, 1984).

Anastasia on Her Own (Houghton, 1985).

Anastasia Has the Answers (Houghton, 1986).

Anastasia's Chosen Career (Houghton, 1987).

Anastasia at This Address (Houghton, 1991).

Anastasia, Absolutely (Houghton, 1995).

Books About Sam

All About Sam (Houghton, 1988).

Attaboy Sam! (Houghton, 1992).

See You Around Sam! (Houghton, 1996).

Contemporary Realistic Fiction

Find a Stranger, Say Goodbye (Houghton, 1978).

Rabble Starkey (Houghton, 1989).

A Summer to Die (Houghton, 1977).

Switcharound (Houghton, 1985).

Other Titles

The Giver (Houghton, 1993).

Number the Stars (Houghton, 1989).

Stay! Keeper's Story (Houghton, 1997).

For More Information About/By the Author

Articles

DiNuzzo, Toni, et al. "Lowry Page: Learning About Lois Lowry." URL: http://www.scils.rutgers.edu/special/kay/lowry.html (Accessed December 1997).

Haley-James, Shirley. "Lois Lowry." *Horn Book Magazine* 66 (July/August 1990): 422–24.

Lowry, Lois. "The Internet Public Library: Lois Lowry." *IPL Youth Division: Ask the Author*. URL: http://www.ipl.org/youth/AskAuthor/Lowry.html (Accessed December 1997).

Lowry, Lois. "Newbery Medal Acceptance." *Horn Book Magazine* 66 (July/August 1990): 412–21.

Lowry, Lois. "Providing an Anchor for Adolescents." *CBC Features* 49, no. 2 (Fall/Winter 1996): 3–4. (Children's Book Council).

Raymond, Allen. "Lois Lowry: 'Anastasia,' and Then Some." *Teaching K–8* (October 1987): 44–46.

Books and Videos

"A Visit with Lois Lowry." [Video]. (Houghton, 1985).

Chaston, Joel. *Lois Lowry* (Twayne, 1997).

Markham, Lois. *Lois Lowry* (Learning Works, 1995).

Patricia MacLachlan

Historical Fiction ◆ Contemporary Realistic Fiction

Cheyenne, Wyoming
March 3, 1938

📖 *Sarah, Plain and Tall*

📖 *Unclaimed Treasures*

📖 *Arthur, for the Very First Time*

About the Author
and the Author's Writing

Patricia was an only child and spent a lot of time with her parents. Sometimes, as she walked home from the library with her mother, she would read as she walked, and, by the time they reached home, she would have already read her book for the first time. But before she took her favorite books back to the library, she read them over and over again. Her father and Patricia spent a lot of time acting out the stories they read. Patricia also made up her own characters. She created kings and queens and many other "friends" to live in her closet. Patricia often watched and listened to conversations that she was not intended to hear.

Patricia MacLachlan was born March 3, 1938, on the Wyoming prairie and heard many stories of her father's life on a prairie farm. Her mother told of a mail-order bride years ago in her family. These stories, bits and pieces of her own life, and the lives of her children and husband have all contributed to MacLachlan's books.

After spending her childhood in Cheyenne, Wyoming, MacLachlan lived in Minnesota, and then moved to the East Coast, entering the University of Connecticut in Storrs. There she met Robert MacLachlan and married. He was a psychologist and eventually became the psychology department head at the university near their Massachusetts home.

For a time MacLachlan served on the board of a family agency. Her duties included writing a series of articles concerning adoption and foster parents. Many of her concerns for families and children have influenced her writing. Although she credits Jane Yolen for luring her into books, it was also her interest and commitment to children's literature that inspired her to write her first book, *The Sick Day* (Harper, 1979). The story was based on a day when her husband stayed home with their daughter, Emily, trying to cope with the sick child and the fever thermometer. After that first book, Patricia MacLachlan has written a book a year (more or less). *Mama One, Mama Two* (Harper, 1982) focuses on the relationship between a child and the foster parent who cares for her until her own mother is able to take her back. MacLachlan plucks incidents out of her life and those of her children to create realistic episodes. For example, it was from her life that she found the hidden places from which Cassie in *Cassie Binegar* (Harper, 1982) listens to conversations that she was not meant to hear. In fact, when MacLachlan sent the manuscript to her mother to read before the book was published, her mother sent it back with the tablecloth under which she used to hide. Her mother knew she was there all the time. It was undoubtedly her years of "listening" that helped her write such convincing dialogue.

MacLachlan admits that Aunt Elda and Uncle Wrisby in *Arthur, for the Very First Time* (Harper, 1980) are really her parents, and that the story of a mail-order bride in her mother's family inspired MacLachlan to write her best-known work, *Sarah, Plain and Tall* (Harper, 1985). The novel was set in the nineteenth century and is told from the viewpoint of Anna, a young girl left motherless shortly after her brother, Caleb, was born. The children's widowered father arranges for the mail-order bride, Sarah, to travel from Maine to their home on the prairie.

The title captured an audience of middle-grade readers and touched the souls of adults as well. The Hallmark Masterpiece Theater optioned the book for a made-for-television movie. MacLachlan consulted on the script for the movie. The producers used most of the book's dialogue but also had to add more to expand the script taken from such a slender book (less than 90 pages). In addition, the movie switched the focus from the child to Sarah, to appeal more directly to an adult audience. The movie was so well received that the producers asked MacLachlan to develop a sequel. Consequently she developed the script and dialogue for *Skylark*. The movie was televised before Harper published the book in 1994. In the sequel, the family's life on the prairie is threatened by drought. Sarah decides to return to Maine for a time and takes her stepchildren, Caleb and Anna, who worry that Sarah will want to remain with her family in Maine.

That one mail-order bride story started MacLachlan writing *Sarah, Plain and Tall*. And she says, "Often a story begins with a small fact, a small fact that once happened. Writing is a bit like painting a picture; you begin with a small sketch, then you apply layers of paint and blend them until the little sketch has been changed into something different and colorful."

MacLachlan borrows freely from the lives of people around her. *The Facts and Fictions of Minna Pratt* (Harper, 1988) is substantially autobiographical and includes her husband, Robert, and all three of her children John, Jamie, and Emily. The family home even appears.

The children are now grown and the family home in Massachusetts is quieter than it once was. Patricia and her husband, Robert, a college professor, divide their time between their 1793 saltbox home and their Cape Cod residence. At times MacLachlan has been a visiting lecturer in children's literature at Smith College. When she is not writing, lecturing, or visiting schools, she can probably be found caring for the family's pets, bird-watching, watering the garden, or playing the cello. She is an accomplished cellist and her husband a viola player. Both also play the piano. The house is often filled with music and always filled with books. "There are books in all rooms of my house. There are books even in my car! I never travel anywhere without a book." For Patricia MacLachlan there will never be enough books.

Books and Notes

Patricia MacLachlan's books all focus on families or family relationships, stories for brothers and sisters, stories about new babies, and families that have a divergent structure. The following is a selective list of her titles.

All the Places to Love. Illustrated by Mike Wimmer. (Harper, 1994).

A boy describes his favorite places on his grandparents' farm.

Arthur, for the Very First Time. Illustrated by Lloyd Bloom. (Harper, 1980).

Arthur attempts to find an identity while he is with his aunt and uncle during a summer.

Baby (Delacorte, 1993).

A baby left with the family at the end of the tourist season occupies the family and helps them cope with the death of an infant son.

Cassie Binegar (Harper, 1982).

Cassie learns to accept change and to find her own niche during the family's summer by the sea.

Journey (Delacorte, 1991).

Unable to cope with her two children, a mother leaves them with grandparents, who attempt to restore a past that the children feel has been erased.

Mama One, Mama Two. Illustrated by Ruth Lercher Bornstein. (Harper, 1982).

A poignant story of a young girl cared for by a foster mother.

Moon, Stars, Frogs, and Friends. Illustrated by Tomie dePaola. (Pantheon, 1980).

Randall the frog longs for a real friend and finds an enchanted prince.

Sarah, Plain and Tall (Harper, 1985).

The widowed father of Anna and Caleb invites a mail-order bride to come live with the family in their prairie home. The children come to love the woman and are hopeful that she will stay.

Seven Kisses in a Row. Illustrated by Maria Pia Marrella. (Harper, 1983).

Emma learns, when her aunt and uncle come to care for her and her brother, that different people do things in different ways and that one is not necessarily right and the other wrong.

Skylark (Harper, 1994).

Sequel to *Sarah, Plain and Tall*. Sarah takes the children back home to Maine during a drought that threatens the financial well-being of the blended family.

Three Names. Illustrated by Alexander Pertzoff. (Harper, 1991).

A great-grandfather tells of going to school on the prairie with his dog, Three Names.

Tomorrow's Wizard (Harper, 1982; Harcourt, 1996).

Murdoch, an unorthodox apprentice to the wizard, makes five important wishes come true in ways that surprise the wishers.

Unclaimed Treasures (Harper, 1984).

Willa thinks she's in love with the father of the boy next door, until she realizes that it is the boy next door who is her "ordinary" love.

What You Know First. Illustrated by Barry Moser. (Harper, 1995).

The daughter of a family that is moving from a farm attempts to remember everything about the family's farm home, so that she might tell her baby brother all about it when he is older.

For More Information About/By the Author

Articles

MacLachlan, Patricia. "The Creative Process: Painting the Air." *The New Advocate* 3, no. 4 (Fall 1990): 219+.

Zolotow, Charlotte, and Patricia MacLachlan. "Dialogue Between Charlotte Zolotow and Patricia MacLachlan: An Illumination of an Old-Style Editor-Author Relationship." *Horn Book Magazine* 65, no. 6 (November 1989): 736+.

Patricia McKissack

◆ Biographies ◆ Nonfiction, African-American themes

◆ Picture Books/Early Readers

Nashville, Tennessee
August 9, 1944

📖 *W. E. B. DuBois*
📖 *The Dark-Thirty: Southern Tales of the Supernatural*
📖 *A Million Fish—More or Less*

About the Author
and the Author's Writing

Patricia McKissack grew up reading and listening. She fondly remembers the hot summer nights when her mother read poetry by Paul Laurence Dunbar. Her favorite poem was Dunbar's "Little Brown Baby."

Patricia L'Ann Carwell McKissack, the daughter of Robert and Erma Carwell, was born August 9, 1944, in Nashville, Tennessee. She grew up in the South, where she often listened to her grandparents tell stories, and where she gathered images and stories. Her grandfather would often use Patricia and her brother and sister's names in the stories. The characters were smart, daring, brave, and clever, and Pat and her sister, Sarah, and brother, Nolan, grew up believing they were smart as well. Patricia became an avid reader.

Later she would use events from her childhood and the stories she heard to create books for other young children to read. She started writing in third grade and says that she has always enjoyed reading and writing. One of her first writing assignments was to write a poem, which her third-grade teacher liked and displayed on the classroom bulletin board. She got into trouble in the fifth grade for talking too much. Her grades were good, but not the best. And, while she was interested in reading and writing, she also loved sports. She played softball, basketball, and track. When she became a teacher, she liked writing for her students and "when I became a mother I enjoyed telling my children stories."

McKissack graduated from Tennessee State University with an undergraduate degree in 1964. On December 12, 1965, she married Fredrick L. McKissack. During the next ten years the McKissacks became parents to three sons, Fredrick Jr. and twins Robert and John. Patricia McKissack also earned a masters degree from Webster University. For a time McKissack taught junior high school English and wrote when she had time. Later, she became a children's book editor and continued her writing. Her first book, written in 1971, *Paul Laurence Dunbar, A Poet to Remember* (Children's Press, 1984), was published during these years. During the next few years she wrote several biographies of important African Americans and became noted for the candor and depth of her topics. She considers 1975 the year that she "started writing professionally." In her nonfiction work, she often included controversial topics, such as racism, and was cited as evenhanded in her writing and presentation of any issue. Patricia and Fredrick McKissack have collaborated on a book for young adults that examines the problem of racism, *Taking a Stand Against Racism and Racial Discrimination* (Watts, 1990). They also coauthored a biography, *W. E. B. DuBois* (Watts, 1990), a scholarly work that examines DuBois's background and life's work to lift up his people.

Patricia Carwell and Fredrick McKissack were acquainted with one another as teenagers, but it was not until both had graduated from Tennessee State University that they became romantically interested. Patricia's degree was in English and Fredrick's degree was in civil engineering. He pursued his own career for ten years, but gradually became involved in writing. He helped research material for the nonfiction books and eventually coauthored several books with Patricia. They have continued to make history come alive for children and write books that make readers aware of the many contributions of African Americans.

McKissack's stories often instruct while conveying a pride in African American heritage. One story, inspired from the author's family, involves the cakewalk, a dance rooted in African American culture. One day McKissack came across a photograph of her grandparents winning a cakewalk. Her grandfather boasted that his wife's dancing had captured the wind. The story became *Mirandy and the Brother Wind* (Knopf, 1988). Fredrick McKissack's grandmother's name was Miranda, but that name jolted the flow of the language, so Patricia changed Miranda to Mirandy. The book also posed some illustration difficulties. For example, Jerry Pinkney had to devise a way to illustrate Brother Wind. As a child McKissack had been associated with the AME (African Methodist Episcopal) Church in Mississippi. At that church she remembered a woman who scandalized the more conservative townspeople by wearing red on Sunday. Ms. Poinsettia is a lot like that woman. When Pinkney began to create an image for her, he drew a picture of a woman who looked a lot like his own wife, Gloria. The illustrations earned a Caldecott honor award.

In *The Dark-Thirty* (Knopf, 1992), McKissack wrote a foreword telling how the 30 minutes before dark were called "the dark thirty." During that time, storytellers often sat on their front porches and spun tales. The book is a collection of stories that might have been told during those dark thirty minutes. The stories have a ring of reality to them, but McKissack says "the stories in *The Dark-Thirty* are all fictional." One of the stories, "Boo Mama," grew out of an event that occurred while McKissack was growing up in Tennessee. A child was lost in the woods for several days, and when the child was found, he had been well taken care of. Investigation revealed that the boy's grandmother designed the hoax to keep the boy herself. Asking "What if?" helped McKissack enlarge the incident to create the full story.

Other ideas, says McKissack, come from many places and people. She keeps a diary and usually creates characters from two or three different people—friends, acquaintances, or family. Her husband, Fredrick, does much of the research for the nonfiction books and gets "excited to find some obscure piece of information that they can use in one of their books."

In a picture book, *Ma Dear's Aprons* (Atheneum, 1997), Patricia McKissack uses aprons to recall what single mothers did to support their children at the turn of the century. McKissack's grandmother and great-grandmother had several aprons that became Patricia's. Her story is based on her great-grandmother's experiences as a domestic worker, and the story views the aprons she wore from a young boy's perspective. The aprons include a blue one with deep pockets for clothespins to wear on washday Mondays, a cheery yellow one to make her smile on ironing Tuesdays, and a flowered one for baking Saturdays. McKissack said,

"I'd like for my readers, especially single parents and their children, to feel that 'family' means unity, and in unity there is strength."

The stories and childhood experiences that spawn McKissack's stories were shared by McKissack's sister, Sarah, and her brother, Nolan. Sarah lives in Nashville and has three adult sons. Nolan lives in Corona, California, and has an adult son and daughter.

Fredrick and Patricia McKissack are partners in a writing service, All-Writing Services, in St. Louis, Missouri, where they live in a large remodeled inner-city home. When they are not writing, the couple enjoy working in their garden, growing roses, and watching old movies. They have three grown sons, Fredrick Jr., a coauthor with his mother of *Black Diamond: The Story of the Negro Baseball Leagues* (Scholastic, 1994); Robert Lewis; and John Patrick. They, along with their cousins, come from a long line of storytellers and are beginning to tell stories of their own. Patricia continues to bring her heritage to readers through the stories she tells. Although she focuses on bringing an awareness of African American culture to readers, she says that she "is not a black writer, but rather a writer who happens to be black—I write for children of all races."

Books and Notes

Patricia C. McKissack's books include wonderful picture books, nonfiction titles, and biographies, as well as several early readers. To each topic she brings a sense of purpose, the skill of storytelling to the printed page, and contributions to the building of bridges between cultures. Many of her books feature strong, determined, and clever female characters.

Biography

A Long Hard Journey: The Story of the Pullman Porter. Coauthored with Fredrick McKissack. (Walker, 1989).

Martin Luther King, Jr.: A Man to Remember (Children's, 1984).

Mary McLeod Bethune: A Great American Educator (Children's, 1985).

Picture Books/Early Readers

Christmas in the Big House, Christmas in the Quarters. Coauthored with Fredrick McKissack. Illustrated by John Thompson. (Scholastic, 1994).

Flossie and the Fox. Illustrated by Rachel Isadora. (Dial, 1986).

Ma Dear's Aprons. Illustrated by Floyd Cooper. (Atheneum, 1997).

Messy Bessey's School Desk. Coauthored with Fredrick McKissack. Illustrated by Dana Regan. (Children's, 1998).
A Rookie Reader.

Mirandy and the Brother Wind. Illustrated by Jerry Pinkney. (Knopf, 1988).

Nettie Jo's Friends. Illustrated by Scott Cook. (Knopf, 1989).

Who Is Who? Coauthored with Fredrick McKissack. Illustrated by Elizabeth M. Allen. (Children's, 1983). A Rookie Reader.

Nonfiction

African-American Inventors. Coauthored with Fredrick McKissack. (Millbrook, 1994).

Rebels Against Slavery. Coauthored with Fredrick McKissack. (Scholastic, 1996).

Red-Tail Angels: The Story of the Tuskegee Airmen of World War II. Coauthored with Fredrick McKissack. (Walker, 1995).

The Royal Kingdoms of Ghana, Mali, and Songhay: Life in Medieval Africa. Coauthored with Fredrick McKissack. (H. Holt, 1994).

For More Information About/By the Author

Articles

Bishop, R. S. "A Conversation with Patricia McKissack." *Language Arts* 69, no. 1 (January 1992): 69–74.

McKissack, Patricia. "The Dark-Thirty." *Bulletin of the Center for Children's Books* 46, no. 4 (December 1992): 117+.

McKissack, Patricia, and Fredrick McKissack. "Sojourner Truth: Ain't I a Woman? Acceptance Speech for the 1993 Boston Globe-Horn Book Award for Nonfiction." *Horn Book* 70, no. 1 (January 1994): 53+.

Books

McKissack, Patricia. *Can You Imagine?* Illustrated with photographs by Myles Pinkney. (Richard C. Owen, 1997).

A. A. Milne

Fantasy ◆ Poetry

London, England
January 18, 1892–January 31, 1956

- 📖 *When We Were Very Young*
- 📖 *The House at Pooh Corner*
- 📖 *Winnie-the-Pooh*

About the Author
and the Author's Writing

Alan Alexander (A. A.) Milne was the third and youngest son of J. B. Milne, a headmaster at a preparatory school. Milne was particularly close to his brother Ken, and together they had many happy boyhood adventures. Some of those adventures inspired episodes in the children's books he wrote many years later.

According to family stories, Alan taught himself to read at an early age (some say at the age of two) and began attending his father's school, Henley House. At Henley House Alan was tutored by the soon-to-be-famous writer H. G. Wells. Alan was excellent in mathematics. He was awarded a scholarship to Westminister School and entered at age 11 in 1903. Later he attended Cambridge to study mathematics. In his second year he became editor of the school's undergraduate newspaper, and from that time became determined to write. Once he graduated from Cambridge, he rented expensive rooms in London and settled down to write. At the end of the year, he had spent the remainder of his Cambridge allowance. Undaunted, he took two cheap rooms in a policeman's house and went on writing. He was a freelance journalist, and at 24 was appointed Assistant Editor of *Punch*. He was associated with *Punch* from 1906 to 1914. He married Dorothy Daphne de Selincourt in 1913 and in 1920 their only child, Christopher Robin, was born. Although an avowed pacifist, Milne served in the Royal Warwickshire Regiment and served in France during World War I.

Milne returned to England and picked up his freelance writing career. His work met with great success. In 1924 he published a volume of verses under the title *When We Were Very Young* (Methuen); many of the verses had been published first in issues of *Punch*.

In 1925 Milne bought Cotchford Farm in Hartfield, Sussex. The forest beyond the farm would eventually provide him with the setting for Pooh's adventures. Milne's son, Christopher Robin, had been given some stuffed animal toys from Harrod's in London. In December of that year, Milne was asked to write a story for the Christmas Eve issue of the *London Evening News*. Milne wrote down one of the stories, *In Which We Are Introduced to Winnie-the-Pooh and Some Bees and the Stories Begin*, that he had invented for his son about his toy bear. The story was published on December 24, 1925, and broadcast by the British Broadcast Company (BBC) on Christmas Day. Daphne Milne is credited with the idea of bringing these animals to life in a children's book. Milne dictated the stories to his wife. She later told that Milne "walked to and fro, puffing at his pipe while I wrote and laughed." The newspaper story became the first chapter to *Winnie-the-Pooh* (Methuen, 1926).

The stories describe the adventures of Pooh and his companions, Piglet, Eeyore, Kanga, Roo, Owl, Rabbit, and Tigger. They all live in the neighborhood of Pooh Corner, which was Cotchford Farm. Piglet, Eeyore, Kanga, and Roo were Christopher's toys, and Ernest Shepard, the illustrator of the tales, is said to have drawn them from the originals. However, some accounts state that Shepard did not use Christopher's bear as a model for the drawings, but rather used "Growler," the much-loved bear owned by his own son, Graham. While Christopher's childhood toys are on display at the Dutton offices in New York, Growler's future was ill-fated. Shepard's granddaughter, Minette, took the much worn Growler with her to Canada during the war, where he was attacked by a Scottie dog in a Montreal garden—the dog won. Piglet suffered a similar fate years earlier in an English orchard, although Piglet survived.

As a child A. A. Milne enjoyed the animal stories of Brer Rabbit in *Uncle Remus* and *Reynard the Fox*, as well as the adventure stories of *Swiss Family Robinson* and *Treasure Island*. He admired the poetry of C. S. Calverly and emulated him throughout his life. Milne's poetry was light and whimsical during a time when whimsicality was very popular.

Milne authored a second book of verse, *Now We Are Six* (Methuen, 1927), the third title to be "taken by children." His fourth was *The House at Pooh Corner* (Methuen, 1928), the final volume of the quartet.

Milne felt that he should be writing something more substantial, such as a detective story. Even after the tremendous success of Pooh, Milne remained doubtful. He did write a detective novel, *The Red House Mystery*, in 1922, and continued to write essays, plays, short stories, and novels. It was his four volumes of light verse and stories about Pooh and his friends that became Milne's legacy. Throughout his life Milne stated that he had not written the stories and poems for children; he intended them for the child within us. He never read the stories to his son, preferring instead to read him favorite authors, such as P. G. Wodehouse. (Note: Wodehouse once described Milne as "about my favorite author.") Christopher Robin liked Wodehouse's stories and is said to have read them to his own daughter, Clare, as she was growing up.

The Pooh books have been published in almost every language, including Latin. Between the years 1926 and 1956, the sales of the four books were said to have been more than 7 million. No one is sure however, because once the figure got above 1 million, the publishers ceased keeping track. Since 1968, it is estimated that Methuen alone has sold more than 20 million copies of the four books. This figure does not include the many copies of books published by Dutton in the United States, or any of the foreign editions of the books. The Russian version, *Vinnie Pookh*, sold more than 3.5 million copies in 1985. And most amazingly, a Latin version, *Winnie Ille Pu*, became the first foreign-language book to become a best-seller in the United States.

Milne was a successful and popular dramatist, novelist, and humorist. Many of his plays were performed to great acclaim in Europe and America. Currently few professional theaters are performing any of his works, although amateur theater groups have used his play in almost every English-speaking country.

In 1952 A. A. Milne had brain surgery, and even though he survived, the surgery left him an invalid. He returned to Cotchford Farm in Sussex, where he spent his final days. His last published work appeared in 1952. He died on January 31, 1956.

The real Christopher Robin Milne was plagued by his namesake character and spent his entire life trying to shake the shadow of being his father's son. While growing up, Christopher spent little time with his father. However, they did share an interest in nature. Even though he disliked the notoriety brought to him by the books, the two developed a close friendship during Christopher's teenage years. Daphne Milne is said to have been too interested in fashion and too busy spending Alan Milne's money to pay much (if any) attention to Christopher. Accordingly, after his father's death, Christopher did not see his mother again, even though she lived for another fifteen years. Christopher's mother, Daphne, died in 1974, and after her death, he discovered that she had destroyed all of his father's papers and personal possessions to keep people from prying into his private affairs. At first he was devastated, but eventually came to think that perhaps she was correct to attempt to keep others from psychoanalyzing Winnie-the-Pooh's author. Christopher Robin died April 20, 1996. Several years before he died he sold all of his interest in the Pooh Trust to the Royal Literacy Fund, founded in 1790 to help writers fallen on hard times. A. A. Milne, although a successful adult author, achieved immortality on four slim volumes of light verse and adventures of "a Bear of Very Little Brain," rather than his huge literary output of plays and novels.

Books and Notes

While there are many editions of the books created by A. A. Milne now on the market, the four original titles were published by Methuen in England and later by Dutton in the United States. Both editions were illustrated with the line drawings of Ernest H. Shepard. Various publishers have been able to acquire rights to publish the stories with colorized versions of Shepard's drawings. Walt Disney Productions bought animation and story rights, and created new cartoon illustrations for their animated versions. They also use those images to illustrate their "Disney" versions of the stories first told by Milne. So many of the stories and verses have been published as single stories or selected versions that it is next to impossible to record every edition or version.

When We Were Very Young. Illustrated by Ernest H. Shepard. (Methuen, 1924).

Winnie-the-Pooh. Illustrated by Ernest H. Shepard. (Methuen, 1926).

Now We Are Six. Illustrated by Ernest H. Shepard. (Methuen, 1927).

The House at Pooh Corner. Illustrated by Ernest H. Shepard. (Methuen, 1928).

For More Information About/By the Author

Books

Thwaite, Ann. *A. A. Milne, His Life* (Faber, 1990).

Thwaite, Ann. *The Brilliant Career of Winnie-the-Pooh, the Story of A. A. Milne and His Writing for Children* (Methuen, 1992).

Nicholasa Mohr

◆ Contemporary Realistic Fiction

New York, New York
November 1, 1939

📖 *Nilda*

📖 *Felita*

About the Author
and the Author's Writing

Pedro and Nicholasa Golpé came to the United States from Puerto Rico in the 1930s. Their daughter, Nicholasa, was born November 1, 1939, in El Barrio, a section of New York City. El Barrio was also known as Spanish Harlem. *El Barrio* means "the neighborhood," and this neighborhood was predominantly Puerto Rican. When Nicholasa's parents immigrated to the United States they brought four small sons; three more children were born in the United States. Nicholasa was the youngest and the only girl. The family moved to the Bronx at about the time Nicholasa started school. She got her first library card when she was seven years old, and the first book she chose was Collodi's *Pinocchio*. Within the year her father had died, and her mother worked hard to keep the family together. When she could no longer work, she had to apply for public assistance. Later in life, Mohr wrote about this period in her book *Nilda* (Harper, 1973). Nicholasa's father had educational goals for his children, and after his death Nicholasa's mother continued to encourage her children to study. Nicholasa enjoyed drawing and creating her own world. Her mother encouraged her artwork and told Nicholasa that she must make an important contribution to the world; she must be somebody. Nicholasa used her art to set herself apart from the other children at school.

When Nicholasa's family moved to an all-white neighborhood they were "beaten, harassed and had to move out . . . and return to our old neighborhood." This time in Nicholasa's life became part of her book *Felita* (Dial, 1979). Like Felita's family, Nicholasa's family managed through very difficult times. While Nicholasa was still in junior high school her mother died and the family had to split up. Nicholasa went to live with an aunt; her six older brothers went to live in other places. In her aunt's home Nicholasa's presence was merely tolerated.

Nicholasa was a very talented artist and wanted to develop her skills. However, a school counselor felt Nicholasa should "learn a trade and not be a burden on society." So the counselor channeled Nicholasa to a trade school instead of encouraging her to strive for a college preparatory course. A poor Hispanic stood little chance of getting a college education, and the counselor's view was that Nicholasa should not take the place of someone who was more likely to go to college. So, Nicholasa went to trade school, but managed to avoid all sewing courses. She disliked sewing and still does. She studied fashion illustrating instead, and eventually managed to study art. When she finished high school, she enrolled in the Art Students' League in New York City, where she studied painting and drawing. During her high school years, she worked in the public library and became acquainted with books that displayed the work of Mexican muralists and artists. She knew that she wanted to go to Mexico to study art, so she saved enough money to spend a semester in Mexico studying printmaking. Seeing the work of the great Mexican muralists helped to shape the direction of her future work.

After returning to the United States Mohr enrolled in the New School for Social Research in New York City, where she met her husband-to-be, Irwin Mohr, a Brooklyn native. Irwin Mohr was working on a doctorate in clinical psychology. After a rather short courtship they married. After their two sons, David and Jason, were born, the family moved to an old wooden house in Teaneck, New Jersey, a suburb of New York City. The house had a huge attic, which Nicholasa converted into an art studio with a printmaking press. She became a successful artist, whose work appeared in many exhibitions and art galleries.

One day at the suggestion of her art agent, who knew that a collector of Mohr's artwork was also an editor, she wrote about the graffiti that often appeared in her prints. (At first she declined, but when she realized how little was written about Puerto Ricans, she decided to try.) She wrote about 50 pages of childhood reminiscences. Mohr later commented, "I found it was very hard to write." The agent and editor who had first requested she try her hand at writing did not like the writing. She wanted more sensational episodes—gang fights, drug dealing, encounters with the police. But that was not Nicholasa's life. So, she declined to rewrite the manuscript. Nicholasa was disappointed, but later offered an editor at Harper & Row her manuscript. Within a week or two, Nicholasa was offered a book contract. Writing the book, which became *Nilda*, was a very difficult experience. Nicholasa took some of her favorite writers—Shirley Jackson, Chekhov, de Maupassant, and went to work on the book at the MacDowell Colony (a community of musicians, artists, and writers in Petersborough, New Hampshire). She spent the summer discovering the magic of storytelling. She discovered that writing was an outlet for her artistic expression; she painted her stories with words. It was then that she decided that writing would be her major vocation. Mohr created nine illustrations for *Nilda* and designed the book jacket as well. Vincent, her second oldest brother, encouraged her to start a second book of short stories. So, *Nilda* was followed by *El Bronx Remembered* (Harper, 1975), twelve short stories and a novella. She had spent several of her childhood years around Prospect and Longwood Avenues in the Bronx, and, in *El Bronx Remembered*, she tells stories of the Puerto Ricans living in the area from 1946 to 1956. She began to concentrate more on her written art and less on her visual art. She has said that from an author's point of view the Bronx is no different than Peoria, Illinois—"it's another American experience."

Writing made her art more accessible to a wider audience. She says that "the world of visual art is very exclusive and expensive." One must have a lot of money to buy a work of art. But a book becomes part of many libraries, and readers can find the book there or buy an inexpensive paperback. *In Nueva York* (Dial, 1977) and *Felita* were published next.

Mohr came to love authors Shirley Jackson, Carson McCullers, and Katherine Ann Porter. Later in life she read the great Latin American writers, like Julia deBurgos and Gabriel Garcia Marquez. From those writers she appreciated "that the more specific you are in your writing, the more universal your appeal. So I write about what I know best." What she knows best is the experience of women and Puerto Ricans growing up in New York City.

Mohr writes fiction, drama, screenplays, and teleplays. She says, "There are still lots of stories for me to write. If I lived two lifetimes, I still couldn't write them all." Nicholasa Mohr no longer works as a visual artist, except for her own personal enjoyment, but concentrates instead on writing fiction and essays. In 1986, *Going Home* (Dial), a sequel to *Felita*, was published. Books by Mohr have garnered the American Book Award, the Jane Addams Children's Book Award, and have been listed on several best- and notable-book lists, including those published by the *School Library Journal* and the American Library Association.

Today Nicholasa Mohr makes her home in the Park Slope area of Brooklyn, where she moved after her husband's death. She has conducted workshops and classes in communities throughout New York and at universities and colleges. In 1989 she became a distinguished visiting professor at Queens College in the Department of Elementary and Early Childhood Education and Services. In May 1989 the State University of New York awarded her an honorary Doctor of Letters degree. Nicholasa Mohr was born in Manhattan's El Barrio, raised in the Bronx, struggled against prejudices, and emerged as Dr. Nicholasa Mohr, successful author and artist.

Books and Notes

Nicholasa Mohr is the author of many short story collections, plays, essays, and books for children, young adults, and adults. Her books for children include many experiences that are part of her own childhood and family background. One of her latest titles, a title for adults, *A Matter of Pride and Other Stories* (Arte Pùblico, 1997), is a celebration of the female spirit in a collection of seven stories of Hispanic women. The stories, set in New York City and the Caribbean, are said to transcend generational and gender barriers with universal themes. Her children's books are among the very few focusing on Hispanic culture that are published by mainstream publishers and which have wide appeal for readers from all cultures. She has retold fairy tales from Puerto Rican culture.

Tales from the El Barrio/Bronx

All for the Better: A Story of El Barrio. Illustrated by Rudy Gutierrez. (Raintree, 1993).

El Bronx Remembered (Harper, 1975; Arte Pùblico, 1985).

Felita. Illustrated by Ray Cruz. (Dial, 1979; Bantam, 1990).

Going Home (Dial, 1986; Bantam, 1989).

In Nueva York (Dial, 1977; Arte Pùblico, 1988).

Nilda (Harper, 1973; Arte Pùblico, 1986).

"Taking a Dare." In *When I Was Your Age: Original Stories About Growing Up.* Introduction by Amy Ehlrich, ed. (Candlewick Press, 1996).

Folktales from Puerto Rico

Old Letivia and the Mountain of Sorrows. Illustrated by Rudy Gutierrez. (Viking, 1996).

The Song of El Coquí and Other Tales of Puerto Rico. Coauthored with Antonio Martorell. (Viking, 1995).

For More Information About/By the Author

Articles

"Wordsmiths Love the Bronx." *Bronx Beat Online.* URL: http://moon.jrn. columbia.edu/BronxBeat/indices/ 051997/writers.html (Accessed February 1998).

Books

Mohr, Nicholasa. *Growing Up Inside the Sanctuary of My Imagination* (J. Messner, 1994).

Phyllis Reynolds Naylor

◆ Contemporary Realistic Fiction

Anderson, Indiana
January 4, 1933

📖 Alice Series

📖 *Shiloh*

📖 *The Grand Escape*

About the Author
and the Author's Writing

When she was young Phyllis Reynolds did not think of becoming a paid writer; it was something she did for fun. Her mother, Lura Shields Reynolds, and sometimes her father, Eugene S. Reynolds, read to Phyllis and her siblings each night until they were well into their teens. They read Mark Twain, the *Bible Story Book*, and Grimm's fairy tales. Sometimes an "occasional dessert" such as *The Wind in the Willow* or *Alice in Wonderland* would be thrown in.

Phyllis Reynolds was born January 4, 1933, in Anderson, Indiana, where she grew up in a household with a brother, John, and a sister, Norma. The entire family enjoyed books. At the age sixteen, a former teacher, who had become the editor of a children's Sunday school paper, wrote to her. She remembered that Phyllis had always liked to write, and asked her if she would like to write a story for the paper. She was paid

$4.67 for it, her first paid writing experience. She was thrilled and began to write other pieces, submitting them to a variety of magazines. She received many rejection slips, but also managed to publish enough stories that she paid a large share of her college tuition when she went off to college to study clinical psychology. She graduated from Joliet Junior College in 1953. In 1960 she married Rex V. Naylor, a speech pathologist. Two sons were born in the next few years, Alan Jeffrey (Jeff) and Michael Scott. She graduated from the American University with an undergraduate degree in 1963. By this time she had a taste of real success. She had been published in many major publications, including the National Education Association's *NEA Journal*, where in 1959 she had written a regular column titled "The Light Touch" based on her early teaching experiences. Writing was her first love, so she opted not to attend graduate school to concentrate on writing full-time. Two years later her first novel, *The Galloping Goat* (Abingdon, 1965), was published.

She says, "I like to write about different things for different ages." Sometimes she writes a picture book, and then writes a piece for retired people, and then perhaps a young adult novel. Each book "begins with an irritation. It's a feeling that I want to say something, an issue that I want to work out for myself, a worry I want to work through. I do all of that by writing."

A number of years ago the Naylors were visiting friends, Frank and Judy Madden, in West Virginia when they found an abused and abandoned dog. Arriving home in Maryland, Naylor was still bothered by the incident. Her husband said, "Well Phyllis are you going to have a nervous breakdown or are you going to do something about it?" That was the beginning of *Shiloh* (Atheneum, 1991). The story was written at "break neck speed." Most of her books concern problems that she wrestled with as a child, but "this book was based on a feeling of discomfort that was still very fresh." She later found out that the Maddens had adopted the stray dog. It seemed as if this was a "first test of justice." Naylor wondered, "What kind of justice is it that I get a book out of this and my friends get stuck with a dog." In fact Naylor not only got a book out of it, but the book earned her the coveted Newbery Award for 1992. Her friends named the beagle Clover.

Her characters and settings come from her life. She is a good observer, and although she tries not to write about the people she knows, she does use aspects of their personalities. Her sons, Jeff and Mike, for example, can find themselves in Naylor's books, no matter how she changes the characters' appearances or situations. Her sons have also assisted her with some incidents. For example, Naylor once paid Jeff $20 to set up a poker game, just so she could sit in a corner and see how it's done. Another time she watched one of her sons and his friends lift weights so she could find out just what they do and say.

Phyllis Naylor says, "Probably every book of mine has a little something of me in it. So many of the embarrassing episodes in my Alice series are based on things that happened to me as a young girl, or that happened to my friends. *Shiloh,* of course, as well as *Shiloh Season* [Atheneum, 1996] and *Saving Shiloh* [Atheneum, 1997] are about an abused dog I found in West Virginia, and *The Keeper* [Atheneum, 1986] is based on the mental illness of my first husband. The cats in *The Grand Escape* [Atheneum, 1993] and *The Healing of Texas Jake* [Atheneum, 1997] are really our own two cats, Marco and Ulysses, renamed Marco and Polo in the books."

The Keeper is the story of a junior high school student, Nick, who must deal with his father, who is plunging fast into serious mental illness. The idea for *The Grand Escape* came when the Naylors' cat Ulysses was found to have a very round tumor in his belly. The Naylors took him to the vet that same day. The vet decided that he would have to operate. Halfway through the operation, the vet called the Naylor residence. He had found 40 yards of Christmas ribbon, 11 rubber bands, grass, and hair, all in Ulysses's belly. Someone commented that "Ulysses is like a lawnmower" and that he should be kept inside because of his antics. *The Grand Escape* is about the little adventures of the Naylors' cats.

Her book *Beetles Toasted Lightly* (Atheneum, 1997) is set in Iowa. The idea was sparked by an article in *National Geographic* that mentioned farmers and the search for nontraditional food products. Because she had often visited her grandparents in Waverly, Iowa, and had spent time on their farm in the summer, it seemed like the right place to set the story.

Shiloh was made into a movie by Warner Brothers and then made available on video. Naylor says, "Although the movie version isn't exactly like the book . . . it is true to the theme and plot, and it was fun for our family to see the actors become the characters we have grown to know so well."

Finding time to write was a struggle for Naylor when her children were young. When Michael was little she would hire a sitter and go to the library to write for eight or nine hours. Before coming home, she would check out picture books for him to read. He thought the books were the ones she had been writing. Michael was quite disappointed to find out that the books were written by someone else.

It was Phyllis's husband who suggested that she put all of her book ideas in a notebook. This would keep her from worrying about keeping all of the ideas together. So in her notebooks, one for each book, she has notes to herself, newspaper clippings, and so forth. Each notebook is labeled. Her first drafts are written in longhand and often her second ones are too. Eventually the manuscript is typed on her computer and the final revisions and rewrites are made there. Her husband is a chess player in his spare time. "He can happily spend an evening over the chess board while I am at the typewriter. But he is my most severe critic (and inspiration), and though I am not always happy with his comments about my characters or plot, his suggestions are always helpful."

When Naylor is not writing books or *thinking* about writing books, she is usually doing something with her husband or family. "I love to go to the theater. I also love taking long walks or swimming. I play the piano, too, and enjoy music and books." Her books have won a number of awards, the Newbery in 1992, the 1985 Edgar Allan Poe Award for Best Juvenile Mystery for *Night Cry* (Atheneum, 1984), literally dozens of nominations and awards in various states, and a similar number of citations on lists for "Best Books of the Year" and other similar lists.

Naylor lives with her husband, Rex, in Bethesda, Maryland, in the same house their sons grew up in. Jeff is married and lives in Minneapolis. He and his wife, Julie, have two daughters, Sophia and Tessa. The Naylors' second son, Mike, is married to Jeanie and they live in New Jersey. "Each year we all rent a house together at the ocean and have a wonderful week swimming, wave running, reading, playing games, and having crab feasts."

Books and Notes

Phyllis Naylor has shown that she is a versatile writer with strength in several genres. Her most popular titles include those in the Alice series, her Shiloh trilogy, and more recently some anthropomorphic fiction titles featuring her cats, Marco and Polo (Ulysses).

Alice Series (YA Titles)

Achingly Alice (Atheneum, 1998).

The Agony of Alice (Atheneum, 1985).

Alice in April (Atheneum, 1993).

Alice in Rapture, Sort Of (Atheneum, 1989).

Alice In-Between (Atheneum, 1994).

All but Alice (Atheneum, 1992).

Reluctantly, Alice (Atheneum, 1991).

Anthropomorphic Fiction

The Grand Escape (Atheneum, 1993).

The Healing of Texas Jake (Atheneum, 1997).

Picture Books

Ducks Disappearing. Illustrated by Tony Maddox. (Atheneum, 1997).

I Can't Take You Anywhere. Illustrated by Jef Kaminsky. (Atheneum, 1997).

Strawberries. Illustrated by Rosalind Charney Kaye. (Atheneum, 1998).

Shiloh Trilogy

Shiloh (Atheneum, 1991).

Shiloh Season (Atheneum, 1996).

Saving Shiloh (Atheneum, 1997).

Other Titles

The Boys Start the War (Delacorte, 1993).

The Fear Place (Atheneum, 1994).

The Girls Get Even (Delacorte, 1993).

Night Cry (Atheneum, 1984).

The Treasure of Bessledorf Hill (Atheneum, 1997).

For More Information About/By the Author

Articles

"Meet an Author." *Frank Schaffer's Classmate* (November/December/January 1986–87): 66–67.

"Meet Phyllis Reynolds Naylor: Write from the Heart." *NEA Today* (May 1992): 9.

Books

Naylor, Phyllis Reynolds. *How I Came to Be a Writer* (Atheneum, 1978).

Stover, Lois Thomas. *Presenting Phyllis Reynolds Naylor* (Atheneum, 1997).

Joan Lowery Nixon

Historical Fiction ◆ Contemporary Realistic Fiction ◆ Mysteries

**Los Angeles, California
February 3, 1927**

📖 Orphan Train Adventures
   Series
📖 Orphan Train Children Series
📖 Casebusters Series
📖 Ellis Island Series

About the Author
and the Author's Writing

Joan Lowery Nixon grew up reading and writing mysteries. "From the time I was very young, I wanted to be a writer. I wanted to write the kind of books I loved to read, stories that made me laugh or cry, and mysteries—especially mysteries." Joan Lowery was born February 3, 1927, and was raised in California. During her childhood she enjoyed reading but also had "weed fights in the vacant lot next door," produced puppet shows, and acted out stories in a dollhouse. Her younger sister and the neighborhood children provided audiences for her theatrics. Once out of high school, she studied and obtained an undergraduate degree in journalism from the University of Southern California and later received a certificate in elementary education from California State College. After marrying Hershell "Nick" Nixon on August 6, 1949, they traveled through several states before settling in Texas, where they have lived since 1960. Their two daughters, Maureen and Kathy, were in grade school when they urged their mother to write a mystery book and to "put us in it." That book, *The Mystery of Hurricane Castle*, was published in 1964 by Criterion. She got 12 rejections for the book before a publisher accepted it. As a way to encourage Nixon, her mother treated her to a housekeeper for a year. The housekeeper read each day to the children, kept an eye on the preschoolers, and kept the house in order; Nixon wrote.

From that beginning she has built a writing career. Many of her books are mysteries, but she has also written humorous picture books, historical fiction novels based on the arrival of immigrants to Ellis Island and orphan children sent West to new homes on "the Orphan Train," and general titles about young adult relationships. But Joan Lowery Nixon remains best known for her mystery books.

A typical writing day for Nixon finds here writing from 8 AM until noon, continuing from 1 PM until 5 PM. She writes at least five days a week and often writes for six.

Nixon says that her ideas come from three sources—newspaper items, incidents that happen to her or her friends and family, and her imagination. She often starts with an incident and the resolution—from that point Nixon constructs a crime, develops the sequence of events, and adds a few clues to pique interest. As Nixon plans the plot, she moves from the climax of the story to make sure all the important clues are there, along with a few red herrings. As Nixon identifies characters, she builds a profile for their personalities, which evolve as the story unfolds. She continually asks herself, "What if?" Nixon explains, "What if I were a 10-year-old boy or a 16-year-old girl and this happened to me? What would I do? As I begin to get the germ of a story idea, I decide on my main character and who she or he should be. My main character and idea come together in my mind to form a plot. It may take a few weeks. In one case it took five years. When I know where I'm going with the story I work on the beginning. I like to open stories with action, or suspense, or both to hook the reader from the opening sentence. When I have the opening firmly in mind, I work on the ending. I never write a word of a story until I know how I'm going to end it. I'm enthusiastic and excited about my story and would hate to lose it by writing into an impossible box. When all this is firmly in mind, I write a proposal for the story for my editor. It runs somewhere between ten and twenty-five pages. I refer to this proposal while writing the story, but I may add characters, make changes, etc. The proposal is flexible."

Several years ago Nixon read an article about a young man in west Texas who was in a semicomatose condition for a number of years, then he suddenly woke up. Nixon began to ask herself what it would feel like to wake up and find yourself four years older. What if a teenager woke up and not only found herself four years older, but came to realize that she was the only witness to a murder committed years ago? That idea and her questions were the beginning of *The Other Side of Dark* (Delacorte, 1986). To research this book she interviewed physicians about the medical details.

Nixon wrote *A Deadly Game of Magic* (Harcourt, 1983) after a friend recounted a story about a car problem on the way home. She stopped and walked in the drizzle to the door of a nearby house. The man who answered let her in. Even though he had to leave, he left her in the house alone to wait for the automobile club to come. Nixon began to think about what might have happened if the man who let her friend into the house was not the homeowner. And what if there was a dead body in a back room?

As Nixon develops a suspense/mystery book, she gives herself a double challenge—that of interweaving two story lines. The main character must have a personal problem and a mystery to solve as well. The solution to the personal problem and the mystery must come together in the climax, while the tale must build a strong element of suspense.

The Nixons live in a modest house in Houston on a cul-de-sac directly across from a dark and mysterious wood. Her home has a rather large foyer, and it was that foyer that became the setting for a murder that takes place in *Whispers from the Dead* (Delacorte, 1989). In that tale a teenager murders a housemaid and an illegal alien. The book's main character, Sarah, survives a near drowning and, as a result, gains an ability to communicate with the dead. Sarah is able to communicate with the murdered housemaid, and ultimately is able to lead the police to the murderer, Adam Holt. This tale is based on a real incident that occurred near Nixon's home. A mail carrier was murdered during her rounds. However, this day the carrier happened to be a substitute and, for some reason, was delivering the mail much earlier than usual. When she did not return to the post office, they retraced her steps and found bloody shoes in the garage. The teenager suspected stated during questioning that he had put the body in a nearby bayou. Later, a tow-truck operator reported that he had pulled the young man's car from a quarry a distance away from the bayou. The body of the mail carrier was found in that quarry, and the young man was charged. The young man's statement about a bayou was not really addressed. Nixon thought that it was strange that the young man would confess to a murder and give the wrong location for the body. She speculated about the possibility of a second murder, perhaps one that the mail carrier witnessed when she arrived earlier than usual at the house. The placement of the mailbox would allow anyone delivering mail to see into the foyer. But who could have been murdered? No one filed a missing persons report. Perhaps someone who did not have anyone to notice whether or not she or he was living. In the Houston area, it is natural to think that perhaps the unreported murder might be that of an illegal alien. From these speculations Nixon developed the storyline for *Whispers from the Dead*. Campaign dirty tricks led Nixon to develop the plot of *A Candidate for Murder* (Delacorte, 1991), and newspaper articles about a kidnapping provided the seed for the plot to *The Kidnapping of Christina Lattimore* (Dell, 1979).

Nixon generally allows three months to write a young adult book, three weeks to one month for shorter books. That time frame does not include research or travel. Nixon has written young adult novels, middle-grade readers, and picture books. She finds young adult books most satisfying because "I have more space in which to develop character and emotion."

Joan Lowery Nixon and her husband, "Nick," a retired petroleum geologist, live in Houston, Texas, where they raised their four children, Kathleen Nixon Brush, Maureen Nixon Quinlan, Joseph M. Nixon, and Eileen Nixon McGowan. They have thirteen grandchildren including Nicole Brush, who not only maintains the Joan Lowery Nixon website, but has coauthored a story, "The Disappearance of Gavin McCann," with her grandmother for *Great Authors and Kids Write Mystery Stories* (Random, 1996). When Nixon is not writing she enjoys traveling and "playing with grandchildren."

Books and Notes

Joan Lowery Nixon is a multifaceted author who is best known for her historical fiction titles and mystery books. Her first sale was a short magazine article sold to *Ford Times*. Her first book was published in 1964, and thirty years later, in 1994, her one hundredth book was published. She has been the recipient of four Edgars from the Mystery Writers of America, two Spurs from Western Writers of America, and eighteen awards from various state organizations that sponsor children's choice awards.

Casebusters

Catch a Crooked Clown (Disney Press, 1996).
Book #8.

Fear Stalks Grizzly Hill (Disney Press, 1996).
Book #9.

Sabotage on the Set (Disney Press, 1996).
Book #10.

The Internet Escapade (Disney Press, 1997).
    Book #11.

Bait for a Burglar (Disney Press, 1997).
    Book #12.

Ellis Island

Land of Hope (Bantam, 1992).

Land of Promise (Bantam, 1993).

Land of Dreams (Bantam, 1994).

Mystery/Suspense

A Candidate for Murder (Delacorte, 1991).

A Deadly Promise (Bantam, 1992).
    Sequel to *High Trail of Danger*.

Don't Scream (Delacorte, 1996).

The Haunting (Delacorte, 1996).

High Trail of Danger (Bantam, 1991).

Murdered, My Sweet (Delacorte, 1997).

The Name of the Game Was Murder (Delacorte, 1993).

Search for the Shadowman (Delacorte, 1996).

The Weekend Was Murder (Delacorte, 1992).
    Sequel to *The Dark and Deadly Pool*.

Orphan Train Adventures

A Family Apart (Bantam, 1987).
    Book #1.

Caught in the Act (Bantam, 1988).
    Book #2.

In the Face of Danger (Bantam, 1988).
    Book #3.

A Place to Belong (Bantam, 1989).
    Book #4.

A Dangerous Promise (Delacorte, 1994).
    Book #5.

Keeping Secrets (Delacorte, 1995).
    Book #6.

Circle of Love (Delacorte, 1997).
    Book #7.

Orphan Train Children

Lucy's Wish (Delacorte, 1998).
    Book #1.

Will's Choice (Delacorte, 1998).
    Book #2.

For More Information About/By the Author

Articles

Brush, Nicole. *Joan Lowery Nixon Book Club*. URL: http://members.aol.com/NikkiB5130/JNixon5130.htm (Accessed December 1997).

"A Conversation with Patricia Windsor and Joan Lowery Nixon." *Dell Carousel* (Fall/Winter 1986–87): 4–6.

James, Dean. "Interview: Joan Lowery Nixon." *Mystery Scene* no. 49 (September/October 1995): 27–49.

Kramer, Barbara. "Interview: Joan Lowery Nixon." *Mystery Scene* no. 21 (May 1989): 31–33.

Nixon, Joan Lowery. "Paving the Way for Future Generations." *Journal of Youth Services in Libraries: Joys* 9, no. 3 (Spring 1996): 233+.

Nixon, Joan Lowery. "Writing Mysteries Young Adults Want to Read." *The Writer* 104, no. 7 (June 1991): 18.

Nixon, Joan Lowery. "Writing the Western Novel for Young Adults." *The Writer* 105, no. 6 (June 1991): 21.

Pavonetti, Linda M. "Joan Lowery Nixon: The Grande Dame of Young Adult Mystery." *Journal of Adolescent & Adult Literacy* 39, no. 6 (March 1996): 454+.

Mary Norton

◆ Fantasy

**Leighton Buzzard,
Bedfordshire, England
December 10, 1903–August 29, 1992**

📖 *The Borrowers*
📖 *The Borrowers Afloat*

About the Author
and the Author's Writing

Mary Pearson was born in the early 1900s in Leighton Buzzard, Bedfordshire, England, where she grew up in the big house that became the setting for *The Borrowers* (Harcourt, 1953). Her father, Reginald Spenser Pearson, was a physician; her mother was Mary Savile Hughes Pearson. Mary Pearson's first ambition was to become an actress, and for a year or more she was a member of the Old Vic Theater Company. She gave up the theater to marry Robert Charles Norton of a famous ship-owning family. His family had established a shipping business in Portugal at the end of the Napoleonic wars. Mary Pearson Norton and Robert Norton moved there, and he worked in the business throughout the Great Depression and into the late 1930s when World War II broke out. During their time in Portugal the Nortons had four children—two sons, Robert George and Guy, and two daughters, Ann Mary and Caroline. She also began to write.

During the war, Mary Norton and the children returned to England. She worked in the War Office and later took the children to New York to work with the British Purchasing Commission. They lived in the United

States from 1940 to 1943. She rented a house in Connecticut and began to write, in earnest, to support her children and pay for the house she had rented. Robert Norton had stayed in Portugal, where he joined the staff of the British Embassy, later joining the British navy as a gunner. She wrote an occasional adult story and some articles. She also began to write down some of the stories she was telling her children, and some editors in America encouraged her writing. In 1943 she returned to London, where she lived in an eighteenth-century house in the Chelsea district, continued writing, and returned to acting.

Her first children's book, *The Magic Bed-knob, or How to Become a Witch in Ten Easy Lessons* (Putnam, 1944), was about a "spinster" who was learning to be a witch, three children, and a flying bed. In 1947 a sequel, *Bonfires and Broomsticks* (Putnam, 1947), was published. When her third book, *The Borrowers*, was published by Dent in 1952, it landed her name in the annals of children's books. Harcourt published *The Borrowers* in the United States the following year. The book won England's prestigious Carnegie Medal for 1952. The story came from her own childhood days when she acted out elaborate plays with small, painted dolls on the floor of the Big House. Three sequels followed: *The Borrowers Afield* (Harcourt, 1955), *The Borrowers Afloat* (Harcourt, 1959), and *The Borrowers Aloft* (Harcourt, 1961). In a 1962 interview Mary Norton said, "*The Borrowers Aloft* is the last of the books about the Borrowers." But nine years later she penned the final tale, *Poor Stainless: A New Story About the Borrowers* (Harcourt, 1971).

Her very first book, *The Magic Bed-knob, or How to Become a Witch in Ten Easy Lessons*, was published in 1944 and reissued in 1957 by Harcourt as *Bed-knob and Broomstick*. Walt Disney Productions made the story into a movie, starring Angela Lansbury, in 1971. In 1994 John Hendersen directed a movie of *The Borrowers*, starring Richard Lewis, Ian Holm, and Sian Phillips.

In the 1960s and 1970s, Mary Norton was living in a cottage in Essex. She was a member of the P.E.N. club, and, when not writing, she enjoyed swimming, riding, and vacation travel. In addition, she had amassed a long list of her own favorite authors. Mary Norton died in Hartland, England on August 29, 1992.

Books and Notes

Mary Norton's *The Magic Bed-knob* is sometimes dismissed as an imitation of P. L. Travers's books about Mary Poppins. Few dispute, however, the appeal of her series of books about the Borrowers, the diminutive Clock Family who live under the floorboards of a quiet country house in England. The tiny family is especially resourceful, creating a very comfortable home with tidbits and trinkets they borrow from the "human beans." Matchboxes become storage containers, postage stamps decorate their rooms as paintings, and two glove fingers become a small pair of Turkish bloomers for Homily to wear while she is "knocking about in the mornings." The books have been issued in many editions since the originals were published in America. Artists Michael Hague, Diane Stanley, Justin Todd, Pauline Baynes, and Sian Bailey have all illustrated various editions of the titles. Paperback editions are from Penguin/Puffin Books.

Bed-knob and Broomstick. Illustrated by Erik Blegvad. (Harcourt, 1957).

The Borrowers. Illustrated by Beth Krush and Joe Krush. (Harcourt, 1953).

The Borrowers Afield. Illustrated by Beth Krush and Joe Krush. (Harcourt, 1955).

The Borrowers Afloat. Illustrated by Beth Krush and Joe Krush. (Harcourt, 1959).

The Borrowers Aloft. Illustrated by Beth Krush and Joe Krush. (Harcourt, 1961).

Poor Stainless: A New Story About the Borrowers. Illustrated by Beth Krush and Joe Krush. (Harcourt, 1971).

For More Information About/By the Author

Books

Stott, Jon. *Mary Norton*. Twayne's English Author Series, no. 508. (Twayne, 1994).

Scott O'Dell

◆ Historical Fiction

**Los Angeles, California
May 23, 1898–October 15, 1989**

📖 *Island of the Blue Dolphins*

📖 *Streams to the River, River to the Sea:
A Novel of Sacagawea*

About the Author
and the Author's Writing

The last years of Scott O'Dell's life were spent with his wife, Elizabeth, in a house near a beautiful wooded lake in northern Westchester County, New York. He was 91 years old. He had become a legend in the world of children's books even though he didn't start writing for children until he was 59 years of age. He cared a lot about nature and the out-of-doors.

O'Dell was born in Los Angeles when there were more horses than cars, and more rabbits than people. Some of his earliest memories include a mountain lion scratching the roof of the family home. The family moved a lot but never far. They lived in San Pedro for a time—it was part of Los Angeles near Rattlesnake Island—Claremont, at the foot of Mount Baldy where the descendants of the first Spanish settlers lived, and in Julian, an old gold-mining town. Julian was at the heart of the Oriflamme Mountains, the ancestral home of the Digueno Indians. The sea was always part of his environment, and he was always close to the traditions and culture of the Spaniards and Indians of the region.

Shortly after graduating from Polytechnic High School in Long Beach, California, where his teachers told him that he was about the brightest student they had ever had, he enrolled in college and quickly found out that he wasn't the brightest college student in the world. That is why he said, "I wandered about from Occidental College to the University of Wisconsin to the University of Rome to Stanford." He eventually gave up completing a degree and took only classes that interested him and those that would help in a writing career. Years later, when asked if it was his education or real life that helped him to develop as a writer, he said, "Without question, I rely upon my experiences. I got very little out of college. Off hand, I can't elaborate on one thing that I learned at all the colleges that I attended."

By the time he was 22 he had published his first book, adult nonfiction. His writing was not making him a living, however, so he went to work at Paramount Pictures and later MGM, where he worked in the camera department. MGM took him to Rome to help with the filming of *Ben Hur*. The filming used the first Technicolor camera, about a foot square in size and made by hand at MIT. When the film crew returned to California, O'Dell stayed and went to Florence, where he wrote his first novel, *Pin Feathers*. He took the novel home to California, rewrote it, and then said, "I read it over, and burned it."

It wasn't until 1934 that his first novel, *Women of Spain*, was published. Ten years later his second novel was published. He did a lot of reading, traveling, and dreaming. Among his favorite authors were Sherwood Anderson, Conrad, D. H. Lawrence, and Willa Cather. Each had their influence on O'Dell's writing. But he credited Sir Walter Scott with having the most influence on his writing career. He admired Scott's perseverance and his efforts to work and pay off a publishing debt, rather than declare bankruptcy. Scott's cousin, Ann, was one of Scott O'Dell's ancestors.

O'Dell's best-known title, *The Island of the Blue Dolphins* (Houghton, 1960), was written when O'Dell was 59 and published when he was 60. The story first came to O'Dell's attention when he read an article published in *Harper's Magazine* during the 1890s about a young girl who had spent 18 years on an island alone. The island was about 60 miles from the California coast near Santa Barbara. O'Dell let the idea languish for years, until he read a second article about hunters coming over the high mountains on the Mexican border killing every creature that walked. He was angered with the mindlessness of men who would do such a thing. The two ideas came together, and he resolved to write a book with two themes—Albert Schweitzer's reverence for all life, and the biblical forgiveness of your enemies. He did not plan to write a children's book, yet his first children's novel won the 1961 Newbery Award. The book however, almost did not get published. He sent it off to his literary agents in New York, and they sent it back, saying that it might sell if he changed the main character to a boy and made it a modern story. He flew to New York and called a close friend at Houghton Mifflin in Boston. They met for lunch in New York City. A few days later his friend called. They wanted to talk about the book, if he could get to New York, and they wanted to publish it as a children's book. It won the Newbery, the William Allen White Award, the Hans Christian Andersen Award of Merit, the Southern California Council on Children's Literature Award, the German Juvenile Book Council International Award, the Rupert Hughes Award, and the Hawaii State Nene Award.

During his life Scott O'Dell acknowledged "that he had been relatively unsuccessful, although three of [his books] had been sold to motion pictures." He did gain success through his children's books. Three additional books won Newbery Honor Awards, and awards from the Catholic Library Association and several states. It usually took six months or so for him to research and complete a book.

Many of the main characters in his books are female, a conscious effort on O'Dell's part. He explained, "Part of my dedication to writing about women comes from the fact that when I was young, women did not have the right to vote. My father could vote; I could vote, but my mother could not vote. I thought at the time, and I've thought since, that women had a bad deal. I take it upon myself to right in some small way the wrong that was done."

O'Dell lived an interesting life. During World War I he was in the Army fighting the battle of Waco, Texas. In World War II he fought the battle of Texas in the Air Force, and then he was in the Coast Guard for a while. For most of the time he lived on or near the ocean. He once sailed the coast from San Diego to Alaska.

In 1981 Scott O'Dell established the Scott O'Dell Award for Historical Fiction. To be eligible for the award, a book must be published in English by a U.S. publisher, and must be set in the New World. (New World being defined as North, Central, or South America.) The award carries a $5,000 prize. The first winner was Elizabeth George Speare in 1984 for *The Sign of the Beaver*. Recent winners have included Katherine Paterson, Mary Downing Hahn, and Paul Fleischman.

Before O'Dell's death, he wrote from about 3 AM until 7 AM, and again after breakfast until 10. He returned to his writing to review it sometime in the afternoon, and perhaps would write for another hour or so. He wrote his books by hand, and his wife typed the stories on the computer. Together they would discuss the stories. Elizabeth O'Dell, his wife, was a magazine editor and writer. Of all of his awards Scott O'Dell said, "I value the Hans Christian Andersen Award more than any I have won." Many feel that it is the top award in children's literature, because it is given for an author or illustrator's body of work, not just one title. Fifteen experts from all over the world judge the author or illustrator's work. At age 86, O'Dell was still writing, traveling and researching, building stone walls, and planting roses—in fact, in the spring of 1985 he planted 125 roses. O'Dell died at age 91 in Mount Kisco, New York on October 15, 1989.

Books and Notes

Scott O'Dell's books were generally based on a historical incident. His name has become almost synonymous with the genre of historical fiction.

Alexandra (Houghton, 1984).
About a girl who, after her father is killed, attempts to help her grandfather by diving off the coast of Florida for sponges, later finding that smugglers are using the sponges to smuggle drugs.

Black Star, Bright Dawn (Houghton, 1988).
A young girl must struggle with the challenges of the Iditarod after her father is injured.

Feathered Serpent (Houghton, 1981).
A Spanish seminarian, who the Mayans consider to be a god, watches as Cortez conquers the Aztec city of Tenochtitlan.

Island of the Blue Dolphins (Houghton, 1960).
A tale of Karana, who survives on an island alone for 18 years.

Sing Down the Moon (Houghton, 1970).
The tale of a Navajo girl who recounts the days of the forced march in 1864 to Fort Sumner.

Streams to the River, River to the Sea: A Novel of Sacagawea (Houghton, 1986).
The story of Sacagawea, who accompanied her cruel husband, along with her infant son, as a guide for Lewis and Clark in the early 1800s.

For More Information About/By the Author

Articles

"Scott O'Dell Papers." *de Grummond Collection.* URL: http://www.lib.usm.edu/~degrum/findaids/odell.htm (Accessed December 1997).
When this website was accessed in December 1997, it listed O'Dell's birthdate as May 23, 1903. That date is inaccurate, according to O'Dell himself. He was born in 1898. However, the rest of the biographical information seems to be accurate.

Random House—Scott O'Dell. URL: http://www.randomhouse.com/teachersbdd/odel.html (Accessed December 1988).

Jerry Pallotta

◆ Nonfiction, Alphabet Books

Boston, Massachusetts
March 26, 1953

📖 *The Ocean Alphabet Book*
📖 *The Icky Bug Counting Book*

About the Author
and the Author's Writing

Jerry Pallotta is a salesman and an author. He was 32 years old and a father when he began writing books for children. He began a fascination with the ocean when he spent childhood summers in the seaside Massachusetts town of Scituate. The beach there was named Peggotty Beach. His first book about the ocean was titled *The Ocean Alphabet Book* (Charlesbridge, 1986). At first he could not find a publisher, so he searched for an illustrator and found Frank Mazzola Jr. Pallotta, determined to get the book in print, made plans to publish the book himself. Pallotta stated that his "wife thought it was a stupid idea." Nevertheless, he poured their savings into publishing the book, and set out to use his sales techniques to replenish their bank account. He began to take flyers to strategic locations, one of the first being the New England Aquarium. When he returned to see what they thought about carrying the book in their gift shop, the man in charge said, "I looked over your flyer, I'll take 5,000." Jerry Pallotta was on his way. He dubbed the book a "Peggotty Beach Book," named after the beach where he went each summer. Officially, the first edition was published by Quinlan Press, but later Charlesbridge Publishing in Watertown, Massachusetts, agreed to publish it. That began the relationship Charlesbridge has had with Pallotta every since.

Jerry Pallotta grew up in Massachusetts and graduated from Georgetown University. In 1979 (at the age of twenty-six) he married his wife, Linda. He began noticing that the alphabet books he was reading to his first child, Sheila, did not really have text. So, he set out to write one. *The Ocean Alphabet Book* became a best-seller, thanks largely to its success at the Aquarium. Its success encouraged Pallotta, and he continued writing. He has written alphabet books on a wide range of topics, from birds, to icky bugs, to dinosaurs, to spices, to butterflies. One of his alphabet books actually masquerades as a counting book. *The Icky Bug Counting Book* (Charlesbridge, 1992) counts "icky bugs" from one to twenty-six, but, if the animals are put in order, back to front, the bugs have also been listed alphabetically. However, a counting book, *The Crayon Counting Book* (Charlesbridge, 1996), that he coauthored with Pam Muñoz Ryan, is *really* a counting book. A rhyming text teaches counting, first by even numbers, and then by odd numbers.

Each of Pallotta's books are carefully researched. He does not hesitate to contact some of the world's leading scientists in his effort to be as accurate as possible. He has spent hours discussing entomology and undiscovered species of rain forest frogs of the Amazon with members of Harvard University's Herpetology Department. In preparation for *The Frog Alphabet Book and Other Awesome Amphibians* (Charlesbridge, 1990), he was searching for an image of a Goliath Frog. He finally found one, but unfortunately it was dead. To capture the image he needed, he photocopied the dead frog. Just because Pallotta is meticulous regarding his research doesn't mean that his books are somber. Pallotta and the illustrators have a lot of fun with the text and illustrations. For example, in *The Bird Alphabet Book* (Charlesbridge, 1986) a bat shows up on the "B" page and is humorously rejected because he is a mammal. Pallotta's favorite book page is the "G" page in *The Ocean Alphabet Book*, which shows the Goosefish. If one looks closely the fish, also known as a "mother-in-law" fish, it resembles one of the book creator's sisters. *The Icky Bug Alphabet Book* (Charlesbridge, 1986) has a moth on the "I" page, which appears to have an owl's face. When flipped over, a "guy with a mustache" will be visible. *The Yucky Reptile Alphabet Book* (Charlesbridge, 1989) sports Pallotta's favorite book cover, and, inside, a look on the "U" page reveals Mickey Mouse ears on the desert cactus. Readers will smile when the heart with "Dawn + Ralph" is located. Illustrator Ralph Masiello is responsible for the inclusion of the "Ralph." Illustrator Leslie Evans "drew on her family" for the borders in *The Flower Alphabet Book* (Charlesbridge, 1991). Pallotta personally selects the illustrators for his many books. Pallotta is a regular speaker at schools and conferences across the United States and continues to come up with new ideas for yet another alphabet book.

Jerry Pallotta grew up in Medford and Scituate, Massachusetts. He attended Boston College High School and Georgetown University. In 1979 he married Linda, and they are now the parents of two daughters and two sons, Sheila, Neil, Eric, and Jill. The family lives in Needham, Massachusetts.

Books and Notes

Jerry Pallotta is known for his non-fiction alphabet titles, and although he has written a couple "non-alphabet" books, none have garnered the popularity of his alphabet books.

The Airplane Alphabet Book. Co-authored with Fred Stillwell. Illustrated by Rob Bolster. (Charlesbridge, 1997).

The Bird Alphabet Book. Illustrated by Edgar Stewart. (Charlesbridge, 1986).

The Boat Alphabet Book. Illustrated by David Biedrzycki. (Charlesbridge, 1998).

The Butterfly Alphabet Book. Co-authored with Brian Cassie. Illustrated by Mark Astrella. (Charlesbridge, 1995).

The Desert Alphabet Book. Illustrated by Mark Astrella. (Charlesbridge, 1994).

The Dinosaur Alphabet Book. Illustrated by Edgar Stewart. (Charlesbridge, 1991).

The Extinct Alphabet Book. Illustrated by Ralph Masiello. (Charlesbridge, 1993).

The Flower Alphabet Book. Illustrated by Leslie Evans. (Charlesbridge, 1991).

The Frog Alphabet Book and Other Awesome Amphibians. Illustrated by Ralph Masiello. (Charlesbridge, 1990).

The Icky Bug Alphabet Book. Illustrated by Ralph Masiello. (Charlesbridge, 1986).

The Ocean Alphabet Book. Illustrated by Frank Mazzola Jr. (Charlesbridge, 1986; 1991).

The Spice Alphabet Book: Herbs, Spices, and Other Natural Flavors. Illustrated by Leslie Evans. (Charlesbridge, 1994).

The Yucky Reptile Alphabet Book. Illustrated by Ralph Masiello. (Charlesbridge, 1989).

For More Information About/By the Author

Articles

Fawcett, Gay. "Please Write a Zillion Books, Jerry Pallotta!" *Ohio Reading Teacher* 27, no. 1 (Fall 1992): 3–4.

Barbara Park

Mt. Holly, New Jersey
April 21, 1947

📖 *Skinnybones*

📖 *My Mother Got Married and Other Disasters*

**About the Author
and the Author's Writing**

Nothing in Barbara Park's childhood would predict that she would grow up to become a writer. She never had a desire to be a writer. However, when she was in school in Mt. Holly, writing was definitely one thing that she did enjoy. She grew up in New Jersey, and graduated from the University of Alabama with an undergraduate degree in education. She then met and married her husband, Richard, a member of the U.S. Air Force, and followed him around the country before settling down in Arizona. They settled first in Phoenix, and then Paradise Valley. Two children later and almost thirty years old, Barbara Park was searching for her "true talents." She thought back to her school days and has said, "being the class clown was not much to base a career on." But she did have, she acknowledges, "an odd sense of humor." So she decided to write. She had no experience, but her parents had instilled a sense of determination and confidence in her. She began to write greeting card verses, short stories, whatever she could, and sent them to all types of publishers. She got rejection after rejection. Finally in 1979 (at the age of 32) she decided to try to write a children's novel. In quick succession Knopf published four book titles: *Don't Make Me Smile* (1981); *Operation: Dump the Chump* (1982); *Skinnybones* (1982); and *Beanpole* (1983). She knew she was where she needed to be—writing children's books.

Barbara Park has two sons, now grown, graduated from college, and "old men" by now. Interestingly, she does not base her characters on her sons. They did, however, provide her with an understanding of how young people talk. Park attempts to tap into universal emotions. For example, when Howard Jeeter has feelings of loss during a move in *The Kid in the Red Jacket* (Knopf, 1987), Park knew the feelings from all those moves with her Air Force husband. But her gift is an ability to see humor in situations. Being able to help Charlie Hinkle deal with his parent's divorce in *Don't Make Me Smile* may help children in the same situation. In its sequel, *My Mother Got Married and Other Disasters*, Charlie's mother remarries. Park's humor helps the reader chuckle at the antics of Charlie's little stepbrother in a way that Charlie probably cannot.

Because she has sons one might assume that Park would enjoy writing about boys, and, in fact, she has written many books with a boy as the chief protagonist. However, the girl characters in *Beanpole* and *Buddies* (Knopf, 1985) are just as interesting, and emerge as unique personalities. Park says, "In fact, Molly Vera Thompson was probably the character I had the most fun creating." (Molly was the female character in *The Kid in the Red Jacket*.) Actually, the way a character deals with an emotion, according to Park, is not dependent on the character's sex, but rather on individual personality. Park says, "I try very hard just to write about feelings in general and not worry too much about whether or not the main character is a boy or a girl."

When Park begins to write a book, she begins with a slim plot idea and then tries to develop some "slightly off-beat characters" to keep the story interesting. The first draft takes from two months to one year to complete, depending on the story. She began to use a computer when she wrote her seventh book, *Almost Starring Skinnybones* (Knopf, 1988), and now says, "I don't know how I ever got along without it."

Her favorite characters are Molly Vera Thompson (*The Kid in the Red Jacket*); Junie B. Jones (all the Junie B. Jones books); and Thomas

Russo (*My Mother Got Married and Other Disasters*). Because little kids say just about anything, she particularly enjoys putting them in her books.

Although Barbara Park has become quite successful as a writer, she says, "Not one single person has ever recognized her in the grocery store and asked for her autograph." She is an avid tennis fan and has been known to walk three to four miles a night. Park says, "Most writers are just regular people," and she seems to be just that, a regular person with two dogs, two sons (Steven and David), one husband, and a regular house in Pleasant Valley, Arizona.

Books and Notes

Almost Starring Skinnybones (Knopf, 1988).

Junie B. Jones and That Meanie Jim's Birthday. Illustrated by Denise Brunkus. (Random, 1996).

Junie B. Jones and the Yucky Blucky Fruitcake. Illustrated by Denise Brunkus. (Random, 1995).

Junie B. Jones Has a Monster Under Her Bed. Illustrated by Denise Brunkus. (Random, 1997).

Junie B. Jones Is a Beauty Shop Guy. Illustrated by Denise Brunkus. (Random, 1998).

Junie B. Jones Is a Party Animal. Illustrated by Denise Brunkus. (Random, 1997).

Junie B. Jones Is Not a Crook. Illustrated by Denise Brunkus. (Random, 1997).

Junie B. Jones Loves Handsome Warren. Illustrated by Denise Brunkus. (Random, 1996).

The Kid in the Red Jacket (Knopf, 1987).

Mark Harte Was Here (Knopf, 1995).

Maxie, Rosie, and Earl—Partners in Grime. Illustrations by Alexander Strogart. (Knopf, 1990).

My Mother Got Married and Other Disasters (Knopf, 1989).

Psst! It's Me—The Bogeyman. Illustrated by Stephen Kroninger. (Atheneum, 1998).

Rosie Swanson: Fourth-Grade Geek for President (Knopf, 1991).

For More Information About/By the Author

Articles

"Barbara Park." *Random House Web Site*. URL: http://www.randomhouse.com/teachers/rc/rc_ab_bpa.html (Accessed December 1997).

Katherine Paterson

Historical Fiction ◆ Contemporary Realistic Fiction

Qing Jiang, Jiangsu, China
October 31, 1932

📖 *Park's Quest*

📖 *Jacob Have I Loved*

📖 *The Bridge to Terabithia*

About the Author
and the Author's Writing

The daughter of Christian missionaries, Katherine Womeldorf learned to speak Chinese as a child. She later learned to speak Japanese. She is settled in Vermont, just being a grandmother and a writer.

When she was a child she lived in China until China's war with Japan started, and the family was forced to leave. They returned to America by way of Southeast Asia and Europe. The family lived in Lynchburg and Richmond, Virginia. Katherine hated being in the United States, and didn't mind at all going back to China. Her family lived in a Chinese house surrounded by Chinese neighbors, so she grew up speaking both Chinese and English.

She was the middle of five children, and had an older brother who "ruled the roost." When World War II began, the family was again forced to flee China. Katherine left China for good when she was eight. She was glad to be leaving China as it was "pretty scary." When the family came back to America, she thought it would be heaven but soon found that it wasn't. Paterson attended thirteen schools during her first eighteen years. The first schools were in China, but back in the United States she found herself attending schools in Virginia, North Carolina, West Virginia, and Tennessee.

During her sixth-grade year she wrote plays that her classmates acted on the school playground, and sometimes on rainy days in the classroom. Paterson said, "I was a very shy child who loved to show off."

After graduation she attended King College in Bristol, Tennessee, and later the Presbyterian School of Christian Education in Richmond, Virginia. She earned a masters degree in English. For a year she taught sixth grade in Virginia. She began thinking about returning to China, but a friend convinced her to go to Japan instead. She spent four years in Japan, two in language school and two living in a Japanese town on Shikoku, where there were no other English-speaking people, so she learned a lot about Japanese language and customs during that time. She assisted eleven pastors with their churches' education programs on the island. She was given a fellowship for further study in Christian Education, and her studies took her back to New York City, where she entered the Union Seminary. In New York she met and married John Paterson. They had four children—two born to them, and two coming by plane.

She was asked to write her first book by officials at the Presbyterian Church. The book was titled *Who Am I?* (Covenant Life, 1966). After that she continued to write, but found it difficult to get her books published. "Nine years later my first novel was published. A mountain of rejection slips had been collected during those years. It took me another four years, when my third novel, *The Master Puppeteer* [Crowell, 1977] won the National Book Award to be declared an 'overnight success.' "

Her books come from a variety of inspirations. *Angels & Other Stories* (Crowell, 1979) is a collection of several stories she had written for her husband's ministry. Each story is about charity and hope. The Reverend John Paterson read one to his congregation each Christmas Eve.

She wrote *The Great Gilly Hopkins* (Crowell, 1978) when she tried to imagine what it might be like if she had been a foster child that the world regarded as disposable. The Patersons were temporary foster parents for a time, and when problems would come up, she would say to herself, "We can't really deal with that, they'll only be here a couple of weeks." She realized that she was treating the children as disposable and began to explore what it would feel like if *she* were the foster child. She decided she'd be very angry. Of course, Gilly's anger comes out in some very inappropriate ways—lying, stealing, and bullying. The language too matches the child's emotions—unhappy, angry, and lost. It's not until Trotter's love begins to turn her around that Gilly finds out what love means.

The Bridge to Terabithia (Crowell, 1977) was written after her son's (David) best friend, Lisa Hill, an eight-year-old, was struck and killed by lightning. She named the children's secret place Terabithia. She thought she had made up that name, a name that sounded like a country. But then one day she was rereading *The Voyage of the Dawn Treader* by C. S. Lewis and came across an island that he put in his book, Terebinthia. At first she was bothered, but then realized that Leslie Burke, the girl who dies in *The Bridge to Terabithia*, had read the book as well. She also realized that C. S. Lewis had also borrowed the name—from the Bible. The Bible mentions the Terebinth Tree in the story of Abraham. Of all of her books, *The Bridge to Terabithia* has sold best and has been published in at least twenty languages. The story is still difficult for her son David to read, as it is really a fictionalization of his story and his friend.

It took Paterson nearly three years to write *Jacob Have I Loved* (Crowell, 1980). It was also one of the most difficult books to write, demanding much research. It also was very demanding emotionally. She began the book in 1977 and struggled first with the setting. Finally, after reading William Warner's *Beautiful Swimmers: Watermen, Crabs, and the Chesapeake Bay* (Atlantic-Little), a gift book from her sister Helen to her son John, she decided to set the book there. Chesapeake Bay was just an hour away from the Paterson home. Before the book was finished came the 1978 Newbery Award announcement for *The Bridge to Terabithia*, the acceptance speech, the notice that after thirteen years in Takoma Park, Maryland, the family would be moving to Norfolk, Virginia, the news of her mother's terminal cancer, the choice of *Gilly* as a Newbery Honor Book, and finally the National Book Award. *Jacob Have I Loved* languished.

She wrote *Come Sing, Jimmy Jo* (Dutton, 1985) after she had a brush with celebrity. She loved some aspects of fame, but hated the parts that seemed to invade her privacy. The situation made her think about a very shy classmate during junior high, Anita Carter, who was also a famous country music singer with her mother, MayBelle, and her two older sisters. No one knew how to treat her. After Paterson wrote the book she sent a copy to Anita Carter. Carter wrote her to tell her how much she loved the book but then said, "I feel terrible I can't picture you." Paterson was not surprised. In Carter's life, she (Paterson) was just like the totally forgettable Will Short.

Most of her books are novels for middle-grade readers, but at least two have been fairy tale picture books. She translated a Japanese folktale, *The Crane Wife* (Morrow, 1981), by Sumiko Yagawa. Paterson wrote *The King's Equal* (Harper, 1992) as a favor to her friend the Russian artist Vladimir Vagin. He is famous for illustrating fairy tales, and Paterson wrote a literary fairy tale for him to illustrate.

As a twelve year old she enjoyed *The Yearling* and also remembers reading *The Scarlet Pimpernel* when she was in junior high, as well as books by Kate Seredy, Frances Hodgson Burnett, Robert Lawson, and Louisa Mae Alcott. She also remembers an eighth-grade study of *Silas Marner*. The teacher had them study the novel in such a way that Paterson did not read another George Eliot book until she was in her fifties. She pleads with teachers, "Don't study a good book to death."

Katherine Paterson sits down to write every morning. "It's day labor." But it is also "the best job in the world." And though the first drafts are usually very difficult, Paterson actually enjoys the rewriting. She continues to visit many schools during a year. Most of the schools are within one hour's drive from her home, because "an author's first responsibility is to her own neighborhood."

Katherine Paterson and her husband, John, a Presbyterian pastor, live in Barre, Vermont, where Katherine writes in a "nice study" in her home. The room has three big windows. From one of them she can see a bit of the Green Mountains of Vermont, and from the other two she can see the huge sugar maple tree in her front yard. When she is not writing, she says, "I love to read and to sing. I play both the piano and tennis badly but still I like to do them." The Patersons have two sons and two daughters. Elizabeth PoLin "Lin" was born in Hong Kong and came to the family six months after their son John Jr. was born. The name *PoLin* is Chinese for "Precious Life." John Jr. was their first born, but Lin is the oldest child. David was born next, and then Mary Katherine Nah-he-sah-pe-che-a (Apache for "a young Apache lady") arrived. Their sons and daughters are grown, and they have "two terrific granddaughters." The entire family plays tennis. All four of the Paterson children are good tennis players "like their dad." Paterson's daughter Mary enjoys a challenging game of Scrabble every time she comes home. Paterson usually wins. Paterson also enjoys crossword puzzles, making quilts, reading, movies, and music of many different types.

Books and Notes

Most of Katherine Paterson's books have been novels; however, she has written three novels set in feudal Japan, a few picture books, and some nonfiction coauthored with her husband, John Paterson. She has won two Newbery Award medals, a Newbery Honor, a National Book Award, and several other awards. She is one of the most-read authors of books for young readers.

Collections of Stories

Consider the Lilies: Plants of the Bible. Coauthored by John Paterson. Illustrated by Anne Ophelia Dowden. (Crowell, 1986; Clarion, 1998).

Images of God: Views of the Invisible. Coauthored by John Paterson. (Clarion, 1998).

A Midnight Clear: Stories for the Christmas Season (Lodestar, 1995).

Novels

The Bridge to Terabithia. Illustrated by Donna Diamond. (Crowell, 1977).

Come Sing, Jimmy Jo (Dutton, 1985).

Flip-flop Girl (Dutton, 1994).

The Great Gilly Hopkins (Crowell, 1978).

Jacob Have I Loved (Crowell, 1980).

Jip: His Story (Lodestar, 1997).

Lyddie (Lodestar, 1991).

Marvin's Best Christmas Present Ever. Illustrated by Jane Clark Brown. (Harper, 1997). Early reading chapter book.

Park's Quest (Lodestar, 1988).

Parzival: The Quest of the Grail Knight (Lodestar, 1998).

The Smallest Cow in the World. Illustrated by Jane Clark Brown. (Harper, 1991). Early reading chapter book.

Picture Books

The Angel and the Donkey. Illustrated by Alexander Koshkin. (Clarion, 1996).

Celia and the Sweet, Sweet Water. Illustrated Vladimir Vagin. (Lodestar, 1998).

The King's Equal. Illustrated by Vladimir Vagin. (Harper, 1992).

The Tale of the Mandarin Ducks. Illustrated by Leo Dillon and Diane Dillon. (Lodestar, 1990).

For More Information About/By the Author

Articles

Buckley, Virginia. "Katherine Paterson." *The Horn Book Magazine* (August 1978): 368–71.

Frew, Andrew W. "Book Strategies: *Park's Quest* by Katherine Paterson." *Booklinks* 1, no. 1 (September 1991): 29+.

"Katherine Paterson." *Internet Public Library*. URL: http://www.ipl.org/youth/AskAuthor/paterson.html (Accessed December 1997).

Namovicz, Gene Inyart. "Katherine Paterson." *The Horn Book Magazine* (August 1981): 394–99.

Paterson, Katherine. "National Book Award Acceptance." *The Horn Book Magazine* (August 1979): 402–3.

Paterson, Katherine. "Newbery Award Acceptance for *Bridge to Terabithia*." *The Horn Book Magazine* (August 1978): 361–67.

Paterson, Katherine. "Newbery Award Acceptance for *Jacob Have I Loved*." *The Horn Book Magazine* (August 1981): 385–93.

Robb, Laura. "Book Strategies: *Three Novels of Feudal Japan* by Katherine Paterson." *Booklinks* 1, no. 4 (March 1992): 20+.

Books

Cary, Alice. *Katherine Paterson* (Learning Works, 1997).

Paterson, Katherine. *Gates of Excellence: On Reading and Writing Books for Children* (Elsevier/Nelson, 1981).

Paterson, Katherine. *A Sense of Wonder: On Reading and Writing Books for Children* (Plume, 1995).

Paterson, Katherine. *The Spying Heart: More Thoughts on Reading and Writing Books for Children* (Lodestar, 1989).

Schmidt, Gary D. *Katherine Paterson* (Twayne, 1994).

Gary Paulsen

Adventure Fiction ◆ Humorous Stories ◆ Historical Fiction ◆ Nonfiction

Minneapolis, Minnesota
May 17, 1939

- 📖 *Hatchet*
- 📖 *Brian's Winter*
- 📖 *The Voyage of the Frog*
- 📖 Culpepper Adventures Series

About the Author
and the Author's Writing

Gary Paulsen was born in Minneapolis, Minnesota, on May 17, 1939. His childhood was difficult, and Gary struggled throughout his growing up days. His father, Oscar Paulsen, was in the military and did not even see Gary until he was seven years old, as he was fighting in the war against Hitler. His mother, Eunice, took him to live with his grandparents.

When Paulsen speaks of his childhood, it is tinged with bitterness and wishes that no child should have a childhood like his. According to Paulsen his parents were "drunks." He fended for himself much of the time. School was not a pleasant place either. He was often not chosen for teams, never had the right clothes. As a teenager he started "taking off." During one summer he hoed sugar beets. During the school year he found things to do at night. One year he set bowling alley pins. He hated school and resolved not to go back. He read poorly.

One year he sold newspapers in bars, and he figured out that if he waited until after the patrons had a few more drinks, they would give him more money for the papers. One night, while he was hanging out waiting for just the right time to begin selling his papers, he slipped into the library to get warm. He credits the librarian who was there for "saving his life." He says he "must have been a sight," but the librarian greeted him and offered him a library card. It was the first time someone had offered him anything. He consented to take the card, and she promptly checked out a western to him. He found an overstuffed chair in the basement of the apartment building where he lived, and hid out to read. The next week he returned to get more books. He began to visit the library regularly. Pretty soon he was taking three westerns, and she slipped in *Moby Dick*. On numerous occasions Paulsen has said, "The only reason I'm here and not in prison is because of that woman. I was a loser, but she showed me the power of reading—that I didn't need to qualify with the right clothes. Everything I am I owe to that woman."

During his teenage years Paulsen read but continued to "be a bum." Then he entered the Army and an sergeant helped him straighten out. He says that he was in the Army for three years, eight months, twenty-one days, and nine hours—and that was enough. He got a job as an electronic engineer on the Gemini shot, tracing satellites. He had a top-secret security badge, but one day he decided to be a writer (although he had not written a thing up to that time). He was twenty-six, going through a divorce, and questioning what he was doing and why he was doing it. He handed in his badge and took off for Hollywood, where he created a phony résumé and went to work as an editor while he studied writing. Later he held down a variety of jobs—truck driver, septic tank installer, dynamite handler, carpenter, teacher, folk singer, Wyoming ranch hand, and North Dakota migrant farm worker.

In the late 1960s he was in New Mexico and began to write seriously. He was also drinking. The FBI investigated him for being a little too factual in a book about the missile business. His second marriage was failing—"[it] lasted three years and should have lasted about 38 minutes." During this time he met Ruth Ellen Wright in Taos, New Mexico. He was standing in line at the local post office when the FBI appeared. He was hoping that they weren't looking for him, but felt a need to "bank" the $20 he had until they left. He turned around and handed the money to the woman behind him saying, "Hold this twenty bucks for me." It was only after the FBI left (they weren't looking for him) that he looked into her eyes. "I fell in love." And even though he wasn't "hunting," he knew this was the woman that he was going to marry.

He spent much of the next six years drinking. To his later regret, he allowed his first wife's second husband to adopt his son and daughter. Paulsen was often suicidal, but finally he tried to quit drinking. In 1973 he joined a national program for help. By then Gary and Ruth were in Colorado, where their son Jim had been born in 1971. Paulsen became sober and cleared his head. His writing had suffered though, and it took him another year or two to restore his sense of literary quality. His books focused on nonfiction adventure topics such as in *Hiking and Backpacking* (Simon, 1978). Eventually he moved into the area of adventure fiction with the publication of *Winterkill* (Nelson, 1976) and *The Foxman* (Nelson, 1977). He and his family moved to Minnesota, and he felt like he was going home. His days with his son were important to Paulsen. "I didn't get a chance to see the older [children] grow up because of my own stupidity, and with the younger one, I have watched him grow, and it's really been neat. Now it's just amazing. He's better at many things than I am."

Gary Paulsen has spent over twenty-five years writing, most of them in "poverty." When *Dogsong* (Bradbury, 1985) was named a Newbery Honor Book in 1986, Paulsen and his family were living in a shack with no electricity and only outdoor toilet facilities. He refers to those days as the days when "we lived under flat rocks and ate bugs." Ruth painted and they "got by." Their combined income was $2,000 to $3,000 a year. They survived by planting a huge garden. They made everything: ketchup, butter, and cheese. Their son had "the longest school bus ride in America," two-and-a-half hours one way.

The success of *The Hatchet* (Bradbury, 1987) brought a change to the Paulsen's economic status as well. It is also the book that catapulted him into many young readers' lives. Gary Paulsen's success did not come overnight. He honed his writing skills for over twenty years. His books represent a wide range of interests and are drawn from firsthand experience. He says that he has lived all of the experiences or has been close to someone who has. As he prepared to write *The Hatchet*, he tried to do everything Brian does in the book. He spent hours in bush planes like the 206 in the book, flying over the north woods and Alaska. He lived off the land as Brian does, even eating a raw snapping-turtle egg. (It tasted a lot like he imagined rotten Vaseline must taste.) He has been attacked more than once by moose, and actually did get a fire started with a rock and a hatchet.

Manny Bustos, the main character in *The Crossing* (Orchard, 1987), is based on a man Paulsen met when he was stationed in Fort Bliss, Texas. And Paulsen, like the sergeant in the book, crossed over to Juarez every night.

The Voyage of the Frog (Orchard, 1989) is the story of a young boy's survival during a Pacific storm. Paulsen once survived a Pacific hurricane in a boat similar to the *Frog*. Such an experience leaves one changed, and never leaves one's memory.

Paulsen's books are populated with interesting people, including war veterans from Vietnam, Korea, and World War II. His characters are farmers, mechanics, ranchers, and others who work hard to achieve human dignity from their strength. Some family relationships are warm and supportive and others debilitating. His books focus on the realities of life, often harsh, but always honest. The stories always seem to have someone on the brink, struggling to survive, just as Paulsen struggled for so many years.

Paulsen's early writing career was prolific. More than forty of his books and numerous articles were published, but then in 1977, a family who felt they recognized themselves in *Winterkill* filed a libel lawsuit against him. The suit went all the way to the Minnesota Supreme Court before being decided in Paulsen's favor. The suit, however, almost broke Paulsen financially, and certainly took a major emotional toll. He gave up writing for two years. Paulsen and his family were living in a remote area of northern Minnesota. Now that he wasn't writing, Paulsen turned to the outdoors, raising and training sled dogs. This interest in dogs eventually inspired Paulsen to return to writing.

The first dogsled race he ran was the Iditarod, a prestigious (and grueling) 1,049-mile dogsled race from Anchorage to Nome, Alaska. Anyone who intends to run the Iditarod must train constantly, and Paulsen was no exception. In the final training, he went to Alaska and did "80s" back to back. That means he would go out with an eight-dog team and go eighty miles. Then he would come back in, get off one sled, step on another, and do another eighty miles. During more than three months of intensive training, the longest time he slept was three hours and twenty minutes. The costs for the Iditarod mounted up fast—to about $14,000. He didn't know where he would get the money, but he succeeded and ran the race. Once in the race, he knew he wasn't going to be competitive; his dog team was too slow. So, he took 750 slides going across the frozen country. That was the first time anyone had every done that. He has selected about eighty of them for a slide show, which he often shares with young people when he is speaking. In 1983 Paulsen finished in 42d place out of 73 contestants. The following year, a violent blizzard foiled Paulsen's efforts to stay in the race. Because of the wretched conditions he is grateful that his dogs survived.

The following year, Paulsen was preparing to run the Iditarod once again when he got word that his agent and friend was dying of cancer. His friend asked him to help. Paulsen knew he would not be able to give his dogs the attention they needed, so he sold everything: the dogs, harnesses, and sled. Paulsen spent every weekend with his friend for the next three months.

It wasn't long before Paulsen began to "get weird." He was looking at boats, airplanes, and anything else that looked like it might provide some adventure. Then he decided to "just get a recreational dog team, four or five dogs." Paulsen and his wife, Ruth, went to the kennels of Jo Carlsen, who had one of the most prestigious dog kennels in the area. Paulsen chose three dogs, and then four, five, and six. He says, "Ruth gave me an elbow jab each time I pointed to a dog." But he did not stop until he had purchased forty-three dogs. Paulsen ran the race one more time, but eventually his hard living caught up with him. In 1985 he found that he was suffering from heart disease. His health forced him to give up the dogs, so he and his wife sold their Minnesota home and bought a ranch in New Mexico. They spend much of the winter months in their La Luz, New Mexico, home, a more than 200-year-old adobe house. They also have a ranch about an hour away from their La Luz home, and a sailboat in the Pacific.

His novels most often feature a tragic character who learns about life's cruelties in realistic and episodic narratives. Paulsen has written many titles in the adult field, as well as young adult novels and children's books. He weaves edge-of-the-seat adventures throughout each book.

Paulsen still seeks adventure. In 1997 he wrote an adult novel, *Pilgrimage on a Steel Ride: A Memoir About Men and Motorcycles* (Harcourt, 1997), based on his ride on a Harley-Davidson motorcycle from New Mexico to Alaska. And he readied his sailboat *Ariel* for a trip from Mexico to Alaska and back again. This time he wanted to continue around to Camp Horn. Surely fodder for more writing.

In 1997 the American Library Association honored Gary Paulsen for his lifetime contribution to writing books for teenagers with the Margaret A. Edwards Award. Paulsen has been married for more than thirty years to Ruth Wright, a fine artist who has also illustrated some of Paulsen's books. His older son, Lance, has a construction firm in Alabama. His daughter, Lynn, has credentials as a high school teacher, and his son Jim is an elementary school teacher. Paulsen's hobbies include sailing, collecting and riding Harley-Davidsons, ranching, and riding horses.

Books and Notes

Gary Paulsen writes for a wide range of readers, including intermediate grades, middle school, young adult, and adult. His books range from adventure to historical fiction to humor. One best-selling series is the Culpepper Adventure series, which stars Dunc Culpepper and his friends, Amos and T.J.

Culpepper Adventure Series

Paulsen has written more than thirty titles for this series. Dunc, Amos, and T.J. work together to solve mysteries and get themselves out of complicated situations. For example, in *Amos Gets Famous* the two best friends, Amos and Dunc, decipher a code they find in a library book and stumble onto a burglary ring. The burglars next target is the home of Melissa, the girl of Amos's dreams. Melissa doesn't even know Amos exists. Being a hero just might make her notice him.

Amos Gets Famous (Yearling, 1993).

Amos Goes Bananas (Yearling, 1996).

Coach Amos (Yearling, 1994).

Dunc and Amos on Thin Ice (Yearling, 1997).

Dunc and the Greased Sticks of Doom (Yearling, 1994).

Dunc's Undercover Christmas (Yearling, 1993).

Super Amos (Yearling, 1997).

Adventure, Historical Fiction, and Other Books

The Boy Who Owned the School (Orchard, 1990).
Jacob, a self-proclaimed wimp and loser, attempts to avoid notice at all costs. A fast-reading, funny story.

Brian's Winter (Delacorte, 1996).
This book is a companion title to *The Hatchet* and *The River*. This story answers the "what if?" question. What would have happened if Brian had not been rescued? What if he would have had to survive in the wilderness for the entire winter?

Canoe Days. Illustrated by Ruth Wright Paulsen. (Doubleday, 1998).
A canoe ride on a northern lake during a summer day reveals the quiet beauty and wonder of nature in and around the lake.

Canyons (Delacorte, 1990).
Set in 1884, a young Apache was killed during his first coming-of-age horse raid. Over 100 years later, 14-year-old Brennan Cole was in the same canyon, and his experiences provide the story of *Canyons*.

The Crossing (Orchard, 1987).
Plucky story of a young Mexican boy and his friendship with the war-damaged Robert.

Dancing Carl (Bradbury, 1983).
He appeared, looking like a bum, during the hockey season in the winter of 1958, in McKinley, Minnesota, where ice skating is everything. His dancing was magic.

Dogsong (Bradbury, 1985).
Russel Suskitt takes a dog team and sled to escape modern ways. His finds his own "song." 1986 Newbery Honor Award.

The Hatchet (Bradbury, 1987).
Brian Robeson is the only survivor of the crash of a 206 bush plane. He is forced to leave his thoughts and worries behind as he focuses on survival. 1988 Newbery Honor Award.

The Island (Orchard, 1988).
Fourteen-year-old Will Neuton finds a "private island."

My Life in Dog Years (Delacorte, 1998).
Chronicles his own life by recalling the lives of some of the dogs that have shared his. Stories of his first dog, Snowball (in the Philippines); Dirk, the dog who protected him from bullies; and Cookie, the hero dog who saved Paulsen's life.

Nightjohn (Delacorte, 1993).
Nightjohn, a slave, is treated horribly, but finds that he must remain courageous if he is to survive and gain his freedom. Sarny is an important friend in this book.

The River (Delacorte, 1991).
A sequel to *The Hatchet*. After surviving in the wilderness and being rescued, Brian now finds himself facing new challenges on "The River."

Sarny: A Life Remembered (Delacorte, 1997).
Continues the adventures of Sarny, the slave girl Nightjohn taught to read, through the aftermath of the Civil War. She teaches other blacks and lives a full life until age ninety-four.

The Schernoff Discoveries (Delacorte, 1997).
Two friends, both hopeless geeks and misfits, try to survive unusual science experiments, the attacks of the football team, and other dangers of junior high school. Based on Paulsen's own life and friendship with the class genius.

Sentries (Bradbury, 1986).
Four teenagers' lives unfold, each in different parts of the country.

Tracker (Bradbury, 1984).
As his grandfather lies dying, John hunts alone for the first time.

The Transall Saga (Delacorte, 1998).
A time-travel tale. Thirteen-year-old Mark falls into a tube of blue light and travels back into a more primitive world, where he must use his wit and skills to survive.

The Voyage of the Frog (Orchard, 1989).
David sails the *Frog* alone—and this time the task is to scatter the ashes of his beloved uncle. A storm threatens his mission.

The Winter Room (Orchard, 1989).
Eleven-year-old Eldon and his brother, Wayne, explore every inch of their family's Minnesota farm. 1990 Newbery Honor Award.

Woodsong (Bradbury, 1990).
An autobiographical book that speaks of Paulsen's life in northern Minnesota and of 17 event-filled days with his 15-dog team.

Worksong. Illustrated by Ruth Wright Paulsen. (Harcourt, 1997).
Illustrations and rhyming text show various work done by different people.

For More Information About/By the Author

Articles

Barron, Ronald. "Gary Paulsen: 'I Write Because It's All I Can Do.' " *ALAN Review* 20, no. 3 (Spring 1993): 27–30.

"Gary Paulsen." *Random House Web Site.* URL: http://www.randomhouse.com/features/garypaulsen OR http://www.garypaulsen.com (Accessed December 1998).

Morris, Dave. "The Adventures of Gary Paulsen." *The Cedar Rapids Gazette: Youth Plus* (Thursday, March 24, 1994): 3Y.

Raymond, Allen. "Gary Paulsen: Artist-With-Words." *Teaching K–8* 23, no. 1 (August/September 1992): 52–54.

Schmitz, James A. "Gary Paulsen: A Writer of His Time." URL: http://borg.lib.vt.edu/ejournals/ALAN/fall94/Schmitz.html (Accessed December 1997).

Originally published in *ALAN Review* (Assembly on Literature for Adolescents) 22, no. 1 (Fall 1994): 15–18.

Books/Videos

Savlner, G. M. *Presenting Gary Paulsen* (Prentice, 1995).

Trumpet Video Visits Gary Paulsen [Video, 24 minutes]. (Trumpet Club, 1993).

Richard Peck

Contemporary Realistic Fiction ◆ Science Fiction

**Decatur, Illinois
April 5, 1934**

📖 *Blossom Culp and the Sleep of Death*

📖 *Lost in Cyberspace*

About the Author and the Author's Writing

Richard Peck was born, April 5, 1934, and raised in the Midwest, in the small town of Decatur, Illinois, where the language of the hard-working men and women was rich and so were the viewpoints. During Peck's childhood the adults around him were struggling to understand the rage and killing of World War II. His parents, Wayne M. (a merchant) and Virginia were among those hardworking people. Peck's father roared off to work each morning in a pair of green coveralls astride a Harley-Davidson. He ran a Phillips 66 gas station that was a hangout for all the elderly men in town. Newspaper carriers also rolled their papers there. The place was always buzzing with ideas and conversation, some of which Peck says, "I was too young to be hearing." His mother was a dietitian and had to struggle with wartime rations. Peck was an only child for many years, and then he "acquired a small sister." She would later become the prototype for many of the heroines in his books for young readers. Peck became the typical older brother.

From early in his school career Peck wanted to go to New York to become a writer. That didn't seem practical, so he decided to become an English teacher—that was as close as he thought he could get to writing. Peck earned a scholarship to DePauw University, where he majored in English. After studying at the University of Exeter in Devon, England, he returned to DePauw University and received his undergraduate degree in 1956. He went on to obtain a masters degree in 1959 from Southern Illinois University. He continued with postgraduate studies at Washington University in 1960–1961 while an English instructor at Southern Illinois University at Carbondale. While Peck served in the U.S. Army at Stuttgart, Germany, from 1956 to 1968, he ghost-wrote some of the chaplain's sermons, and then returned to teach English at the college and high school levels until 1971, when he turned to writing full-time.

He did not start writing until he found a readership, and he had found them in his students, at least the thoughtful students willing to learn. He has said about giving up teaching, "I didn't want to, but teaching had begun to be more involved in psychiatric social work, and I wasn't trained for that." So he turned in his pension and hospitalization plan and moved his typewriter into the garden of his Brooklyn apartment, and began to write a novel for the students he had left behind.

He draws on his past and present to find voices for his writing. He says, "I was born in the midwest and grew up at mid-century. The elders of my family, and the people next door, recalled earlier times, and I'm still retelling their memories. The oral tradition of a time and place, when people lived near their roots and their neighbors, still fuels my fiction."

He visits about one hundred classrooms a year in this country and others, hoping to hear from young people what his next novel will be about. "This visiting inspires my writing—the turns of phrase, the fads, the local color, the universal challenges of being young."

When there was an "epidemic of adolescent suicide raging," Peck wrote *Remembering the Good Times* (Delacorte, 1985). He says, "I wrote the book to dramatize the warning signs—those signals that despairing people send out to those nearest them. Young people need to know and evaluate these signals to alert help for their friends. In most schools and homes, this grim problem is not being discussed." This book, says Peck, "elicits the most thoughtful responses."

He became interested in writing *Are You in the House Alone?* (Viking, 1976) when he became aware that rape was one of the fastest-growing, least-reported crimes, and its typical victim was a teenage girl. Peck began to see the victims as one of his own readers, a girl who, being a teenager, doesn't have a lawyer, a girl who believes none of her friends would ever hurt her. A girl who believes that crime is in the inner city, not in her safe suburb. "My sources were more than willing to give me the profile of both victim and criminal. They are the people who volunteer at rape crisis centers. They were pleased when they heard I wanted to write a novel to alert teenagers to the legal ramifications of this crime, but they said the book was needed for younger children, increasingly rape victims." For many years this was one of his most widely read books, and still may be.

Dreamland Lake (Holt, 1973) came from his observations as a seventh-grade teacher in a girls school. It seemed that friendships at his age "consisted of one leader, one follower, and one common enemy to give them a cause." He noticed the same pattern, every day. In order to establish distance he told the story about boys. The novel "is a diatribe against being a follower."

During Peck's visits to classrooms he "sees things no parent would dare know. And I receive letters every day from the young who write to a stranger what they would never say to a friend (or an adult they can see.)"

His four books about Blossom Culp and her "second sight" have a special life all their own. "Blossom receives mail that I do not. My format of choice is humor, including supernatural humor. The young are basically humorless. Most of their laughter comes from nervousness or derision. I'd like them to know that humor has better uses."

Peck remembers his great-uncle, Miles Peck, an 80-year-old rogue and journeyman carpenter who rode through Decatur, Illinois, in his Model A Ford outfitted with a carpentry box in place of the rumble seat. At 85 he was still looking for pretty women and had a keen nose for scandal. He also had a great memory for other people's pasts—pasts he did not hesitate to mention at inopportune times. He had married several times, but was as free as Peck "hoped adults were."

Richard Peck's great-uncle Miles "made an emphatic entrance in a book called *The Ghost Belonged to Me* [Viking, 1975]." The Mystery Writers of America presented the Edgar Allen Poe Award to Peck for the book. *The Ghost Belongs to Me* is the first of four books about Blossom Culp and Alexander. Set in the 1910s in the small Illinois town of Bluff

City (a fictionalized version of Peck's own Decatur), the Blossom Culp books are supernatural comedies written in response to repeated requests from Peck's readers to "write a ghost story." Blossom is a strong, resourceful female character who is willing and able to make her own decisions. Three more Blossom Culp titles continued the story.

In 1997 Richard Peck was working on "revisiting my grandmother [Miles Peck's sister-in-law] in a series of short stories, one of which is called, 'Shotgun Cheatham's Last Night Above Ground.' Happily, I didn't grow up in a suburb, but most of my readers are doing just that, and I want to share with them the riches of my childhood in a family and community now vanished."

Richard Peck lives in New York City and travels a lot. "Like most writers, when I'm not writing, I'm thinking about writing. Since I'm aging and my young readers aren't, I move among them as much as I can and wherever I'm invited. The visiting inspires my writing—the turns of phrase, the fads, the local color, the universal challenges of being young. Luckily, I was born with itchy feet and to give my far-flung wanderings a purpose, I say I'm doing research. Otherwise, it would only be snooping."

Richard Peck has been awarded the American Library Association's 1990 Margaret A. Edwards Award and the National Council of Teachers of English 1990 ALAN Award, both for outstanding contributions to young adult literature. He has also been awarded two Edgar Allan Poe Awards from the Mystery Writers of America.

Books and Notes

While Richard Peck is known for his young adult novels, he is also well known for his four books about Blossom Culp and Alexander Armsworth. The same-age reader will enjoy *Lost in Cyberspace* and its sequel, *The Great Interactive Dream Machine*. Books that were written to appeal to an older audience draw themes from the lives of readers he meets or who write him letters. He says, "A novel is never an answer; it's always a question. All my novels end with a door opening on a new beginning."

Blossom Culp Series

Blossom Culp and the Sleep of Death (Dell, 1986).
Blossom aids the restless spirit of a long-dead Egyptian princess.

The Dreadful Future of Blossom Culp (Dell, 1984).
Blossom finds herself caught in a time warp when she travels through time from 1914 to 1984.

The Ghost Belonged to Me (Dell, 1975).
The first book in the series. Uncle Miles makes his entrance in this title. Alexander Armsworth (from the "right

side" of the tracks) and Blossom Culp (from the "wrong side" of the tracks) are the chief protagonists. Together they meet the ghost of a young Creole girl from the Civil War era who is haunting the barn. Uncle Miles is the one who knows the secret story behind the ghost, whose body must be exhumed and then laid to rest.

Ghosts I Have Been (Dell, 1977).
    As Blossom's gift evolves, both Blossom and Alexander are involved in a series of adventures into the supernatural.

Cyberspace Books

Lost in Cyberspace (Dial, 1995).
    Josh Lewis, a sixth-grader, is having difficulties at home. Once at a New York prep school, Josh and his friend Aaron find they can use the school's computer to travel through time, learning secrets from the school's past and improving Josh's home situation.

The Great Interactive Dream Machine: Another Adventure in Cyberspace (Dial, 1996).
    Sequel to *Lost in Cyberspace*. Josh and Aaron find themselves uncontrollably transported through space and time.

Other Titles

Are You in the House Alone? (Viking, 1976).

Bel-Air Bambi and the Mall Rats (Delacorte, 1993).

Desirable Digs (Viking, 1998).

Father Figure: A Novel (Viking, 1978).

The Last Safe Place on Earth (Delacorte, 1995).

Remembering the Good Times (Delacorte, 1985).

Secrets of the Shopping Mall (Delacorte, 1979).

Strays Like Us (Dial, 1998).

Voices After Midnight: A Novel (Delacorte, 1989).

For More Information About/By the Author

Articles

"Random House: Richard Peck." URL: http://www.randomhouse.com/teachersbdd/peck.html (Accessed December 1997).

Books

Gallo, Donald R. *Presenting Richard Peck* (Twayne, 1989).

Peck, Richard. *Anonymously Yours* (Beech Tree, 1995).

Peck, Richard. *Love and Death at the Mall: Teaching and Writing for the Literate Young* (Delacorte, 1994).

Robert Newton Peck

Contemporary Realistic Fiction ◆ Historical Fiction

Vermont
(rural area near Lake Champlain)
February 17, 1928

📖 *A Day No Pigs Would Die*

📖 Soup Series

About the Author
and the Author's Writing

Robert Newton Peck was born in Vermont on February 17, 1928, where he was raised on a farm near the shores of Lake Champlain. He grew up in the Shaker tradition, the son of a pig butcher, F. Haven Peck. Peck's mother was Lucille Peck. Peck attended a one-room schoolhouse for the first six years of his school life, but eventually dropped out and did not attend school again until later in life. The one-room schoolhouse had twenty to thirty children in grades one through six. Many of the children were sons and daughters of mill workers, farmers, or lumberjacks, and many of their parents could not read. At a young age, Peck went to work as a lumberjack and later worked in a papermill, killing hogs, and as an advertising executive. During World War II, at the age of 17, Peck joined the Army and served as a machine-gunner in the U.S. Army 88th Infantry Division. When he returned, he entered Rollins College and earned his undergraduate degree in 1953. He studied law at Cornell University, but left after just one year.

Peck's first writing experiences began with music and radio jingles, which gained him employment with an advertising agency. It wasn't until he was in his forties that he set down to write a book. His first book, published in 1973, was an instant success. Robert Newton Peck wrote his autobiography, *A Day No Pigs Would Die* (Knopf, 1973). In the story he talks of his hard times on a Vermont farm, the death of his father, and his early forced entry into manhood when the farm, his mother, and aunt became his responsibility. The book also reveals why Peck feels one should never give a pig a name. In an April 1980 speech made at the Children's Literature Festival at Central State Missouri State University, Peck told of writing his most successful book, *A Day No Pigs Would Die*, in two-and-one-half weeks, and that the book had earned him $500,000 in 1980.

Later Peck gained additional notoriety when he created the Soup series. One of the major characters draws heavily on a real person, Miss Kelly, a lovable but tough school teacher. Peck praises Miss Kelly and other teachers for their desire to get their students to read. He says, "I was lucky to have Miss Kelly for my real-life teacher." Some of the books Peck views as most influential were those that Miss Kelly read aloud. She read *Ivahoe*, *Tom Sawyer*, and *The Wind in the Willows*.

Not one to waste words, when an interviewer asks Robert Newton Peck a question, the answer will be bare bones. If the answer can be yes or no he is likely to answer "Yup!" And as for his writing schedule he says, "I get up at 6 AM have breakfast at 6:15, and go back to bed at 6:30." Before his success as a children's book author he says he was a "soldier, farmer, and advertising copywriter."

Peck says that he "writes books to earn [money]." Adults sometimes gasp at his honesty, but children do not. Peck also writes because he loves the "work of it," but the main reason is that it is a good way to make money. He does not like his books to be tagged as "adolescent literature." His books, he says, "are for readers, not age groups." He tries to spin yarns that are strong and clean, but says, "I am still a Vermont farmer."

In 1958 Robert Newton Peck was married to Dorothy Houston, a librarian. His best friend, Fred Rogers, of *Mister Roger's Neighborhood*, was the best man. The couple had two children, Christopher Haven and Ann Houston. While Christopher was growing up he played football and

Ann played the piano, something Robert Newton Peck also enjoyed. At conventions he often serenaded the attendees with his rendition of "The Chappaquiddick Rag." For meetings of librarians, when Virginia Kirkus was a powerful figure in book reviewing circles, he sang his special song, "Who's Afraid of Virginia Kirkus?"

In addition to his many fiction books Peck has written two books for other writers, that is, books to advise writers how to write books themselves. Not lacking in modesty, Peck is said to have described one of his books as "probably the best book in creative writing ever written."

Since 1974 Peck has been a full-time writer and says, "I'm in citrus, cattle, banking, insurance, airports, pro football, broadcasting, and publishing." For over twenty years Robert Newton Peck has lived and worked in Longwood, Florida.

Books and Notes

Most of Peck's books reflect his experiences growing up in Vermont, but because he has lived in Florida for so long many of his titles are also set there. His books about writing, although seemingly egotistic, do give some entertaining and sound advice about writing. Many of his novels for young readers are based on historical events. The accuracy of time and place becomes the most important aspect of the setting. For example, in his book *Fawn* (Little, Brown, 1975), Peck displays a great deal of knowledge about Fort Ticonderoga and includes an authentic map of the attack on the fort. The story itself, because of the historical data, becomes gripping and suspenseful.

Books for Writers

Fiction Is Folks: How to Create Unforgettable Characters (Writer's Digest Books, 1983).

Secrets of Successful Fiction (Writer's Digest Books, 1980).

Novels for Young Readers

Arly (Walker, 1989).

A Day No Pigs Would Die (Knopf, 1973).

Eagle Fur (Thorndike, 1992).

Higbee's Halloween (Walker, 1990).

Kirk's Law (Doubleday, 1981).

Little Soup's Birthday. Illustrated by Charles Robinson. (Dell, 1991).

Little Soup's Bunny. Illustrated by Charles Robinson. (Dell, 1993).

Nine Man Tree: A Novel (Knopf, 1998).

A Part of the Sky (Knopf, 1994).

Spanish Hoof (Knopf, 1985).

Soup Vinson Series

The "Soup" books are based on Robert Newton Peck's childhood in Vermont and his friendship with a pal, Luther Wesley "Soup" Vinson. Every time something is going on, Soup is right in the middle of it and somehow finds a way to involve Rob. The books are wild, hilarious, and by some standards outrageous.

The first book was published in 1974 and a new volume has appeared every year or two since—in hardback first, and, later, most have appeared in paperback. The following is a very selected list of titles.

Soup. Illustrated by Charles Gehm. (Knopf, 1974).

Soup 1776. Illustrated by Charles Robinson. (Knopf, 1995).

Soup Ahoy. Illustrated by Charles Robinson. (Knopf, 1995).

Soup in Love. Illustrated by Charles Robinson. (Dell, 1992).

Soup's Hoop. Illustrated by Charles Robinson. (Dell, 1990).

For More Information About/By the Author

Articles

"Author Admits He Is Just Out for Money." *School Library Journal* 26, no. 6 (August 1980): 14–15.

Jack Prelutsky

◆ Poetry

Brooklyn, New York
September 8, 1940

  📖 *The New Kid on the Block*

  📖 *A Pizza the Size of the Sun*

  📖 *The Dragons Are Singing Tonight*

About the Author
and the Author's Writing

Jack Prelutsky had drawn two dozen or so simple little imaginary animals. Eventually he wrote some poems to go with them but put them aside. Those poems brought him into the world of children's literature.

He was born September 8, 1940, in Brooklyn, New York. The family lived on the top floor of a six-story apartment building where everyone knew everyone else. That is also where he and four friends hung out. The friends eventually made their appearance in Prelutsky's *Rolling Harvey Down the Hill* (Greenwillow, 1980). Prelutsky was known as the absent-minded, strange-looking, clumsy kid. His four best friends were Harvey, Lucky, Tony, and Willie. Prelutsky describes Willie as being smart, strong, fast, a good friend, and very handsome. Then he says, tongue-in-cheek, "Willie was exactly like me." The two were always competing. They had a secret agreement—if one did something different, the other one would do the same thing right then, right there on the spot. One day, when Prelutsky was ten, there was "a worm eating contest in my neighborhood—nobody won!" Willie spotted a worm and said, "That looks good." He "slurped" down the worm. Prelutsky recounts, "I had to eat a worm. Willie had eaten a big, long, fat red juicy worm." That incident became "Willie Ate a Worm" in *Rolling Harvey Down the Hill*.

Prelutsky says, "[A]s a kid, I loved anything to do with dinosaurs. Now I have a book of dinosaur poems titled, *Tyrannosaurus Was a Beast* [Greenwillow, 1988]. 'Gussie's Greasy Spoon' from *The New Kid on the Block*, was based on a lunch I had in a small town diner, one of the few meals I've ever consumed that was worse than school cafeteria food!"

Many of Prelutsky's other poems come directly from his life experiences and questions he asks about events. One day he was sitting in the bathtub and reading a story in an old *National Geographic* about wolves. He thought about wolves doing their laundry and eventually the idea of a "Wash-and-Were Wolf" was formed. Another time he was in a grocery store and thought about boneless chickens, wondering what kind of eggs a boneless chicken would lay.

He wrote a poem about his mother's singing. The song was about the "worst singer in the world." However, he did not want to tell that the singer was his mother. He says that, "My mother's singing would make the plaster peel from the ceiling and accidents happen in the street. That took some doing, since we lived on the top floor of a six-story apartment house."

From the time Prelutsky was young he wanted to be the best at whatever he attempted. For a time he was paid to sing at weddings and was given free voice lessons by the choir master of the Metropolitan Opera. But when Prelutsky heard Pavarotti sing, he knew he could not be the best. After graduating from high school in 1958, he took night classes at Hunter College but found the courses quite boring. He says he "flunked seven languages (eight if one counts English)." However, he has translated books from German and Swedish into English. Once he decided he wasn't going to be an opera singer, he held a number of jobs—bus driver, coffeehouse folk singer, potter, photographer, meat truck driver, and sculptor.

His love of poetry was not fostered during his childhood. The poems he heard in elementary school left him to believe that poetry was "the literary equivalent of liver. I was told it was good for me, but I didn't believe it." He says that he doesn't think he wrote any poems when he was a kid, but that was a "long time ago." He does remember liking word games and puzzles, so he did like to play with language. During his twenties, Prelutsky rediscovered poetry and liked it. A college professor of his was very fond of poetry, and Prelutsky also had a girlfriend who was working on a Ph.D. in literature. Her dissertation was about poets. These connections sparked Prelutsky's interest. He was working in a music store when, fancying himself as an artist, he drew several sketches and added some poems to showcase the sketches. When a friend convinced him to show the drawings and poetry to a children's editor, the editor rejected both the drawings and the poetry. The second editor he showed them to, Susan Hirschman at Greenwillow, was interested in the poems (but not the drawings). She told him that he had the talent to become one of the best poets in the world.

Prelutsky tends to write in spurts and professes to have little in the way of a writing schedule. Sometimes he writes for weeks at a time, and sometimes just for a day or two. When he does write, he writes around the clock. When the flow of words stops, he does not write again for several months.

When he wrote the poems for *The New Kid on the Block* (Greenwillow, 1984), the writing took seven weeks, but he had about ten years' worth of notes that went into the writing. The time it takes Prelutsky to write a book varies. The dedication page of *The New Kid on the Block* says, "To Susan Hirschman—20 years." Prelutsky credits Hirschman as being "entirely responsible for my career as a children's poet."

Prelutsky usually carries a notebook and has a stack of notebooks (taller than he is) in his home. He jots down any jokes or ideas that pop into his head. Once he is at home, he transfers the information to his word processor. His writing style takes him back and forth between his computer and recliner. Once he prints out his thoughts from the computer, he settles back into the recliner and scribbles changes and ideas that eventually create a poem. Sometimes he begins with an idea, rhyme, sentence, or sometimes even a single word. Sometimes he begins at the beginning, sometimes the end, and sometimes he begins in the middle. He has said that *Nightmares: Poems to Trouble Your Sleep* (Greenwillow, 1976) was a pivotal book in his career, because he wrote it after a two-year-long writer's block. But *The New Kid on the Block* was his favorite for many years because "it is my largest book of original poems." Since *The New Kid on the Block* was published, Prelutsky has authored two more substantial volumes of original poetry, *Something Big Has*

Been Here (Greenwillow, 1990) and *A Pizza the Size of the Sun* (Greenwillow, 1996).

Prelutsky writes his poetry in a studio in his home. The studio contains his writing desk, a computer, and his library of reference books and children's literature, including a large collection of children's poetry. He has a "lot of stuff" in his studio and admittedly has a difficult time throwing anything away. Among his many books sit some of his collection of frogs (all kinds except living). He has never counted all of his frogs but says he may possibly have more than a thousand, maybe even three thousand. His wife has given him a frog tie and once in awhile someone gives him a live frog, but he always lets it go. He also has a collection of windup toys. At one time his favorite toy was a gorilla pencil sharpener, but his favorite changes from time to time. Several of the toys in his studio have become poems. Other poems come from things he remembers happening to him as kid—like the day his mother came home from the hospital with a new baby brother. Sometimes he writes about his likes or dislikes. One of his poems was about spaghetti, and he loves spaghetti.

Prelutsky has visited hundreds of schools across the United States. He often sings his poems to the accompaniment of his guitar. It was on one such trip to Albuquerque, New Mexico, that he met his wife, Carolynn. She was a librarian and was the person who was designated to show him around the area during his visit. Within five minutes of meeting her, he had proposed. She accepted the next day, and a few months later, near Christmas in 1979, they married. They lived in Albuquerque for eleven years. She was quite the opposite of him. He had been so disorganized that for years he had a joint checking account with his editor (Susan Hirschman) because he couldn't keep track of his money. Carolynn was organized. He is creative, and she is more managerial. At one time he said, "I'm not sure whether she's working for me, with me, or over me." In the early 1990s they moved to Washington state, where Prelutsky's studio window lets him see the trees and many kinds of birds. He says, "Everywhere! Everything I see or hear can become a poem." The Prelutskys have had cats and dogs as pets, but other times they have been without pets. Prelutsky says he has "many interests besides writing poetry. I enjoy photography, carpentry, creating 'found' sculpture, collages, and games. I also collect art, children's poetry books, and frog miniatures. I studied music as a young man and still attend the opera and symphony whenever I get the chance. I also eat out a lot!"

In early 1996, the Prelutskys moved to a house only three miles from the first one. They spent much of February "getting ready to move, . . . packing, and picking out colors, carpets, and lighting fixtures, and finding painters and carpenters and floor refinishers and roofers and so on." The Prelutskys are now settled into their new home in Olympia in western Washington state.

Books and Notes

Prelutsky's poetry books include collections of his own poetry as well as anthologies of poetry written by others. He often includes selections of his own poetry in the anthologies as well.

Poetry by Prelutsky

Monday's Troll. Illustrated by Peter Sis. (Greenwillow, 1996).

The New Kid on the Block. Illustrated by James Stevenson. (Greenwillow, 1984).

A Pizza the Size of the Sun. Illustrated by James Stevenson. (Greenwillow, 1996).

Rolling Harvey Down the Hill. Illustrated by Victoria Chess. (Greenwillow, 1980).

Something Big Has Been Here. Illustrated by James Stevenson. (Greenwillow, 1990).

Poetry Selected by Prelutsky

A. Nonny Mouse Writes Again! Poems. Illustrated by Marjorie Priceman. (Knopf, 1993).

Beauty of the Beast: Poems. Illustrated by Meilo So. (Knopf, 1997).

Dinosaur Dinner with a Slice of Alligator Pie: Favorite Poems. By Dennis Lee. Selected by Jack Prelutsky. Illustrated by Debbie Tilley. (Knopf, 1997).

For Laughing Out Loud: Poems to Tickle Your Funnybone. Illustrated by Marjorie Priceman. (Knopf, 1991).

For Laughing Out Louder: More Poems to Tickle Your Funnybone. Illustrated by Marjorie Priceman. (Knopf, 1995).

Hooray for Diffendoofer Day! By Dr. Seuss and Jack Prelutsky. Illustrated by Lane Smith. (Knopf, 1998).

Imagine That! Poems of Never-Was. Illustrated by Kevin Hawkes. (Knopf, 1998).

Read-Aloud Rhymes for the Very Young. Illustrated by Marc Brown. (Knopf, 1986).

For More Information About/By the Author

Articles

McElmeel, Sharron L. "Jack Prelutsky." In *The Poet Tree* (Teacher Ideas Press, 1993): 91–96.

Raymond, Allen. "Jack Prelutsky . . . Man of Many Talents." *Early Years* (November/December 1986): 38–42.

Ivy Ruckman

Hastings, Nebraska
May 25, 1931

📖 *Night of the Twisters*
📖 *In a Class by Herself*
📖 *This Is Your Captain Speaking*
📖 *In Care of Cassie Tucker*

About the Author
and the Author's Writing

Ivy Ruckman is firmly established in the world of children's books. A former high school English teacher, she has built a reputation for writing very believable novels dealing with contemporary issues for the older intermediate and middle-school reader.

Ivy Myers Ruckman, the youngest of seven children, was born May 25, 1931, and grew up during the Depression, near the farming community of Hastings, Nebraska. Of her youth Ruckman says, "My earliest memories are of sitting on my father's lap—wide-eyed, I'm sure—listening to hair-raising tales of life in western Nebraska's ranch country." She and her brother would often beg for just "one more." They were never disappointed. "The stories and storyteller were first-rate, with subjects ranging from rattlesnakes to twisters, and including every variety of outhouse prank."

Ruckman says her mother was "deprived, by hardship, of books and her girlhood, didn't often tell stories. She read them to us instead, including *Robinson Crusoe*, long before I was able to understand most of it. She was the one who took my brother Bill and me by the hand for the mile-long trek to the Hastings Carnegie Library, somehow returning home in time to cook supper for nine."

Her older (and closest in age) brother, William, contributed to her sense of imagination and creativity as the two spent days thinking up new adventures. When Ivy was just twelve years old, William introduced his sister to the Salvation Army, and for the next few years they spent their days outshining each other in piety. They shared interests in biology and Shakespeare. He became a cardiovascular surgeon; she became an English teacher with junior high students, later teaching high school English.

She says, "I now know how lucky I was to grow up in a story-loving family in a quiet prairie town during the Great Depression. My days were long and leisurely. Play and make-believe were my whole life.

"My first 'published' work was a play in verse, inspired by the fairy tales I'd discovered at Morton Elementary. A teacher decided it should be performed for the entire school, and appointed me director. Naturally, I gave myself the best part (the prince), then flew into costuming and directing with a relish that now makes me smile.

"At home I read. I read sitting in the cottonwood tree, at meals, hunched over the furnace grate. My mother excused me from doing dishes if I happened to be reading or practicing the piano, and so I became somewhat skilled at both. I also wrote. On sidewalks, on backs of old wallpaper rolls, in discarded bookkeeping ledgers, on an unsightly slab of slate Mama installed in the living room forever. Always I loved the kind of outdoor play and school assignment that allowed me to make things up. There was no television, but action-packed, dialogue-laced stories ran nonstop in my head."

Coming from a long line of ministers and teachers who valued "the word," it was little surprise that Ruckman would become a teacher. She attended Hastings College and taught in Wyoming and Utah. At the age of 24 she married, but after eight years, in 1963, the couple divorced. Two years later she married Stuart Allan Ruckman, a dentist. Together they became avid rock climbers, as did their three children, Kim, Bret (William Bret), and Stuart.

It took twenty years (after college) for Ruckman to become a published writer. One of her most popular titles, *Night of the Twisters* (Crowell, 1984), is set just twenty-five miles from her hometown, Hastings, Nebraska. She says about the book, "Both the research and the writing took me home, literally and figuratively. The voices in the book are out of my past, although I never experienced the kind of destructive tornadoes Dan and his community witnessed that night.

"Regularly I rummage through my private ragbag for ideas and feelings that breathe life into a story. When a favorite cousin lost everything in a tragic tornado, goose bumps raked my scalp and refused to go away. All my early fears (and the stories) came surging back. 'Head for the cellar!' I could hear my father shout again as we braced against the basement wall, waiting. Two years after the Grand Island tornado disaster I began to write *Night of the Twisters*, a family-centered story that has bonded me with readers more profoundly than any of my other work.

"Many of the details used in the story came from real life. There really was a woman who escaped from her basement by climbing bed springs. There was a Deputy Sheriff Kelly (Buck) who was a hero that night in Grand Island, and my cousin's family did take refuge in the jail after their house was destroyed. The storm and its behavior are as accurate as I could make them, but the characters and the story are fiction. Except for the two street names bordering the neighborhood, the setting also is real. I named Fonda Way after Henry Fonda, who was born in Grand Island and was one of my favorite actors; I called the other street Sand Crane Drive because of the sand hill cranes that visit Mormon Island in the Platte River. In reference to the dedication in *Night of the Twisters*, Cindy, Mark, and Ryan are the names of my cousin's children. Tia was the family cat that was never found after the tornado. The family (later) got a new cat, Tia II."

The book *Night of the Twisters* was made into a movie in 1996. The ninety-seven minute movie, now available in video format, is distributed by GoodTimes Entertainment and stars John Schneider, Devon Sawa, and Lori Hallier. The movie aired on the Family Channel, and, according to the Channel, the movie (as of early 1998) still held the record for numbers of viewers for its premier in February. The movie continues to be shown, periodically, on the Family Channel and is available in retail stores. Ruckman says, "I was invited to Toronto where it was being filmed, where I met Devon Sawa and others in the cast and was able to watch two days of studio shooting as they wrapped up the TV movie.

After being consulted all the way through the writing, and even the film-ing, (which is unusual) I became interested enough in the process to want to adapt one of my other books for possible use as a screenplay." The script she developed was based on *No Way Out* (Crowell, 1988). No producer has yet committed to produce the script, but she says, "I'm keeping my fingers crossed."

When Ruckman wrote *In a Class by Herself* (Harcourt, 1983) she presented the story through two viewpoints. The two characters were suggested by two former students, a troubled, street-tough, but funny and charismatic girl, and a talented boy who suffered a crippling shy-ness. A subplot in the book was taken from her own high school creative writing class, which sold a script to ABC's *Room 222*. The show was actually aired and rerun. She says, "I have a personal stake in this book because of its classroom setting and its larger Salt Lake City setting. I may also feel more committed to the ideas this book espouses because they are my philosophies—acting out of love *can* make a difference; young people in trouble *can* turn their lives around; age, economic, cul-tural differences *are* insignificant in the long run. We're all human first, and we need each other. I confess to loving all my books, but each per-haps for a different reason." She cites *Night of the Twisters* because it is her "scariest"; *What's an Average Kid Like Me Doing Way Up Here?* (Delacorte, 1983) for its humor; and *The Hunger Scream* (Walker, 1983) because of its maturity.

In 1983 Ruckman's husband, Allan (Stuart Allan Ruckman), died in a mountain climbing accident. "Two books, *This is Your Captain Speak-ing* [Walker, 1987] and *No Way Out* grew out of the emotional turmoil of those next few years. The more light-hearted *Who Invited the Under-taker?* [Crowell, 1989], although still dealing with the subject of loss, clearly signals my return to a happier state of mind."

In 1997 Ruckman turned to writing historical fiction, her first his-torical novel for intermediate and middle-school readers. "My grand-parents and great-grandparents were early settlers of south-central Nebraska, arriving to claim and farm land just before the turn of the century. Both sides of the family were headed by ministers, called 'preachers' then, who farmed and raised large families. Their early strug-gles to remain independent through drought, disease, and crop failures left them living near the poverty level, but always with a strong belief that every child should read books and love music. After two of my aunts wrote their moving memoirs, I knew that someday I'd like to draw on some of these same family stories to write a novel for young readers. *In Care of Cassie Tucker* [Delacorte, 1998] is that book.

"Similar to what happens in the story, my own father was injured as a result of bronc-busting and lay in a coma a frighteningly long time. His mother, although hampered with arthritic hands and feet herself, kept him alive by her vigilant administering of simple remedies.

"There really was a pet crow who plucked clothespins off the line; there really were blizzard deaths every winter; these pioneering families *were* largely suspicious of outsiders, even as they were clannish and neighborly, often going to great lengths to help each other. Adult responsibilities, to help with everything on the farm, fell on very young shoulders among my forebears. Indeed, the older children of eight in the family often became mothers and fathers to the ones coming up.

"I was touched by my own mother's story of being forbidden to swim. Her family lived near the Little Blue River on what I believe was called 'Pawnee Creek.' The one time she went in the river (in overalls) with her older brothers, a neighbor lady spied and told on her. My grandmother forbade her to go near the river again. My own love of swimming gives this incident poignancy it might not have otherwise and, of course, insured it a place in this Nebraska novel."

Ruckman has also drawn much material from her three children. Their concerns were part of *Melba the Brain* (Dell, 1991) and *Melba the Mummy* (Dell, 1991). Their enthusiasm for adventure contributed to *No Way Out*, and her daughter's marathon running played a part in *Hunger Scream*, the novel about an anorexic teenager. Her sons' rock-climbing became the passionate pursuit of characters in two of her novels.

Ivy Ruckman has lived in Salt Lake City for over twenty years. Her three children, Kim, Bret, and Stuart, are grown, and although they have other occupations, all three have published books. Stuart and Bret have used their mutual interest in rock climbing to collaborate on two titles, *Climber's Guide to American Fork Canyon, Rock Canyon* (Chockstone Press, 1995) and *Wastach Climbing North: Big Cottonwood Canyon, Little Cottonwood Canyon, Lone Peak and Others* (Chockstone Press, 1991).

Ruckman has been a full-time writer since 1974. Today when she is not "reading, swimming, or answering mail" her time is divided between speaking and writing. She says, "I've become a traveling teacher, one who loves meeting readers face-to-face in schools across the country." Traveling to schools and for pleasure and research are a major part of Ruckman's life. She counts among her friends fellow Salt Lake City resident and writer Gloria Skurzynski. Ruckman remains particularly interested in nature and the outdoor world, and often writes in the out-of-doors. She enjoys making (and eating) brownies and a good glass of Russian tea.

Books and Notes

Most of Ruckman's books are contemporary realistic fiction, although she has written two mystery/suspense books, *Spell It M-U-R-D-E-R* and *Pronounce It Dead* as well as her first historical fiction title, *In Care of Cassie Tucker*.

In Care of Cassie Tucker (Delacorte, 1998).

Night of the Twisters (Crowell, 1984).

No Way Out (Crowell, 1988).

Pronounce It Dead (Bantam, 1994).

Spell It M-U-R-D-E-R (Bantam, 1994).

This Is Your Captain Speaking (Walker, 1987).

What's an Average Kid Like Me Doing Way Up Here? (Delacorte, 1983).

Who Invited the Undertaker? (Crowell, 1989).

For More Information About/By the Author

Limited information on flaps of book jackets. Check general reference sources.

Cynthia Rylant

Contemporary Realistic Fiction ◆ Poetry

Hopewell, Virginia
June 6, 1954

📖 *Waiting to Waltz: A Childhood: Poems*
📖 *When I Was Young in the Mountains*
📖 *Missing May*
📖 Henry and Mudge Series
📖 Mr. Putter and Tabby Series

About the Author
and the Author's Writing

Cynthia Rylant was born June 6, 1954, in Hopewell, Virginia. Her parents, John Tune and Leatrel Rylant Smith, separated when she was just four years old and divorced some time later. Cynthia's mother decided she would be able to care for Cynthia better if she had a profession, so she decided to go to nursing school. Leatrel Rylant took Cynthia to live with her grandparents, Elda and Ferrell Rylant, in Cool Ridge, West Virginia, so that she could attend nursing school. Cynthia grew up in the poorest part of West Virginia. The house had no electricity or running water. She never traveled far from home because the family did not have a car. They didn't read many books because the family was poor, and there weren't libraries nearby. She loved her grandparents. Her grandfather died before Rylant wrote her first book, but one piece of advice from her grandfather has stayed with her, "Always do the best you can with what you've got." While she was loved and well cared for at her grandparents', she was always waiting for her parents to come back. One did; one didn't. Her grandfather worked twenty-four years in the coal mines and returned home each night covered with coal dust. Rylant told the story of her early years in *When I Was Young in the Mountains* (Dutton, 1982).

Rylant was unable to identify with many of the illustrations in the published book. The little girl on the cover was wearing a shirtlike dress. That was not her. Originally, the picture depicting her grandfather returning from the coal mines showed him with only a dirty hat on his head. The art had to be revised to show his clothing covered with the fine film of coal dust that is constantly present in a coal miner's life. Diane Goode made the changes before the book was published. The book received a Caldecott Honor Award for Goode's illustrations.

Rylant wrote two books that were published by Dutton, but later moved to Bradbury and editor Richard Jackson. Stephen Gammell was chosen to illustrate her third book, *The Relatives Came* (Bradbury, 1985). Gammell called Rylant and said, "Cynthia this is the weirdest manuscript I've ever read. It sounds like aliens coming." Actually the story is true. Every summer Rylant's grandmother's sister, Aunt Agnes, and her family would come from Virginia. The children were always welcomed and treasured. Their two- to three-week stay was filled with activity and love. Gammell agreed to illustrate the book, and, from the title page on, his illustrations depict the flurry of people and activity and love. Gammell included his own family within the book. His father is shown cutting a young man's hair in the upper corner of one page, and Gammell shows himself as a bearded, bespectacled, guitar-playing young man in red sneakers on the following page. Next, Gammell's wife is shown, barefoot, in jeans and a red shirt, taking a family picture. On one of the last pages, Gammell's mother is shown in her nightgown watching the relatives as they drive away at the first light of day. Rylant dedicated the book to her aunt.

Another of Rylant's books, *Waiting to Waltz: A Childhood: Poems* (Bradbury, 1984), depicted Rylant's childhood years in Beaver, West Virginia. When Rylant's mother completed nursing school, she returned and established a home for Cynthia. They moved to Beaver, a small town, and while her mother worked, Cynthia went to school. After school she spent time walking up and down the streets. She was a restless fourteen-year-old anxious to get out of Beaver. "My mother was a single parent and I was a single kid." It was the first time she remembered sidewalks and indoor plumbing. The main street of Beaver "goes about 500 feet and then it quits." Beaver Creek ran through the town.

She sat down to write the poems for the collection *Waiting to Waltz: A Childhood: Poems* on Mother's Day. Rylant tends to write quickly, and on that Sunday morning she went out into the yard and sat down in a lawn chair. Only a dog's barking punctuated the silence. That morning she wrote sixteen poems, and the next day she wrote seven. The following day she wrote the final poems.

Rylant had sent an odd number of poems off to Jackson, 29, since, as Rylant has said, "My editor has a 'thing' about odd numbers." Jackson responded that she must write one more poem. It was a poem about her father dying, something she had thus far refused to acknowledge. Her father had left when she was four, and her only memories of him were tucking her into bed. He died when she was just a teenager, never having returned. He had been in the war and was an alcoholic. Both had taken their toll on his life while he was alive, and now his death took a toll on Cynthia. The poem came in a tidal wave and was sent to complete the poetry volume. "Forgotten" was perfectly complemented by Gammell's drawing of an empty chair. In its own way *Waiting to Waltz* continues Rylant's story *When I Was Young in the Mountains*, although *Waiting to Waltz* is intended for intermediate-aged readers.

Miss Maggie (Dutton, 1983) is a story of a woman that Rylant really knew. The woman lived across the cow pasture and was the ugliest woman one could ever meet. She lived in a dark house that was rumored to have snakes. In the book the young character is a boy instead of a girl, but he feels all the feelings that Rylant felt.

She describes her years in Beaver by saying, "Mom and I had an apartment. It was heated with old gas heaters, no carpet, and there were spiders in the bathtub. From the front window I could see Todd's junkyard. There was always some talk about the ghost of Todd's father." She had little access to books although she could manage to obtain comic books. She gathered pop bottles from ditches to buy comic books. She desired better things, and after high school, she decided to go to college. "As long as I stayed in Beaver I was somebody special. When I went away. . . ." She began school at what is now known as the University of Charleston. Since her father had died when she was thirteen, she was a "war orphan" and was able to go to college free. The first time she set foot in a library or museum was when she attended college. Later, she attended Marshall University and earned a masters degree. She worked in the Akron Public Library, and it was there that she read Donald Hall's *Ox-Cart Man*. She knew then that she wanted to write books. She read many, many children's books and completed a masters degree in library science at Kent State University. She also began writing. She checked out market possibilities in *Writer's Market* and sent her stories off. After six months trying to interest someone in her writing, she managed to sell her first book, *When I Was Young in the Mountains*. Her son, Nate, was nine months old. She is a prolific writer and since then has written more than seventy-five books. In just a three-year time period, 1997–2000, she will have twenty-five titles published.

During her early college days she had tried to be a hippie, but during graduate school she "tried to look intellectual." The birth of her son also brought about changes in her lifestyle. She says, "I did not have time to iron Indian shirts anymore." Her change also had a lot to do with the birth of her writing.

For a period of time in the late 1970s and early 1980s, Rylant was married to a man who enjoyed large dogs. One of those dogs became the model for Mudge, the dog in the Henry and Mudge books. Rylant's son, Nate, born in 1979, gave her many ideas for the books that rival the popularity of the touchstone of emerging readers, Arnold Lobel's Frog and Toad series.

Rylant feels that it is important to present a collaboration of text and illustrations. After her disappointment with the illustrations for her first book, she wanted as much control as possible when her other books were published. When the illustrations for *Miss Maggie* were being created by Thomas Di Grazia, she sent a photo of the cabin where the real Miss Maggie had lived. The artist used the picture, and when the book was published the illustration of the cabin gave Rylant a personal connection. When the boy is shown entering the home, Rylant felt as if she had walked through that very same doorway. The book is dedicated to her son, Nate, whose name was used for the boy in the story.

When Peter Catalanotto first drew the sketches for the artist's whale picture in *All That I See* (Orchard, 1988), he draw the paintings as a cartoon-type whale. But it was important that the reader view Gregory as a real artist, not as someone who was emotionally or mentally disturbed. Rylant therefore requested that the artist's picture show a real whale. Catalanotto complied and the book gained the dimension that Rylant was striving to achieve.

In recent years, Rylant has even tried her own hand at illustration. She illustrated *Dog Heaven* (Blue Sky Press, 1995) and *Cat Heaven* (Blue Sky Press, 1997). The illustrations were very childlike and somewhat reminiscent of those characteristically created by her good friend and author/illustrator Dav Pilkey.

Rylant's first book was published in 1982, but it was not until 1985 that she felt her writing was making enough money to quit her part-time job. For many years she and her son, Nate, lived in Kent, Ohio. During those early years as a writer another writer was also attending Kent State University as an art major. When a creative writing professor encouraged him to write professionally, he wrote the manuscript for *World War Won* and entered it into a contest for student writers. The manuscript was selected for publication. After the book was published, the writer, Dav Pilkey, moved back to Kent. It was then that he "met Cyndi Rylant at a writer's group." According to Pilkey, "It didn't take long before Dav and Cyndi fell in love, and they have been sweethearts ever since." In 1990, after a dream that Pilkey says told him he was supposed to move to Oregon, the couple decided to move west.

Rylant arranged to donate her manuscripts to the library at Kent State University, and the two of them packed up their dogs and cats and made the trek westward. They settled in Eugene, Oregon, in 1993. Pilkey lives in a small house surrounded by tall trees and more than 100 rhododendron and azalea bushes. Rylant lives just down the street. They often walk their dogs and meet at each other's houses for conversation and tea. She says, "I go to movies every chance I get, and I see my favorites over and over, as many as seven or eight times." She regards her grandparents as having had a profound influence on her writing. "The tone of my works reflect the way they spoke, the simplicity of their language, and, I hope, the depth of their own hearts."

Books and Notes

Cynthia Rylant is a versatile and prolific author. *When I Was Young in the Mountains* was her first book, and within a fifteen year period she has written (and published) more than 75 books, an average of five books a year. She has written picture books (two of which she illustrated), early chapter books, novels for the intermediate reader, and books for young adults.

Henry and Mudge Series

Since the first title was published in 1987, Rylant has written more than fifteen additional titles. Henry and his large dog, Mudge, romp and play by the "forever sea," get in "puddle trouble," and do many of the same things other little boys and their dogs do. Mudge is based on the personality and character of a big dog that Cynthia and her son, Nate, once owned. During Nate's childhood, his antics and romps with the large dog provided many incidents that later show up in the books. James Stevenson illustrated the first two books published in 1987. The rest of the books in the series have been illustrated by James Stevenson's daughter, Suçie Stevenson.

Henry and Mudge. Illustrated by James Stevenson. (Bradbury, 1987).

Henry and Mudge and Annie's Good Move. Illustrated by Suçie Stevenson. (Simon, 1998).

Henry and Mudge and the Best Day of All. Illustrated by Suçie Stevenson. (Bradbury, 1995).

Henry and Mudge and the Careful Cousin. Illustrated by Suçie Stevenson. (Bradbury, 1994).

Henry and Mudge and the Sneaky Crackers. Illustrated by Suçie Stevenson. (Simon, 1998).

Henry and Mudge and the Starry Night. Illustrated by Suçie Stevenson. (Simon, 1998).

Henry and Mudge in the Family Trees. Illustrated by Suçie Stevenson. (Simon, 1997).

Henry and Mudge Under the Yellow Moon. Illustrated by Suçie Stevenson. (Bradbury, 1988).

Mr. Putter and Tabby Series

Three titles in this series were published in 1994, and during the next four years, an average of two titles appeared each year. Mr. Putter, his cat, Tabby, their neighbor, Mrs. Teaberry, and her dog, Zeke, are the main characters in these tales. Mr. Putter bakes a cake (he

knows nothing about doing such a thing), takes a train, picks pears, and does many other ordinary things that he and his constant companion, Tabby, manage to make extraordinary. Selected titles follow.

Mr. Putter and Tabby Bake the Cake. Illustrated by Arthur Howard. (Harcourt, 1994).

Mr. Putter and Tabby Fly the Plane. Illustrated by Arthur Howard. (Harcourt, 1997).

Mr. Putter and Tabby Row the Boat. Illustrated by Arthur Howard. (Harcourt, 1997).

Mr. Putter and Tabby Take the Train. Illustrated by Arthur Howard. (Harcourt, 1998).

Mr. Putter and Tabby Toot the Horn. Illustrated by Arthur Howard. (Harcourt, 1998).

Other Titles

Cynthia Rylant has written picture books, middle-grade novels, and novels for young adults. The settings for many of her books (as well as her poetry) are sensed more than blatantly specific. Much of her writing emerges from memories of her youth in the Appalachian region, and the scenery in her books reflects that. Diane Goode was given a 1984 Caldecott Honor Award for the illustrations for Rylant's first book, *When I Was Young in the Mountains*, and Rylant herself was awarded a Newbery Award for her book *Missing May*.

Appalachia: The Voices of Sleeping Birds. Illustrated by Barry Moser. (Harcourt, 1991).

Explore the countryside and people of Appalachia.

The Bird House. Illustrations by Barry Moser. (Blue Sky Press, 1998).

An orphan girl finds an unexpected home.

A Blue-Eyed Daisy (Bradbury, 1985).

Eleven-year-old Ellie and her family live in a coal mining town in West Virginia.

But I'll Be Back Again: An Album (Orchard, 1989).

Tales from growing-up years in a small West Virginia town. Autobiography.

A Fine White Dust (Bradbury, 1986).

A traveling preacher comes to a small North Carolina town and has a profound impact on the life of thirteen-year-old Peter.

The Islander (DK Ink, 1998).

An orphan, ten-year-old Daniel, lives with his grandfather on an island off British Columbia. His loneliness brings him to make connections with a mermaid.

Miss Maggie. Illustrated by Thomas Di Grazia. (Dutton, 1983).

Young Nat is afraid of old Miss Maggie and her rotting log house.

Mr. Grigg's Work. Illustrated by Julie Downing. (Orchard, 1989).

The Old Woman Who Named Things. Illustrated by Kathryn Brown. (Harcourt, 1996).

An old woman who has outlived all of her friends resists becoming too attached to the stray dog that shows up at her home each day.

The Relatives Came. Illustrated by Stephen Gammell. (Bradbury, 1985).

This Year's Garden. Illustrated by Mary Szilagyi. (Bradbury, 1984).

The seasons of the year reflect the growth, life, and death of the garden of a large rural family.

When I Was Young in the Mountains. Illustrated by Diane Goode. (Dutton, 1982).

Reminiscences of life with her grandparents in the mountains.

Poetry Collections

Rylant's interest in poetry dates back to her college days when she visited a display of poet David Hubble. She especially loved "Paper Boy," a poem with very strong characters. Her own poetry celebrates the lives of ordinary people living their lives in quiet, strong ways.

Soda Jerk: Poems (Orchard, 1990).

Poems spoken by a young soda jerk in a small town as he views the people of that town (Beaver, WV).

Waiting to Waltz: A Childhood: Poems. Illustrated by Stephen Gammell. (Bradbury, 1984).

Thirty poems from Rylant's childhood memories in the Appalachian Mountains.

For More Information About/By the Author

Articles

Antonucci, Ron. "Rylant on Writing: A Talk with 1993 Newbery Medalist Cynthia Rylant." *School Library Journal* (May 1993): 27–29.

"Cynthia Rylant, Papers." *Kent State University Library*. URL: http://www.library.kent.edu/speccoll/children/rylant.html (Accessed January 1998).

Cynthia Rylant Web Site. URL: http://rylant.com (Accessed December 1998).

Books

Rylant, Cynthia. *Best Wishes*. Illustrated by Carlo Ontal. (Richard C. Owen, 1992).

Louis Sachar

Humorous Stories ◆ Contemporary Realistic Fiction

East Meadow, New York
March 20, 1954

📖 *Sideways Stories from Wayside School*

📖 *There's a Boy in the Girl's Bathroom*

📖 Marvin Redpost Series

About the Author
and the Author's Writing

During his first week of law school, Louis Sachar's first novel was accepted for publication. By the time he graduated, he had written two more books, and decided to become a writer rather than an attorney.

Sachar was born on March 20, 1954, in East Meadow, New York, the son of Robert J. Sachar, a salesperson, and Ruth Raybin Sachar, a real-estate broker. He spent the first nine years of his life in East Meadow, where he attended Barnum Woods School. During those days he remembers "staying away from the woods across the street" where the "older, tougher" boys would be. Looking back, he realizes those boys were probably no more than eleven or twelve years old. When he was nine his family moved to Tustin, California, where he attended Red Hill School. He and his friends often cut through the orange groves to school and along the way home had "orange fights." Most of these groves are now paved over and fast food restaurants, offices, and housing developments have moved in.

He enjoyed school, especially math, got good grades, and played little league baseball. In the late 1960s when he entered high school, he began to enjoy reading. After high school he entered Antioch College in Ohio, and soon after received word of his father's death. Sachar was only eighteen and the death was difficult for him. He took a semester off from college and moved home to California to be near his mother. After a few months selling Fuller brushes, Sachar returned to college—this time to the University of California at Berkeley. He majored in economics, but also took creative writing classes and read his favorite authors. Sachar enrolled in a Russian course thinking that he might be able to read his favorite Russian novelists in the original language. He came to quickly realize that he probably would not become fluent in Russian, and, three weeks into the semester, he decided to drop Russian. He then set out to fill that 3-credit-hour void. From a handbill he learned about a volunteer position at a local school that would yield 3 hours of credit. He applied, and soon was not only volunteering, but he also became a paid "yard supervisor." To the students he became known as "Louis, the yard teacher."

He read Damon Runyon's *Our Town*, which is a collection of short stories told from the perspective of different members of the town. Sachar had the idea to combine multiple "authors" of stories and some of his school observations and his first book was begun. Sachar graduated from Berkeley and took a job in a sweater factory in Connecticut. He began to write *Sideways Stories from Wayside School* in the evenings. After about seven months he was fired from his job and decided to return to school. He began to send out his manuscript and applications to law schools. He was accepted at the University of California and had just begun his first week of graduate school in 1977 when his manuscript was accepted. *Sideways Stories from Wayside School* was first published by Follett in 1978. Later it was published by Knopf (1990) and in 1998, Morrow Junior Books published the latest edition. For the next six years Sachar attended classes and wrote children's books. All the while, he struggled with whether he would be an attorney or a writer.

Before he passed the bar (1980), he had written two more children's books. For a time he did part-time legal work. He wrote in the morning and practiced law in the afternoon. At first his *Sideway Stories from Wayside School* was not highly successful, but reading motivator Jim Trelease began to use the book as an opening read-aloud in many of the seminars he presented to teachers and parents. The book became very popular, partially due to Trelease's promotion, and by 1995 the book had sold over 1 million copies.

Sachar had difficulty finding a publisher for *There's a Boy in the Girl's Bathroom* (Knopf, 1987), and when several readers wrote asking for a sequel to the Sideways stories, he decided to comply. One editor who expressed an interest in *There's a Boy in the Girl's Bathroom* wanted Sachar to rewrite the book so that there was just one viewpoint, rather than alternating viewpoints as Sachar had originally done. So while Sachar worked in the morning rewriting *There's a Boy in the Girl's Bathroom*, he worked in the afternoons making up puzzles for *Sideways Arithmetic from Wayside School* (Scholastic, 1989), puzzles that would help young readers know that reading is fun.

Many of the children in the class where Sachar worked became characters in the Wayside School stories. The class was taught by Mrs. Jukes, who became Ms. Jewell in his Wayside School books. Mrs. Jukes was the model of a patient, caring teacher. Sometimes Sachar combined the traits of two or more students to create a composite character. Mrs. Jukes is the mother of another author, Mavis Jukes, who has written several novels about mending families. After Sachar had become an author of note, his editor came to California and invited two of her clients to lunch. One client was Sachar and the other was Mavis Jukes. It was then that the two discovered their connection.

A group of young readers in Plano, Texas, helped Sachar make another connection. They loved his books and thought he ought to meet their unmarried teacher. He eventually accepted an invitation to visit the school to meet with the children and their teacher. He says that the teacher was nice, but that he liked the counselor better. As luck would have it, the counselor was single.

He and Carla Askew were soon married, and she moved with him to San Francisco. He continued to write, and she taught school. The Sachar family soon included daughter Sherre. Later they moved back to Texas, this time settling in Austin. Louis still spends mornings writing and the afternoons answering letters from young fans, and doing some part-time legal work.

Carla Askew became the inspiration for the counselor in *There's a Boy in the Girl's Bathroom*. That character, Carla Davis, got her last name from the school where Sachar first met the real-life Carla. Many of the phrases the counselor uses are those of Sachar's wife. However, the two Carlas are also very different. For example, in one place in the book, Carla says, "I like messy rooms." The real Carla would never say such a thing, preferring to have things orderly and clean.

Sachar's Wayside School stories are about the boys and girls who attend a fictional school built mistakenly 30 stories high, with one classroom on each floor, instead of one story high with 30 classrooms on one floor. Some of the characters in Sachar's other books are memorable. Angeline in *Someday Angeline* (Avon, 1983; Morrow, 1998) just wants to fit in with classmates. Marvin Redpost, a main character in several titles, is a nine-year-old outcast in his third-grade class.

Louis Sachar and his family live in Texas, where Louis has taken up bridge and regularly plays at a bridge club in the Austin area. He also enjoys playing chess, skiing, playing the guitar, and being with his family. Carla continues to teach and Louis continues to write funny books.

Books and Notes

Sachar is known for his humor-filled books, but he also tries to write books that help children take a look at their own behavior and at the way they treat other children. Sachar's Wayside School series has been immensely popular with intermediate readers, and readers who are just becoming comfortable with chapter books often choose his Marvin Redpost books.

Marvin Redpost

Marvin Redpost has a lot of problems with his classmates. Sachar's tales deal with these problems with humor and sensitivity. Readers will gain insights into the feelings of those around them— and will be laughing at the same time.

Marvin Redpost: Alone in His Teacher's House. Illustrated by Barbara Sullivan. (Random, 1994).

Marvin Redpost: Is He a Girl? Illustrated by Barbara Sullivan. (Random, 1993).

Marvin Redpost: Kidnapped at Birth? Illustrated by Neal Hughes. (Random, 1992).

Marvin Redpost: Why Pick on Me? Illustrated by Barbara Sullivan. (Random, 1993).

Other Titles

The Boy Who Lost His Face (Knopf, 1989).

Dogs Don't Tell Jokes (Knopf, 1991).

Holes (Farrar, 1998).

Johnny's in the Basement (Morrow, 1998).

Monkey Soup. Illustrated by Cat Bowman Smith. (Knopf, 1992).

Someday Angeline. Illustrated by Barbara Samuels. (Morrow, 1998).

There's a Boy in the Girl's Bathroom (Knopf, 1987).

Wayside School Stories

Louis Sachar's first title, *Sideways Stories from Wayside School*, gained popularity and spawned several more titles about Wayside School. Each collection takes place at the school providing interesting commentary on events in our elementary schools. Several of the titles cited below were previously published, but have been reissued by the publisher cited below.

Sideways Arithmetic from Wayside School (Scholastic/Apple, 1997).

Sideways Stories from Wayside School. Illustrated by Julie Brinckloe. (Morrow, 1998).

Wayside School Gets a Little Stranger. Illustrated by Joel Schick. (Morrow, 1995).

Wayside School Is Falling Down. Illustrated by Joel Schick. (Lothrop, 1989).

For More Information About/By the Author

Articles

McElmeel, Sharron L. "Louis Sachar." In *Educator's Companion to Children's Literature, Volume 1: Mysteries, Animal Tales, Books of Humor, Adventure Stories, and Historical Fiction* (Libraries Unlimited, 1995): 84–87.

Marilyn Sachs

◆ Contemporary Realistic Fiction

New York, New York
December 18, 1927

- 📖 *The Bears' House*
- 📖 *A Pocketful of Seeds*
- 📖 *Veronica Ganz*
- 📖 *The Big Book for Peace*

About the Author
and the Author's Writing

Marilyn Stickle Sachs was born in New York City on December 18, 1927. When she was just four years old the family—her parents, an older sister, and Marilyn—moved to Jennings Street in the east Bronx, a borough of New York City. Apartment houses, side by side, five stories high, stood on one side of the street. Each one had a "super" who lived in the basement and took care of the building. The apartment buildings were most likely once very fancy homes, but when the Stickle family lived there they housed several families, all of them quite poor. The street did not have any trees, grass, birds, or flowers. Across the street was a junior high school and a large schoolyard. The children played in the streets, sat on the apartment building stoops (steps), or sneaked through the bars on the schoolyard gates to play on the playground.

Marilyn was just four when her mother sent her off to school. Her mother said she was five. Later, after her mother got sick, her father sent Marilyn and her sister to summer camp so that their mother could rest. Campers were supposed to be eight, but Marilyn was only six. When the camp counselors found out, they decided to let her stay. The scary stories told there and other unsettling things made Marilyn hate going to camp. For many summers, Marilyn and her sister were sent to camp despite their dislike for the experience. The camps were all charity camps for poor children from the city who needed to learn the beauty of the countryside.

Marilyn's school days were plagued by bullies—it seems like hundreds. And then there was the day in first grade that her teacher would not let her go to the bathroom until someone else needed to go too (so they could go together). When the class got up to play "The Farmer in the Dell," it was too late for Marilyn. While the moment was unbelievably embarrassing for her at the time, she used it forty-five years later in the first chapter of her book *Class Pictures* (Dutton, 1980).

By the time Marilyn was six her mother was quite ill, and the family moved to an apartment on the first floor, because her mother could no longer climb four floors to get to their old apartment. In third-grade Marilyn's mother was very ill, and Marilyn spent much of the year crying. That year her third-grade teacher was a "lovely young woman" named Mrs. Powers. Previously Mr. Powers had built his wife a replica of the house where the three bears lived. It was filled with exquisite little handmade furniture and a pantry full of dollhouse food. The dining room held a table with a red checkered cloth and the chairs of the three bears. Upstairs were the three bears' beds, each with their own sheets and pillows. In the smallest bed was a little golden-haired doll, Goldilocks. Since Mrs. Powers was not returning the following year, she had decided that at the end of the year she would give the house to the "best child" in the class. All the children were permitted to play with the house, but the last day of school was actually a dreaded day—only one of them would get the house. Classes then always had "best" and "worst" children and most of them knew exactly where they stood. Gold stars were given for behavior, and always if one got 100 percent in spelling or math. Marilyn seldom got a gold star because she was always crying. But at the end of the year, Marilyn was delighted to be the one who received the house. It took Marilyn, her sister, and several other sixth-graders to take the Bears' House home.

That house and school year became the inspiration for *The Bears' House* (Doubleday, 1971). Though Fran Ellen's family had different circumstances from Marilyn's, their joy over the Bears' House is very similar.

Marilyn spent much of her time at the Morrisania Branch of the New York Public Library. There, she has said, "My life as a writer began." The lines to get into the library often extended into the street. Children had to go upstairs to the top floor, and once inside were admonished to be quiet, or they would be sent out. Two library clerks inspected their returned books to make sure they were not soiled or damaged. Then they could select two books to take home. Often the librarian wanted to suggest stories about girls going across the country in covered wagons. Those were not the type of books Marilyn wanted to read, so she quietly put them back on the shelf and selected the books that she wanted. Her favorites were those by Caroline Dale Snedeker, Howard Pyle, Jeffrey Farnol, Sir Walter Scott, and, as she matured, Alexandre Dumas. She also read comic books, series books, such as the Bobbsey Twins, and books her sister recommended. Marilyn's sister became increasingly important in her life, especially when their mother died, when Marilyn was twelve years old. Seldom did the girls actually own a book, but for her eighth birthday Marilyn received her favorite book, *Rebecca of Sunnybrook Farm*. This was the only book her mother ever read to her. On her ninth birthday she received *Grimm's Fairy Tales*, and as a ten-year-old she received *Uncle Tom's Cabin*.

Marilyn's father was the youngest of eight children and for a time his sister, Aunt Bertha, a prim and proper lady, lived with the family, telling wonderful stories about the family. She also told stories about the great-grandmother who hid fugitive slaves before the Civil War. Marilyn loved to hear them all.

Her father also told stories, often epic stories and stories from the Bible. He changed details to make drama, a trait some noticed in Marilyn. However, when Marilyn embellished her everyday stories, she was considered to be a liar. She lied a lot. Marilyn's mother's family came from Russia and the family also had many great stories. Her grandmother became the mother in *Call Me Ruth* (Doubleday, 1982).

In 1938 Marilyn's father ran for the New York state legislature. He lost but his involvement in politics sparked Marilyn's interest and has stayed with her. She graduated from junior high school in a dress worn by her sister a few years earlier, and her father gave her a corsage of red roses. Life without her mother was difficult and things were never the same. One of her closest friends was a boy named Seymour, and the friendship lasted until they married—each to someone else. That friendship, years later, became the basis for *Peter and Veronica* (Doubleday, 1969).

By the time Marilyn was fifteen her father remarried and the family moved from Jennings street. Their new neighborhood was in the west Bronx, a little better neighborhood. By now Marilyn was writing a lot of stories and was a rather good writer. When she received an 86 percent in an English class and other students were getting 90 percent or better, she was disappointed. She asked the teacher many times why she had only gotten an 86. Later the teacher explained that the 86 was a "compliment" intended to let her know that she was capable of so much more. That teacher and the summer's experiences showed up in Sachs's *A Summer's Lease* (Dutton, 1979). Sachs dedicated the book to that teacher.

Marilyn Stickle graduated from Morris High School in 1944 and soon was attending Hunter College. Marilyn found college to be difficult, and began to wonder if she should even be going to college. Her father was not encouraging because girls, in his estimation, would end up married and mothers anyway. That attitude was a motivating force to Marilyn. She moved out of her father's home to Brooklyn and began to make her own way. She met her husband-to-be, Morris Sachs, when she was eighteen. He was a twenty-three-year-old veteran of the war and was attending college on the GI Bill. They met during a rally to raise money to get black players into the major league baseball teams. They married on January 26, 1947. The two of them moved to North Brother's Island in the East River, where many other college students were living. She graduated in 1949, and, even though she wanted to be a writer, took a job with the Brooklyn Public Library. Morris became a teacher in the New York City school system. Along the way Marilyn Sachs went to Columbia, earning a masters degree in library science. Morris Sachs gave up his teaching to become a sculptor. She needed to commit time to writing if she was ever going to be an author, so the couple saved $500 and she took a six-month leave of absence from her job. They spent $200 on a piece of artwork, and then settled down at their work. He created a sculptor's studio in the front of the apartment, and she worked on a typewriter in the back of the apartment. In four months she finished the manuscript for *Amy Moves In* and sent it to an editor she knew at Knopf. The book was rejected by several publishers; it seemed no one wanted it. The book did not get published for ten years. The story was too "realistic" to be published at that time. Editors wanted her to change the book, to put in some Jewish holidays, to make the parents more acceptable, to make everything turn out all right by book's end. Sachs did not want to change it so she kept working.

In 1961 the Sachs moved to San Francisco. By then they had two children, Anne, born in 1957, and Paul, born in 1960. She began working part-time in the San Francisco Public Library. Then she received a letter from a friend with whom she had worked at the Brooklyn Public Library. She was now editor at Doubleday and wanted to see her manuscript. Sachs promptly sent it, and within two weeks she received an acceptance letter.

From that time on she was an author, writing about a book a year. Her first books featured Amy and Laura, who came straight out of her childhood. *Veronica Ganz* (Doubleday, 1968) came next, a longtime favorite of Sachs herself. Veronica Ganz was a composite of all of those bullies Sachs had encountered as a child. Sachs wanted to "kill" Veronica in the book, but her daughter told her not to do that. The cover illustration of Veronica, drawn by Louis Glanzman, is exactly right according to Sachs. The reason Glanzman could draw it so perfectly is because, "I knew what Veronica looked like . . . she was in my sixth grade class."

Anne has been her mother's strongest critic and best supporter. She now lives in New York, where she is in education, but she continues to read each new book. Paul was not as interested in his mother's writing, and, in an effort to get him to read something that she had written, she wrote two picture books, *Matt's Mitt* (Doubleday, 1975) and *Fleet-Footed Florence* (Doubleday, 1981). Another of her books, *Laura's Luck* (Doubleday, 1965), began as an "anti-camp" book, but actually turned out more positive than Sachs intended. Many children write and tell her that they wish to go to "Camp Tiorati."

Although most of her books are contemporary realistic fiction, one title was historical fiction. *A Pocketful of Seeds* (Doubleday, 1973) became a story of the contrast of how people lived during the years of World War II. Sachs was dancing and laughing in the American canteens. Years later she met a woman her age who had lived in France during the war. While Sachs was dancing, her friend's parents and little sister were being taken to Auschwitz because they were Jews. Her friend was in hiding.

Marilyn Sachs's life and interests continue to appear in her books. Her daughter, Anne, and son, Paul, are grown and there are "three enchanting granddaughters, Miranda, Lena, and Sarah." Marilyn Sachs's husband, Morris, is still a sculptor; they celebrated their 50-year wedding anniversary on January 26, 1997. When the couple celebrated their 25-year wedding anniversary, Anne and Paul gave them a wonderful surprise party. In *Another Day* (Dutton, 1997) Genevieve and Ernest do the same thing. Genevieve and Ernest are based on Anne and Paul. "Anne was an angel, and my son . . . was not." And Sachs says, "The recipe for the chocolate chip cake is really a family favorite."

Sachs states, "Every book I write is a new experience for me, a new journey. I feel very lucky to have had the privilege of writing for children over more than thirty years. Probably the book I'm proudest of is *The Big Book for Peace* [Dutton, 1990], a peace anthology that I co-edited and for which I wrote one story. We had many famous and generous authors and illustrators contribute pieces and none of us accepted any royalties for our work. Instead, we ended up contributing over one-half million dollars to five peace organizations."

When Marilyn Sachs is not writing, she says, "I'm reading. When I'm not reading, I'm babysitting, walking, seeing friends, and suffering over the San Francisco Giants baseball team." Marilyn and Morris Sachs live in San Francisco in the house where they have lived for more than twenty-five years.

Books and Notes

Marilyn Sachs's first book was *Amy Moves In*. Since then she has written more than 30 books of contemporary fiction. Other than that first book, all were written while she lived in San Francisco. Her first six books were set in the Bronx during the 1940s. Her more recent titles have been set in the present and have dealt with a number of problems common to young readers. She has said, "I usually write about 'losers' because I felt I was a loser as a child."

At the Sound of the Beep (Dutton, 1990).
Ten-year-old twins Mathilda and Matthew run away because their separating parents plan to split them up. They intend to stay with an uncle in San Francisco, but he is away. The two resort to sleeping in Golden Gate Park, where someone is murdering homeless people.

The Bears' House. Illustrated by Louis Glanzman. (Doubleday, 1971).
Everybody in Fran Ellen's class knows her name, and that she sucks her thumb and smells bad. But nobody really knows anything important about Fran Ellen. Her mother is sick; her father is not in the house; and nobody is there to take care of the children.

The Big Book for Peace. Edited by Ann Durell and Marilyn Sachs. (Dutton, 1990).
Collection of stories about peace.

Call Me Ruth (Doubleday, 1982).
Ruth and her mother emigrate to the United States from Russia.

Class Pictures (Dutton, 1980).

Pat traces the history of her friendship with Lolly.

A Pocketful of Seeds. Illustrated by Ben Stahl. (Doubleday, 1973).

A tale of two young women during the years of World War II, one in the United States, and one in France fleeing the German Nazis.

A Summer's Lease (Dutton, 1979).

Gloria needs to be the assistant editor of the high school literary magazine. Mrs. Horne is the kind of English teacher who could help her attain her goal. Set in the 1940s.

Thunderbird. Illustrated by Jim Spence. (Dutton, 1985).

A Greenpeace animal lover and a Thunderbird-loving mechanic meet at the library, quarrel, and fall in love.

Veronica Ganz. Illustrated by Louis Glanzman. (Doubleday, 1968).

This book is about the composite bully that plagued Sachs throughout her school life.

For More Information About/By the Author

Limited information on the flaps of books. Check standard reference sources.

George Selden

◆ Animal Fantasy

**Hartford, Connecticut
May 14, 1929–1989**

📖 *Cricket in Times Square*
📖 *Tucker's Countryside*
📖 *The Genie of Sutton Place*

About the Author
and the Author's Writing

George Selden [Thompson] became well known as an author with *Cricket in Times Square* (Ariel, 1960). Thompson used his first two names, George Selden, as his writing pseudonym to avoid being confused with another George Thompson who was also a writer. Now there is also another George Selden who has written many nonfiction books about science topics.

George Selden Thompson was born May 14, 1929, in Hartford, Connecticut, where he grew up. He attended Loomis School and Yale University and then spent a year (1951–52) on a Fulbright Scholarship in Italy. He traveled all over Europe and had that "great American experience in Europe." Once he returned to the United States, he settled in Greenwich Village in New York City. His first writing efforts were dismal failures, and he was not particularly proud of his work. But Thompson persisted and kept honing his skills.

Late one night Thompson heard a cricket chirp in the Times Square subway station. "The idea for a story developed immediately." His characters were Mario Bellini and his parents, who operate an unsuccessful newsstand in Times Square; Chester, the liverwurst-loving cricket, who had been carried there in a picnic basket from his Connecticut home; Tucker, a mouse; and Harry, the lovable cat. When the story *Cricket in Times Square* (Ariel, 1960) was published, it was a great success. Hundreds of readers wrote to request a sequel, and eventually Thompson wrote three of them. His personal favorite was *Tucker's Countryside* (Farrar, 1969), about which he has said, "I put the writing of a sequel off until I thought I had an equally good idea." The conservation theme was one that was important to Thompson. He used his own childhood home and the meadow across the street for the book's setting. He considered some of the book's passages among his best children's writing. *Chester Cricket's Pigeon Ride* (Farrar, 1981) and *Chester Cricket's New Home* (Farrar, 1983) also featured the same characters as *Cricket in Times Square*.

Thompson's favorite books as a young reader were *The Lord of the Rings* and *The Hobbit*, both by J. R. R. Tolkien. He enjoyed music, archaeology, and J. R. R. Tolkien. For much of his adult life and until his death in 1989, Thompson lived in New York City.

Books and Notes

George Selden (Thompson) claimed his spot in children's literature when his book *Cricket in Times Square* was published in 1960. Later, he wrote a number of animal tales, including other books featuring the same characters as those in his first successful title. Garth Williams's well-executed drawings helped endear the story to young readers. *Cricket in Times Square* was a Newbery Honor Book.

Chester Cricket's New Home. Illustrated by Garth Williams. (Farrar, 1983).

Cricket in Times Square. Illustrated by Garth Williams. (Ariel, 1960).

Harry Kitten and Tucker Mouse. Illustrated by Garth Williams. (Farrar, 1986).

The Old Meadow. Illustrated by Garth Williams. (Farrar, 1987).

Oscar Lobster's Fair Exchange. Illustrated by Peter Lippman. (Avon, 1962; 1982).
Originally published as *The Garden Under the Sea*.

Tucker's Countryside. Illustrated by Garth Williams. (Farrar, 1969).

For More Information About/By the Author

Limited information on the flaps of books. Check standard reference sources.

Shel Silverstein

◆ Poetry

Chicago, Illinois
1932

📖 *Falling Up*

📖 *A Light in the Attic*

📖 *Where the Sidewalk Ends*

About the Author
and the Author's Writing

Shel Silverstein was well known as a writer of adult books before he began writing for children. In fact, he *never* planned to write for children. Silverstein's friend, Tomi Ungerer, a well-known children's book author, insisted that Silverstein meet with book editor Ursula Nordstrom. Soon Silverstein had written the manuscript for *Where the Sidewalk Ends* (Harper, 1974), and people all over the world were reading his poems. His books have been translated into 14 languages.

Shel Silverstein was born in Chicago, Illinois, in 1932. The actual day of his birth eludes researchers, and for years, even his publisher, HarperCollins, had very limited biographical information about him. There is so little biographical information, that one might suspect that Silverstein is a pseudonym. However, according to Nicole Hoyt, a biographer of Danielle Steel, the popular adult romance writer once met Silverstein at a gathering at Hugh Hefner's Playboy mansion. Poet William Cole is also said to have met Silverstein in the 1960s in the Simon &

Schuster publishing offices. (The occasion was Cole rejecting a manuscript by Silverstein.) That manuscript was *The Giving Tree*. Cole is said to have told Silverstein that the book fell between adult and children's literature and would never sell. Eventually Harper & Row published the title, and it sold over 14 million copies.

In 1969 Hal Drake, a senior writer with the Army publication *Pacific Stars and Stripes*, interviewed Silverstein. The last interview seems to have been in 1975 when Jean F. Mercier interviewed him for the February 24, 1975, issue of *Publishers Weekly*. At that time he was quoted as saying, "I won't give any more interviews," and he has not.

Other than a few bits and pieces, little is known about Silverstein. He is said to have appeared in the 1971 film starring Dustin Hoffman, *Who Is Harry Kellerman and Why Is He Saying Those Terrible Things About Me?* He did create some musical scores for the movie, notably "One More Ride" performed by Silverstein and Dr. Hook.

In the early 1950s (1953–1955) he was a member of the U.S. Armed Forces, serving in both Japan and Korea. During that time he drew cartoons for *Pacific Stars and Stripes*. From the Army he became a cartoonist, composer and lyricist, folk singer, movie actor, and writer. His cartoons have appeared in various adult magazines.

He is a folk singer and composer, as well as a poet. Brenda Lee, Jerry Lee Lewis, and Johnny Cash are among those who have sung and recorded some of Silverstein's songs. Johnny Cash popularized Silverstein's song "A Boy Named Sue." Silverstein's most popular album seems to be *The Great Conch Train Robbery*. In addition to songs, Silverstein wrote several plays, including *The Lady or the Tiger* and *The Crate*. A movie screenplay for *Things Change* was coauthored with David Mamet.

Silverstein told Mercier that he couldn't play ball, and he "couldn't dance. Luckily the girls didn't want me; not much I could do about that. So I started to write and draw."

Silverstein was first introduced to children's books by Tomi Ungerer. Ungerer thought that Silverstein could (and should) write for children. Silverstein did not think he could, but editor Ursula Nordstrom convinced him to try. By the time Silverstein was thirty-one, his first book, *Uncle Shelby's Story of Lafcadio, the Lion Who Shot Back* (Harper, 1963), was successful enough that Silverstein wrote *The Giving Tree* (Harper, 1964) and *A Giraffe and a Half* (Harper, 1964). Just ten years later Silverstein's popular verses and drawings were published in *Where the Sidewalk Ends* (Harper, 1974). In 1980 alone the book sold over 250,000 copies. William Cole, a fellow poet, lauded Silverstein's poetry as being "tender and humorous." Cole felt the verses were "just right for all ages," including his own.

Seven years later, just before Christmas, another volume of Silverstein's poetry appeared. *A Light in the Attic* (Harper, 1981) was an immediate success. Although it was marketed as a children's book, it immediately captured the number one spot on the *New York Times* adult nonfiction best-seller list. The book was at the top of the list for several weeks and the publisher tallied more than a half million copies sold during that first year. No other book has stayed on the list that long in the list's fifty-five year history.

Silverstein prefers privacy and has declined requests for interviews and publicity tours for years. He even asked his publisher not to give out any biographical information about him. He was married for a time and is the father of a grown daughter. He is associated with Grapefruit Productions in Brooklyn, New York. The most recent information available indicates that he divides his time between homes in Greenwich Village in New York City; Key West, Florida; and his houseboat, which was docked near Sausalito, California, for a time.

Books and Notes

Although he is most well known for his books of poetry, Silverstein has also written some popular picture books, which have appealed to children and adults. Some adults have objected to Silverstein's books of poetry on the grounds that the poems are too gross and disrespectful of adults. However, Silverstein's poetry has consistently attracted readers from early primary to adult.

Poetry

Falling Up: Poems and Drawings. Illustrations by Shel Silverstein. (Harper, 1996).

A Light in the Attic. Illustrations by Shel Silverstein. (Harper, 1981).

Where the Sidewalk Ends: The Poems and Drawings of Shel Silverstein. Illustrations by Shel Silverstein. (Harper, 1974).

Picture Books

The Giving Tree. Illustrations by Shel Silverstein. (Harper, 1964).

The Missing Piece. Illustrations by Shel Silverstein. (Harper, 1976).

The Missing Piece Meets the Big O. Illustrations by Shel Silverstein. (Harper, 1981).

Who Wants a Cheap Rhinoceros? Illustrations by Shel Silverstein. (Macmillan, 1983; 1964).

For More Information About/By the Author

Books

MacDonald, Ruth K. *Shel Silverstein* (Twayne, 1997).

Seymour Simon

Science ◆ Mystery

New York, New York
August 9, 1931

- 📖 *The Paper Airplane Book*
- 📖 *Wolves*
- 📖 *Soap Bubble Magic*
- 📖 The Anatomy Series
- 📖 The Astronomy Series
- 📖 The Earth Science Series
- 📖 The Einstein Anderson Series

About the Author
and the Author's Writing

Seymour Simon is a native New Yorker, born there in 1931. At a young age he became interested in science, learning the names of dinosaurs and planets along with baseball and basketball players on his favorite teams. His interest in science fiction began as a "junior scientist" when he was "just a kid." He loved reading science fiction magazines and eventually became interested in astronomy and technology. He spent hours in the New York City museums. The American Natural History Museum sponsored a Junior Astronomers Club. He joined and became president a few years later. He wrote his first book when he was in third grade. It was a story about a visit to an interplanetary zoo. He made up all the animals in the book and drew pictures of them. He attended the Bronx High School of Science, which is a specialized school within the New York Public School System. After high school he enrolled in the City College of New York City (CCNY), where he investigated and expanded his interest in animals and their behavior. In the early 1950s Simon spent some time in the U.S. Army and later pursued a teaching career. He studied science topics, psychology, literature, history, and philosophy in graduate school.

During twenty-three years as a science teacher, he developed a direct, conversational writing style that appealed to young readers. He says, "I try to write the same way that I talk. I'm always thinking about the effect my sentences will have on children when the words are read aloud." Seymour Simon, according to *Kirkus Reviews*, has "done more than any other living author to help us to understand and appreciate our planet and our universe." In the early 1980s Simon retired from teaching to concentrate on writing (and editing) full-time. However, he continues to visit classrooms and regularly talks to students about science-related topics. Some of his best book ideas come from classrooms across the United States. "Interesting questions come up in class discussions."

For many years he taught school and wrote in the evenings, during the summer, and whenever he could find time outside of the school day. He said, "Every teacher I knew had a second job; the salary just wasn't quite enough. When I began to write I was delighted that I could add to my income by doing something I enjoyed."

Simon has written over 150 science books; over half have been named Outstanding Science Trade Books for Children by the National Science Teachers Association. He writes about a great assortment of topics, such as light, earthquakes, volcanoes, and paper airplanes. When Simon writes about a nonfiction topic, he is also responsible for finding and arranging for the illustrations, and many are illustrated with photographs. Many of these come from public domain sources, a lot from the National Archives. The National Aeronautics and Space Administration's (NASA) archives have been the source from many of the photographs in his books about the planets. He also contacts photographers who are known for specific topics, such as mountains or glaciers. He must pay for permission if he uses photographs taken by private photographers, but photographs in government archives can be used without any fee. The problem is to locate the photographs to use. The catalog lists less than 2 percent of those available. However, when he was writing about volcanoes, he decided that he should really take some of the pictures himself. A great place to find volcanoes was Hawaii, and of course he thought a trip to Hawaii would be pleasurable. Now, more than before, Simon is using his own photos as his photography skills develop. Simon takes or culls through anywhere from 300 to 1,000 photographs before he selects 24 photographs to illustrate a book.

Simon's books have been honored with many awards, including the New York State Knickerbocker Award for Juvenile Literature (1994), and the Hope S. Dean Memorial Award (1996).

He is not interested in merely reciting a list of facts about a topic. His goal is to write science books that excite the reader about the topic being explored. "I hope to make the reader as fascinated about the topic as I am." He begins his books with a hook, something that will entice the reader further into the book. The content must be "interesting, factual, and current." Simon has said, "If you say you're bored by science, you are really bored by life."

Dinosaurs are among the most popular science topics but Simon wrote 60 or 70 books before writing about dinosaurs—and then it had a distinct twist. *The Smallest Dinosaur* (Crown, 1989) looked at the dinosaur from an unconventional perspective. One of his books challenged readers to answer questions such as, "What color were dinosaurs?" Children will often say grey, green, or brown. The truth is no one actually knows, because there were no humans living at the time to record any information about the color and only a few pieces of skins have been found. And, those pieces are so old that the color of the skin has long ago faded. Dinosaurs may have actually been brilliant colors.

Simon often uses analogies to help his readers visualize animals and events in science. For example, a humpback whale is longer than a semi-trailer; the tongue of a humpback whale weighs more than an elephant; in one day a baby whale drinks 100 gallons of milk and gains as much as 200 pounds; and the heart of a blue whale is as large as a small car.

He continues to write and photograph from a house on a hill in New York's Hudson Valley, Great Neck. He and his wife, Joyce (a travel agent), have two grown sons, Robert and Michael. Robert and his wife Nicole are the parents of Simon's two grandsons, Joel and Benjamin. Chloe, Simon's first granddaughter, was born to Michael and his wife Debra. When Simon is not writing (or visiting schools), he enjoys music, traveling, playing tennis, reading, and visits from his grandchildren.

Books and Notes

Seymour Simon has written several dozen magazine articles and a multitude of books. In addition to his nonfiction series, he has written individual books on eclectic topics. He has also written a series of science-based mystery books for the intermediate reader.

The Anatomy Series

This series focuses on human body systems. More titles are forthcoming.

Bones: Our Skeletal System (Morrow, 1998).

The Brain: Our Nervous System (Morrow, 1997).

The Heart: Our Circulatory System (Morrow, 1996).

Muscles: Our Muscular System (Morrow, 1998).

The Astronomy Series

Planets and other bodies in the celestial skies are each the focus of a book in this series. This series has produced several outstanding science trade books for children.

Comets, Meteors and Asteroids (Morrow, 1994).

Destination, Jupiter (Morrow, 1998).

Mercury (Morrow, 1992).

The Universe (Morrow, 1998).

Venus (Morrow, 1992).

The Earth Science Series

Ecosystems and weather-related topics are part of this series. All have been well researched by Simon with photographs selected to illustrate the text.

Deserts (Morrow, 1997).

Mountains (Morrow, 1997).

Storms (Morrow, 1997).

Volcanoes (Morrow, 1988).

The Einstein Anderson Series

This fiction series combines science with mystery. Einstein Anderson, science sleuth, is a young science genius and lover of bad puns. He solves mysteries in ten episodes in each book. The reader is given a chance to solve the puzzle and learn something about science in the process.

The Gigantic Ants and Other Cases. Illustrated by S. D. Schindler. (Morrow, 1997).

The Halloween Horror and Other Cases. Illustrated by S. D. Schindler. (Morrow, 1997).

The Howling Dog and Other Cases. Illustrated by S. D. Schindler. (Morrow, 1997).

The Invisible Man and Other Cases. Illustrated by S. D. Schindler. (Morrow, 1997).

The On-Line Spaceman and Other Cases. Illustrated by S. D. Schindler. (Morrow, 1997).

The Time Machine and Other Cases. Illustrated by S. D. Schindler. (Morrow, 1997).

Wings of Darkness and Other Cases. Illustrated by S. D. Schindler. (Morrow, 1997).

Other Titles

Animal Fact/Animal Fable. Illustrated by Diane deGroat. (Crown, 1979).

The Optical Illusion Book (Morrow, 1998).

The Paper Airplane Book. Illustrated by Byron Barton. (Viking, 1971).

Ride the Wind: Airborne Journeys of Animals and Plants. Illustrated by Elsa Warnick. (Browndeer Press, 1997).

Spring Across America (Hyperion, 1996).

Strange Mysteries from Around the World (Morrow, 1997).

They Swim the Seas: The Mystery of Animal Migration. Illustrated by Elsa Warnick. (Harcourt, 1997).

Wild Babies (Harper, 1997).

For More Information About/By the Author

Articles

"Seymour Simon." *The Internet Public Library.* URL: http://www.ipl.sils. org/youth/AskAuthor/simon.html (Accessed December 1997).

Seymour Simon Children's Science Books. URL: http://www.users.nyc. pipeline.com:80:/~simonsi/ (Accessed December 1997).

Gloria Skurzynski

Mystery ◆ Adventure Fiction ◆ Nonfiction, technology

**Duquesne, Pennsylvania
July 6, 1930**

- 📖 *Zero Gravity*
- 📖 *Cyberstorm*
- 📖 *Know the Score: Video Games in Your High-Tech World*

About the Author and the Author's Writing

On the front of her author brochure Gloria Skurzynski quotes a old Chinese saying, "May you live in interesting times." And in her own words, "Life is exciting!" Gloria Skurzynski's thirst for new knowledge and enthusiasm for sharing that knowledge have resulted in more than two dozen books for young readers. From the Middle Ages to adventures in today's world to an exploration of the future, Skurzynski has investigated it all and has managed to share her enthusiasm and interest with readers. Her writing career has spanned three decades and has produced picture books, folktales, middle-grade adventure stories, novels, young adult nonfiction titles, "futuristic" novels for young adults, and most recently a series of mystery/science books coauthored with her daughter Alane Ferguson.

Gloria Skurzynski says that she is different from most authors in two ways: "First, I didn't know I wanted to be a writer until I was a grown-up woman with five children. Second, I grew up in a home with very few books. When I was seven, and forced to stay in bed because of tonsillitis, a friend of my parents gave me a copy of *Heidi*—the first book I ever owned." She was an only child who filled her days with characters from books and movies. When she was ten she received a copy of *Hans Brinker and the Silver Skates* for Christmas and shortly after bought herself a copy of *Aesop's Fables* for 10¢. "Now, [over] fifty years later, I still have all three books. The pages are dry and crumbling and the bindings are falling apart, but I treasure them. . . . I loved books from the moment I turned that first page of *Heidi*, and I still love them—the touch, the smell, and most of all, the wonderful worlds found in the pages of books." It was her love of good writing and her admiration of authors that prompted her to write a fan letter to Phyllis McGinley, who had just won the Pulitzer Prize in 1965. Their correspondence grew into a friendship, and McGinley encouraged Gloria to try her hand at writing. Her first published story, accepted after fifty-eight submissions, was a story about her daughter Serena's broken leg. Eventually she published several magazine articles, and later, as her children grew, she began to turn to novels for their age category, 7 to 13 years of age.

Gloria Skurzynski was born in Duquesne, Pennsylvania, on July 6, 1930. She was an only child who turned to movies and books to fill her days. Her father often told stories about his own childhood. She knew that his story should be told one day but she did not think about becoming a writer until she was the mother of five daughters.

One of her books, *The Tempering* (Clarion, 1983), is based on her father's childhood and the stories he told her during her childhood in Pennsylvania. She began to write his story only a year before her father died. One of the most dreadful scenes, in which Karl's foot was burned with molten lead, actually happened. Another book, *Good-Bye, Billy Radish* (Bradbury, 1992), took her storytelling back to her childhood home, to the "smoky, sooty, western Pennsylvania town where flames set fire to the night." From her memories and her parents' stories, she re-creates the time and place. She writes the stories so others will continue to "remember the rumbles and shrieks of the mills, the smell of the smoke, the blaze of the furnaces, and the enormous power of the steel mills over the townspeople."

Skurzynski became an outstanding author of adventure fiction for intermediate-age readers with her Mountain West Adventures series. For a dozen years Skurzynski's family—her husband, Edward, and all five daughters—camped in the Utah desert at least once each summer. After a time, she began to observe more closely the desert animals, plants, and insects. She researched the effects of dehydration on the body. From these observations and research emerged *Lost in the Devil's Desert* (Lothrop, 1982). Several years later, she and her husband made a weekend trip to the redrock cliff country of southern Utah and northern Arizona. "The night we arrived, a fierce thunderstorm dumped rain on the mesa tops and into the canyons, creating spectacular waterfalls and a flash flood. The next morning the water was gone, but evidence of the flood remained. A full-sized automobile flipped on its roof in a stream bed, boulders flung helter-skelter like pebbles, a road washed out completely." These images planted the seeds for another adventure title, *Trapped in the Slickrock Canyon* (Lothrop, 1984). The book, set in Arizona, incorporates the flash flood into a story of two cousins fleeing from criminals who have reason to want Gina and Justin stopped from reaching safety. Skurzynski continued the series with a story set in Idaho that recounts the worst earthquake there in twenty-five years. *Caught in the Moving Mountains* (Lothrop, 1984) tells the story of the October 28, 1983, earthquake that centered on Mt. Borah, Idaho. A story set in Nevada, *Swept in the Wave of Terror* (Lothrop, 1985), focuses on an actor, performing in Las Vegas, who plans to destroy part of the Hoover Dam and plunge the city into darkness.

But Gloria Skurzynski has not been content to bask in the popularity of her adventure novels. Her nonfiction explores the world of high technology, and her most recent novels have futuristic twists or a science bent. "It isn't wise for an author to go off in too many directions . . . [but] I dislike confining myself to any one type of book. The world is just too full of fascinating topics and challenging genres."

She says, "Adventure novels are a lot of fun to research and write, but high-tech research lets me meet people who are working on the cutting edge of next-century technology. When they see that I'm really interested in their work, they open up and share things with me that I can't wait to share, in turn, with my readers. I don't know enough to really understand, in depth, how these technologies work, but I can learn enough to introduce them to kids and to make them aware that these marvelous creations exist. And there's always the hope that my young readers will get motivated to become creators themselves when they grow up." Although the research is often time consuming, she says, "None of the high-tech titles was really difficult to research. I become so enthused about the subjects that I can't wait to talk to the people who work in those fields, which means I learn as much as I can before I even contact them. They sense my enthusiasm and it all turns into a big, happy party."

Thus far she has investigated and written about robots, simulations, telecommunications, video games, zero gravity, and has incorporated information about the U.S. Postal Service's automated procedures. In *Cyberstorm* (Macmillan, 1995) she uses the concept of teleporting (separating at the molecular level and moving through time and space over some unknown electromagnetic wavelength) and the possibility of reliving one's past life through virtual reality. "*Cyberstorm* is my first venture into science fiction, although I prefer to think of it as a futuristic novel, rather than science fiction, because I tried to base it pretty much on what the world will actually be like in the year 2015." Skurzynski's characters are well drawn and the plot is fast-moving and full of adventure and suspense.

Her nonfiction high-tech books are illustrated with photographs, most of which Skurzynski takes herself. Other photographs are selected and arranged by her. "I'm doing almost all of my own photo illustrations these days, because I know what it is I want to show in the picture. When I can't take my own, as in *Zero Gravity* [Bradbury, 1994], since NASA wouldn't let me go up in the shuttle, I actually visited both NASA/Kennedy in Florida and NASA/LBJ in Texas. As always, I've studied the subjects ahead of time so I know what I'm looking for." At times she uses her grandchildren as subjects in her photographs. With the publication of *Waves: The Electromagnetic Universe* (National Geographic Society, 1996), all seven of her grandchildren will have appeared in photographs in her books.

In 1996 *Mystery of the Spooky Shadow* (Troll), the first of several collaborations between daughter Alane and Skurzynski, was published. Alane Ferguson is a well-known writer of mystery titles. So Ferguson "does the mystery part" and Skurzynski "does the science." *Wolf Stalker* (National Geographic Society, 1997) and *Rage of Fire* (National Geographic Society, 1998) are recent collaborations. Skurzynski says, "We love working together, and it looks as though we'll be under contract for many additional titles." Alane is the only daughter who still lives within driving distance. However, "when we work together, we most often connect by modem."

Gloria Skurzynski uses a computer to write her books and regularly accesses the Internet/World Wide Web. She recently mounted her own Website. Skurzynski views herself as "an observer, as I usually am in the real world, too—just cruising around quietly to see what other people are up to, not letting myself become too conspicuous."

Her interest in technology, new learning, and creative thinking is shared by her family. Her husband, Edward, is a retired aerospace engineer who "loves computers." Their oldest daughter, Serene Nolan, practices medicine. Jan Skurzynski met her husband, Dale Mahoney, on the Internet. She works for Hewlett Packard and performs throughout the Northwest as half of the music duo Black Diamond. The Skurzynskis' third daughter, Joan Alm, designs Western clothing for Southwest boutiques. The youngest two daughters are Alane Ferguson, the mystery writer, and Lauren Thliveris, a computer engineer.

When Gloria and Ed have spare time they "watch movies, dink around on the computer, or travel." She enjoys hearing from readers and prefers to receive messages by e-mail.

Books and Notes

Gloria Skurzynski's books range from early readers to those for the young adult reader. In general, her books appeal to the middle-grade/middle-school reader. Her nonfiction books and a few of her novels deal with technology-related topics.

Mystery and Science Fiction

Cyberstorm (Macmillan, 1995).

Mystery of the Spooky Shadow. Co-authored with Alane Ferguson. Illustrated by Jeffrey Lindberg. (Troll, 1996).

Rage of Fire. Coauthored with Alane Ferguson. (National Geographic Society, 1998).

The Virtual War (Simon, 1997).

Wolf Stalker. Coauthored with Alane Ferguson. (National Geographic Society, 1997).

Zero Gravity (Bradbury, 1994).

Nonfiction (High-Tech)

Here Comes the Mail (Bradbury, 1992).

Know the Score: Video Games in Your High-Tech World (Bradbury, 1994).

Waves: The Electromagnetic Universe (National Geographic Society, 1996).

Other Titles

Caitlin's Big Ideas. Illustrated by Cathy Diefendorf. (Troll, 1995).

The Ministrel in the Tower. Illustrated by Julek Heller. (Random, 1988).

For More Information About/By the Author

Articles

Gloria Skurzynski. URL: http://redhawknorth. com/gloria (Accessed December 1998).

Skurzynski, Gloria. "The Best of All (Virtual) Worlds." *School Library Journal* 39, no. 10 (October 1993): 37.

Alfred Slote

Contemporary Realistic Fiction ◆ Science Fiction

Brooklyn, New York
September 11, 1926

📖 *Finding Buck McHenry*
📖 *The Trading Game*
📖 *My Robot Buddy*

About the Author
and the Author's Writing

Born in Brooklyn on September 11, 1926, Alfred Slote grew up with a younger sister. The neighborhood children often played ball in the streets, and as a young boy, Alfred Slote loved sports. He played all kinds of ball—baseball, football, basketball, and even tennis and squash. When neighborhood youngsters played roller skate hockey in the street, they used phone books wrapped around their shins as guards. Several times his mother came out in the street to get him for his piano lesson, but most embarrassing was the time his music teacher actually came out onto a field where he was playing football and made him go home for his lesson.

Alfred's mother also saw to it that he visited the public library branch on a regular basis. He enjoyed reading, and his favorite authors included John R. Tunis, Ralph Henry Barbour, and Rafael Sabatini. His mother often read to him and his younger sister, and there were always books in the house. After high school, at the age of eighteen, he entered the University of Michigan. He attended for two semesters before he joined the U.S. Navy. He served from 1944 to 1946, and then returned to Michigan. During this second year at the university, he began writing seriously. He earned his undergraduate degree in 1949. While he was at the university, he was awarded the Avery and Jules Hopwood Award for creative writing. He collected enough rejection slips to paper the ceiling of his room. The following year, 1950, he earned a masters degree and was awarded a Fulbright Scholarship in Comparative Literature to study at the University of Grenoble. He lived with a French family there, but never did study literature. He did learn to ski and finished writing a first novel. "It was a terrible novel." By this time he had met his future wife, and she was finishing her final year at Mount Holyoke.

Alfred Slote's younger sister was attending Mount Holyoke College and brought her friend home for Christmas. After traveling all night from Michigan he arrived home to see a strange woman wearing his old Navy jacket. She had not brought enough warm clothes to Brooklyn. They married by the end of 1951 even though they only saw each other in person six times before. Henrietta "Hetsy" Howell was from Philadelphia and lived in the city center. It was 1950, but she still had her mail delivered by horse and wagon.

The couple moved to Ann Arbor, where Hetsy earned her masters degree in English while Slote taught as a fellow in the English department. She obtained a Fulbright Scholarship to France, and this time they both went. They lived in Lyons and Nice. While living in Nice, Slote received copies of his first novel. Before returning to the states, Slote interviewed for and received a position as an English instructor at Williams College in Williamstown, Massachusetts. He taught there from 1953 to 1956. While living in Massachusetts the Slotes' first two children were born. Hetsy contracted polio, but completely recovered. Slote enjoyed teaching, but he found that one hour of teaching was like four hours of work in the outside world, and he wanted to write. Writing and teaching, he believed, drew on the same energies. In 1955 an old radio drama friend from Massachusetts invited him to return to Ann Arbor to become involved in educational television. In the summer of 1956 Slote left Massachusetts and returned to Ann Arbor to become a producer-writer and associate director at the University of Michigan Television Center. For the next seventeen years he wrote and produced various prize-winning children's television programs. During this time he continued to write—three adult novels, two adult mysteries, and one book of non-fiction. The Slotes' third child, Ben, was born in Michigan.

During the course of producing educational children's shows, he searched for a folktale about communication. Because he couldn't find one, he sat down and pieced together a short story, "The Princess Who Wouldn't Talk." His agent immediately sold it to Bobbs-Merrill as a picture book. In 1964 Bobbs-Merrill published that literary folktale. He earned a $750 advance and thought he was rich. *The Princess Who Wouldn't Talk* (Bobbs-Merrill, 1964) was followed by two story collections, *The Moon in Fact and Fancy* (World, 1967) and *Air in Fact and Fancy* (World, 1968).

However, picture books were not really his strength. His agent called to tell him that Lippincott wanted an author to write two sports books a year that another author had been writing. Slote's agent thought he ought to give it a try. He didn't think he could do it, but after a few minutes on the phone, he went to his office and began to type on his old Royal Standard typewriter. The writing seemed to come easily; he was writing in his own voice.

His first sports title, *Hang Tough, Paul Mather*, was published by Lippincott in 1974. His interest in sports began in childhood but involvement with his sons' high school sports events contributed as well. His first love was baseball, but Slote's sons' hockey games provided background for a controlled-vocabulary hockey story, *The Hotshot* (Watts, 1977). He followed that hockey book with a title about tennis, *Love and Tennis* (Macmillan, 1979). Although Slote writes about all sports, he prefers using baseball as a backdrop: "Baseball has gaps in it, silences and pauses that are so important." Those gaps allow the writer to let the reader know what is going on in the character's head.

After writing several sports books, he was invited to speak at a college in California. The professor wanted him to talk about his books that the professor said were written on the exact same theme—fathers and sons and their relationship. At first Slote did not want to believe that he had merely been writing the same book (plot and theme) over and over, but when he acknowledged it, he stopped writing. He did not want to write the same story/plot/theme.

In the process he began to write science fiction books. He wrote three titles about the same character, Jack Jameson, who has a mechanical friend. Of the three titles, *My Robot Buddy* (Lippincott, 1975) is probably the best known.

Recently Slote has returned to baseball titles with two immensely popular novels. *The Trading Game* (HarperCollins, 1990) details the dilemma of Andy, who desperately wants a baseball card that features his grandfather, a little known major league player. That card is worth a quarter or less, and his friend has the card but refuses to part with it unless Andy gives up a valuable Mickey Mantle card. Andy is not a wise card trader—he inherited his collection from his dad. But Tubby, the boy with the card featuring Andy's grandfather, knows the value and is still willing to demand the Mantle card in exchange. Only when their mutual friend enters the picture does the plot come to light. She turns the table on Tubby. The grandfather, who was a professional baseball player and pushed his son to play ball, was loosely based on Slote's own mother. He thinks, "my mother and Andy's grampa are the same person, even though my mother never played for the Detroit Tigers." Slote himself is the eleven-year-old in his books. He is Jake, Danny Gargan, Paul Mather, Aaron Henry, Jason Ross, and Andy Harris.

Most of his books have been composed using a Royal Standard typewriter, but he does use a computer. He has two home offices, one in which he actually writes, and one in which he does all the other things associated with writing, such as answering letters from readers. It takes from six weeks to two years to write a book. The usual length required is about one year.

Finding Buck McHenry (Harper, 1991) is perhaps Slote's most popular title yet. It is a compelling tale of a group of school children who convince themselves that an African American custodian working in their school is actually a famous Negro league ballplayer that has dropped out of the limelight. When the custodian offers to coach their little league baseball team, the children just know that they have correctly identified him. Surprises are in store for both the children and the custodian.

Slote writes every day. He prefers to write in the morning, as that is his most productive time. He writes, rewrites, and rewrites. Children often ask if his children "helped" him with his writing when they were growing up. The answer is "No." Slote says, "After all, I was the eleven-year-old."

His sons and daughter are grown now. John is a writer in New York state. He has two daughters, Sophia and Franny. Elizabeth is married to Galen Gilbert and lives in Boston. She is an art editor for Houghton Mifflin and an author as well. Her two books, *Nellie's Garden* and *Nellie's*

Grandmas, were published by Tambourine Press (a division of William Morrow). Elizabeth illustrated one of Slote's books, *Clone Catcher* (Lippincott, 1982). Elizabeth has two children. Ben has a doctorate in American literature and teaches at Allegheny College in Pennsylvania. He and his wife Susan have two children, Audrey and Joe.

Alfred Slote says he loves being a grandparent but otherwise leads a pretty "dull life." He and his wife live in Ann Arbor, Michigan, where he writes full-time. In 1998 he was just finishing a screenplay (cowritten with David Field) for Hallmark and Showtime based on his book *Finding Buck McHenry*. In addition to his children's books, he writes screenplays and adult novels.

Books and Notes

Slote's books basically fall into two categories, science fiction and sports. However, Slote is quick to point out that the science fiction is more science fantasy, and the sports books really focus on other problems. For example, *Hang Tough* is a book about a boy who is dying; *Matt Gargan's Boy* is about a child's efforts to reunite his divorcing parents; *Jake* is about a child looking for his father; *The Trading Game* is about a war between generations; and *Finding Buck McHenry* deals with a lot of topics—one of which is racism.

Science Fiction

C.O.L.A.R.: A Tale of Outer Space. Illustrated by Anthony Kramer. (Lippincott, 1981).

My Robot Buddy. Illustrated by Joel Schick. (Lippincott, 1975).

My Trip to Alpha I. Illustrated by Harold Berson. (Lippincott, 1978).

Omega Station. Illustrated by Anthony Kramer. (Lippincott, 1983).

The Trouble on Janus (Lippincott, 1985).

Sports Fiction

Clone Catcher. Illustrated by Elizabeth Slote. (Lippincott, 1982).

Finding Buck McHenry (Harper, 1991).

Jake (Lippincott, 1971).
This book was adapted as an ABC *After School Special* titled "The Rag Tag Champs."

Make-Believe Ballplayer. Illustrated by Tom Newsom. (Lippincott, 1989).

Stranger on the Ball Club (Lippincott, 1970).

The Trading Game (HarperCollins, 1990).

For More Information About/By the Author

Limited information on the flaps of books. Check standard reference sources.

Virginia Driving Hawk Sneve

Contemporary Realistic Fiction ◆ Poetry ◆ Nonfiction, Native Americans

Rosebud, South Dakota
February 21, 1933

- 📖 *Dancing Teepees*
- 📖 *Jimmy Yellow Hawk*
- 📖 First Americans Series
    - 📖 *The Sioux*
    - 📖 *The Nez Perce*

About the Author
and the Author's Writing

Virginia Driving Hawk Sneve (rhymes with *navy*) says her childhood was "happy and secure. . . . We were poor, but I didn't know that because so was everyone else on the reservation." Virginia Driving Hawk Sneve was born on the Rosebud Indian Reservation in South Dakota on February 21, 1933. Her parents were James H. Driving Hawk and Rose Driving Hawk. Her father was a Sioux Episcopal priest. Her family included one brother and her grandparents. Virginia's early schooling took place in Bureau of Indian Affairs' schools. After the sixth grade, Virginia Driving Hawk attended St. Mary's School for Indian girls in Springfield, South Dakota. The girls were given piano and organ lessons, taught how to serve a tea, dance, set a table, and care for a home and children. They were also taught how to do laundry, knit, crochet, sew, and embroider. The school had a physical education program with track and field and basketball. The academic program was focused on preparation for college. She was encouraged to read beyond the small school library, and she was encouraged to write. She graduated from St. Mary's in 1950 and went on to the South Dakota State College in Brookings, graduating in 1954. She returned to the same university, renamed South Dakota State University, to obtain her masters degree in 1969.

Her father was her hero during her childhood. He sang, played the saxophone, taught her how to dance, drive a car, and hunt pheasants. He stressed education as the only way Native Americans would be able to survive in a modern world. Virginia's father died when she was just 14.

One time an eastern church congregation sent a rummage box to her family's rectory home, where she found books by Louisa May Alcott. Jo from *Little Women* set her to writing. It was her father's belief in the importance of education that encouraged Virginia to continue beyond high school. She taught music and English in public schools in White and Pierre, South Dakota, and then taught English, speech, and drama with Native Americans in the Flandreau Indian School in Flandreau, South Dakota—first as an English teacher, and then as a guidance counselor. In the 1970s she began working as an editor for the Brevet Press in Sioux Falls. She and her husband settled in Rapid City, South Dakota, where Virginia Driving Hawk Sneve became a counselor at Rapid City Central High School, working with Native American youth. She also was an associate instructor in English for Ogalala Lakota College Rapid City Extension.

As both a writer and educator, Sneve strives to correct inaccurate information about Native Americans. She is one of the few Native American writers to emerge in the mainstream publishing industry. Initially Sneve was able to crack the barrier when she entered a contest sponsored by the Interracial Council of Minority Books for Children. Her manuscript, which later became *Jimmy Yellow Hawk* (Holiday, 1972), won that contest in the Native American category. Her stories reflect the spirit of the Native American existence. Historical events, such as the Battle of the Little Big Horn and the 1862 uprising, are part of her stories. Each of those stories are brought into the present through Sneve's fictionalized dialogue and incidents.

Sneve has also collected poems of young Native Americans in a book titled *Dancing Teepees* (Holiday, 1989), illustrated by Stephen Gammell. Chief Oren Lyons, a member of the Turtle Clan of the Onondaga Nation, illustrated her novels. At the time he illustrated the books, he was living on the Onondaga reservation in Nedrow, New York. He was also an associate professor in American studies at the State University of New York at Buffalo. Some of his work was painted on hand-tanned elk hide, while others are pen-and-ink drawings.

Sneve says, "Stephen Gammell was the first non-Indian to illustrate my books. His illustrations for *Dancing Teepees* are beautiful and true to the Native-American artistic tradition. The soft, near pastel colors he used are like the traditional subdued native colors, because they were made from natural elements—roots, berries, bark, etc.—not the bright colors of chemically produced oils or acrylics."

Sneve's First Americans series of nonfiction books about Native American Indian tribes are illustrated by Ron Himler. She says, "I'm pleased with Ron Himler's illustrations. He makes every attempt to accurately depict the topic tribe and is open to suggestions. I also approve each stage of the illustrations from pencil to final watercolor."

She says her work as an editor and writer evolved from her career as an educator. She feels that she still educates through writing. "The general reading public has little, and often inaccurate information about Native Americans, and I can correct inaccuracies as a writer/editor." She says, "I want readers of my books to know that they are accurate representations of Native American life. I want them to see us as a living people who value our past as we live in the present."

However, there is a lament. According to Sneve, "Few contemporary Native American stories are published because they don't sell. Legends and historic settings do sell, because that is how the general public wants to view us and publishers continue the fantasy."

In June of 1995, Virginia Driving Hawk Sneve retired from her education positions. Her husband, Vance M. Sneve, once an industrial arts teacher, and later an employee of the Bureau of Indian Affairs, retired as well. In retirement, Virginia continues to write and Vance continues his role as "helper." He encourages Virginia when she gets discouraged and proofreads her manuscripts; he also does housework and cooks when she is busy writing. Virginia uses a computer to write and now has learned to use the Internet for much of her research. Fiction generally requires a greater period of concentrated writing than nonfiction. She says,

"Nonfiction can be set aside and easily picked up again, but I can't do that with fiction." She composes directly on the computer when writing fiction, but when she begins her nonfiction titles, she uses paper and pencil to brainstorm ideas. Later, after creating an outline, she composes on the computer. Poetry is written with pencil and then recorded on the computer. She says one of the most exciting parts of being an author is "getting letters from children all over the United States and Canada." In 1992 she received the University of Nebraska's Native American Prose Award; in 1996, the Author-Illustrator Human and Civil Rights Award from the National Educational Association, and the Spirit of Crazy Horse Award. In 1994 she was the recipient of the South Dakota Education Association Human Service Award.

The Sneves have three children and four grandchildren. Their daughter, Rose (named for Virginia's mother), and two sons, Paul and Alan, are grown now and have homes of their own. Family and preserving family traditions are an important part of the Sneves' lives. For example, a few years ago Grandma Rose Driving Hawk (who lived in California) visited the Sneves and brought Indian dolls for the Sneves' grandchildren (Grandma Rose's great-grandchildren), Bonita (Bonnie) and Madeline. Her older great-granddaughter, Joan, had been given her Indian doll several years earlier. The girls, along with Nickolas (Nick), a great-grandson, spent the time during the visit listening to their great-grandmother's stories and learning how to cut strings of paper dolls from folded paper. "Grandma Rose taught the children how to pronounce words to the Lakota hymns we all sang."

Virginia Driving Hawk Sneve's own leisure-time activities include playing the piano and organ, gardening in the summer, and quilting in the winter. She also enjoys golfing, concerts, the theater, and continues to read prolifically.

Books and Notes

In the early 1970s Sneve wrote several contemporary realistic fiction stories about young people who are caught in contemporary mysteries or situations. Although substantially out-of-print, a couple of these titles have been reprinted in the 1990s. Elements of the youngster's Native American culture are woven into the setting. Sneve's efforts to help others respect and recognize contemporary Native Americans have resulted in a collection of Native American poetry, *Dancing Teepees*. Early in the 1990s, Holiday asked Sneve to write a series of books about various Native American tribes. Those books are the First Americans Series.

First Americans Series

The Apaches (1997); *The Cherokees* (1996); *The Cheyennes* (1996); *The Hopis* (1995); *The Iroquois* (1995); *The Navajos* (1993); *The Nez Perce* (1994); *The Seminoles* (1994); *The Sioux* (1993). All illustrated by Ron Himler. (Holiday)
Discusses the history, culture, and present situation of the specified tribe of Native Americans.

Poetry

Dancing Teepees: Poems of American Indian Youth. Illustrated by Stephen Gammell. (Holiday, 1989).
Poems collected from young Native Americans, representing various tribes.

Other Titles

The Chichi Hoohoo Bogeyman (University of Nebraska, 1993).
While visiting their Sioux grandparents, three cousins are convinced they've found the real bogeyman.

Completing the Circle (University of Nebraska, 1995).
Vignettes from the lives of Sneve's female ancestors, including Flora Driving Hawk.

High Elk's Treasure. Illustrated by Oren Lyons. (Holiday, 1992).
Joe High Elk and his sister, Marie, find a "treasure" in a cave used by their ancestors to hide prize mares from thieving soldiers. The treasure holds important clues to the past.

Jimmy Yellow Hawk. Illustrated by Oren Lyons. (Holiday, 1972).
"Little Jim" must earn his place in the family. Set in the story's background are the excitement of a rodeo, a lost mare in a dangerous storm, and a tribal dance contest.

The Trickster and the Troll (University of Nebraska, 1997).
Iktomi, a Lakota trickster, and a troll from Norway meet and become competitors.

When Thunders Spoke. Illustrated by Oren Lyons. (University of Nebraska, 1994).
Originally published by Holiday, 1994. Story of Norman Two Bulls, a boy from the Dakota reservation.

For More Information About/By the Author

Articles

McElmeel, Sharron L. "Author Profile: Virginia Driving Hawk Sneve." *Library Talk* 7, no. 5 (November/ December 1994): 20+.

"Virginia Driving Hawk Sneve." *The Internet Public Library—Native American Authors*. URL: http://www.ipl. org/cgi/ref/native/browse.pl/A118 (Accessed January 1998).

Virginia Driving Hawk Sneve Biography. URL: http://www—personal.si.umich. edu/~lmon/snevebio.html (Accessed January 1998).

Zilpha Keatley Snyder

Fantasy   ◆   Contemporary Realistic Fiction

Lemoore, California
May 11, 1927

- 📖 *The Egypt Game*
- 📖 *Black and Blue Magic*
- 📖 *The Headless Cupid*

About the Author
and the Author's Writing

Zilpha Keatley Snyder's grandparents were homesteaders in Southern California during the late 1870s. Her mother grew up there, and Zilpha was born in Lemoore, California, to a household of storytellers. Both her mother and father shared accounts of past events in their lives. Zilpha had an urge to tell stories too, but her past was not nearly so rich as her parents', so she sprinkled her early storytelling with images from her vivid imagination. By the time she was eight, she knew she wanted to be a writer. She was a very good reader and writer and experienced no difficulty at school until sixth grade, when she suddenly began to feel like a "misfit." Her many animals brought her friendship, but her other friends came in books. Libraries became a haven. There was no television, few movies, and no travel—books were her window on the world.

On her way to school she played imaginary games like "Cracking the Whip" as she drove a team of oxen across a desert on her way to the California gold rush. She made up stories about nearly everything. Her mother often said, "Just tell it, don't embroider it."

For a time she felt her talent for making up stories was simply a source of scoldings, but eventually she discovered that some people actually made a living writing down stories. Writing fiction became her goal.

During her elementary and junior high school years she wrote poems, short stories, and unfinished novels. All of her stories and poems were handwritten, as the family did not own a typewriter. She just knew that after putting herself through college with part-time jobs, waitressing, and living on scholarships, that she would find an attic somewhere and spend all of her time writing. However, when reality set in she became a teacher to be financially responsible. She also met her future husband, Larry A. Snyder. They married and moved to New York, where she taught school and he earned a masters degree at Eastman School of Music. Larry Snyder joined the Air Force and the family (which eventually included three children) traveled to Texas and Alaska.

With nine years of teaching behind her, the family settled in Marin County, just across the Golden Gate Bridge from San Francisco. Her husband was now out of school and her youngest child was just starting it. It seemed the right time for her to return to writing. Her teaching career and children seemed to be the forces that motivated her to write for children. In 1964 Atheneum published her first children's book, *Season of Ponies*.

Many of her books are fantasies, but even her realistic titles include some mysterious or magical elements. She is interested in reaching a wider knowledge and experience than what is readily available to the five senses. However, she says, "I don't really hold seances, and I've never really seen a ghost."

While much of her writing comes from imagination, elements do come from her own life. *The Velvet Room* (Atheneum, 1965) included "ghosts of my own childhood." *Black and Blue Magic* (Atheneum, 1966) came from one of her son's childhood experiences. One of her most memorable books, *The Egypt Game* (Atheneum, 1967), actually began when she was in fifth grade and became interested in almost everything Egyptian. The interest never completely faded, and eventually came together with ideas from students in Berkeley and from a game her daughter was playing at the time.

Research for her books requires excursions to libraries to brush up on Egyptian mythology, fog patterns in San Francisco, deer hunting in California, and also to small towns on the coast of northern California to observe teenage culture and mores. For *The Headless Cupid* (Atheneum, 1971) she read many books on poltergeists. *And Condors Danced* (Delacorte, 1987) includes a family whose life parallels the homesteading period of Snyder's own maternal grandparents. Although the book's family was not specifically modeled on her grandparents' family, many of the social situations, minor events, and much of the flavor of the times come from her mother's stories about her family's history. She used memories of holidays, marriages, births, storms and fires, accidents and illnesses. Many details surrounding the characters in her books are gleaned from people who made even brief appearances in her life.

For more than thirty years Zilpha Keatley Snyder has written books for children. Her personality is solitary and she has said that her only "unchanging trait is my adaptability." Her minor hobbies often change. One year she is focused on horseback riding, another year it's exercise tapes. However, her major hobbies tend to remain constant—she enjoys reading and traveling and she says, "writing continues to be my favorite avocation as well as my vocation."

For a time, Larry Snyder was dean at the San Francisco Conservatory of Music but in the middle 1990s he retired from the music department of Sonoma State University. After living in the country, with all kinds of animals, including horses, the Snyders now live in Mill Valley, a small town not far from San Francisco. Their daughter, Melissa, and two sons, Ben and Douglas, are grown and have homes of their own.

Books and Notes

Whether Snyder is writing fantasies or realistic fiction there is always a touch of the mysterious, the magical, and definitely the unusual. *The Egypt Game* was given a Newbery Honor Medal in 1968 as well as named to several honor lists. In 1970 the book was given a Lewis Carroll Shelf Award. Five of her books have been recorded, unabridged, on cassette tape. Included are *Cat Running, The Egypt Game, Song of the Gargoyle, The Witches of Worm*, and *The Headless Cupid*. All are available from Recorded Books, Inc., in New York City.

The Birds of Summer (Atheneum, 1983).

Black and Blue Magic. Illustrated by Gene Holtan. (Atheneum, 1966; Aladdin, 1994).

Cat Running (Delacorte, 1994).

And Condors Danced (Delacorte, 1987).

The Egypt Game. Illustrated by Alton Raible. (Atheneum, 1967).

Fool's Gold (Delacorte, 1993).

Gib Rides Home (Delacorte, 1998).

The Gypsy Game (Delacorte, 1997).

Song of the Gargoyle (Delacorte, 1991).

The Trespassers (Delacorte, 1995).

The Truth About Stone Hollow (Atheneum, 1974).

The Witches of Worm. Illustrated by Alton Raible. (Atheneum, 1972).

For More Information About/By the Author

Articles

Random House/Zilpha Keatley Snyder. URL: http://www.randomhouse.com/teachersbdd/snyd.html (Accessed December 1998).

Zilpha Keatley Snyder. URL: http://www.microweb.com/lsnyder/ (Accessed December 1997).

Elizabeth George Speare

◆ Historical Fiction

**Melrose, Massachusetts
November 21, 1908–November 15, 1994**

📖 *The Sign of the Beaver*
📖 *The Witch of Blackbird Pond*

About the Author
and the Author's Writing

Elizabeth George Speare was born in Melrose, Massachusetts, the daughter of Harry Allan and Demetria (Simmons) George. She spent many childhood days exploring the fields and woods around Melrose. The city of Boston was close, so the family frequently attended the theater or concerts there. During the summer, the family went to the shore where they had a hilltop home overlooking the ocean and fields of daisies and blueberries. Elizabeth and her younger brother often took walks along the winding trails through the woods. They were the only children in the area. One of the previous owners of the shoreside home had left behind a shelf of children's books, and Elizabeth soon discovered Dorothy, the Land of Oz, and Mark Twain. Among her favorite books was a thin green volume that was most likely in a series, the Dearfoot series. Elizabeth spent endless hours reading, thinking, and dreaming. Her dreams and thinking turned into stories. She wrote those stories and others throughout her high school years.

Elizabeth attended Smith College for a year and then entered Boston University, where she earned her undergraduate degree in 1930 and went on to obtain a masters degree in 1932. She went on to teach English in Massachusetts high schools. Teaching English seemed a unparalleled opportunity to share her love of reading and writing. She spent vacations as a camp counselor. One summer was spent traipsing through Europe.

By 1936 she had met and married Alden Speare, an industrial engineer, and had moved to Connecticut. During the next fifteen years their son, Alden Jr., and daughter, Mary, were born. Life was filled with piano practices, camping, and other family activities. There seemed no time to write stories. By the time Alden Jr. and Mary were in junior high, Elizabeth found herself with long days. She took out her pencil and paper and began writing again. She wrote about things the family had done together. Her first article was about a family skiing trip. She frequently visited local libraries searching for magazine markets and reading.

One day she came across a history of the Connecticut River Valley and a story, "A Narrative of the Captivity of Mrs. Johnson." It was the story of a woman, Susanna Johnson, who had written about her experiences as an Indian captive. Johnson's husband and children, and Susanna Johnson's teenage sister, Miriam Willard, were captured by Indians and taken to Montreal, Canada. Susanna gave birth to the couple's fourth child during the journey north. The baby was named Elizabeth Captive. Johnson provided many details about the years she spent as a captive, but it was Miriam's story that intrigued Speare. At the time of the capture Miriam was approximately the same age as Speare's daughter at the time. She began to research the period and to speculate about the fate of the captives, particularly the fate of Miriam. The story that developed became *Calico Captive* (Houghton, 1957).

For over twenty years Elizabeth Speare lived in Wethersfield, Connecticut, where, in 1687, the citizens in the town believed in witches. During this early period many English children were sent from Barbados to Boston for an education. Knowledge about that period of time led Speare to speculate about what life would be like for a young woman who might be suspected of being a witch. For over a year and a half she put the story, *The Witch of Blackbird Pond* (Houghton, 1958) down on paper. Kit Taylor comes to Connecticut from a warm Barbados. The friendship she develops with Hannah Tucker leads Kit to be suspected as a witch. The book was the 1959 Newbery Award winner.

Speare's third book, *The Bronze Bow* (Houghton, 1961), was criticized by some reviewers as having a "density [which is] an overwhelming obstacle." This story is about an ancient Israelite, an "angry, young man," who views the conquering Romans in harsh terms until Jesus convinces him that love is stronger than hate. The book was the 1962 Newbery Award winner.

Speare's fourth book was an adult novel, and she did not publish again for over twenty years, until *The Sign of the Beaver* (Houghton, 1983) appeared. This book was based on a short anecdote she found in a history of Milo, Maine, about a thirteen-year-old who accompanied his father to new territory and was left to guard the family's land claim. Unbeknownst to the boy, Matt, his father is detained when he finds his family is ill. While Matt waits for his father's return with the family, he loses his food supplies to an invading bear. He survives only with the help of compassionate members of a local Indian tribe, who help him fish and hunt. In return for Attean's help, Matt helps him learn to read.

The Sign of the Beaver turned out to be a very popular book. When Speare was asked what she thought was her most popular book, she responded, "*The Witch of Blackbird Pond* seems to have the widest appeal." Many authors tend to use incidents in their own life to anchor their writing, but Speare was never "conscious of ever having done so."

After growing up in Massachusetts, Elizabeth George Speare lived the rest of her life in Connecticut, where she and her husband, Alden, raised their son, Alden Jr., and their daughter, Mary. In 1988 the couple had five grandchildren and delighted in visits from them. The Speares spent much of their time traveling widely and bird-watching. Elizabeth George Speare died November 15, 1994. Six days later she would have celebrated her 86th birthday.

Books and Notes

While Speare's writing career spanned a thirty-year period, she was not particularly prolific. She only wrote four books for young readers. However, she earned numerous honors with these books, including two Newbery Awards (1959 and 1962), a Newbery Honor Award (1984), the Laura Ingalls Wilder Award (1989), the Scott O'Dell Award for Historical Fiction (1984), the Child Study Committee Award (1983), and the Christopher Award (1984).

The Bronze Bow (Houghton, 1961).

Calico Captive. Illustrated by W. T. Mars. (Houghton, 1957).

The Sign of the Beaver (Houghton, 1983).

The Witch of Blackbird Pond (Houghton, 1958).

For More Information About/By the Author

Articles

Cosgrave, Mary Silva. "Elizabeth George Speare." *Horn Book* (July/August 1989): 465–68.

Random House/Elizabeth George Speare. URL: http://www.randomhouse.com/ teachersbdd/spea.html (Accessed December 1997).

Speare, Elizabeth George. "Newbery Award Acceptance: Report of a Journey." In *Newbery and Caldecott Medal Books: 1956–1965* (Horn Book, 1965).

Jerry Spinelli

◆ Contemporary Realistic Fiction

**Norristown, Pennsylvania
February 1, 1941**

📖 *Maniac Magee*

📖 *Wringer*

📖 *Who Put That Hair in My
Toothbrush?*

About the Author
and the Author's Writing

Jerry Spinelli, an Italian-American, was born February 1, 1941, in Norristown, Pennsylvania. His parents were Louis A. Spinelli, a printer, and Lorna Mae (Bigler) Spinelli. Spinelli "grew up in a dead-end street neighborhood with railroad tracks, coal piles, red hills, a creek, woods, and alleyways—a great geography for a kid. My grandfather on my father's side traveled by ship alone to this country from Naples, Italy when he was only 14. My mother's family were Pennsylvania Dutch." Jerry Spinelli loved sports and dreamed of becoming a major league baseball player. "Then," says Spinelli, "I wrote a poem about an exciting football game; it appeared in the local newspaper, and I decided to become a writer. It never occurred to me it would take so long to get published. My first four novels nobody wanted. Then one day I found the fried chicken that I was going to take to lunch was missing. I knew one of my kids had eaten it. I began writing about the incident at work that day. That was the start of what would become my first published book."

Spinelli enrolled in Gettysburg College and earned an undergraduate degree in 1963 and a masters degree the following year from Johns Hopkins University. By 1966 he had begun working as an editor for an engineering magazine for Chilton Company. He also joined the Naval Reserves. He used his lunch hours, after-work hours, and any available time he could find to write books for adults. None were published. In 1977 he married Eileen Mesi, a writer and mother of five children. One night Spinelli was living alone in a third-floor efficiency apartment, and the next day he was in a house with a wife, stepchildren, and a hermit crab. During the next five years he continued to write with little success.

Concerning this time Spinelli said, "Before going to bed one night, I wrapped some fried chicken and put it in the refrigerator for work the next day. In the morning I went to get it, and it was gone. Six kids were sleeping upstairs. I knew one of them had snatched it. I also knew it was gone forever. I went to work that day fried-chickenless, and over lunch I began to write about a kid who snatched his father's lunch. I didn't know it at the time, but I was beginning to write my first published novel, *Space Station Seventh Grade* [Little, 1982]." Spinelli was 41 years old. He continued to write over his lunch hour.

His second book, *Who Put That Hair in My Toothbrush?* (Little, 1984), was published two years later. The main characters, ninth-grader Greg and his younger sister, Megin, use alternating chapters to describe their sibling rivalry and lives in general. Spinelli drew the characters from his family. "*Who Put That Hair in My Toothbrush?* is really the only book inspired by my own kids (in that case, Molly and Jeffrey, who were always fighting). The reference point for most of my books is the memory of my own years as a child." Funny and true to life, *Who Put That Hair in My Toothbrush?* is one of his most humorous books. He also gets ideas for stories from newspapers and incidents that happen around him. One day he read a story about a girl who competed on her high school wrestling team. That inspired the book *There's a Girl in My Hammerlock* (Simon, 1991). Spinelli says one of his favorite characters in that book is a girl named Bernadette. She's a rat. At the time Spinelli had a real pet rat by that name. Bernie would scoot across the floor in his office and hop onto his foot, up his leg and chest, and kiss him on the nose. "Bernadette was so proud when I put her in the story." Now Bernie is dead and buried out by the berry patch.

During the next five years, three more novels were published. In April of 1989 he says, "I quit my job as magazine editor. I try to write from 10–12 in the morning and from 8–12 at night." The next year brought him immeasurable success with the publication of *Maniac Magee* (Little, 1990). Spinelli says, "There are many sources [for the book]. Probably the first is something a friend told me some years ago. An orphan, he used to run—not walk, not bike—everywhere he went, up to six miles to the nearest movie theater. That appealed to me, the idea of a kid who runs everywhere he goes. I tucked it away and waited for the right story to come along." In 1991 he was awarded the Newbery Award for *Maniac Magee*.

Nine more titles followed. In 1997 he published three titles, *The Library Card*, *Blue Ribbon Blues*, and *Wringer*. *Wringer* was named a Newbery Honor winner in 1998. *Wringer* was based on an event that occurs every year in a little town in Pennsylvania. He read an article in a local newspaper and used that story as the basic premise. However, the book is not strictly about the town nor did he attempt to focus on the event in that town or the people living there. He's never been to the town and he conducted no interviews.

In 1998 Knopf released the autobiography *Knots in My Yo-Yo String: The Autobiography of a Kid*, which tells about Spinelli's early life in Norristown and his emergence as a world-class writer. Spinelli's wife, Eileen, is also an author. She was born in Pennsylvania as well. Eileen says that their house "overflows with books and papers." When their children and grandchildren visit, their house is also overflowing with people. When the couple is not writing they are apt to be visiting flea markets, garage sales, gardening, and visiting New England. Jerry Spinelli enjoys country music and has been known to pick wild berries, grill superior barbecued hamburgers, devour chocolate almond ice cream, and search for Sunday buffets.

In a final word, Spinelli has this to say about reading: "There's a tendency to view reading and living as an either/or proposition. You either read a lot, or you live a lot. Kids who believe that wind up lopsided. A kid who reads a lot has a fuller life, a kid who lives a lot gets more out of what he or she reads. Books are not Xerox® copies of life. Books are part of life, like spring and pizza. Books are words at their best—and try to get very far without words. Question: Which is the best kind of kid—the one who gets down and dirty on the football field, or the one who reads a poem? The answer: The one who does both."

Books and Notes

The Bathwater Gang. Illustrated by Meredith Johnson. (Little, 1990).

The Bathwater Gang Gets Down to Business. Illustrated by Meredith Johnson. (Little, 1992).

Blue Ribbon Blues. Illustrated by Donna Nelson. (Random, 1997).

Crash (Knopf, 1996).

Do the Funky Pickle (Scholastic, 1992).

Dump Days (Little, 1988).

Fourth Grade Rats. Illustrated by Paul Casale. (Scholastic, 1991).

Jason and Marceline (Little, 1986).

The Library Card (Scholastic, 1997).

Maniac Magee: A Novel (Little, 1990).

Night of the Whale (Little, 1985).

Picklemania (Scholastic, 1993).

School Daze: Report to the Principal's Office (Scholastic, 1991).

Space Station Seventh Grade (Little, 1982).

There's a Girl in My Hammerlock (Simon, 1991).

Tooter Pepperday (Random, 1995).

Who Put That Hair in My Toothbrush? (Little, 1984).

Wringer (Harper, 1997).

For More Information About/By the Author

Articles

"Jerry Spinelli." *Random House Web Site.* URL: http://www.randomhouse.com/teachers/rc/rc_ab_jsp.html (Accessed January 1998).

Keller, John. "Jerry Spinelli." *Horn Book* 67, no. 4 (July/August 1991): 433–35.

Spinelli, Jerry. "Catching Maniac Magee." *Reading Teacher* 45, no. 3 (November 1991): 174.

Spinelli, Jerry. "1991 Newbery Acceptance Speech." *Journal of Youth Services in Libraries* 4, no. 4 (Summer 1991): 335; or *Horn Book* 67, no. 4 (July/August 1991): 426–32.

"Writing Spinelli Style." *Teaching Pre-K–8* 27, no. 2 (October 1996): 42.

Books

Spinelli, Jerry. *Knots in My Yo-Yo String: The Autobiography of a Kid* (Knopf, 1998).

Robert Lawrence (R. L.) Stine

Humorous Stories ◆ Horror Fiction

Columbus, Ohio
October 8, 1943

📖 Goosebumps Series
📖 Fear Street Series
📖 Ghosts of Fear Street Series

About the Author
and the Author's Writing

For a number of years Robert Lawrence Stine called himself Jovial Bob Stine to distinguish himself from the "at least forty-eight other Bob Stines or Steins in publishing in New York." However, since 1992 he has been writing and marketing his Goosebumps books as R. L. Stine, and few young readers need to be told who R. L. Stine is.

R. L. Stine was born in 1943 in Columbus, Ohio, where he also grew up. His home had a large attic and one day, during elementary school, he discovered an old typewriter. He started using it to type joke books and was still typing joke books thirty years later (and probably "using a lot of the same jokes)." One day he brought home some "Tales from the Crypt" comics from the barbershop. His mother would not let him keep them. During the next few months, Stine had one of his shortest haircuts as he would return to the barbershop every two weeks just so he could read the new comics. *Mad* magazine was also one of his favorite reads.

Stine had a powerful radio, which he used to attempt to listen to New York stations. He often spent hours tuning the radio just right, and did manage to get Jean Shepherd on WOR. The stories were fabulous.

When, as a teenager, his parents suggested he get a summer job, he said he was busy writing a novel. He never did work during his childhood or young adult life. He wrote for his school newspaper in Columbus. After high school he entered college at Ohio State and soon became editor of the humor magazine, *The Sundial*. He was editor of the humor magazine for three out of his four years of college, and, to create some kind of personality in the magazine, R. L. Stine dubbed himself "Jovial Bob Stine." The magazine was the same one that James Thurber had edited fifty years before.

After college, Stine went to New York. He had the idea that that's where all writers lived and wanted to have his own humor magazine. Stine became associated with Scholastic, Inc., and, as an editor of some of their most successful magazines, he began to learn the nuances of editing and publishing.

At first he worked with *Junior Scholastic*, and in 1971 the company was reorganized to launch a new magazine. *Search* was for junior high students who read at a fourth-grade level. It was a magazine with a social studies focus, which did not interest Stine in the least. But as editor Stine began to do "all kinds of things in disguise, interviews, simulations, and so forth." The kids loved it. The rest of Scholastic's magazines were very straight; this one was weird. *Search* was followed by *Dynamite*, which became Scholastic's number one seller. At one time it had over 1 million subscribers. *Dynamite* was for fourth- and fifth-graders and was so successful that Scholastic wanted to duplicate it for older students. They figured television and humor would attract them, so Stine created a magazine, *Bananas*, which became immensely successful. He went on to create a second magazine, *Maniac*. For a year he edited both *Search* and *Bananas*. Eventually he had to choose one, and he chose *Bananas*.

During all of this he also met his future wife. Jane had come to Scholastic as the new editor for *Dynamite*, and they eventually married. They coauthored some humor titles. Then Jane Stine left Scholastic to run their packaging company, Parachute Press. It was Parachute Press that put together the proposal that resulted in Scholastic's publication of the

Goosebumps series and Simon & Schuster's publication of the Fear Street and the Ghosts of Fear Street series. By 1995 the Fear Street books had sold more than 41 million copies; the Ghosts of Fear Street had nearly 8 million copies in print. Stine's series have been at the top of every list since 1995. *USA Today* regularly lists his books at the top of their best-seller list. In 1995 the *New York Times* listed the series as the number four best-selling series for children. Stine himself has appeared on almost every major talk show. Several news magazines have featured articles about him and his books. Stine's theory is that books should not have to teach children anything specifically, they "can be just for fun."

Stine's first books were humor. He wrote books with such titles as *How to Be Funny: An Extremely Silly Guidebook* (Dutton, 1978) and *Don't Stand in the Soup: The World's Funniest Guide to Manners* (Bantam, 1982). He was 28 when his first book was published. His books were funny, but did not enjoy the phenomenal success that his scary books have. He has, he says, "two ideas a month, one for *Fear Street* and one for *Goosebumps*." Sometimes he will get a title first, sometimes an image (such as a boy in a bathtub with worms), and sometimes he will think of a plot. He began his Goosebumps series in July 1992. Just three years later there were more than 130 million copies of his books in publication. While Stine likes to scare his readers, he says there is only one book that actually scared him. That book was *Something Wicked This Way Comes* by Ray Bradbury. He did scream a few times during a showing of the movie *Jurassic Park*, however. Among his favorite authors is Chris Van Allsburg. He says he buys all of Van Allsburg's books and considers him very talented and original.

Jane and R. L. Stine have one son, Matthew, who would not read any of his father's books—simply because Matthew knew it would drive his dad crazy. The first scary book that Stine wrote, *Blind Date*, took him three months. Now it takes about 8 days to write a Goosebumps title and about 12 days to write a Fear Street title. Before he begins to write a book, he carefully outlines it—a chapter-by-chapter list of everything that happens. Only then does he write the book.

Educators and parents have vilified some of his books. Because they are easy to read and scary, they do attract readers—and they get children reading. They also attract a group of youngsters who pick them up because it is the "in" thing to carry around a Goosebumps book or put a Goosebumps book on the corner of a desk. His first Goosebumps book, *Welcome to Dead House,* has sold over 3 million copies and is the series best-seller. Says Stine, "It is much scarier than the others. The rest are toned down, with more humor. I decided I didn't want to have dead kids books." So in a way Stine has come back to humor, his first love.

R. L. Stine is often asked if he writes all of the series books himself or if he recruits other writers. His answer is "Yes, I write them all." The question is raised because it is well known in the industry that most series writers hire others to flesh out the outlines. Once the basic dialogue is written, "the" writer takes the manuscript and tweaks it so they have "written it." At one time the going price for contracting to write a series book such as Goosebumps was in the neighborhood of $5,000. Stine's sister-in-law does write the spin-off series Give Yourself Goosebumps.

Jane continues to work as a book packager with Parachute Press. When he is not busy writing, Stine enjoys watching old black-and-white movies, and reading. He enjoys mystery writers like Agatha Christie and Stephen King. He also likes to explore New York City with his son and wife—they live on the Upper West Side of Manhattan. Jane also edits the Fear Street series. Matthew Stine, according to R. L. Stine, "is getting too old to be interested in my work," but does continue to provide insight into the lives of teens. Stine continues to spy on their music, how they dress, and how they talk. Soon enough the information is woven into yet another book by R. L. Stine.

Books and Notes

R. L. Stine began as an author of humor books and evolved into an author of scary books for the intermediate child (Goosebumps series). He then developed a series for the older reader (Fear Street series). Since Fear Street books were published by Simon & Schuster, they wanted to have a series that appealed to the intermediate reader as well. Soon another scary series was developed for them (Ghosts of Fear Street series). With literally dozens of titles being put out each year, it is difficult to keep up. The following list is just a sample of available titles.

Fear Street Series

Silent Night (Archway, 1991).

Switched (Archway, 1995).

The Face (Archway, 1996).

Goosebumps Series

Deep Trouble (Scholastic, 1994).

One Day at Horrorland (Scholastic, 1994).

The Haunted Mask (Scholastic, 1995).

Go Eat Worms (Scholastic, 1995).

Legend of the Lost Legend (Scholastic, 1996).

Humor Books
(by Jovial Bob Stine)

The Cool Kids' Guide to Summer Camp. Coauthored with Jane Stine. Illustrated by Jerry Zimmerman. (Four Winds, 1981).

Everything You Need to Survive Homework. Coauthored with Jane Stine. Illustrated by Sal Murdocca. (Random, 1983).

101 Vacation Books (Scholastic, 1990).

Pork and Beans: Play Date. Illustrated by Jose Aruego and Ariane Dewey. (Scholastic, 1989).

For More Information About/By the Author

Articles

"R. L. Stine." *Scholastic Web Site.* URL: http://www.scholastic.com/Goosebumps/high/stine/index.html (Accessed December 1997).

"Stine Gives Kids 'Goosebumps' with Frightening Speed." *USA Today Books Web Site.* URL: http://usatoday.com/life/enter/books/leb606.htm (Accessed January 1998).

Books

Wheeler, Jill C. *R. L. Stine* (Abdo, 1996).

Mary Stolz

Contemporary Realistic Fiction   ◆   Historical Fiction

Boston, Massachusetts
March 24, 1920

📖 *The Bully of Barkham Street*

📖 *A Ballad of the Civil War*

📖 *Coco Grimes*

About the Author
and the Author's Writing

Mary Slattery Stolz was born March 24, 1920, in Boston, Massachusetts. She was educated at the Birch Wathen School in New York City, where she studied literature and history. During her school days she developed an interest in writing and served as assistant editor of the school's newspaper, *Birch Leaves*. After graduating from Birch Wathen, she enrolled at New College of Columbia University and the Katharine Gibbs School. At New College she was encouraged to write poetry and fairy tales and at Katharine Gibbs she learned to type—a skill that was to become useful later.

Stolz attended New College from 1936 to 1938. In 1938 she married and devoted herself to being a homemaker and later caring for her son, Bill. She developed an interest in riding horses and baseball and for the next eleven years lived a genteel life.

However, throughout her marriage Stolz experienced chronic pain. By 1949 the pain was so intense that she was confined to her home. Her doctor, Dr. Thomas C. Jaleski, suggested she find an interest to occupy her time. Initially she could only think about her interest in riding horses, but acknowledged that at one time she had been interested in writing. Jaleski encouraged her to develop that interest. She located a secondhand typewriter and a ream of yellow paper and set out to write her first novel. The manuscript, *To Tell Your Love*, was accepted and published by Harper in 1950. That book was a teenage romance novel focusing on a "first love." Once successful, she kept right on writing. Her pain eventually disappeared, but her friendship with Dr. Jaleski continued. In 1956 Stolz divorced her husband, and nine years later married her doctor. During this time Stolz cultivated a writing career.

Most of her books have been fiction and many deal with problems and concerns of teenagers. She also wrote picture books, intermediate-grade novels, and more recently has penned a number of historical fiction titles. In addition she has written at least one nonfiction adult novel and has written many articles for magazines such as *Cosmopolitan*, *Ladies' Home Journal*, and *Seventeen. Belling the Tiger* (Harper, 1961) and *The Noonday Friends* (Harper, 1965) were named Newbery Honor Books in 1962 and 1966 respectively. Several other titles have received honors and awards. In 1982 Stolz received a George G. Stone Recognition of Merit Award for her entire body of work.

Stolz and her husband, Thomas C. Jaleski, live on the Gulf Coast in Longboat Key, Florida. In addition to her writing, Mary Stolz has interests in the social and environmental arenas. She also enjoys reading, cooking, and baseball.

Books and Notes

Mary Stolz's early years in college focused on literature and history. In later years she developed an interest in baseball, an interest shared by her son, Matthew. Her writing has come to reflect both her interest in history and baseball.

A Ballad of the Civil War. Illustrated by Sergio Martinez. (Harper, 1997).

A Union solider reflects on his childhood and the reasons he and his twin brother have ended up fighting on opposite sides in the war.

The Bully of Barkham Street. Illustrated by Leonard Shortall. (Harper, 1963).

A bully attempting to reform his behavior meets continual failure until his performance at a school assembly changes things.

Cezanne Pinto: A Memoir (Knopf, 1994).

A former slave recalls his days as a slave on a Virginia plantation.

Coco Grimes (Harper, 1994).

Focuses on the Negro Baseball League.

The Explorer of Barkham Street. Illustrated by Emily Arnold McCully. (Harper, 1985).

A contemporary fiction account of life on Barkham Street.

Go Fish. Illustrated by Pat Cummings. (Harper, 1991).

An intergenerational picture book.

Quentin Corn. Illustrated by Pamela Johnson. (Godine, 1995).

An animal fantasy; a pig disguises himself as a boy and makes friends with a girl.

Stealing Home (Harper, 1992).

Examines how life changes when Great-Aunt Lizzy comes to stay. Thomas and his grandfather have been used to just baseball and fishing.

The Weeds & the Weather. Illustrated by N. Cameron Watson. (Greenwillow, 1994).

A former teacher, Mrs. Weeds, and her dog and cat watch the seasons and the changes that the seasonal weather brings.

Zekmet, the Stone Carver: A Tale of Ancient Egypt. Illustrated by Deborah Nourse Lattimore. (Harcourt, 1988).

A beautifully illustrated account of ancient Egypt.

For More Information About/By the Author

Articles

"Mary Stolz Papers." *de Grummond Collection Web Site.* URL: http://www.lib.usm.edu/~degrum/findaids/stolz.htm (Accessed December 1997).

Mildred D. Taylor

◆ Historical Fiction

Jackson, Mississippi
September 13, 1943

📖 *Roll of Thunder, Hear My Cry*
📖 *The Road to Memphis*

About the Author
and the Author's Writing

Mildred Delois Taylor was born in Jackson, Mississippi, on September 13, 1943. After her father was involved in a racial incident, the family moved to Toledo, Ohio, where Taylor grew up. Mildred Taylor heard stories from her father, Wilbur Lee Taylor. Some stories came from the experiences of her parents and her grandparents and were about the everyday, but sometimes dangerous, events that occurred in the lives of the family and those around them. The stories taught Taylor a different history than the one she was learning in school.

When Taylor read history books at the local library, the mention of African Americans was minimal—Booker T. Washington, George Washington Carver, Marian Anderson, and Dr. Ralph Bunche. As a group, African Americans were portrayed as a docile, subservient people happy with their fate—both before, during, and after slavery in the United States.

Mildred Taylor wanted to present a picture of African Americans as people who were full of dignity and pride. Her stories of the Logans present a picture of just such a family during the Depression and the Vietnam War era.

The Taylor household was an environment that focused on building pride and self-confidence—both traits that can be found in Taylor's books about the Logans. From the time Taylor was in high school she created stories, elaborate daydreams in her mind. She decided to write her stories, confident that she would someday be a writer. After Taylor graduated from high school in Toledo, she entered the University of Toledo and earned an undergraduate degree in 1965. For two years she worked in Ethiopia with the Peace Crops as an English and history teacher. She returned to the United States to teach and recruit for the Peace Corps, and then went on to earn a masters degree in journalism from the University of Colorado in 1969. For a time she stayed to work in the black studies program at the university, but eventually resigned to move to Los Angeles. There she obtained a nominal day job and wrote at night.

Taylor remembered the stories told by her father of African Americans filled with pride and knowledge of self-worth. The stories he told were of ordinary people, some brave, and some not so brave—but all proud and heroic in some way. Some of the stories he had heard from his parents and grandparents, and many of those stories had come from generations before. Many of the stories were also firsthand accounts of things that had happened to him. Taylor says, "I was fascinated by the stories, not only because of what they said or because they were about my family, but because of the manner in which my father told them. I began to imagine myself as a storyteller."

There was one special story about the cutting of some trees on her family's land. At first she tried to tell the story from her grandmother's point of view and found that it wasn't working. Eventually she created eight-year-old Cassie to tell the stories. She says, "I didn't have a really good typewriter at home, so my friends at work covered for me while I sat in a little back room and typed up the manuscript." Her coworkers proofed it for her, and she was able to mail the manuscript that same night—the deadline for entering the story in a competition sponsored by the Council on Interracial Books for Children. The book won the 1973 first prize in the African American category. The council flew Taylor to New York, where she accepted her award and found that the council had sent her story around to publishing houses. Several publishers were interested. That story, *The Song of Trees*, published by Dial in 1975, was her first published book.

Taylor says that after writing about Cassie in *The Song of Trees,* she was not ready to let Cassie go. She decided to continue the stories of the Logans with *Roll of Thunder, Hear My Cry* (Dial, 1976), *Let the Circle Be Unbroken* (Dial, 1981), and *The Road to Memphis* (Dial, 1990). Through Cassie and her three siblings, the story of the Logans unfolded. The siblings were Stacey, a thoughtful leader; Christopher-John, a happy, sensitive mediator; and Little Man, the prideful, manly six-year-old. As she wrote *Roll of Thunder, Hear My Cry*, she attempted to weave facts about which she had read or heard into the story.

Although the stories are set in the 1930s, a decade or more before Mildred Taylor herself experienced hardships of life in the South, she wove some of her own childhood feelings into the tapestry. As a child she traveled with her family south to Mississippi—at least once or twice a year. On those trips Mildred and her sister would go to their father's boyhood school and would be sent into the fields to pick cotton, so they would know what life there was like. On the trip South, once the family crossed the Ohio River (from Toledo on the way to Mississippi) it seemed to be a different world. Taylor's parents would tell them that when a white person addressed them they should not answer, but rather let their parents do the talking. Taylor learned that gas stations often did not have restrooms or water fountains that blacks could use. They could not stay at motels, nor could they find places to eat unless they went in the kitchen door. When they drove through the countryside they literally crept through the towns in order not to break any laws. There was always one time during each trip that the police would stop them. Several times the police would make their father "spread eagle" so they could frisk him. Because they could not stay at motels, when Taylor's father would get too tired, he would pull off the road to sleep for an hour or so. While he slept, the rest of the family had to keep watch.

Taylor's impression of those incidents was incorporated into accounts of similar incidents retold by Cassie. Cassie was intentionally created as a very bright and pretty child. Those qualities gave her confidence, and that confidence helped her achieve.

Mildred Taylor's father was just 56 when he died, before he could see his storytelling legacy fully realized in *Roll of Thunder, Hear My Cry*. The book was named the Newbery Award Book in 1977. It was five years before the next book, *Let the Circle Be Unbroken*, was published, and although *The Road to Memphis* was originally scheduled for publication in 1985, it was not released by Dial until 1990. A fourth book about the Logans, *The Well: David's Story* (Dial, 1995), tells a story of well water sharing during the drought, amid an atmosphere of racial violence. Between the publication of these novels Taylor has published several novellas each focusing on one major incident from the 1930s. Those titles include *Mississippi Bridge* (Dial, 1990), *The Friendship* (Dial, 1987), and *The Gold Cadillac* (Dial, 1987). In the 1990s *The Song of the Trees*, originally published in 1975, was reissued by Dial.

Taylor's writing style includes mapping out the story line and then revising again and again. She first thinks through the story in her head. Eventually, she sits down to write the full outline. When she is ready to write a chapter she makes an outline and figures out scenes that might be included. Sometimes she even maps out the chapter, but by the time she actually gets to the chapter, the outline may be inappropriate to the way the story line is going.

Taylor tries to write each day, but if the words are not coming particularly easy, she doesn't write. She finds that she just ends up throwing away the work anyway if she writes on those days. Instead, she researches for background information or reads. On other days she'll find that the words come easily and she'll sit down and write for seven or eight hours. She prefers to compose her text directly into a memory writer—she hates most to type something from longhand. She does write in longhand, however, if she is in the mountains away from modern writing tools.

The closeness of her family was demonstrated the night she accepted the Newbery Award for *Roll of Thunder, Hear My Cry*. Thirty family members were present in Detroit, Michigan, as she accepted the award in her father's name. In 1983 she was teaching at the University of Colorado, but seems to no longer be affiliated with them. Recent information from Penguin Publishers indicates that she still lives in Colorado.

Books and Notes

In *The Song of the Trees*, Cassie is eight years old. In *Roll of Thunder, Hear My Cry*, Cassie is nine; she is ten and eleven in *Let the Circle Be Unbroken*. In the next book about the Logans, Cassie is sixteen/seventeen. In *Let the Circle Be Unbroken*, one of the Logans' friends, T.J., is accused of murder. The experiences of the Logans basically center around their Southern community. In a sequel to those two books, Cassie is taken into young womanhood. *The Road* to Memphis takes place at the brink of World War II (1941), and through its story Taylor attempts to show World War II from a black point of view.

The Friendship. Illustrated by Max Ginsburg. (Dial, 1987).

The four Logan children witness the tension created and the resulting outrage and violence when Tom Bee addresses a white storekeeper by his first name.

The Gold Cadillac. Illustrated by Michael Hays. (Dial, 1987).

When the family takes the Cadillac on a visit South, they encounter racial prejudice for the first time.

Let the Circle Be Unbroken (Dial, 1981).

Continues the story that was begun in *Roll of Thunder, Hear My Cry*. The prejudices surrounding black and white friendships and incidents involving a cousin from a "mixed" marriage all fill in the story of the inner struggle to keep the family circle unbroken.

Mississippi Bridge. Illustrated by Max Ginsburg. (Dial, 1990).

During a heavy rainfall in the 1930s, a rural Mississippi ten-year-old boy observes a bus driver demanding that all black passengers get off the bus. The bus sets off across the raging Rosa Lee River, leaving the black passengers behind.

The Road to Memphis (Dial, 1990).

Cassie is finishing high school and is planning on going to college. She meets a handsome lawyer from Memphis. Many of their friends are going off to war.

Roll of Thunder, Hear My Cry (Dial, 1976).

The first story in the Logan saga. Four children and their parents live in the South in the 1930s plagued by poverty and injustice. They must also face the Depression, which plagues everyone.

The Song of the Trees. Illustrated by Jerry Pinkney. (Dial, 1975).

Set during the Depression when money is scarce, especially for poor Mississippi blacks. Money sent home by Cassie's father is often stolen from the envelope before it reaches the family. Then the white men come to cut down the Logans' trees. Cassie's father, David, comes home and at least part of the forest is saved. This story is based on an experience of Taylor's family.

The Well: David's Story (Dial, 1995).

Set in the early 1900s, David's family generously shares their well water with whites and blacks alike. But it is all David can do to keep the peace when some of the white boys are antagonistic and create an atmosphere that has the potential for racial violence.

For More Information About/By the Author

Articles

Random House/Mildred D. Taylor. URL: http://randomhouse.com/teachersbdd/tayl.html (Accessed December 1998).

Sherrod, Barbara. "Writers at Work: A Conversation with Mildred Taylor." *Writing* (January 1985): 24–26.

Theodore Taylor

Statesville, North Carolina
June 23, 1921

📖 *The Cay*
📖 *The Trouble with Tuck*

About the Author
and the Author's Writing

Theodore Taylor was born in Statesville, North Carolina, on June 23, 1921, and still thinks of himself as a part of that quiet "red clay" country by the Catawba River. Taylor was 10 when his family moved to the Tidewater area of Virginia, to a village outside Portsmouth called Cradock. His father was an iron molder, an Irish American, and worked at the Navy yard in nearby Norfolk. His mother was a housewife, a German American, a unique woman with a great zest for life. He had four older sisters. Three were already away from home—one was living in London, another teaching in California, and the third was living in New York. His fourth sister was at home but very "sophisticated." She introduced Taylor to Hemingway when Ted was just eleven. She was collecting everything Hemingway had written.

Ted thought Hemingway's writing was pretty heady stuff. Ted began writing at the age of thirteen, having landed a sportswriting job with the

Portsmouth Star. He was paid 50¢ a week. He continued working on the paper in high school, and when he was unable to pass freshman math, which he needed to graduate, he dropped out in his senior year. At age 17 he was a copy boy for the Washington, D.C., *Daily News*. When World War II broke out, he joined the Navy as an AB seaman. Later he was a radio writer, boxing manager, merchant seaman, naval officer, Hollywood press agent, and documentary filmmaker. At the age of 25, in 1946, he met and married Gweneth Goodwin. At first he wrote for adults and combined books with his film work. While serving as a press officer in the Pentagon, he wrote at night. Later he worked as a public relations officer for the Navy and met producer William Perlberg, partner of director George Seaton. In 1955 Taylor moved to Hollywood to work as a press agent for Perlberg and Seaton's production company. Taylor, his first wife Gweneth, and their three children moved to Laguna Beach in 1961. He commuted to Hollywood for the next decade, and flew to remote locations such as Taiwan, continuing to write books in his spare time. His writing was not lucrative enough to support his wife and family, so he continued to work in the movie industry. He worked on *Tora! Tora! Tora!*, but the glamour was not long lasting. By 1970 his income from writing was substantial enough to support his family.

His first book for young readers was the result of movie work, *People Who Make Movies* (Doubleday, 1967). Probably his best-known work is *The Cay* (Doubleday, 1969), the story of a prejudiced white boy saved from drowning by a black West Indian sailor. *The Cay* was written in three weeks—the culmination of 11 years of on-and-off thought. "I do not have a good imagination so all the books are based on truth and I'm usually involved, one way or another." The idea for *The Cay* first emerged while reading research for another book. The incident took place during the war and involved a German submarine that torpedoed a Dutch ship in the Caribbean. The ship was severed in half, and the few survivors crawled onto a lifeboat. The survivors looked back and saw a young boy climbing onto a raft. They assumed he was going to be safe, but the submarine surfaced and blocked their view. Once the submarine moved, the boy and raft were nowhere in sight. Taylor based the character on a boy he had known in Statesville whose parents had molded him into one of the most prejudiced young people Taylor ever knew. He put the boy on the raft with a black man upon whom his very life would depend. The black man was a composite of West Indians Taylor sailed with during the war as well as an old man he drank and fished with in St. Croix in the Virgin Islands.

Despite criticism as being offensive and reinforcing racial stereotypes, the book has earned classic status, and, by 1997, the 137-page book had sold over 4 million copies. It is required reading for fifth- and sixth-graders in 33 states and has garnered 11 literary awards. Even though the book was published in 1969, Taylor still receives as many as 500 letters a month from around the country. In 1974 the book was the basis for an NBC movie starring James Earl Jones. For years he received countless requests (actually more than 200,000 at one count) to write a sequel, and he finally did. Even Taylor does not expect *Timothy of the Cay* (Harcourt, 1993) to attain any measure of success compared to *The Cay*.

Several years after writing *The Cay* and before writing the sequel Taylor wrote a book about a blind dog. He based the book on the true story of a family and their dog, Tuck. One day a family friend invited him to dinner at his house in San Francisco. Another guest at the dinner said, "You wrote a story about a blind boy. Now let me tell you a story about a blind dog." "That story," says Taylor, "became *Tuck*. It happened to a San Francisco family, but I am not acquainted too much with San Francisco, so I changed the locale to Los Angeles and substituted a girl (a daughter of a friend) for one of the five boys, eliminating three of the original family. I turned non-fiction into fiction in this case. I hope it rings true."

In fact, Taylor says, "*The Trouble with Tuck* [Doubleday, 1981] is 80 percent true. Tuck went blind at the age of three-and-a-half. The Orser family provided a seeing eye dog for Bonanza, trained one themselves, and Bonanza, suffering from retinal atrophy, guided on one until he died at the age of eleven-and-a-half."

Most mornings one can find Ted Taylor and his golden Labrador walking on the nearly deserted beach. He met his second wife, Flora, on a similar walk along the beach in 1977. He was walking along the beach when his dog "attacked her dog." Flora, a widow, was a librarian at the El Morro Elementary School in Laguana Beach. He called that evening to apologize and because he was separated from his first wife at the time, invited her to dinner and a movie. They saw the movie *Rocky* that night. In 1981 they married. Each morning Taylor is at his writing desk by 8:30 AM. His golden Labrador, Hyra, pads into the office with him. He obtained Hyra from a guide dog school in Northern California where he did research for *The Trouble with Tuck*. He breaks for one-half hour for lunch and then is back at his desk until 4:30 PM (except during football season, when he stops to watch college games on Saturday and professional games on Sunday). With the exception of fishing off the coast in a friend's outboard motorboat and traveling, which is usually in connection with research or promotion for a book, Taylor spends every day, seven days a week, writing. In addition to his own schedule for books, he has ghost-written several adult books ranging in subjects from ESP and hyperactive children to an autobiography of a famed Hollywood comedian. His "clients" include Jerry Lewis and the Amazing Kreskin. As a measure of his stature one might compare the advance he received for *The Cay*, which was $500, and the six-figure advance Harcourt Brace gave him to write the prequel-sequel to *The Cay*, *Timothy of the Cay*.

Theodore and Flora Taylor now live in a "house in the woods." Their home, two blocks above the Pacific Coast Highway, is a two-story, white board-and-batten house nestled among a quarter-acre grove of oak, sycamore, elm, and eucalyptus trees. They enjoy visits from their children, six in all. Flora, now retired, accompanies Taylor on his research travels around the world. An expansive garden is Flora's special domain. On the southern end of the house, between two brick patios, is a pushed-out section of the house that serves as Ted's office—that is his domain. He says, "Many mornings I can't wait to get there to go to work. I enjoy writing, and I want to write, and I do it."

Books and Notes

Theodore Taylor's books are filled with adventure and often have a hint of the sea. Taylor loves travel and the sea.

The Bomb (Harcourt, 1995).

The Cay (Doubleday, 1969).

To Kill the Leopard (Harcourt, 1993).

Maria, a Christmas Story (Harcourt, 1992).

Sweet Friday Island (Harcourt, 1994).

Timothy of the Cay (Harcourt, 1993).

The Trouble with Tuck (Doubleday, 1981).

Tuck Triumphant (Doubleday, 1991).

Walking Up a Rainbow: Being the True Version of the Long and Hazardous Journey of Susan D. Carlisle, Mrs. Myrtle Dessery, Drover Bert Pettit, and Cowboy Clay Carmer, and Others (Harcourt, 1994).

For More Information About/By the Author

Articles

Hubbard, Kim. "Return to the Cay." *People Weekly* 40, no. 25 (December 20, 1993): 105–6.

Yoshiko Uchida

Historical Fiction ◆ Folktales

Alameda, California
November 24, 1921–June 21, 1992

📖 *The Best Bad Thing*
📖 *Journey to Topaz*
📖 *The Dancing Kettle and Other Japanese Folk Tales*

About the Author
and the Author's Writing

Yoshiko Uchida (Oo-chee-dah) was born in Alameda, California, November 24, 1921. Her mother, Iku Uchida, wrote poetry. Her father, Dwight Takashi Uchida, was a San Francisco businessman. To the end of her life Yoshiko remembered the days during World War II when her family was held in concentration camps, where Americans of Japanese heritage were sent after the bombing of Pearl Harbor. The family lived in Berkeley, California, in a small house with a large yard. Her mother cooked Japanese foods, and they spoke Japanese at home. Yoshiko and her older sister sometimes wore kimonos for special programs at school. The family celebrated traditional Japanese holidays. The third day of March was Dolls Festival Day. A tea party would be held to show off special dolls put on display. The family had many books from Japan and her parents often read stories from those books to Yoshiko and her sister. The Uchidas even traveled to Japan once.

Yoshiko also read Louisa May Alcott's *Little Women* and *Little Men*, Frances H. Hodgson's *The Secret Garden*, and Anna Sewell's *Black Beauty*. As a young writer, she often wrote her stories on brown wrapping paper.

Yoshiko was a senior at Berkeley High School when Pearl Harbor was bombed in December 1941. All Japanese in the United States, even if they were born in this country and were U.S. citizens, were ordered to leave their homes and to go to relocation centers (now referred to by historians as internment camps). At first the Uchidas were sent to live in a horse stall at the Tanforan Race Track. After five months they were sent to Topaz, a guarded camp, in the Utah desert. Yoshiko received her high school diploma by mail in a cardboard tube. After receiving a fellowship to study at Smith College, Yoshiko was released. Her family was released later that same year.

After earning her masters degree, Yoshiko began her teaching career at a Quaker school in Philadelphia. She moved to New York City and worked as a secretary while trying to start a writing career. In 1952 the Ford Foundation granted her a fellowship to travel to Japan so that she could collect material for more books. She was to spend one year in Japan, but she liked it so much that she stayed for a second year. While in Japan she was able to collect folktales and study folk art. When she returned to the United States she became the West Coast correspondent for *Craft Horizon Magazine*. She lived for a time in Oakland and eventually was able to write full-time. She wrote stories for many magazines, including *Woman's Day*, the magazine that first accepted one of her stories. Her first children's book, *The Dancing Kettle and Other Japanese Folk Tales*, was published by Harcourt in 1949.

Uchida's early stories focused on settings and tales from Japan. Her first three books were collections of Japanese folktales. After the death of her mother in 1966, Uchida wanted to write a book for her parents that would reflect and acknowledge the hardships that all first-generation Japanese had gone through. That book, *Journey to Topaz: A Story of the Japanese-American Evacuation* (Scribner, 1971), became an account of her own family's experiences in the World War II camps. The story is told through the eyes of 11-year-old Yuki. *Journey Home* (Atheneum, 1978) continues the story and tells of the Sakane family's return to Berkeley. At that time Berkeley residents harbored a lot of hostility. The family goes into partnership with other Japanese Americans and establishes a grocery store. The story departs from Uchida's own family's experiences; however, her stories reflect those of many Japanese Americans after they were released from the internment camps.

Just one year before her death, Yoshiko Uchida sat for an interview and said, "I've always loved children's books and wanted to share with American children the wonderful Japanese folk tales I'd heard as a child. Sharing stories, I hoped, would help them understand other cultures and see that people everywhere have the same hopes, fears, and joys." Uchida talked about the parts of her life that appeared in some of her books. "A good bit of me is in Rinko, the child in my trilogy, *A Jar of Dreams*, *The Best Bad Thing*, and *The Happiest Ending* [McElderry, 1981, 1983, and 1985], although the stories are fictional and not about my family. Also, *Journey to Topaz* is based on my experiences during World War II when we were interned by our government, so there is much of me in Yuki. Her story continues in *Journey Home*."

Yoshiko Uchida's childhood writing began as a 10-year-old with a book she wrote on the brown wrapping paper. The day she finished elementary school, she began a "Journal of Special Events." As an adult she taught elementary school for a short time, but teaching did not give her enough time for writing. Her writing career spanned more than 40 years.

In the mid-1980s Yoshiko Uchida was diagnosed as having Chronic Fatigue Immune Dysfunction Syndrome, which kept her from traveling and going to the theater. Her writing career came to a standstill. However, she continued to enjoy reading, painting, and walking. In 1990 she was able to begin writing again, something she had not been able to do for five years or more. Her writing garnered several honors. In 1981 the University of Oregon bestowed on her an award for "having made a significant contribution to the cultural development of society . . . and . . . [helping] to bring about a greater understanding of the Japanese-America culture." In 1991 Julian Messner/Silver Burdett published *The Invisible Thread: An Autobiography*. Shortly before her death, Uchida had completed two picture books. In 1993 McElderry published *The Magic Purse*, and Philomel published *The Bracelet*. Yoshiko Uchida was living in an apartment in Berkeley when she died of a stroke on June 21, 1992.

Books and Notes

Yoshiko Uchida collected Japanese folktales and told stories that reflected her Japanese heritage. Those who read her novels will glean much information about the imprisonment of Japanese Americans during and immediately after World War II.

Historical Fiction

The Best Bad Thing (McElderry, 1983).
Sequel to *A Jar of Dreams*.

The Birthday Visitor. Illustrated by Charles Robinson. (Scribner, 1975).
Emi's seventh birthday turns out to be one of the best ever.

The Bracelet. Illustrated by Joanna Yardley. (Philomel, 1993).
A young girl in an internment camp loses a bracelet given to her by a friend, but finds that their friendship is stronger.

The Forever Christmas Tree. Illustrated by Mizumura. (Scribner, 1963).
A Christmas celebration among people who do not worship in the Christian manner.

The Happiest Ending (McElderry, 1985).
A third book in the trilogy that begins with *A Jar of Dreams* and *The Best Bad Thing*.

Hisako's Mysteries. Illustrated by Susan Bennett. (Scribner, 1969).
Mysteries set in Japan in the 1960s.

A Jar of Dreams (McElderry, 1981).
First book in a trilogy that begins during the Depression in 1935.

Journey to Topaz: A Story of the Japanese-American Evacuation. Illustrated by Donald Carrick. (Scribner, 1971).
Set during World War II after the bombing of Pearl Harbor.

The Rooster Who Understood Japanese. Illustrated by Charles Robinson. (Scribner, 1976).
A view of a middle-class Japanese American home.

Folktales

The Dancing Kettle and Other Japanese Folk Tales. Illustrated by Richard C. Jones. (Harcourt, 1949; Creative Arts, 1986).
Tales of royal beings, monsters, ogres, and gods.

The Magic Listening Cap—More Folk Tales from Japan. Illustrated by Yoshiko Uchida. (Harcourt, 1955; reissued by Creative Arts, 1987).
Fourteen tales with universal themes.

The Magic Purse. Illustrated by Keiko Narahashi. (McElderry, 1993).
A family finds a purse that fills with gold.

For More Information About/By the Author

Limited information on the flaps of books. Check standard reference sources.

Cynthia Voigt

◆ Contemporary Realistic Fiction ◆ Fantasy ◆ Mystery

Boston, Massachusetts
February 25, 1942

📖 Crisfield Stories
📖 *Homecoming*
📖 *Dicey's Song*
📖 *Building Blocks*
📖 *The Callendar Papers*

About the Author
and the Author's Writing

Cynthia Voigt dreamed of becoming a writer, but she married and became a teacher. She enjoyed teaching but she renewed her interest in writing when she found a library filled with children's books. When her son was born, she found time to write. Voigt says that *Building Blocks* (Atheneum, 1984) was begun after her husband built a "tower out of giant blocks, into which I watched my son crawl early one morning. What if . . . ? I thought, watching, remembering how his father had built it." While she was working on *Building Blocks*, Voigt saw some children sitting in a car and wondered what would happen if no one came back for them. She put aside the *Building Blocks* story to write the manuscript that was to become *Homecoming* (Atheneum, 1981). The book begins the saga of the Tillerman family—Dicey, James, Maybeth, and Sammy.

Voigt has said that Sammy is much like her own son, Peter, and Gram is the woman she would like to become.

Cynthia Voigt was born February 25, 1942, in Boston, Massachusetts, as Cynthia Irving. She was the second child of Elise Keeney and Frederick C. Irving, a corporate executive. Cynthia's childhood years were spent in southern Connecticut. She first decided to become a writer when she was in high school, because she liked books. Her career was sidetracked when she first married in 1964. She attended Smith College, where she obtained her undergraduate degree and later did graduate work at St. Michael's College. She earned her teaching certificate from Christian Brothers College. She worked at an advertising agency, as a secretary, and, after earning her teaching certificate, she taught high school English in Glen Burnie and Annapolis, Maryland. She was department chair from 1971 to 1979. During this time her first marriage ended, and she married Walter Voigt, a fellow teacher in 1974. Her family brought new responsibilities that took time away from her writing, but also provided inspiration for plots, specific incidents, and character traits for her books.

When Voigt was teaching, she decided to write books for young readers. She wrote short stories and poetry in high school and college. Her first effort focused on writing *Building Blocks*, but her first book to be published was *Homecoming*. The book's sequel, *Dicey's Song* (Atheneum, 1982), earned Voigt the prestigious 1983 Newbery Award. She has added five more titles to what Voigt calls her Crisfield Stories to her list of published books.

Many of her books are set in places where Voigt and her family have lived—Maryland, New Mexico, and Maine. The Chesapeake Bay plays an important role in several of her books. She says, "My stories are permeated with the world as I've seen it. My own sense of how much is actual and how much imaginative is best expressed when I admit that I feel as if I'm discovering stories that are already there." As Voigt begins to shape a scene, she will often sit outside and draw the structures that she wants to write about. The drawing helps her to keep the details of the story straight. For example, she drew the shop Dicey worked in so that she would always have the doors and the windows in the right places.

Voigt prefers to write in the morning between the hours of 8 AM and noon. She works from an outline, but sometimes characters just appear and must be included later. That happened when she was writing *Homecoming*. "Gram sprang into my mind, full-blown, so the book became twice as long." After *Homecoming*, Voigt says, "I knew I had to write *Dicey's Song* to complete the mother's story." And, when Jeff appeared in *Dicey's Song*, "I knew I had to tell his story next." That story was *A Solitary Blue* (Atheneum, 1983). Next came *The Runner* (Atheneum, 1985). *The Runner* told a story from a generation earlier, the story of Dicey's uncle, Bullet. By most readers' standards Bullet does not seem very likable; he's angry and bigoted. Voigt, however, has said, "[I] can't worry about that." She loved the character and did not want any harm to come to him. She continued the saga of the Tillermans in *Come a Stranger* (Atheneum, 1986) and *Sons from Afar* (Atheneum, 1987).

Her teaching background inspires classroom scenes in her books, but she does not hesitate to write about ineffective teachers. Voigt's editors have watched that she does not dwell on one classroom topic/problem for too long. She also realizes that what she imagines a scene to be might not be what readers draw from the same writing. She says, "I believe that fiction is a lie, and that people who deal in it ought to remember that they're lying."

When Cynthia Voigt is not writing she is probably reading, eating, playing tennis, or watching movies. She particularly enjoys her husband, Walter; daughter, Jessica; and son, Peter. After living in Massachusetts; Connecticut; Annapolis, Maryland; and New Mexico, Cynthia Voigt now lives in Deer Isle, Maine. In 1995 she was honored with the Margaret A. Edwards Award for her contributions to the field of literature for young adults.

Books and Notes

Cynthia Voigt's writing career blossomed with her first book about the Tillerman family—Dicey, James, Maybeth, and Sammy—in 1981. That book was an American Book Award Nominee and a Notable Children's Trade Book in the Field of Social Studies. *Dicey's Song* was awarded the 1983 Newbery Medal. She was awarded the Mystery Writer's of America Edgar Allen Poe Award for *The Callendar Papers* in 1984. For many years she published all of her books with Atheneum. Recently Scholastic has published some of her books. Two of those recent books feature Margalo and Mikey, two girls who meet in Mrs. Chemsky's fifth-grade class. In their second book they attempt to prevent the divorce of Mikey's parents, but the scheme is foiled by a new girl at school.

Tillerman Stories

Come a Stranger (Atheneum, 1986).

Dicey's Song (Atheneum, 1982).

Homecoming (Atheneum, 1981).

Sons from Afar (Atheneum, 1987).

Mystery

The Callendar Papers (Atheneum, 1983).

Fantasy

Building Blocks (Atheneum, 1984).

Other Titles

Bad, Badder, Baddest (Scholastic, 1997).

Bad Girls (Scholastic, 1996).

When She Hollers (Scholastic, 1994).

The Wings of a Falcon (Scholastic, 1993).

For More Information About/By the Author

Articles

Voigt, Cynthia. "1995 Margaret A. Edwards Award Acceptance Speech: Thirteen Stray Thoughts About Failure." *Journal of Youth Services in Libraries* 9, no. 1 (Fall 1995): 23–25.

Books

Reid, Suzanne Elizabeth. *Presenting Cynthia Voigt* (Twayne, 1995).

E. B. (Elwyn Brooks) White

◆ Animal Fantasy

Mt. Vernon, New York
July 11, 1899–October 1, 1985

📖 *Charlotte's Web*

📖 *Stuart Little*

📖 *The Trumpet of the Swans*

About the Author
and the Author's Writing

E. B. White was born July 11, 1899, in Mt. Vernon, New York. He was the youngest of six children. His father was the president of a piano manufacturing company. White attended Cornell University on a scholarship, and left Cornell in 1918 to serve as an army private during World War I. He returned to Cornell and graduated in 1921. At Cornell he got the nickname "Andy." While at Cornell he studied under the grammarian William Strunk Jr.

After college White spent time traveling. He and a friend drove out West in a Model T. White's writing career started as a reporter with the *Seattle Times*. He worked for years in an advertising agency as a production assistant, copywriter, writer, and contributing editor. He rarely kept regular hours. He eventually made his way to New York and his first article for the *New Yorker* was published in 1925. That was the year that he met a distinguished editor at the *New Yorker*, Katharine Sergeant Angell. In 1927 he joined the staff of the *New Yorker* as an associate editor. Eventually he became the major contributor to the column "Notes and Comment." One of his closest friends was James Thurber. They shared an office in the early days of their careers. White is said to have taught Thurber the art of writing that helped Thurber's career as a cartoonist.

During White's association with the *New Yorker*, he came to respect Katharine Angell. She had married Ernest Angell in 1915 and they had become parents of a daughter, Nancy, and a son, Roger. Their marriage ended in 1928 with a "painful dissolution." On November 13, 1929, Katharine Angell and E. B. White married. They had one son, Joel McCoun White.

In 1938 the Whites purchased an old farm in North Brooklin, Maine. The Whites left New York and moved to the farm. He was equally as comfortable writing from his home in Maine as he had been from his apartment in New York. On the farm White spent hours writing in an old boathouse for *Harper's* magazine. His books, essays, and letters were also published and read around the world.

His first children's book, *Stuart Little* (Harper, 1945), was written as a treat for his six-year-old niece. The book told of a mouse born into a human family. Seven years later *Charlotte's Web* (Harper, 1952) was published. Charlotte is a very intelligent spider who displays the ultimate in love and friendship when she sacrifices her own life for her friend, Wilbur the pig. White has said that he got the idea for the book from watching a spider spin a web on his farm. Some feel that E. B. White wrote *Charlotte's Web* to show children the inherent value of each individual, the need for tolerance and understanding, and the strength of love for another. E. B. White has discussed his inspiration for the characters, saying, "Well I like animals, and it would be odd if I failed to write about them. Animals are a weakness with me, and, when I got a place in the country, I was quite sure animals would appear, and they did." His last children's book was *The Trumpet of the Swans* (Harper, 1970). He learned about swans to make sure that the facts in this fantasy were accurate.

His wife, Katharine, died after 48 years of marriage. Katharine White retired from the *New Yorker* in 1960 at the age of 68. Debilitating illnesses and financial concerns marred her last years. She died July 20,

1977, at the age of 85. E. B. White continued essay writing and living on the farm. In his later years, White suffered from Alzheimer's disease. He died eleven years later, in 1985, at the age of 86.

E. B. White was considered an "esteemed essayist" whose prose works were legendary at the *New Yorker*, where he contributed regularly from the 1930s to the 1970s. His writing brought him many honors, including the Presidential Medal of Freedom (1963), the Laura Ingalls Wilder Award (1970) for his "lasting contribution to children's literature," and a special Pulitzer Prize citation for the body of his work in 1978.

Books and Notes

E. B. White said he had "two or three strong beliefs about the business of writing for children." Those beliefs included never kidding about anything; transmitting his/her own love of life; showing an appreciation of the world; and maintaining accuracy, even within a web.

Charlotte's Web. Illustrated by Garth Williams. (Harper, 1952).

Stuart Little. Illustrated by Garth Williams. (Harper, 1945).

The Trumpet of the Swans. Illustrated by Edward Frascino. (Harper, 1970).

For More Information About/By the Author

Articles

The E. B. White Home Page. URL: http://www.tiac.net/users/winlib/ebwhite.htm (Accessed December 1997).

"A Neighbor's Farewell to E. B. White." *Yankee* (February 1986): 156+.

Obituary. *Newsweek* (October 14, 1985): 79.

Obituary. *Time* (October 14, 1985): 105, 2c.

"Tomorrow Is Another Day." *U.S. News & World Report* 115, no. 16 (October 25, 1993): 84.

Books

Berg, Julie. *E. B. White* (Abdo, 1994).

Collins, David R. *To the Point: A Story About E. B. White*. Illustrated by Amy Johnson. (Carolrhoda, 1989).

Gherman, Beverly. *E. B. White, Some Writer! A Biography* (Atheneum, 1992; Beech, 1994).

Rylant, Cynthia. *Margaret, Frank, and Andy: Three Writer's Stories* (Harcourt, 1996).

Tingum, Janice. *E. B. White: The Elements of a Writer* (Lerner, 1995).

Laura Ingalls Wilder

◆ Historical Fiction

Rural Wisconsin
February 7, 1867–February 10, 1957

📖 Little House Series

📖 *Little House on the Prairie*

📖 *On the Banks of Plum Creek*

About the Author
and the Author's Writing

Laura Elizabeth Ingalls Wilder was born February 7, 1867, the daughter of Charles and Caroline Ingalls. She was forty-four when she and her husband, Almanzo, began to write for *Missouri Ruralist*. It was not long before their daughter, Rose Wilder Lane, a journalist in San Francisco, was encouraging her mother to write some of her childhood tales. Her first drafts were written in big, rough school tablets. She wrote in pencil on both sides of the paper. Harper & Row published her first manuscript in 1932 as *Little House in the Big Woods*. Laura Ingalls Wilder was sixty-five years old.

The stories Laura wrote concerned her family and their pioneer days in the Midwest. Her first book, *Little House in the Big Woods*, is the story of life in a log cabin in the big woods of Wisconsin in the 1860s. Real people became the characters in the stories—Pa (Charles), Ma (Caroline), her older sister, Mary, Laura herself, and the youngest child, Carrie. Ma baked bread on Saturdays, and Pa played his fiddle. Charles Ingalls was born in 1835 in Cuba, New York. Caroline was born five years later in Wisconsin. They began their married life in Wisconsin, where their first three girls, Mary, Laura, and Carrie, were born. Pa (Charles) often got restless, so the family moved about. First they lived in Wisconsin, and then Minnesota. For a time the family operated a hotel in Burr Oak, Iowa, and during another period of time, they moved from Minnesota to Indian Territory in Oklahoma. When the family settled on Indian land, they were ordered off. So once again they packed their wagon. This time they crossed from Kansas to Missouri, through Iowa, settling back in Minnesota in a sod house on the banks of Plum Creek. Eventually the family settled near DeSmet, South Dakota, where the last five of the Little House stories were set.

Laura was teaching school when Almanzo Wilder began to court her. He would come to her schoolhouse every Friday and take her home for the weekend. On August 25, 1885, Laura and Almanzo married in DeSmet. She was eighteen, and he was twenty-eight. The following year, their daughter, Rose, was born. Rose was just two when Laura and Almanzo became ill with diphtheria in 1888. Almanzo never completely recovered from the illness. That fall, on August 12, 1888, Laura and Almanzo had a baby boy who died shortly after he was born. He was buried in DeSmet. The story of Laura and Almanzo's courtship is told in *These Happy Golden Years* (Harper, 1943). By the time this story was published, Laura was seventy-six years old, and all of the Ingalls family except Carrie had died. (Pa died in DeSmet in 1902; Ma in 1924; Mary died at Carrie's home in Keystone, South Dakota, in 1928; and Grace died in 1941.)

After suffering from diphtheria, Laura and Almanzo moved to Florida, thinking the climate would help Almanzo recover. They had relatives there and stayed two years. But Almanzo did not seem to be any better in the South, so they returned to DeSmet. Almanzo suffered a stroke, and Laura and Almanzo decided to move to a milder climate, after a time traveling to Missouri. There they found forty acres of rough and rocky land, which they could buy with the $100 Laura had saved. The only building on the land was a one-room log cabin with a rock fireplace. The cabin had one door, but no windows. When the door was closed the light came between the logs where the mud chinking had fallen out. After a year, Almanzo had recovered from the stroke suffered in South Dakota.

Together with neighbors, the Wilders built a log barn for his horses and a hen house. Eventually Laura and Almanzo expanded their farm to 200 acres, stocked it with a fine herd of cows, good hogs, and a very good egg-laying flock of leghorn hens. They lived on the farm, which they called Rocky Ridge Farm, with their daughter, Rose.

Rose Wilder left home at the age of seventeen for Kansas City. She soon moved to San Francisco, married (and later divorced) Gilbert Lane, and became a successful journalist and writer. Along the way, Rose made friends with Berta Hader, who later coauthored and illustrated with her husband, Elmer, *The Big Snow* (Macmillan, 1948), the 1949 Caldecott Award winner.

Laura and Almanzo remained on Rocky Ridge Farm. Almanzo worked with his dairy herd, and Laura set about increasing her flock of leghorn hens. In addition to helping to care for the farm and the animals, Laura was organizer and secretary of the Mansfield Farm Loan Association, which issued over $1 million of loans to Ozark farmers during the Depression. Her work with her poultry helped her to become an expert, and she was often asked to give speeches about her success with leghorn hens. Once when she was too busy to go in person, she sent a written speech. An editor of a weekly farm journal heard the speech and was impressed enough to ask Laura to write on a regular basis. The first article in the *Missouri Ruralist* appeared just after her forty-fourth birthday. For over ten years she wrote a regular column for the newspaper and championed the image of women in farming. She was poultry editor of the St. Louis *Star* and home editor of the *Missouri Ruralist*.

Her daughter, Rose, encouraged her to write for the "big markets," and during a visit to see Rose in San Francisco, Laura began to write her stories. She later completed a manuscript in the big, 5¢ tablets. Her first manuscript covered a long period in her life, and it lacked some of the charm of her later work. She was dissatisfied and reworked the stories to cover a shorter time period.

Rose was involved with getting the manuscript published. Apparently Rose contacted her old friend Berta Hader and asked her to influence her editor to at least get the book looked at. Virginia Kirkus, who at the time was an editor at Harper & Row, confirms part of the story. Kirkus's interest in the Little House books began with a mysterious phone conversation. An acquaintance thought Kirkus might be interested in the manuscript. Children's books were entering an era of great popularity, but the Great Depression had just hit. So when the call came that "an elderly lady was writing a true story—in fictional form—about her pioneer childhood," Virginia Kirkus was not sure that she wanted to read the manuscript. When she did, she was enchanted with *Little House in the Big Woods*.

Kirkus left Harper while the second book, *Little House on the Prairie*, was still in the making. Helen Sewall and Mildred Boyle illustrated the first edition of the books. In 1943 Laura and Almanzo had stopped farming, but they were still active. Laura kept up the ten-room house and cooked, baked, and churned their butter. A few years later, Ursula Nordstrom, the editor at Harper, investigated the possibility of a newly illustrated, uniform-sized collection of the Wilder books. Nordstrom asked Garth Williams, a new illustrator at Harper, to reillustrate the books. Williams traveled to all the Ingalls family's home sites and used photographs as models. The covers Williams created had more drama than those of the previous editions. The uniform edition with Williams's illustrations was published in 1953.

Laura had begun to pen the story of her married years, starting with the first four, but died February 10, 1957, before it was published. She was ninety years old. Rose Wilder Lane, Laura and Almanzo's daughter, edited an account of the family's move from the Dakotas to Missouri. In 1962 Harper published Laura's book *On the Way Home*, edited by Rose Wilder Lane. Rose died in 1968. In 1971 Laura's unfinished story *The First Four Years* was published by Rose's lawyer, the son of a longtime friend of Rose Wilder Lane, Roger MacBride. He is often referred to as Laura's adopted grandson. It was MacBride who arranged (and co-produced with "Laugh-In's" Ed Friendly) for the television series based on *Little House on the Prairie*, which aired in the 1970s.

As a boy, Roger MacBride was extremely close to Rose and would regularly ride his bike 20 miles to visit her and discuss philosophy. Rose was one of the great twentieth-century libertarian pioneers. She had been a Communist early in her life, but after visiting Stalin's Soviet Union she was so disillusioned that she rejected her earlier beliefs, becoming a staunch individualist libertarian. She introduced MacBride to libertarianism. He became an important member of the Libertarian Party, as it became the third largest political party. He later rejoined the Republican Party and worked to move it more toward the goals of the libertarians. Roger was a Harvard-educated lawyer, won a seat in the Vermont State Legislature as a Republican, and in 1976 became the Libertarian Party's presidential nominee.

When Rose died, Roger inherited Little House rights, as well as an enormous pile of manuscripts written by Rose. He was asked to donate many of his libertarian papers to the Herbert Hoover Presidential Library & Museum at West Branch, Iowa. He agreed and inquired if the museum was interested in obtaining the papers and correspondence of Rose Wilder Lane. Because she had a connection to the Libertarian Party, as well as to Herbert Hoover (she had penned a biography of Lou Henry Hoover), the museum was eager to obtain those papers. Consequently, the Herbert Hoover Museum has many pieces of important correspondence between Rose and her mother. Some of those papers indicate that Rose perhaps had an important involvement with the writing of her mother's books.

Roger Lea MacBride died of heart failure at his home in Miami Beach at the age of 66. His daughter, Abigail Adams MacBride, became the literary heir not only to her father's literary estate, but those of Rose Wilder Lane and Laura Ingalls Wilder as well.

Books and Notes

Laura's recollections of childhood were written in the last decades of her life. Since their first publication, the books have been reissued and reprinted many times. The first edition was illustrated by Helen Sewall and Mildred Boyle, but the most well-known edition was issued in the 1950s featuring illustrations created by Garth Williams. The following book list presents the books in chronological sequence of the setting/time period. All the books have been published by Harper.

The Little House Books

Little House in the Big Woods—Book 1

Little House on the Prairie—Book 2

Farmer Boy—Book 3

On the Banks of Plum Creek—Book 4

By the Shores of Silver Lake—Book 5

The Long Winter—Book 6

Little Town on the Prairie—Book 7

These Happy Golden Years—Book 8

The First Four Years—Book 9

On the Way Home: The Diary of a Trip from South Dakota to Mansfield, Missouri, in 1894. Edited by Rose Wilder Lane—Book 10

Adaptations

In 1990 Harper began packaging chapters and episodes from the Little House books into picture books and beginning chapter books. Illustrations created for a specific chapter are combined to create a picture book in the "My First Little House Books," and various thematic chapters from several books are combined to create single thematic-based, beginning chapter books in "Little House Chapter Books." For example, the publishers have selected chapters that focus on Laura's relationship with her sisters. Those chapters became the contents for *Pioneer Sisters*.

My First Little House Books (all adapted from the Little House Books)

Bedtime for Laura. Illustrated by Renee Graef and Susan McAliley. (Harper, 1996).

Christmas in the Big Woods. Illustrated by Renee Graef. (Harper, 1995).

County Fair. Illustrated by Jody Wheeler. (Harper, 1997).

Dance at Grandpa's. Illustrated by Renee Graef. (Harper, 1994).

The Deer in the Wood. Illustrated by Renee Graef. (Harper, 1995).

A Farmer Boy Birthday. Illustrated by Jody Wheeler. (Harper, 1997).

A Farmer Boy Christmas. Illustrated by Jody Wheeler. (Harper, 1999).

Going to Town. Illustrated by Renee Graef. (Harper, 1994).

Going West. Illustrated by Renee Graef. (Harper, 1996).

Happy Birthday, Laura. Illustrated by Renee Graef. (Harper, 1995).

Hello, Laurie! Illustrated by Renee Graef and Susan McAliley. (Harper, 1996).

Laura Helps Pa. Illustrated by Renee Graef and Susan McAliley. (Harper, 1996).

Laura's Garden. Illustrated by Renee Graef and Susan McAliley. (Harper, 1996).

A Little House Birthday. Illustrated by Doris Ettlinger. (Harper, 1997).

A Little Prairie House. Illustrated by Renee Graef. (Harper, 1998).

Merry Christmas, Laura. Illustrated by Renee Graef. (Harper, 1995).

My Little House ABC. Illustrated by Renee Graef. (Harper, 1997).

My Little House 1-2-3. Illustrated by Renee Graef. (Harper, 1997).

Prairie Day. Illustrated by Renee Graef. (Harper, 1997).

Springtime in the Big Woods. Illustrated by Doris Ettlinger. (Harper, 1999).

Sugar Snow. Illustrated by Renee Graef. (Harper, 1997).

Summertime in the Big Woods. Illustrated by Renee Graef. (Harper, 1996).

Winter Days in the Big Woods. Illustrated by Renee Graef. (Harper, 1994).

Winter on the Farm. Illustrated by Renee Graef. (Harper, 1996).

Little House Chapter Books

The Adventures of Laura and Jack. Illustrated by Renee Graef. (Harper, 1997).

Animal Adventures. Illustrated by Renee Graef. (Harper, 1997).

Farmer Boy Days. Illustrated by Renee Graef. (Harper, 1998).

Hard Times on the Prairie. Illustrated by Renee Graef. (Harper, 1998).

Laura & Nellie. Illustrated by Renee Graef. (Harper, 1998).

Little House Farm Days. Illustrated by Renee Graef. (Harper, 1998).

Little House Friends. Illustrated by Renee Graef. (Harper, 1998).

Pioneer Sisters. Illustrated by Renee Graef. (Harper, 1997).

School Days. Illustrated by Renee Graef. (Harper, 1997).

For More Information About/By the Author

Articles

Irby, Rebecca, and Phil Greetham. *Laura Ingalls Wilder—PG Home Page.* URL: http://ourworld.compuserve.com/ homepages/p_greetham/ingalls/ home.html (Accessed January 1998).

"Laura Ingalls Wilder: Teacher Resource File." URL: http://falcon.jmu.edu/ ~ramseyil/wilder.htm (Accessed January 1998).
     Website provides a number of excellent links to other Laura Ingalls Wilder sites.

Slegg, Jennifer. *My Little House on the Prairie Home Page.* URL: http://www. pinc.com/~jenslegg/laura.htm (Accessed January 1998).

Books

Anderson, William. *Laura Ingalls Wilder: A Biography* (Harper, 1992).

Blair, Gwenda. *Laura Ingalls Wilder* (Putnam, 1981).

Giff, Patricia Reilly. *Laura Ingalls Wilder: Growing Up in the Little House* (Viking, 1987).

Wallner, Alexandra. *Laura Ingalls Wilder.* Illustrated by Alexandra Wallner. (Holiday, 1997).

Wilder, Laura Ingalls, and Rose Wilder Lane. *A Little House Sampler* (University of Nebraska, 1988).

Elizabeth Winthrop

Contemporary Realistic Fiction ◆ Fantasy ◆ Picture Book Fiction

---

Washington, D.C.
February 14, 1948

📖 *The Castle in the Attic*

📖 *Maggie and the Monster*

📖 *As the Crow Flies*

About the Author
and the Author's Writing

Elizabeth Winthrop was born in Washington, D.C., February 14, 1948. She grew up in a rambling house with five brothers. Her father was journalist Stewart Alsop, so Elizabeth often came home to the clacking of her father's old Underwood typewriter. She often saw her father reading newspapers and talking to people before he wrote his stories. He had such power of concentration, that only the jingle of a phone could get his attention. The family installed a second phone in his office so they could call him when they needed (or wanted) to talk to him.

Elizabeth liked to tell stories because "they took me away from the parts of my life I didn't like." As a youngster she got the idea that writing was easy—one could talk to people, go out to dinner, and read all the time—so she announced that she was going to become a writer. She wrote her first story at the age of twelve about a family of mice who lived in the White House. Unfortunately (or perhaps fortunately), she left it on a seat in a bus. In high school she began to write short stories.

She attended Miss Porter's School in Farmington, Connecticut, and went on to earn her undergraduate degree from Sarah Lawrence College. One of her instructors, Jane Cooper, suggested she try writing children's books. She graduated in 1970, and that same year married Peter Mahony, an architect. From 1971 to 1973 she worked as an editor for Harper & Row. Her first book, *Bunk Beds*, was published in 1972 by Harper, and by 1973 she was writing full-time. Their first child, Eliza, was born in 1974; their second child, Andrew, was born in 1976. She has now written over forty books for children, including novels for middle-grade/middle-school readers and picture books for younger readers.

When she began writing, she took her manuscript to her father for comments. One of her scenes described a character leaving a room in painful detail. Her father noted that unless the character crawled out of the room, that she (Winthrop) could probably just say, "Emily left the room." In other words, keep the writing simple. For a long time she kept a sign, "Emily left the room," pasted in front of her desk, a sign to remind her of her father's advice.

Her most successful book probably came in 1985 when her fantasy novel, *The Castle in the Attic*, was published by Holiday. That book featured William, who casts a spell on his beloved Mrs. Phillips to keep her with him forever. He soon learns that by making her a prisoner, he loses love and respect. To undo his selfish spell, he must embark on a terrifying mission. The book was nominated for twenty-three state book awards and won the Dorothy Canfield Fisher Award in Vermont and the Young Readers Award in California. Movie rights have been purchased, and, in 1994, a sequel, *The Battle for the Castle*, was published by Holiday. In addition to writing picture books and novels for young readers, she has also retold a few folktales and written at least one adult novel.

Winthrop has written about miniature knights in *The Castle in the Attic*; pigs that kiss in *Sloppy Kisses* (Macmillan, 1980); alcoholic parents in *Knock, Knock, Who's There?* (Holiday, 1978); guilt over walking away from a grandfather's death in *Walking Away* (Harper, 1973); and a dog named Fishface in *Belinda's Hurricane* (Dutton, 1984). She writes four to six hours a day, first in a journal, and then on a computer. So that she is not distracted while she writes, she turns off the telephone and tries to stay out of the kitchen. Her ideas come from her emotions and those she had as a child. She remembers clearly trying to fit into the crowd, helplessness when her parents argued, and devastation when her best friend found someone else to play with. Other ideas come from her children.

She reads as much as she can and tries to find just the right character to tell her stories. The stories must mirror real feelings. She characterizes herself as a "city lover." She was born in Washington, D.C., and now lives in New York City with her son and daughter. She loves the arts and enjoys the theater and arts available in the city. When she is not writing she enjoys swimming, playing tennis, riding bicycles, and enjoys eating anything chocolate—especially brownies.

Books and Notes

Winthrop is a versatile writer. She has written novels for the older reader and picture books for the younger reader, in addition to retelling a few folktales.

Folktales

The Little Humpbacked Horse: A Russian Tale. Illustrated by Alexander Koshkin. (Clarion, 1997).

Vasilissa the Beautiful: A Russian Folktale. Illustrated by Alexander Koshkin. (Harper, 1991).

Novels

The Battle for the Castle (Holiday, 1993).

The Castle in the Attic (Holiday, 1985).

Knock, Knock, Who's There? (Holiday, 1978).

Miranda in the Middle (Holiday, 1979).

Picture Books

As the Crow Flies. Illustrated by Joan Sandin. (Clarion, 1997).

Bear and Mr. Duck. Illustrated by Patience Brewster. (Holiday, 1988).

Bear and Roly-Poly. Illustrated by Patience Brewster. (Holiday, 1996).

Belinda's Hurricane. Illustrated by Wendy Watson. (Dutton, 1984).

Lizzie and Harold. Illustrated by Martha Weston. (Lothrop, 1986).

Maggie and the Monster. Illustrated by Tomie dePaola. (Holiday, 1987).

Shoes. Illustrated by William Joyce. (Harper, 1986).

For More Information About/By the Author

Articles

Elizabeth Winthrop. URL: http://www.absolute—sway.com/winthrop/ (Accessed December 1998).

David Wisniewski

Legends (Literary and Retold) ◆ Biographies

Middlesex, England
March 21, 1953

📖 *Sundiata: Lion King of Mali*

📖 *Golem*

📖 *Rain Player*

About the Author
and the Author's Writing

David Wisniewski (pronounced wiz-NESS-key) was a freelance illustrator looking for a way to make a living when he attended a seminar for children's books. He was told that he should take a portfolio to New York City and make the rounds of the publishers. He should also have a book idea, so the editors would think of him as an illustrator with an idea. The first editor he presented his idea and illustrations to, Dorothy Briley, liked the art and the story so much that she offered to turn it into a book.

David Wisniewski began to draw when his mom taught him how to link circles and ovals together to form human figures. By the time he was in the fourth grade he was "the kid who could draw." But it wasn't until after ten years of experience in shadow theater that he realized he had honed his talent into a skill he could market. His writing also developed in the puppet theater. As a child he hadn't ever been "big on writing, but it was something I *had* to do when faced with the need for scripts in our pup-pet theater." It was through that experience that, "I practically absorbed the basics of writing: the mechanics of plot, the development of charac-ters, the tricks of pacing, and other elements necessary to the develop-ment of a good story. In a way, I became a writer by being a reader."

Born in Middlesex, England (his father was in the Air Force stationed at South Ruislip AFB), March 21, 1953, David lived with his parents and one brother in Nebraska, Alabama, Germany, and Texas before settling down in the Washington, D.C., area. In addition to establishing his art ability as a fourth-grader, he also learned to love reading. He was particularly fond of science fiction and fantasy. Ray Bradbury is still his favorite author and his favorite book is *The Martian Chronicles*. In high school he was involved in the visual arts and drama, but drama was his first choice when he decided to attend the University of Maryland. After a semester or two he realized that he wasn't going to get any good roles—they all went to juniors and seniors. He had also run out of money for tuition, so he joined the Ringling Brothers Circus and spent two years as a clown and one year with a California tent show called Circus Vargas.

At the end of the three years he was tired of traveling and wanted to settle down, so he returned to Washington, D.C., and looked for a job. He interviewed with Donna Harris for a job with the parks department with their puppet theater troupe. He was hired because of his experi-ence creating props. He and Donna began to specialize in shadow pup-petry and to use flat jointed figures against a lit screen. Six months later, David and Donna married, and, in 1980, founded their own shadow thea-ter troupe and toured throughout the United States. Their second child, Alexander, was born in 1985, and their daughter, Ariana (who had been born in 1981), was nearing school-age. They realized that they would need to look for alternatives to the constant travel. David began to look for freelance art assignments. He wore out a pair of shoes searching for jobs before he got the advice about entering the children's book field. Two weeks before he was to have his first interview, he sat down and wrote the first draft for *The Warrior and the Wiseman* (Lothrop, 1989). During his work with the shadow puppet theater, he had developed an interest in reading folklore, which the couple used for their puppet presentations.

Research for one of Wisniewski's books takes two to three months before he can even begin to formulate the story. After submitting the package of writing and illustrations to the editor, he spends time correcting and incorporating the editor's request for changes into revised sketches. Finally, after he is given the okay, he begins to cut and assemble the final art. The entire process takes nine to ten months.

His art editor, Dinah Stevenson, is very exacting about Wisniewski's sketches. She often asks him to revise the sketches, and the effort and diligence seem to have paid off. His art for *Golem* (Clarion, 1996) earned him the Caldecott Award in 1997.

Each of Wisniewski's books espouse a point of view. *Elfwyn's Saga* (Lothrop, 1990) is set in Iceland and "tells a story about the danger of distraction from the important things of life by the fleeting and trivial. In fact, the vision-crystal in the book represents television and its unending torrent of distracting entertainment and commercials. In *Rain Player* [Clarion, 1991] the young hero challenges fate and the opinion of the majority to emerge victorious." *Sundiata: Lion King of Mali* (Clarion, 1992) shows that courage and perseverance can help overcome many handicaps—physical handicaps as well as poverty and social disgrace. Wisniewski's *The Wave of the Sea-Wolf* (Clarion, 1995) takes place among the Tlingit Indians of the Pacific Northwest. Two cultures clash when one views nature with respect and care, while the other views nature with a condescending attitude. It is, of course, respect and care that prevails. *Golem* tells the Jewish legend of Rabbi Loew, who shaped a giant man from clay and brought him to life to save an oppressed people.

Wisniewski does much research for each story, but he sometimes takes artistic license in constructing his stories and the illustrations. *Elfwyn's Saga* is an original tale, but draws on the legend of the hidden folk that are said to live in Iceland. In the author's note at the end of the book, Wisniewski explains that "Gorm's distinctive helmet is much more decorative than those usually worn, being of earlier Swedish origin. Most Viking warriors (when they had helmets at all) wore the Norman variety, a pointed steel cap with nosebar." Although Iceland is essentially treeless now, in the time of the Vikings there was an abundance of birch trees, but none so massive as the oak tree beneath which Elfwyn rides her pony.

In *The Warrior and the Wiseman* Wisniewski took liberties with the design of the sword on the title page, because an authentic representation would have been "impossible to render in cut paper."

Sundiata: Lion King of Mali is a biography of a king who lived in Africa over 800 years ago. Battle pennants were used in thirteenth-century

Africa, but little is known about their appearance. Designs for the banners were drawn from other objects found in ruins from the Mande, Malinke, or Fon people of neighboring Benin.

The "witches" of Mali would have dressed no differently than the rest of the community. Wisniewski chose to dress them in the cotton head wrap of the desert-dwelling Tuaregs of northern Mali. The "foreign" costume was used to heighten the sense of mystery and fear. Many of the objects in the illustrations are shown with a turtle motif. While researching the culture of West Africa, Wisniewski determined that the pottery from that area would have used lizards, snakes, and turtle motifs as decorations. He concluded that they may have been used on other objects as well.

In *Rain Player* it would be very unusual for a jaguar and a quetzal to be found in the same area as a cenote (a crevice below the surface). Jaguars are in nearly every segment of the Maya region; however, quetzals are usually in the southern highlands and the cenotes are only in the Yucatan region, where the porous ground absorbs the rainfall, creating underground rivers that erode the limestone to form a natural well. But pok-a-tok was a favorite game of the Maya and the *hetzmek* ceremony welcoming a new child into the community is still performed in the Yucatan. Wisniewski admits to one unintentional story error. After *Rain Player* had been out several months, he received a letter from a fifth-grader in Michigan telling him that although he depicted the quetzal in the story with long blue tail feathers, it was only the male bird that had such plumage. Wisniewski had referred to the bird as "she." The young reader was correct.

After writing several of his own books, he began to have difficulty with getting his story ideas accepted but his art was in demand. He illustrated a picture book, *Ducky*, by Eve Bunting (Clarion, 1997). His illustrations help tell the story of a small plastic duck that is part of a spill of thousands of plastic toys in the Pacific Ocean. The story and illustrations follow the duck from the middle of the ocean to the shores of Alaska.

He was asked to illustrate some short poems about tools by Andrew Clements. Wisniewski wanted to make the pictures more than just an inventory list of tools, so he developed a visual subtext focusing on a carpenter's apprentice who is constructing a carousel in the 1920s.

For several years he attempted to diversify his writing to appeal to a variety of readers. One idea was a humorous book that explains to young readers why parents tell their children to do such things as "comb your hair." That title, *A Kid's Guide to the Secret Knowledge of Grown-Ups*, was "revealed and illustrated" by David Wisniewski and published by Lothrop in 1998.

As an artist and writer, Wisniewski has little "free" time. He usually writes in the evenings, after everyone is in bed and the house is quiet. When he is not writing or working on illustrations he enjoys reading. He also enjoys an occasional round of "X-Wing"—a "really neat Star Wars flight simulator game." If he is alone in the house he plays the guitar. He currently lives in Monrovia, Maryland, with his wife, Donna, and their two children, Ariana and Alexander.

Books and Notes

Wisniewski's literary folktales and his biography of Sundiata all have a recurring story element—the individual triumphs against overwhelming odds. Wisniewski says, "If your characters are in a tight spot, but they have principles and remain faithful to their principles, then the principles are faithful to them." That theme is carried through in many great pieces of literature in many variations.

Literary Legends

Elfwyn's Saga. Illustrated by David Wisniewski. (Lothrop, 1990).

Golem. Illustrated by David Wisniewski. (Clarion, 1996).

Rain Player. Illustrated by David Wisniewski. (Clarion, 1991).

The Warrior and the Wiseman. Illustrated by David Wisniewski. (Lothrop, 1989).

The Wave of the Sea-Wolf. Illustrated by David Wisniewski. (Clarion, 1995).

Biography

Sundiata: Lion King of Mali. Illustrated by David Wisniewski. (Clarion, 1992).

Other Titles

Ducky. Written by Eve Bunting. Illustrated by David Wisniewski. (Clarion, 1997).

A Kid's Guide to the Secret Knowledge of Grown-Ups. Revealed and illustrated by David Wisniewski. (Lothrop, 1998).

Workshop. Written by Andrew Clements. Illustrated by David Wisniewski. (Clarion, 1999).

For More Information About/By the Author

Articles

"David Wisniewski." *Harrison Elementary School Web Site.* URL: http://www.cedar-rapids.k12.ia.us/Harrison/DavidW.html (Accessed January 1998).

"David Wisniewski." *Houghton Mifflin's Education Place Web Site.* URL: http://www.eduplace.com/rdg/author/wisniewski/index.html (Accessed January 1998).

McElmeel, Sharron L. "Author & Illustrator Profile: David Wisniewski." *Library Talk* 8, no. 2 (March/April 95): 16+.

Betty Ren Wright

**Wakefield, Michigan
June 15, 1927**

📖 *The Dollhouse Murders*
📖 *The Ghost in Room Eleven*

About the Author
and the Author's Writing

Betty Ren Wright was born in Wakefield, Michigan, June 15, 1927. Her family soon moved to the Milwaukee, Wisconsin, area, where she grew up. Her father taught school there, but died suddenly when Betty was five, leaving Betty and her mother with few resources to survive. Her mother returned to school to study for a teaching degree and eventually taught fourth-grade students for thirty years. Betty Ren Wright was just eight when she began to copy poems into a notebook with her name lettered across the cover. That was the beginning of her career as a writer. Her writing continued throughout childhood, although there was an interruption when she lost a year of school at age fourteen to have surgery for a spinal curvature. She remembers that time as the one filled with visitors coming to see the "girl in head-to-toe plaster."

After high school she attended Milwaukee-Downer College and graduated in 1949. By graduation she was already submitting articles to publishers. During the following years she became an editor with Western Publishing, a job she held for thirty years. She worked on children's books during the day and wrote adult short stories and some picture books in the evening. In 1976 she married George Fredericksen and moved from a small city apartment to a hundred-year-old house near lake Michigan. Their home was surrounded by woods, fields, wildflowers, and mysterious night noises. When Wright married she acquired three stepchildren and five (now eight) grandchildren.

Wright had been writing picture story books and magazine articles in addition to working as an editor. Two years after her marriage in 1978, she decided to concentrate on freelance writing. She thought she would be writing adult fiction, but decided to try one novel for younger readers. She has stayed with books for young readers ever since.

When Wright became a stepmother in 1976, her new family was warm and welcoming, but inside she was imagining how hard it might have been if there had been a step grandchild who did not want a new grandmother in the family. That provided the idea for *Getting Rid of Marjorie* (Holiday, 1981).

Two incidents inspired *The Dollhouse Murders* (Holiday, 1983). For several years Wright had been interested in miniatures. Knowing that, an artist friend invited Wright to clean house one sunny afternoon. The house was an exquisite Victorian dollhouse that the friend had constructed as an exact replica of her grandparents' home. The smallest detail was accurate. The house opened a floodgate of memories, both joyful and sad, for Wright's friend. Wright reasoned that if the dollhouse could hold all those memories, it ought to hold some ghosts as well. On another afternoon Wright watched two brothers, one with severe mental disabilities, share a picnic lunch at a roadside park. She had written about this relationship in several short stories, but wanted to deal with the topic in a full-length novel. The two afternoons came together to form the central plot of *The Dollhouse Murders*.

"Like most writers, I rely a lot on personal experiences for inspiration. Sometimes a very brief contact or experience turns out to be the starting point for a book. For example, *The Ghost in Room Eleven* [Holiday, 1998] grew out of memories of a rural school I visited years ago. It provided the setting, and a letter from a reader telling me about his haunted school provided the motivation for this particular story. Even though he hadn't seen a ghost, he very much wanted to believe there was one, and so did I!"

In *Out of the Dark* (Scholastic, 1995), the little schoolhouse in the story is on display in a nature preserve not too far from Wright's home. *Too Many Secrets* (Scholastic, 1997) features Aunt Rosebud, whose character came out of an association Wright had with a woman she had met years earlier. That woman made her own elaborate hats and wore them while she did her housework.

After her husband's death in 1995, Betty Ren Wright moved from their rather isolated rural home to a condo-duplex in Racine. She says, "I am enjoying the setting very much. My 'live-in' family consists of Gracie, a small black cocker-poodle mix, and Nougat, a rangy tiger of a cat." The rest of her family, three stepchildren and many grandchildren, are close by and ready to share their adventures and concerns. Her condo gives her "a delightful spot for writing, with a green view, lots of birds, and an occasional rabbit to drive Gracie and Nougat into a frenzy."

Wright has had many satisfying moments in her career writing children's books. One is when she gets a letter from a child who declares that, after reading one of her books, she or he "now reads all the time." In the spring of 1997, Wright received the Harry and Lynde Bradley Major Achievement Award for her writing.

She still enjoys watching birds and walking, but her favorite pastimes are reading and spending time with her family and friends. She lives in Racine, Wisconsin.

Books and Notes

Betty Ren Wright draws readers into her books by creating believable plots and characters juxtaposed with a supernatural element. By then the reader is hooked and accepts the ghost or ghostly event along with the characters. The ghosts remain real. Wright does not explain them away with ideas like the ghost "might have been a tree limb brushing against a window pane."

Christina's Ghost (Holiday, 1985).

Getting Rid of Marjorie (Holiday, 1981).

The Ghost in Room Eleven (Holiday, 1998).

Out of the Dark (Scholastic, 1995).

The Pike River Phantom (Holiday, 1988).

Rosie and the Dance of the Dinosaurs (Holiday, 1989).

Too Many Secrets (Scholastic, 1997).

For More Information About/By the Author

Limited information available on some book flaps. Check general reference sources.

Elizabeth Yates

Historical Fiction ◆ Nonfiction: Writing

Buffalo, New York
December 6, 1905

📖 *Amos Fortune: Free Man*

About the Author
and the Author's Writing

Elizabeth Yates was born December 6, 1905, and raised in Buffalo, New York. Her family included seven children. Elizabeth was the sixth child in the family. The family spent hours in the outdoors on their father's large countryside farm south of Buffalo. There was plenty of work—gardening, making butter, and caring for the animals. There were many playmates—brothers and sisters, dogs, and horses.

Elizabeth spent her childhood in a house filled with books. Reading and being read to were common pastimes in the Yates household. On many occasions Yates would mount one of the family horses and go riding through the countryside for a day at a time. She often stopped by a brook to eat a sandwich and drink from the brook. She was alone, but she talked to the horse and "wrote" stories in her head. Elizabeth also had a secret place in a unused pigeon loft where she copied down the stories she had thought up.

The winter days were spent in Buffalo, where she attended Franklin school from kindergarten through twelfth grade. The school emphasized the classics and English literature. She loved writing and knew she wanted to be a writer. After completing her last year at Franklin, she went to a boarding school, spent a summer abroad, and then went to New York, where she worked for three years. In the summer she taught riding at a girls camp. During her time in New York she met William McGreal, a young American engineer, whose business was in London. They married when she was twenty-three. From 1928 to 1938 Elizabeth Yates and William McGreal lived in London. She spent hours interviewing people, writing articles, editing, and ghost-writing. In addition to writing, she spent long hours in the British Museum and the London Library. While the couple lived in England they traveled widely in the British Isles and throughout Europe. They climbed mountains and met many interesting people.

One of those people was a British illustrator, Nora Spicer Unwin. She was a part-time teacher, as well as a painter and illustrator of children's books. The women became close friends.

In 1938 Yates's first book was published. *High Holiday* (A. & C. Black, 1938) concerned her favorite activity, mountain climbing in Switzerland and Iceland. The book was published in England, but not in the United States. Eventually, the topic was covered in republished titles, *Iceland Adventure* (Journey Books, 1997) and *Swiss Holiday* (Bob Jones University Press, 1996) with illustrations by Gloria Repp.

McGreal had a recurrent and serious eye problem that caused the couple to return to the United States in 1939. They settled in a 150-year-old farmhouse in Peterborough, New Hampshire, surrounded by 67 acres. They had mountains, lakes, and small village shops nearby.

Yates spent her writing time in a little loft in one end of the house. She generally worked from 8:30 AM to 1 PM each day. The room was heated with an old-fashioned wood stove, and she worked at a large table facing a window. She could gaze out across a small valley and pine woods to the mountains from her writing loft. Yates and McGreal modernized the house and named it Shieling from memories of the Isle of Skye and a type of shelter for shepherds called "shielings."

In the winter of 1939, in an attempt to correct the eye problem, McGreal had eye surgery. The surgery was unsuccessful, and McGreal was left blind. Her husband's encounter with blindness brought Yates to write *The Lighted Heart* (Dutton, 1960). With the exception of days when there were special guests in their house, Yates kept to her writing routine faithfully. Her books began to earn her awards and accolades as early as 1943 when *Patterns on the Wall* (Dutton, 1943) won a New York *Herald Tribune* Spring Festival Award. *Patterns on the Wall*, set in New Hampshire in 1816, concerned Jared Austin, an apprentice and then journeyman painter.

In 1946 Yates's friend Nora Unwin immigrated to the United States and lived with Yates and her husband for a time. Unwin illustrated some of Yates's books, and at least two won special distinction. *Mountain Born* (Dutton, 1943) was a Newbery Honor Book, and *Amos Fortune: Free Man* (Dutton, 1950) was named the Newbery Award winner in 1951. That book also won the *Herald Tribune* award.

One summer evening in the late 1940s Yates was planning to attend a presentation that was part of the Amos Fortune Lecture Series in a little town, Jaffrey Center, about seven miles from her home in Peterborough. On her way she decided to stop in the churchyard to view the hilltop graves of Amos Fortune and his wife, Violet. She wanted to know more. For the next year she researched the life of the African prince Amos Fortune, who had been sold into slavery in Boston in the early 1700s. Amos Fortune was born in Africa in 1710 and at the age of sixty bought his freedom. Yates visited Freeman's home, studied his personal items and papers, his will, and African slave trading. From her inch-thick notes, she began to fashion a story.

Elizabeth Yates continued to maintain the Peterborough farm after her husband's death in 1963. For many years Yates and her sheltie, Sir Gibbie (who was the subject of a book by her), roamed the paths around the farm. She enjoyed canoeing, swimming, climbing, talking, reading, and trips, many of them with the Sierra Club. She canoed the border waters of Canada and Minnesota, went on a pack trip up the Smoky Mountains, and snowshoed in the winter. As a trustee for the Peterborough Town Library, she was very proud of her community and its resources.

Eventually she left 45 acres of her farm to the state of New Hampshire. The area is known as the Shieling State Forest at Peterborough and is described as "[a]n area of 45 acres of tree covered ridges and valleys with wildflower preserve, trails for walking, (dogs on leash permitted) cross country skiing, and snowshoeing." Recreational brochures acknowledge the forest as a gift "from well-known author Elizabeth Yates McGreal." The New Hampshire Division of Forests and Lands maintains the Shieling State Forest. Throughout her life Yates has continued to enjoy reading, writing, gardening, and traveling.

Books and Notes

Elizabeth Yates wrote historical fiction, collected folklore from Cornwall, and wrote religious tracts. The following list presents just a few of her more than 80 publications.

Amos Fortune: Free Man. Illustrated by Nora S. Unwin. (Dutton, 1950).

The Journeyman (Bob Jones University Press, 1990).
Originally published as *Patterns on the Wall* (Dutton, 1943).

The Next Fine Day (Bob Jones University Press, 1994).

Pixie Folklore and Legend (Gramercy Books, 1996).

A Place for Peter. Illustrated by Nora S. Unwin. (Bob Jones University Press, 1994).

Sarah Whitcher's Story. Illustrated by Nora S. Unwin. (Bob Jones University Press, 1994).
Originally published by Dutton, 1971.

Being a Writer

Elizabeth Yates was a journal and diary keeper. She published three books (republished as one) that chronicled her evolution as a writer, and another with advice for the new writer.

Someday You'll Write (Bob Jones University Press, 1995).
Originally published by Dutton, 1962.

Spanning Time: A Diary Keeper Becomes a Writer. Foreword by Barbara Elleman. (Cobblestone, 1996).
A collection of diary entries from 1917 to 1950 portraying the life of an aspiring writer. Includes the previous publications: *My Diary, My World*; *My Widening World*; and *One Writer's Way*.

For More Information About/By the Author

Limited information available on some book flaps. Check general reference sources.

Jane Yolen

Folk Tales ◆ Fantasy ◆ Biographies

New York, New York
February 11, 1939

📖 *Dragon's Blood*
📖 *The Devil's Arithmetic*

About the Author
and the Author's Writing

Jane Yolen is a study in activity. She considers herself a full-time writer and a full-time wife and mother (and since March 25, 1995, a grandmother). She has served as president of the Science Fiction and Fantasy Writers of America and as a member of the Board of Directors of the Society of Children's Book Writers and Illustrators since its beginning. She often appears at major writing and reading conferences. She is a master storyteller and founding member of the Western New England Storytellers Guild. In addition, she is on the editorial board of several magazines and holds memberships in several other guilds and writers groups.

Jane Yolen was born February 11, 1939, in New York City, the daughter of Will Hyatt Yolen and Isabelle Berlin Yolen. "I always enjoyed reading. When I was young, I particularly enjoyed reading fairy tales."

Her father, a public relations executive, wrote, compiled, and edited several books. Her mother's family had an academic bent, so it was not surprising that Jane became an avid reader and writer by the second grade.

"I love writing and have always been good at it. I started as a poet and writer of songs. I still do both. My first big success as a writer came in first grade where I wrote the class musical. It was all about vegetables and I played the chief carrot. We all ended up in the salad together! In junior high I wrote my big class essay about New York State Manufacturing in verse, with a rhyme for Otis Elevators I have—thankfully—forgotten. In college I wrote my final exam in American Intellectual History in rhyme and got an A+ from a very surprised teacher."

At the age of thirteen, her family moved to Westport, Connecticut. This is where she got her first job as a library page. She received her undergraduate degree from Smith College in 1960 and became a production assistant for the *Saturday Review Magazine*. Later she was associate editor at Knopf. She sold her first children's book on her twenty-second birthday in 1961. She married David W. Stemple, a professor of computer science, in 1962. They lived for a time in Conway, Massachusetts, before purchasing a small farm, Phoenix Farm, in Hatfield, Massachusetts, not far from Boston. Jane comes from a long line of storytellers.

"Both my parents were writers. My father was a journalist, my mother a short story writer, who also created crossword puzzles and double acrostics for magazines and books. I just assumed all grownups were writers. Since my brother is a journalist, and my three grown children all write well, in our family at any rate, that is true."

Jane's great-grandfather was a storyteller, too. He did not write them down, however. He owned an inn in a small remote Russian village. Anyone who came to stay the night had to listen to one of his stories. Jane's visitors only listen to her stories if they want to. She does keep her books out, however, just in case they are interested. Sometimes she sings and accompanies herself on the guitar, autoharp, or fairy bells.

Her father and the folk culture he helped to instill in her were great influences. She read many folktales and fairy stories while growing up. She borrowed dozens from the public library. Her late father, playing the guitar and singing, introduced her to folk songs. She learned some Old English, Scottish, Irish, and Appalachian love songs and ballads. During college she made a little money singing at fraternity parties and mixers with a friend.

She says, "My first published book, *Pirates in Petticoats* (McKay, 1963), came out when I was twenty-three. It was about women pirates." In 1965 Yolen became a full-time professional writer. She spent some time writing and traveling in Europe. She often wrote short stories and some of them have evolved into novels. For example, *Dragon's Blood* (Delacorte, 1982) "began with a short story I wrote, 'Cockfight' for an anthology of dragon stories called *Dragons of Light* (Ace, 1980). I like the boy Jakkin and the dragon Heart's Blood so much. I wanted to know more. But the only way I could know more was to write about it myself." She wrote *Dragon's Blood* based on the short story and then continued the story with a sequel, *Heart's Blood* (Delacorte, 1984). In the second novel, Jakkin is a young master and plans to enter his own dragon in the gaming pits of Austar IV. *A Sending of Dragons* (Delacorte, 1984) is the final book of the trilogy.

Yolen has written many types of books and has garnered awards from all corners of the children's literature world. Jane Yolen says, "I began as a poet and a journalist and quite by accident fell into children's books, where (except for an occasional foray into adult poetry or novels) I have lived happily ever after." *Owl Moon* (Philomel, 1987), written by Yolen and illustrated by John Schoenherr, earned Schoenherr the Caldecott Award in 1988 for his exquisite watercolors, and another book, *The Emperor and the Kite* (Philomel, 1967) with intricate paper-cut illustrations by Ed Young, brought Young a Caldecott Honor Award in 1968.

The Devil's Arithmetic (Viking, 1988) was awarded the Jewish Book Award; *The Girl Who Loved the Wind* became a Lewis Carrol Shelf Award winner; and several of her books have been awarded state children's choice awards. Her body of writing has been honored with the Kerlan Award, the Regina Award, and the Keene State Children's Literature Award. "But awards," says Yolen, "just sit on the shelf gathering dust. The best awards are when young readers love my books." Her books have been translated into Japanese, French, Spanish, Chinese, Afrikaans, Zulu, German, Swedish, Norwegian, Danish, and Braille.

The sources for her book ideas are as varied as the subjects themselves. She says that where ideas come from does not matter as much as what is done with them. Ideas come from family, friends, newspapers, music, paintings, eavesdropping, and even from dreams. Sometimes the ideas sit awhile, only to be activated by a second incident or person. She says, "I have a creative memory in which bits and pieces of my own personal history (or my husbands' or my parents' or my friends') find their way into my stories." She says, "I wrote *Owl Moon* because my husband used to take our children owling when they were younger. The little girl in *Owl Moon* is not me, but is based on my daughter, Heidi, who is now an adult with her own little girl, Maddison Jane. We are looking forward to the time that Maddison is old enough to be taken out owling."

The Emperor and the Kite (Philomel, 1967; 1988) is based on Yolen's own relationship with her late father, Will Yolen, who was an international kite-flying champion and described as "the world's leading kite-flying expert."

The Devil's Arithmetic addresses the Holocaust. It is a subject that interests Yolen both as a Jew and as a citizen of the world. Her family, both sides, came to the United States at the beginning of this century. There was no family left in either Ukraine or Latvia during World War II. While she was writing the book, she said "I am writing a time travel novel about a Jewish girl who is suddenly whisked back to the time of Nazi Germany." With those few words she described what would become a griping and powerful novel. *The Devil's Arithmetic* is indeed a "daring, uncompromising new story that blends elements of fantasy, and historical fiction with the grim truth about the Holocaust." Her own family, she says, "is a product of the *dis-memorification* we so highly prize. My children have Hebrew names as well as English ones. They identify themselves as Jews. But other than a couple of Bar Mitzvahs and a Sedar or two, they know little about it. But some things should not be forgotten." Yolen said *The Devil's Arithmetic* was for Heidi/Chaya, Adam/Adom, and Jason/Jacob, and for the eighth-graders in Indianapolis "who were shocked and surprised when I told them about the concentration camps. They thought I had made it all up."

Jane Yolen and David Stemple have lived for several decades in rural Massachusetts. Yolen's beautifully decorated office is "the size of most struggling writer's entire apartments." It is, she says, one of the small rewards of having worked for two decades in "the vineyards." The office is located in the third-floor attic of the home, a huge, old, New England farmhouse. The attic, full of bookcases, consists of two rooms. One room is for editing and the other for writing. The writing room has three wings—a writing area, a copier/filing cabinet area, and a reading area where a sofa sometimes serves a dual role as a comfortable place to sit and an "in" basket. The house is surrounded by fifteen acres of farmland (usually rented out to truck farmers). Her library is filled with a wall of folklore and mythology books, one of poetry, two walls of science fiction and fantasy, and a collection of children's literature.

Yolen has scaled back her speaking schedule, but considers very carefully those requests that come from locations near any one of her three children's homes. She delights in being a mother and absolutely adores being a "Nana." Jane Yolen's family includes her husband, a daughter, Heidi Elisabet, and two sons, Adam Douglas and Jason Frederic. Jane became a grandmother for the first time on March 25, 1995. Maddison Jane was born to daughter Heidi and her husband.

Books and Notes

Jane Yolen writes for all age levels and has written literally hundreds of titles. Among those titles are picture books, books of historical fiction, fantasy, science fiction, stories of magic, and many literary folk stories.

Dragon Fantasy

Dragon's Blood (Delacorte, 1982).

Heart's Blood (Delacorte, 1984).

"Early Readers"

Commander Toad and the Big Black Hole (Coward-McCann, 1983).

Commander Toad in Space. Illustrated by Bruce Degan. (Coward-McCann, 1980).

Historical Fantasy

The Devil's Arithmetic (Viking, 1988).

Picture Books

The Emperor and the Kite. Illustrated by Ed Young. (Philomel, 1967; 1988).

The Giants Go Camping. Illustrated by Tomie dePaola. (Seabury, 1979).

Owl Moon. Illustrated by John Schoenherr. (Philomel, 1987).

Pegasus, the Flying Horse. Illustrated by Li Ming. (Dutton, 1998).

Piggins. Illustrated by Jane Dyer. (Harcourt, 1987).

Raising Yoder's Barn. Illustrated by Bernie Fuchs. (Little, 1998).

A Sending of Dragons (Delacourt, 1984; Harcourt, 1997).

The Seventh Mandarin. Illustrated by Ed Young. (Seabury, 1970).

Sleeping Ugly. Illustrated by Diane Stanley. (Coward-McCann, 1981).

Other Titles

The Book of Fairy Holidays. Illustrations by David Christiana. (Blue Sky, 1998).

House/house. Illustrated with photographs by the Howes Brothers and Jason Stemple. (Marshall Cavendish, 1998).

Moon Ball (Simon, 1999).

The Mystery of the Mary Celeste. Co-authored with Heidi E. Y. Stemple. (Simon, 1999).

Once Upon Ice and Other Frozen Poems. Illustrated with photographs by Jason Stemple. (Wordsong/Boyds Mills, 1997).

The Originals: Animals That Time Forgot. Illustrated by Ted Lewin. (Philomel, 1996).

For More Information About/By the Author

Articles

"Approaching the Edge: Doesn't Everyone Grow Up to Write? An Interview with Jane Yolen." *The Leading Edge* no. 2 (1992): 82+.

Elleman, Barbara. "Water and Waterways (with Jane Yolen and Barbara Cooney on Letting Swift Water Go)." *Booklinks* 2, no. 1 (September 1992): 7+.

"History's Other Voice: Children's Book Author Jane Yolen Tells Why She Wrote *Encounter*, the Story of Columbus's First Meeting with the Taino Tribe." *Instructor* 102, no. 2 (September 1992): 42+.

"Interview: Jane Yolen." *Storytelling Magazine* 8, no. 1 (January 1996): 22+.

"Interview: Jane Yolen: Telling Tales." *Locus* 39, no. 2 (August 1997): 4+.

Koch, John. "An Interview with Jane Yolen." *The Writer* 110, no. 3 (March 1997): 20+.

"Meet the Author: Jane Yolen." *Instructor* 105, no. 7 (April 1996): 61+.

Scales, Pat. "The Gift of Sarah Barker (by Jane Yolen)." *Booklinks* 4, no. 5 (May 1995): 40+.

Books

Yolen, Jane. *A Letter from Phoenix Farm*. Illustrated with photographs by Jason Stemple. (R. C. Owen, 1992).

An autobiographical account of the prominent author Jane Yolen and how her daily life and writing process are interwoven.

Appendix

Photography Credits

Photograph of David A. Adler by David Godlis, courtesy of David A. Adler and reprinted with his permission.

Photograph of Lloyd Alexander by Alexander Limont, courtesy of David A. Adler and reprinted with his permission.

Photograph of Judy Blume, courtesy of Judy Blume and reprinted with her permission.

Photograph of Bill Brittain by Virginia Brittain, courtesy of Bill Brittain and reprinted with his permission.

Photograph of Eve Bunting by Hans Gutknecht, courtesy of Eve Bunting and reprinted with her permission.

Photograph of Betsy Byars by Ed Byars, courtesy of Betsy Byars and reprinted with her permission.

Photograph of Matt Christopher, courtesy of Little, Brown Publishers and reprinted with the permission of Cay Christopher.

Photograph of Eth Clifford, courtesy of Eth Clifford and reprinted with her permission.

Photograph of Christopher Collier, courtesy of Christopher Collier and reprinted with his permission.

Photograph of Ellen Conford by David Conford, courtesy of Ellen Conford and reprinted with her permission.

Photograph of Pam Conrad by Sharron L. McElmeel, and reprinted with permission.

Photograph of Judy Delton, courtesy of Judy Delton and reprinted with her permission.

Photograph of Aileen Fisher, courtesy of Aileen Fisher and reprinted with her permission.

Photograph of Paul Fleischman by Becky Mojica, courtesy of Paul Fleischman and reprinted with his permission.

Photograph of Sid Fleischman, courtesy of Sid Fleischman and reprinted with his permission.

Photograph of Paula Fox, courtesy of Paula Fox and reprinted with her permission.

Photograph of Russell Freedman, courtesy of Russell Freedman and reprinted with his permission.

Photograph of Jean Fritz by Jill Krementz, courtesy of Jean Fritz and reprinted with her permission.

Photograph of Jean George by Ellan Young, courtesy of Jean George and reprinted with her permission.

Photograph of Patricia Reilly Giff by Tornberg Associates, courtesy of Bantam Doubleday Dell Publishers and Patricia Reilly Giff and reprinted with her permission.

Photograph of Jamie Gilson by Matthew Gilson, courtesy of Jamie Gilson and reprinted with her permission.

Photograph of Carol Gorman by Sharron L. McElmeel, courtesy of Carol Gorman and reprinted with her permission.

Photograph of Mary Downing Hahn by Norm Jacob, courtesy of Mary Downing Hahn and reprinted with her permission.

Photograph of Clifford B. Hicks by Sarah Sneeden, courtesy of Clifford B. Hicks and reprinted with his permission.

Photograph of Lee Bennett Hopkins is an Egita Photo, and is reprinted courtesy of Lee Bennett Hopkins with his permission.

Photograph of Johanna Hurwitz by Amanda Smith, courtesy of Johanna Hurwitz and reprinted with her permission.

Photograph of Suzy Kline, courtesy of Suzy Kline and reprinted with her permission.

Photograph of E. L. Konigsburg, courtesy of Simon & Schuster and reprinted with permission.

Photograph of Phyllis Reynolds Naylor © 1996 by Janet Mills and reprinted courtesy of Phyllis Reynolds Naylor and Janet Mills.

Photograph of Joan Lowery Nixon, courtesy of Joan Lowery Nixon and reprinted with her permission.

Photograph of Richard Peck by Don Lewis, courtesy of Richard Lewis and reprinted with his permission.

Photograph of Ivy Ruckman, courtesy of Ivy Ruckman and reprinted with her permission.

Photograph of Marilyn Sachs by Morris Sachs, courtesy of Marilyn Sachs and reprinted with her permission.

Photograph of Shel Silverstein, courtesy of and reprinted by permission of HarperCollins.

Photograph of Gloria Skurzynski by Ed Skurzynski, courtesy of Gloria Skurzynski and reprinted with her permission.

Photograph of Alfred Slote, courtesy of Alfred Slote and reprinted with his permission.

Photograph of Virginia Driving Hawk Sneve by Sharron L. McElmeel, and reprinted with permission.

Photograph of Zilpha Keatley Snyder, courtesy of Zilpha Keatley Snyder and reprinted with her permission.

Photograph of Jerry Spinelli by Chuck Cully, courtesy of Jerry Spinelli and HarperCollins and reprinted with permission of Jerry Spinelli and HarperCollins.

Photograph of Theodore Taylor by John Graves, courtesy of Theodore Taylor and reprinted with his permission.

Photograph of David Wisniewski by Sharron McElmeel and reprinted with permission.

Photograph of Betty Ren Wright by Raymond Houte, courtesy of Betty Ren Wright and reprinted with her permission.

Photograph of Jane Yolen, courtesy of Jane Yolen and reprinted with her permission.

Genre Index

Information about the authors and those genres associated with specific authors may be accessed by going to the chapter(s) about the cited authors listed with each genre. This reference volume is arranged in alphabetical order by each author's last name, thus page numbers are not included with this index.

General Index

In this index, the page numbers that refer to the main entry for each author are included in bold type. Titles that are within the narrative about each author are included with references to the appropriate page numbers. References to titles in the selected bibliographies at the end of each chapter are not included in this index. References to specific genres written by authors included in this volume can be found in the genre index.

About the Author

Sharron L. McElmeel has developed a national reputation in the area of children's literature and technology and its integration into every corner of the curriculum. Born in Cedar Rapids, Iowa, Sharron obtained an undergraduate degree in education and later earned a master's degree at the University of Iowa. She taught in the Iowa public schools for many years as a classroom teacher and as a library media specialist at both the elementary and secondary levels. She is a full-time educational writer and editor and a nationally recognized consultant on the use of literature and technology in the classroom. She regularly works with organizations and school districts in locations as widespread as Canada, Arkansas, and Virginia.

Her interest in children's and young adult literature and in those who create it has grown over two decades. She is a frequent contributor to professional publications, including *Library Talk* and *Book Report* where her World Wide Web columns and articles about books and authors are a regular feature. She has authored 20 books, including the popular Author-a-Month and Bookpeople titles from Libraries Unlimited. Among her most recent publications for Libraries Unlimited are *Educator's Companion to Children's Literature, Volume 1: Mysteries, Animal Tales, Books of Humor, Adventure Stories, and Historical Fiction* and its companion volume *Children's Literature, Volume 2: Folklore, Contemporary Realistic Fiction, Fantasy, Biographies, and Tales from Here and There.*

Sharron L. McElmeel lives in a serene rural area near Cedar Rapids, Iowa where her home, surrounded by bustling fields and the hum of those passing by, is filled with thousands of books. Her favorite book this year is Jacqueline Briggs Martin's *Snowflake Bentley* (Houghton, 1998), whose illustrations earned Mary Azarian the 1999 Caldecott Award. Other favorites may be viewed on her website at http://www.5thseason.net/~mcelmeel.